A GLIMPSE OF SION'S GLORY

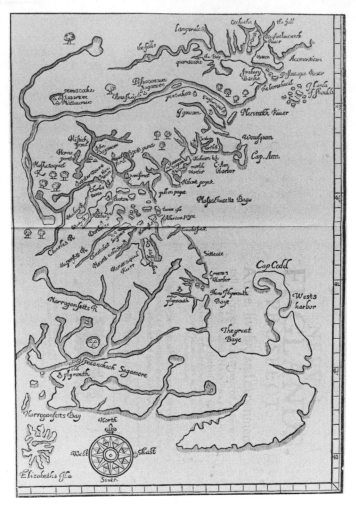

The South part of New-England, as it is Planted this yeare, 1634.

Map of New England, circa 1634, from William Wood's *New Englands Prospect* (London, 1634).

A GLIMPSE OF
SION'S GLORY

PURITAN RADICALISM
IN NEW ENGLAND,
1620 – 1660

Philip F. Gura

WESLEYAN UNIVERSITY PRESS
Middletown, Connecticut

Also by Philip F. Gura

THE WISDOM OF WORDS
Language, Theology, and Literature
in the New England Renaissance

CRITICAL ESSAYS ON AMERICAN
TRANSCENDENTALISM (*with Joel Myerson*)

Chapter 10 appeared, in somewhat different form, in *William and Mary Quarterly*, 3rd Ser., 36, no. 1 (January 1979). Chapter 11 appeared, in somewhat different form, in *William and Mary Quarterly*, 3rd Ser., 39, no. 3 (July 1982).

All inquiries and permissions requests should be addressed to the Publisher, Wesleyan University Press, 110 Mt. Vernon Street, Middletown, Connecticut 06457

Distributed by Harper & Row Publishers,
Keystone Industrial Park, Scranton, Pennsylvania 18512

LIBRARY OF CONGRESS CATALOGING IN PUBLICATION DATA

Gura, Philip F., 1950– . A glimpse of Sion's glory. Bibliography: p. Includes index. 1. Puritans—New England—History—17th century. 2. Radicalism—New England—History—17th century. 3. New England—Intellectual life. 4. United States—Civilization—To 1783, I. Title.
F7.G87   1984   974'.02   83-21831
ISBN 0-8195-6154-1

Manufactured in the United States of America

First published in 1984 by Wesleyan University Press
Wesleyan Paperback, 1986

For Alan Heimert in one way

"He had an uncommon thirst for Knowledge, in the pursuit of which, he spared no Cost or Pains. . . . Tho' his Principles were *Calvinistic*, yet he called no Man, Father. He thought and judged for himself, and was truly very much of an Original."

and for Leslie in so many others

"High experiences and religious affections in this person have not been attended with any disposition at all to neglect the necessary business of a secular calling . . . but worldly business has been attended with great alacrity, as part of the service of God. . . . These things have been accompanied with an exceeding concern and zeal for moral duties . . . and an uncommon care to perform relative and social duties. . . . Now if such things are enthusiasm, and the fruits of a distempered brain, let my brain be evermore possessed of that unhappy distemper!"

PREFACE

The mark of a fine teacher is, as often has been noted, the ability to ask the right kinds of questions, and the genesis of this book is directly related to one such teacher and at least one such question. Many years ago, during my doctoral examination, Alan Heimert had what I then considered the audacity to question me about one of the most obscure figures in early New England history. "Did Samuel Gorton typologize Christ?" he asked. Of course I hadn't the foggiest notion; but several years later, after I had serendipitously purchased a copy of the nineteenth-century reprint of Gorton's *Simplicities Defence against Seven-Headed Policy*, I undertook to answer him as thoroughly as I could. Though I then did not know it, the result of that inquiry (published in the *William and Mary Quarterly* in 1979) was the starting point for this study.

This project received another unsought-for boost during 1980–1981, when as a Fellow of the Charles Warren Center for Studies in American History at Harvard, I had begun work on an intellectual history of the Connecticut Valley in the seventeenth century. I started at the beginning, with William Pynchon, one of the first settlers in the valley, and discovered that he, like Gorton, was a much misunderstood (because little read) representative of radical Puritan thought in New England. A reader's report for the *William and Mary Quarterly*, to which I had submitted an essay on Pynchon, included the following comment: "The author . . . seems to be well on his way to writing a New England version of Christopher Hill's *World Turned Upside Down* in the finest non-Marxian sense." Until then I had no such intention, but I began to follow the lead

so generously given and shifted my research to the numerous representatives of Puritan radicalism whose stories are recorded in New England
town histories; in church, town, and colony records; and in many seventeenth-century works from and about the area.

The result is, I admit unabashedly, intellectual history pure and simple,
for I am not a social historian nor pretend to be. I have been most interested, first, in describing the numerous representatives of radical Puritan
ideology in New England and in relating them to the complex Puritan
culture in England during the same period, a culture so richly described
by Christopher Hill and Keith Thomas, among other English historians.
I will be the first to admit that there is an important book to be written
about the socio-economic status of those in New England who were attracted to radical ideology—indeed, as early as 1962, long before the proliferation of demographers, Emery Battis attempted just such a study of
Anne Hutchinson and her followers—but before such work can proceed,
we have to understand what such individuals believed and how those beliefs were related to radical ideology across the Atlantic.

Second, I have sought to understand the effect of radical Puritan ideology on the development of what historians have enshrined as the "New
England Way," and here I do nod politely to the Marxists. I believe that
the ecclesiastical and doctrinal underpinnings of New England theology
evolved as a result of a constant dialectic between nonseparating congregationalists and those in the population who argued for more radical
reorganization of seventeenth-century society. If we believe, then, that
the New England mind has indeed contributed something basic to that
nebulous thing called the "meaning" of America, we also have to be
ready to acknowledge that in many ways our national ideology was
formed by a co-optation of a more radical agenda for our political and
social priorities. I leave it to others to articulate what such an ingrained
conservatism has meant, say, to the development of our politics in the
eighteenth century and beyond.

My work has been most facilitated by the scholarship of Geoffrey Nuttall and Christopher Hill, as well as by two American scholars who for
many years have explored the byways of New England history. As far
back as 1956 J. F. Maclear pointed out the importance of what he termed
"the mystical element" in Puritanism, and his more recent essays on millennialism and Christian mortalism in New England helped to focus
many of my concerns. Similarly, Stephen Foster, particularly in his recent
essay on Puritan radicalism in transatlantic perspective, has made me
aware of the complexity of the relationship between English and Ameri-

can Puritanism. With regard to New England Puritan radicalism these two individuals have been pioneers on the American strand.

Michael McGiffert has given unsparingly of his historical knowledge and editorial expertise to make my work on Gorton and Pynchon more lucid, an objective easily conceived but, given my subject matter, less readily attainable, as anyone who has read in the gnarled prose of radical Puritan theology knows full well. Part of chapter ten and chapter eleven first appeared in the *William and Mary Quarterly*, under his editorship. Jeannette Hopkins, Director of Wesleyan University Press, has supported this project from its inception; her encouragement has been most welcome, as has been that of Edwin S. Gaustad and Sacvan Bercovitch. Carolyn Dameron again has had the patience to bear with me through several drafts of this book; her typing and editorial skills have saved me literally months of time.

I wish to thank the Administrative Committee of the Charles Warren Center for Studies in American History, with Stephan Thernstrom as Director, for providing me with a year in which I could read in the Harvard University and Boston-area libraries, and the Committee on Research and Creative Work at the University of Colorado for a travel grant to make possible another visit to these resources. My wife, Leslie, herself immersed in work toward the C.P.A. examination during the period in which I completed the first draft of this study, provided much-needed affection, support, and an environment with the least number of distractions. To her, and in a very different way to the teacher who asked the right questions, I give most thanks.

PHILIP F. GURA
Boulder, Colorado
1983

CONTENTS

LIST OF ILLUSTRATIONS

AND CREDITS

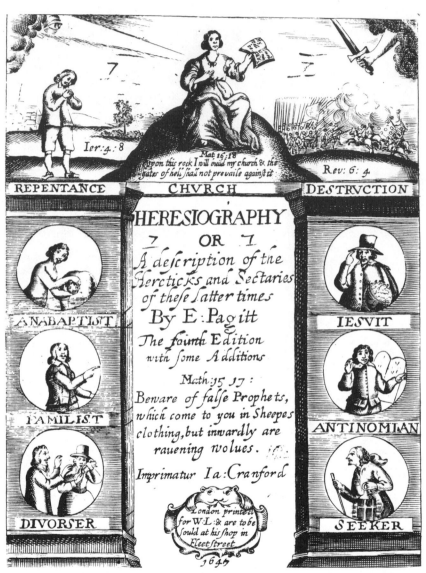

Title page of *Heresiography*, by Ephraim Pagitt (London, 1654), which went through several editions; the book contains lengthy descriptions of several groups of sectaries.

If there be many Prophesies and Promises in Scripture that are not yet fulfilled; and the fulfilling whereof will bring the *Church* into a more glorious condition then ever it was yet in the world: then there is a glorious Time a coming. . . . The nearer the Time comes, the more clearly these things shall be revealed. And because they begin to be revealed so much as they doe now, we have cause to hope the Time is at hand. . . . Take heed that you lose not this opportunity.

THOMAS GOODWIN
A Glimpse of Syons Glory (1641)

For whom the Lord hath given once a glimpse of his glory, the soul it can not be at rest, but it breatheth for more of that mercy and presence.

THOMAS SHEPARD
"Ineffectual Hearing of the Word" (c. 1641)

I am now prest for service of our Lord Jesus Christ, to re-build the most glorious Edifice of Mount Sion in a Wildernesse.

EDWARD JOHNSON
The Wonder-Working Providence of Sions
Saviour in New England (1651)

A GLIMPSE OF SION'S GLORY

PROLOGUE

NEW ENGLAND PURITAN
RADICALISM:
AN OVERVIEW

On 6 July 1631 the *Plough*, a small ship from London, anchored in Boston harbor in the Massachusetts Bay Colony. A year earlier its ten passengers and two score other Londoners had formed a group called the "Husbandmen" and petitioned Sir Ferdinando Gorges for a patent of land in the New World; Gorges, to whom King James had given vast acreage in the northeastern parts of New England, granted them title to a large parcel of unsettled land near Sagadahock, in what now is southeastern Maine. In the winter months before their arrival at Boston the "Company of the *Plough*" (as they also were called) had visited Sagadahock, but, disappointed by the region's harsh weather and rocky soil, they explored the possibility of establishing themselves elsewhere in the New World. After a brief visit to Charlestown and Watertown in the Bay Colony, the *Plough* embarked for the more hospitable climate of the West Indies, where other English outposts were being established, only to return to New England within three weeks, so storm-ravaged that its crew would not consider recrossing the Atlantic to England. By the late summer of 1631, the Husbandmen found themselves

members of the larger Puritan settlement at the mouth of the Charles River.[1]

In his journal Governor John Winthrop had noted the *Plough*'s arrival. Whether he then knew anything specific about its passengers is unclear. But within a year, after two more contingents had arrived in the colony within days of each other, he quickly learned that, whatever their commercial ties, these individuals were linked most strongly by religious views that differed in important particulars from those held by the majority of the Massachusetts settlers. Because of their beliefs, over the next decade—first in Saugus and Lynn, then in Ipswich, Yarmouth, and Newbury, and finally across the Merrimack River in Hampton and Exeter—the Husbandmen caused Winthrop and other leaders of the colony no small degree of consternation. Led by Stephen Batchelor, a seventy-year-old Hampshireman whom the group had chosen for their minister, they insisted on their prerogative to covenant together to practice the Puritan faith as they understood it, whether or not their understanding coincided with that of the colonial government. Although the Husbandmen clearly were "Puritans," because they were inclined, as Winthrop later noted sharply, toward a more spiritually egalitarian form of Puritanism called "familism," they represented an element of English Protestantism too radical for the governor and his associates to tolerate.[2]

Between 1630 and 1660, among the approximately twenty thousand colonists who settled in New England there were many individuals, ministers as well as laymen, whose Puritanism was not consonant with the official ideology of the Bay Colony and whose difficulties with its government paralleled those of Batchelor and his followers. The Massachusetts Puritans attempted to limit the colony's population to those whose religious views were compatible to their own, and as the decade of the 1630s wore on, compatibility more and more meant agreement with the principles of nonseparating congregationalism. Nevertheless, the great Puritan migration that, beginning in 1629, brought to New England a cross section of old England's population, included many who had been influenced by theological views more radical than those officially sanctioned in Massachusetts and who subsequently sought to promulgate them in the communities where they settled. By the 1640s New England's congregationalists (as well as their conservative English critics) complained that the colonies harbored self-declared (or scarcely disguised) separatists, antinomians, familists, Seekers, anabaptists, Ranters, Adamites, and Quakers, all implicitly aligned against the established church system because of their insistence that an individual's personal religious experience supersede the demands of ecclesiastical tradition and civil law. In many cases, theirs were the same Protestant principles Winthrop and others earlier had defended in England yet, under pressure to settle a wilderness and codify their ecclesiology, soon enough condemned as seditious or heretical.

The experiences of the Husbandmen and other radical Puritans in seventeenth-century New England have not been studied with any completeness because of a prevailing disposition among historians of colonial America to regard American Puritanism as relatively homogeneous and the American sectarians only as weak, if prophetic, advocates of religious toleration. To be sure, accounts of early New England history invariably mention such prominent dissenters as Roger Williams, Anne Hutchinson, and the Quakers; still, no historian has attempted to document either the widespread presence of radical Puritans in New England or their complex and extended relationship to their English counterparts.[3] A number of studies—most notably those of Christopher Hill and Keith Thomas—do describe the radical Protestant sects that flourished in England between the death of Queen Elizabeth and the Restoration, but historians of American Puritanism have insistently portrayed it as but one branch of an English plant and not itself a vigorous if slender rootstock that brought forth the same exotic varietals as its English counterpart.[4] Williams, Hutchinson, and the Quakers, as significant as were their challenges to the New England Way, offer only the most memorable examples of an inescapable fact: between 1630 and 1660 the doctrinal and ecclesiastical, as well as the imaginative, development of American Puritanism was nurtured in soil thoroughly turned by radical elements in the New Englanders' midst.

This resistance to an acknowledgment of the radicals' effect upon New England Puritanism can be traced to the still-pervasive influence of Perry Miller, who in his magisterial account of "the New England mind"— what he termed his "map of the intellectual terrain of the seventeenth century"—continually emphasized what he considered the New England Puritans' supreme achievement. To him this achievement was the theological and ecclesiastical synthesis known as nonseparating congregationalism, an ecclesiastical system under which individual congregations maintained their autonomy while at the same time claiming their continued allegiance to the hierarchy of the Church of England. But in his desire to illustrate the extent to which the American Puritans were successful in promulgating and defending this world-view, Miller was too willing to believe that "after the New England divines had weathered the storm of 1637–1638 they were never seriously threatened by any form of Antinomianism, though they were horrified by the sectarian outbursts in England . . . and magnified the few Quakers who ventured within their jurisdiction." He sketched the contours of his "map" of New England's intellectual development under the assumption, too readily accepted by other scholars, that "the first three generations in New England paid almost unbroken allegiance to a unified body of thought, and that individual differences among particular writers or theorists were merely minor variations within a general frame." In the two decades since Miller's death, it has become all too clear that the "liberty" he took of "treating the whole literature as though it were the product of a single intelligence" reveals more about his own desire for order than it does of the full complexity of the New England mind in the seventeenth century.[5]

Miller's eagerness to identify those characteristics that distinguished American Puritanism from its English and Continental counterparts and his insistence that the American wilderness guaranteed such distinctions, led him to claim that through the early eighteenth century the "official cosmology" of the Bay Colony remained unmarked by any challenge to its legitimacy. Even in *From Colony to Province* (1953), a study devoted to the institutional development of New England Puritanism, he maintained that "such developments as took place [in the colonists' ideology]" only affected "lesser areas of church polity, political relations, or the contests of groups and interests." Miller admitted that some of these developments had been "intense and shattering experiences" for those who were involved in them, yet, he believed, these events did not cause "any significant alterations" in the "doctrinal frame of reference" within the colony.[6] But the sheer intellectual vigor of Miller's narrative in this work (and in other works of his that deal with seventeenth-century New England) undercuts his assumption: the intensity of the conflicts over matters of church polity and colonial politics, as well as over theological doctrine, indicates that, no matter how decidedly the Puritan authorities "triumphed" in these "contests of groups and interests," the various challenges to the magistrates' authority initiated by dissenting colonists had an undeniable effect upon the future course of New England's history. Miller viewed New England dissent as a sideshow to the events on the main stage of New England's intellectual and social history.

I will argue, in contrast, that in large measure New England Puritanism developed as it did because of, and not in spite of, the criticism of the colony from those in the population whose vision of the kingdom of God in America differed significantly from John Winthrop's.

In the last decade some scholars of early American history and culture have begun to recognize this fact. Larzer Ziff, for example, in his wide-ranging study *Puritanism in America: New Culture in a New World*, has argued (as had Kai Erikson in his *Wayward Puritans*) that "dominant Puritan culture had in the 1630s defined itself through defining deviancy from it," but Ziff limits his discussion of the "deviants" only to the standard figures: Williams, Hutchinson, and Rhode Island's Samuel Gorton. Ziff realizes that the "triumphant [Puritan] culture was not to continue to grow without weaving into its fabric threads from the concepts of its opposers," yet does not rend the fabric of New England society fully enough to discern its true warp and woof. Like Miller, he concludes that "the many signs of dissension in the Massachusetts of the 1640s combined ultimately to underline the great strength of the culture that could adjust to them without a significant shift in its particular conception of reality."[7]

A perusal of church, town, and colony records of seventeenth-century New England reveals, however, a surprisingly wide range of theological opinion in the colonies before the Restoration and a complex relation of such diversity to the internal development of American Puritan doctrine. *Heterogeneity*, not unanimity, actually characterized the colony's religious life. Darrett Rutman, who has gone as far as anyone to challenge Miller's conclusions about the existence of a unified body of thought called "American Puritanism," noted that, contrary to the observations of Miller and other historians, "orthodox New England possessed the semblance but not the substance of unity."[8] In such works as *Winthrop's Boston: Portrait of a Puritan Town* and *American Puritanism: Faith and Practice*, Rutman argues that, even among the ministers in the colony, "disparity of doctrine and even practice was the rule, not the exception." For him, American Puritanism can best be explained as a chance confluence of diverse cultural and religious forces; "if what eventually emerged was uniquely American," he writes, "it was only because one found here a continuing juxtaposition of varied elements which could not be duplicated anywhere." In New England "there was no Puritan way, no constant to be injected" by the settlers into the waiting body of the new continent. There were merely the "actions, reactions, interactions" of the heterogeneous population themselves.[9]

Rutman's astute assessment addresses itself specifically to the range of theological opinion in colonial New England; his conclusions are derived from detailed demographic analyses. If he fails finally to explore the significance of the dialectic between the dissenters and more moderate Puritans in New England for the development of Puritan doctrine, or the dissenters' role in what in effect was a transatlantic debate about the nature and extent of the Puritan renovation of society, Rutman at least calls attention to the ideological blinders that narrowed Miller's delineation of the intellectual contours of the New England mind. As one recent student has said of the Antinomian Controversy—in seventeenth-century New England the most important radical challenge to the ideology of nonseparating congregationalism: "it was apparent from the outset that not all who came to the Bay Colony had been listening to the same spirit or brought the same notions about the nature of the New England enterprise." [10] Here, in the very complexity of English Puritanism on the eve of the colonization of New England, we must seek an understanding of the true import of what Miller and others hitherto have dismissed as "minor" events in the development of American Puritanism.

In 1936 Charles M. Andrews noted that the large influx of settlers to New England between 1630 and 1640 had "brought an unusual number of ministers . . . whose interpretations of scripture and the purpose of God in his relations with men . . . represented many shades of opinion." It is also important to recognize that the New England mind was formed as much, if not more, by the laity, by what another historian has called "the spontaneous, irrepressible aggregation of like-minded saints in shifting voluntary groups . . . seeking comfort and enlightenment for themselves from the Gospel." [11] A full understanding of seventeenth-century New England Puritanism depends on an acknowledgment that many of those who migrated to America did not share a fixed ideology or commitment to an agreed-upon ecclesiastical program as much as a common spiritual hunger and a disenchantment with the Church of England's refusal to address the nation's spiritual famine. Further, English Puritans—including those who later emigrated to the New World—had not tempered their intellectual and social bonds at any single ideological forge but over the spiritual flames of countless private devotional meetings or "conventicles" throughout England. [12] From these private meetings, which perhaps more than any institution or idea provided Puritans with a group identity, sprang not only the likes of John Winthrop, Thomas Hooker, Thomas Shepard, and others who became staunch supporters of nonseparating congregationalism, but also those individuals who by the mid-1640s had helped to generate a myriad of radical Puritan sects that threatened to fulfill the prophecy of Acts 17:6 and turn the known world upside down. In England the soon-to-be settlers' experience as "Puritans" had been as varied as the regions from which they came. This fact must inform any examination of the variety of American Puritanism.

From what we know of the persistence of English local institutions in the various New England towns that have been examined by such historians as T. H. Breen and David Grayson Allen, it should come as no surprise that once in the New World many Puritans sought to replicate the form and quality of their previous religious experience.[13] They replicated precisely what one would expect from English Puritanism between 1630 and 1660: everything from the most structured presbyterianism to the religious and social radicalism of antinomians, Seekers, and Ranters. Moreover, in the free air of the New World, English Puritans had every right to anticipate that what they had learned in the privacy of their conventicles would form the basis of a new social order. History would prove their dreams illusory. Many individuals, once as powerless before the bishops as other of their brethren, who had justified their resistance to the Church of England through appeals to individual religious experience similar to those that led others to more radical positions, in the New World assumed a more conservative posture. They came to believe that, no matter what their experience with more radical forms of Puritan thought in England, they must establish and maintain strict doctrinal orthodoxy to achieve civil order in a new society. Most historians have minimized the resistance to the institution of such a unified body of doctrine in New England. It is clear, nevertheless, that the experience of English Puritanism was too varied to have been so easily transformed without serious challenge by those whose understanding of the logic of the Gospel plan differed at many points from that of the leaders of the more conservative colonies. Miller would have us marvel at how compelling the colonists found the New England Way. Rather, we should ask why anyone who had experienced the range of English Puritan thought, and the spiritual and social liberation it offered, would accept the ideological limitations of New England congregationalism.

Consider Samuel Gorton, founder of Warwick, Rhode Island, a radical spiritist with many connections to the sectarian underground in England, particularly to the General Baptist groups. Frequently linked to such prominent English radicals as John Saltmarsh and William Dell, Gorton was instrumental in preparing the way for the reception of the Quakers in his colony. Or John Clarke, of Newport, also in the Rhode Island colonies, a Particular Baptist who, along with Obadiah Holmes and John Crandall, openly challenged the relationship of church and state in Massachusetts. He maintained close contact with his doctrinal counterparts in London, particularly Henry Jessey and John Tombes, two of the signers of the famous Baptist Confession of 1644.[14] Then, too, there was William Pynchon, first settler of Springfield in the Connecticut Valley of Massachusetts, who took his inspiration from such English latitudinarians or "Socinians" as Anthony Wotton and John Goodwin. Pynchon's tracts published in the 1650s display his advocacy of an enlightened rationalism in religion, particularly as a basis for toleration of diverse Christian opinions; his settlement in the Valley initiated that region's long-standing challenge to the supremacy, religious and otherwise, of the clergy of eastern Massachusetts. William Aspinwall, one of the antinomians disarmed in 1637, later returned to England to become a prolific pamphleteer for the cause of the Fifth Monarchy; his conception of a divinely instituted church state was reviewed and accepted by some of the most advanced radicals of the 1650s. One of his followers, Thomas Venner, left his trade as a wine cooper in Boston to lead the major Fifth Monarchy uprising in London in 1661; he was hanged, drawn, and quartered, and his head was placed on a pike atop one of the city gates.[15] These are but a few of the more prominent spokesmen for Puritan radicalism in New England. Many have received insufficient attention.

The response of the Bay Colony and of Connecticut to the presence of such radicals was complicated by the fact that some of the points of doctrine which from the outset of the migration had been central to the evolution of the New England Way encouraged the same radical conclusions about church and society advanced by the sectarians, both at home and in England. Note, in particular, the colonists' fervent millennialism and their belief in both a gathered church of Christian saints and, more important, the animating power of the Holy Spirit.[16] These emphases within New England Puritanism, especially the Puritans' stress on the witness of the Spirit in each saint and on the saint's obligation to bring Christ's kingdom to earth, were irreducible elements of the religious culture within which the colonists had lived in old England. It was by fully addressing the ideological implications of such beliefs that the leaders of Massachusetts and Connecticut could implement their own more conservative plans for the renovation of the English church. The nature and extent of the dialogue between representatives of nonseparating congregationalism and those among the settlers who, at least initially, refused to relinquish their own very different plans for the establishment of a Christian commonwealth lies at the center of any appreciation of the complexity of New England's religious culture in the mid-seventeenth century.

The radicals' ideas, in addition to affecting the officially sanctioned theology of New England Puritanism, contributed significantly to the social and political development of the New England colonies. This was particularly so in the ways in which Massachusetts and Connecticut congregationalists protected themselves against the further spread of radical ideas, and in their response to the increasing criticism of their repressive policies levelled at them by their English brethren.[17] Further, the radicals' various challenges to the New England Way also had profound effect on the Puritans' imaginative conception of themselves and their social experiment. It is the underlying premise of Sacvan Bercovitch's *The American Jeremiad* that since their earliest days in the New World the Puritans had adhered to a "myth of America" that involved the creation and maintenance of an ideological community most clearly defined not by its territorial or political integrity but by its members' incessant rhetorical self-justification of a divinely ordained purpose.[18] Scholars of American Puritanism, including Miller and Bercovitch himself, have described the development of this myth of American exceptionalism in terms of the colonists' adoption and subtle modification of the principles of nonseparating congregationalism, particularly in light of an increasing awareness of their physical and ideological distance from old England.[19] But what is apparent in the colonists' elaborate definitions and justifications of their ecclesiastical polity and evident in their polemics against dissenters is that the New Englanders' ideological self-image was shaped less by any set of ecclesiastical principles than by an unyielding effort to neutralize the influence of those who argued for a much more radical reorganization of the society. The "middle-class culture" that defined New England from its earliest days was the result not merely, as Bercovitch suggests, of the New Englanders' freedom from the feudal restrictions of Europe, of a corrupt opportunism in the face of New World opportunity, or of an antipathy to the Arminian tendencies of the Church of England,[20] but also of a sharp and continual debate with those who from their English Puritan experience had formed a particularly democratic notion of their errand into America's wilderness.

I am concerned with the social and political, as well as with the religious, implications of the radical Puritans' presence in New England. Like Miller, Ziff, and Bercovitch, I recognize the importance for American history of the ideological consensus that later generations of Americans discerned in the first decades of New England's settlement. But, once aware of the nature and extent of the radical challenges to this consensus, we have every right to ask why seventeenth-century New En-

gland did not become *more* radicalized and *more* democratic than it did.
Such scholars of English Puritanism as William Haller and Christopher
Hill have taught us that the Puritan sectarians fundamentally challenged
many of the traditional assumptions on which their society was based.
In the religious sphere they raised searching questions about the proper
relationship of church and state, the minister and his congregation, the
word of the Bible and the witness of the Spirit. They also reexamined the
moral bases of society: they challenged the established relationship of
the sexes in both the religious and domestic spheres; they questioned the
very existence of heaven and hell, and of sin, and wondered aloud if in
an age of impending apocalypse an educated ministry was at all necessary. As Haller himself noted many years ago, to attempt to reform the
Church of England in the seventeenth century was quite simply "to attempt the reorganization of society."[21] Why, then, did the New England
Puritans, three thousand miles away from the iron grasp of the bishops,
refuse to incorporate into their society more of the ideas the radicals advocated? If, as the Woburn, Massachusetts, militia-captain Edward Johnson wrote, New England was "the place where the Lord will create a
new Heaven, and a new Earth in, new Churches and a new Commonwealth together," what prevented the colony from being modeled after
the spiritual utopia of a John Saltmarsh, or the political democracy of a
John Lilburne?[22]

Such speculation is not out of line, for a large number of those who
came to New England in the 1630s and 1640s, before the advent of the
English civil wars had shifted the Puritans' focus back to England, clearly
believed that their transatlantic voyage had been undertaken for much
more than an escape from ecclesiastical persecution. Since the 1620s they
had heard countless Puritan preachers remind them of the Books of
Daniel and Revelation, in which it was apparent that "there be many
Prophesies and Promises . . . that are not yet fulfilled; and the fulfilling
whereof will bring the *Church* into a more glorious condition than ever it
was yet in the World." For many who came to America in those two decades it seemed perfectly plausible that in their new home such prophecy
would be fulfilled. From New England one could view not only the return of Christ, but the staging of his triumph over Satan's legions.[23] New
Englanders were not hesitant to raise Christ's standard and march in the
vanguard of his armies, for they believed that they were a chosen people.
As Edward Johnson put it, "God hath . . . caused the dazeling brightnesse of his presence to be contracted in the burning-Glasse of [their]
zeal." New England was destined to be more than a shining beacon upon

a hill. Its spiritual ardor would set Christ's fire to the whole world, its flames never quenched "till it hath burnt up Babilon Root and Branch."[24]

Thomas Tillam, who later returned to England a fervent Fifth Monarchist, in a poem written "Upon the first sight of New-England, June 29, 1638," hailed a "holy-land wherein our holy lord/Hath planted his most true and holy word" for the sake of a society in which he and his fellow colonists, "free from all annoye," could "Injoye" Christ's presence in every aspect of their lives. A similar eschatological hope compelled Ezekiel Rogers of Rowley to remind Governor Winthrop in 1639 that the "worke of the Lorde in bringing so many pretious ones to this place is not for nothing." Like Boston's minister, the renowned John Cotton, who that same year began to preach the sermons that would comprise *An Exposition upon the Twelfth Chapter of the Revelation*, Rogers looked forward to the reappearance of Christ on earth and the bestowal of his blessing on "none but [the] downright godly ones" who had prayed for his reappearance; Rogers was sure that the Saviour first would be seen in New England. By 1647 Samuel Symonds of Ipswich knew enough of New England to proclaim that the days of the New Jerusalem had indeed commenced: "Is not government in church and Common weale (according to gods own rules) that new heaven and earth promised, in the fullnes accomplished when the Jewes come in; and the first fruites begun in this poore of New Engl[and] . . . ?" Similarly, Sir Symonds D'Ewes, writing in his autobiography in 1638 from the perspective of England, believed the New England experiment of paramount importance, "a true type of heaven itself" in which the colonists, "in the main, aim simply at God's glory, and to reduce the public service of God to that power and purity which it enjoyed in primitive times." In 1651 his sentiment was echoed by none other than Oliver Cromwell, who begged John Cotton to write to tell him "What is the Lord a-doing? What prophecies are now fulfilling?"[25]

New England, then, was settled in the belief that it was to become nothing less than a fulfillment of biblical prophecy, a land in which the life of the spirit informed all behavior and so would mark the spot of the New Jerusalem. Within such a context of millennial expectation the Puritan radicals presented plans, which they believed to be as firmly grounded in Scripture as the more conservative Puritans did theirs, for the religious and social reformation that would initiate Christ's holy commonwealth.

The radicals' challenge to the church and state in England was effectively defused by the political and religious settlement of the Restoration. By the 1660s in the New World, however, compromise had taken a different form: the dissenters seemingly had become *bona fide* members of the congregational order on which Winthrop, Hooker, Shepard, and others had expended so much intellectual effort. In New England, where the Church of England never had been institutionalized, one found instead the gradual evolution of an ideological system that, while it could not fully satisfy the spiritist longings of the radicals, harnessed enough of the potential energy of their ideas to garner the support of the majority of the settlers. Only at the fringes of Massachusetts and Connecticut—in the Rhode Island communities (which one observer called "the receptacle of all sorts of riff-raff people, and . . . the sewer of New England") and to the north in what eventually became New Hampshire and Maine—did the inhabitants continue to press for a different social order from that overseen by Winthrop or Thomas Dudley.[26] At the meetings of the Synod of 1662, which set the direction of the New England Way for the next fifty years, those who represented congregationalism—"a speaking *Aristocracy* in the face of a silent Democracy," in the words of the Hartford minister Samuel Stone—emerged with enough power to end the plans of more radical Puritans for the establishment of a New Canaan.[27]

The manner in which the supporters of both the Synods of 1648 and 1662 gathered such power to themselves of course is of great interest, for the compromises over polity and doctrine to which the colonies' leaders were forced by their more radical brethren also led to the American Puritans' most impressive achievement, the sublimation of radical ideology into the emerging "myth of America" described by scholars like Bercovitch and Robert Middlekauff in their accounts of the New England mind.[28] Through the rhetorical power of the ministers' jeremiads and the subtle redefinition of New England's errand within the terms of scriptural typology, much of the original force of the radicals' criticism of seventeenth-century society was subsumed into the millennial component of Puritan thought that always had formed a significant part of the Puritans' understanding of their position in the New World.

The full co-optation of the radicals' program into what Bercovitch elsewhere calls "the American self" had to await the second generation of American Puritans, who had missed both the excitement of life in outlawed conventicles and the heady delight of viewing the New World as "a new Indes of heavenly treasure" where "yet more . . . may be."[29] But even as the foundation of the New England Way was being laid in the years before 1660, Puritans in both old and New England had begun to worry whether the colony was fulfilling the divine destiny to which it was called. In 1644, for example, Roger Williams thought it a "monstrous Paradox" that within the Bay Colony "Gods children should persecute Gods children" and reported "the Speech of an honourable Knight of the Parliament" who, on hearing of the intolerance of the Massachusetts leaders, exclaimed: "What, Christ persecute Christ in New England?" Isaac Penington, arguing against John Norton's defense of the colony's persecution of the Quakers in the 1650s, asked New Englanders to consider whether they really had felt themselves "to grow in the inward life, upon [their] coming into *New-England*, or did that [life] begin to flag and wither, and [their] growth chiefly consist in form and outward order?" Even Peter Bulkeley, minister to the frontier outpost of Concord and a strong supporter of Shepard, warned that unless the colonists rearranged their priorities "God [may] remove thy Candlesticke out of the midst of thee" and change Massachusetts from "a Citie upon an hill, which many seek unto," to "a Beacon upon the top of a mountaine, desolate and forsaken." Though John Cotton, as his grandson Cotton Mather reported, may indeed have written to John Davenport that in New England "*the order of the churches and commonwealth . . . brought to his mind the new heaven and the new earth,*" it is essential to realize that his sentiment simply was not shared by all the population. Some had very different expectations for the future of the colony.[30]

In the place of the spiritual and, by implication, political democracy the radicals demanded, the New Englanders erected only a half-way house on the road to a more democratic society—the congregationalism that played so large a part in the liberation of radical ideology in England but which, when institutionalized as it was in New England, more often than not produced supporters as harsh and intolerant as the English prelates.[31] But some historians—Stephen Foster, for example—argue that the colonists "actually put into practice the Independents' most visionary and apparently unachievable goals," specifically, an "insistence on the rule of the saints, on government of and by the regenerate."[32] More important, for the first four decades of New England's history individuals and groups who represented the full range of English Puritan thought fertilized the New England mind with much more novel, and sometimes downright startling, ideas carried with them from their English experience.

PART I

THE VARIETIES OF
NEW ENGLAND
PURITAN RADICALISM

A NURSERY OF

SCHISMATICKES

Writing in 1644 to a friend in England, Thomas Shepard lamented "the late differences and breaches among the godly" in that country and warned against "the spreading of the contagion of corrupt opinions." "Such cracks and flames in the new building of the Reformation portend a fall," he continued; to avoid "worse dayes than ever England yet saw" English Puritans would have to follow New England's example and move decisively to crush dangerous heterodoxies before the contagion became epidemic. The Massachusetts Bay Colony had not hesitated to suppress antinomians and familists, Shepard told his correspondent, and therefore "The Churches here are in peace; The Common Wealth in peace; The Ministry in most sweet peace; The Magistrates (I should have named first) in peace."[1]

A few years later, Shepard's co-worker in Christ's ministry in New England, Nathaniel Ward, echoed his sentiments. Under the guise of the "Simple Cobler of Aggawam in America" he warned the English people that their nation could be saved from the religious and social chaos brought on by the civil wars only if Parliament and the King agreed upon a policy that would eliminate the increasing support for religious toleration, itself responsible for the proliferation of sects in his native land. "Either I am in an Apoplexie," Ward wrote, "or that man is in a Lethargie, who doth not now sensibly feele God shaking the heavens over his

head, and the earth under his feet" because of England's religious difficulties. The inhabitants of England, he continued, now "stagger like
drunken men"; and "no marvel," for they had "transgress[ed] the Lawes,
chang[ed] the Ordinances, and brok[en] the Everlasting Covenant" with
God. Ward's advice to his homeland, where Satan fished in "royled wa-
ters," was the same as Shepard's: to follow New England's example and
crush radical sectarians wherever they arose. "I dare take upon me," the
Ipswich minister announced, "to bee the herauld of *New-England* so
farre, as to proclaime to the world, in the name of our colony, that all
Familists, Antinomians, Anabaptists, and other Enthusiasts shall have
free Liberty to keepe away from us."[2]

With respect to the success of the Massachusetts Puritans in controlling
the "Opinionists" in their midst, Shepard and Ward in fact were whis-
tling in the dark. In the mid-1640s, for example, Samuel Gorton, leader
of a group of radical spiritists in Warwick, Rhode Island, had successfully
pressed his case in Parliament against Massachusetts for the colony's
harsh treatment of him and his followers, and in 1648 he returned to
Boston under the protection of none other than the Earl of Warwick.[3] In
the mid-1640s, too, several groups of "Anabaptists" flourished at the
southern borders of the Bay Colony, and, despite the stringent law against
the sect passed in 1644, more and more individuals within the Massachusetts churches risked punishment to proclaim their sympathy with baptist principles.[4] If that were not enough, in the very year Ward published
his *Simple Cobler of Aggawam* (1647), Robert Childe, William Vassal, and
other opponents of the strict congregationalism of the Bay circulated a
petition in which they called for open church membership and few restrictions upon those who held liberal theological views. Thus, although
in his *Simple Cobler* Ward had complained that among many Englishmen, the Massachusetts settlers had unjustly been "reputed a Colluvies of
wild Opinionists, swarmed into a more remote wilderness to find elbow-
roome" for their "phanatick Doctrines and practises," in many respects
the description was apt.[5]

There is no denying that the Massachusetts and Connecticut theocrats
were able to prevent their colonies from disintegration into various war-
ring camps, particularly if one considers their successful repression of
Anne Hutchinson and her supporters in the Antinomian Controversy of
1636–1638 and the severe chastisement of the Quakers in the late 1650s.
For too long, however, these two episodes in early New England history
have been taken as indications that opponents of the New England Way
had little effect upon the development of American Puritanism. If, on the

other hand, close attention is paid to the frequency of disciplinary cases that appear in town, church, and colony records, it is apparent that between 1630 and 1660 New England Puritanism experienced an ideological fragmentation similar, though on a smaller scale, to that of its English counterpart. Although the leaders of the two largest New England colonies were able to prevent any single radical group from holding a significant degree of power, throughout the first three decades of New England's history the emergent synthesis we now call "American Puritanism" was constantly challenged by individuals and groups who did not readily accept the principles of nonseparating congregationalism advocated by the majority of the settled ministers. The influence of these dissenters was subtle but important, for as representatives of more radical Puritan ideology they strongly pressed the ministers and magistrates to adjust their understanding of New England's mission to the demands of those in the population who found the ecclesiastical polity of a John Cotton or a Thomas Hooker an insufficient approximation of a true Christian commonwealth.

It has long been noticed that, as a movement that focused on what one historian has described as the "personal experience of the Spirit's regenerating work," teaching "that individuals, unencumbered by ecclesiastical tradition, could discover God's will directly in scripture by the Spirit's illumination," Puritanism was "inherently susceptible to sectarian proliferation."[6] Students of Puritanism's English and continental forms have stressed its centrifugal tendencies; Henry Ainsworth, writing in his *Communion of Saints* (1607) about his congregation's difficulties in their exile in Holland, referred to the saints' predilection "(if they be not wary, and have their wits exercised to discover good and evil) to be carried about with divers and strange doctrines" and so to "fall into errors, heresies, & idolatries."[7] But it has been generally assumed that what characterized *American* Puritanism was a strong orthodoxy that kept the population massed around a common center of belief and discouraged any doctrines which threatened to delay the construction of a conservative, hierarchical social order.

Many contemporary accounts from the first thirty years of New England's history belie this simplistic generalization and indicate that, as hard as they tried, the moderate Puritan leaders of the colonies could not contain the Reformation's effervescent new wine in bottles left over from the Middle Ages. As early as 1624 in the tiny settlement at Plymouth, for example, John Lyford, an Anglican clergyman whom the Pilgrims refused to ordain as their minister, had written to England to expose the divisions within the infant colony between "saints" and non-church members that had prevented his election. And throughout the early 1630s the colony labored under the ministry of Ralph Smith, whose extreme separatist position further encouraged schismatic tendencies.[8] In 1633, only a few years after the settlement of a large group of English Puritans around Trimount (later Boston), Edward Howes, who from England was closely watching the colony's progress, told John Winthrop the Younger that he had heard "that your ministers preach one against the other's doctrines," a situation he regarded as "a great scandall," one which "if not reformed in tyme," might "prove . . . fatal" to the people's hopes for the colony.[9] By the time John Clarke, the future leader of the Particular Baptists in Rhode Island, arrived in Massachusetts early in 1636, he encountered the factionalism that shortly thereafter threatened to tear apart the colony in the famous Antinomian Controversy. "I thought it not strange to see men differ about matters of Heaven, for I expect no less on Earth," he wrote; "But to see that they were not able to bear [with] each other in their different understandings and consciences, as in those utmost parts of the World to live peaceable together," was more than he could bear.[10] Not for that had Clarke braved the Atlantic in winter, and almost immediately he journeyed out of the limits of Massachusetts, to the wilderness of Rhode Island.

During the period between 1636 and 1638 the New England Puritan leaders were preoccupied with their case against John Cotton and the Hutchinsonians, but even after scores of individuals had been banished in the aftermath of the Synod of 1637 the colony still was bothered by sectarian ferment, increasingly organized by those whom Ezekiel Rogers of Rowley called those "Anabaptisticall Spiritts among us." In 1639 Rogers complained to Governor Winthrop—in what has to be one of the classic understatements of this period of American history—that "truly, Sir, we are not yet (the body of the land, I meane) as we must be." His plea for the magistracy "to clense our mixtures and filth" before the colony was visited by a "sore scourge" soon was echoed by ministers like Concord's Peter Bulkeley, whose series of sermons, published in 1646 as *The Gospel-Covenant*, addressed the Puritans' confusion in the aftermath of Hutchinson's challenge to the clergy's supremacy. Bulkeley lamented a "generation in the Land, that are altogether looking after new light, and new truths," a generation with "itching eares, itching mindes, and itching tongues also, itching to be fed with, and to be venting novelties." It may indeed be "the blemish of our English nation," he continued, "that they have been alwayes new-fangled, running after new fashions, taking up with the fashions of every Nation," but it also had become only too evident that in Massachusetts, where "every one is forward to vent his own imagination, and hath libertie to so doe, every one saying, I have seene, I have seene," the colony had become filled "with idle fancies, which breed questions, rather than godly edifying."[11]

Bulkeley identified as staggering drunk on "old poysoned errors" the radical sectarians who preoccupied New England's moderate Puritan leaders. By the mid-1640s, when the colony's difficulties with Samuel Gorton were at the front of everyone's attention, Winthrop and others clearly feared that, even apart from the tension Gorton had caused with some of the native Americans around his settlement at Shawomet, he was most dangerous because of the wide appeal of his spiritist ideas, that is, his belief that God literally dwelled in the heart of the true Christian.[12] In 1644 John Endecott of Salem had warned Winthrop that "Wee have heere divers that are taken with Gortons opinions" and asked whether "it were not best to bynde" over one of these troublemakers to the Massachusetts General Court "to make such a one exemplarie, that others might feare." To Endecott and Salem's minister, Edward Norris, who had had first-hand experience with such English spiritists (called "Antinomians" because they purportedly obeyed the voice of the Spirit within rather than the moral law) as John Traske, it was apparent that "both with you & with us, & in other places [,] that heresie doth spread which at length may prove dangerous." The General Court's speedy release of the Gortonists from their sentences of hard labor in the various communities in which they had been placed and their subsequent banishment from Massachusetts further indicate the authorities' fears that it was a great risk to leave these individuals in towns where they might garner more support for their ideas.[13]

And so it went through the late 1640s and 1650s. The Plymouth court records indicate that "after the . . . business about Gorton" the "error of Anabaptistry" noticeably increased.[14] In 1655 the Massachusetts clergy were worried about the colony's infiltration by even more radical ideas that had spread through England after the execution of King Charles and the consequent struggle for political power. In that year Charles Chauncy, the minister at Scituate in Plymouth Colony, who had succeeded Henry Dunster as president of Harvard College, was deeply disturbed by both the "contempt of the word of God and his Ordinances" throughout New England, and, even more ominously, the "listening to lying books & pamphlets, that are brought over into the country, whereby multitudes" were "poysoned" against the ordained ministry.[15] Chauncy had foremost in mind the works of William Dell, who had been carrying on a sharp campaign against "university" men; and before too long the doctrines for which Dell, John Saltmarsh, and other advanced English Puritan radicals had argued found their way across the Atlantic. There also was support among the population for those derisively called "Quakers," who sought to destroy the very conjunction of church and state the New England leaders had worked so hard to maintain. By 1656 the Massachusetts authorities felt so threatened by these newest of "new Lights" that they sentenced several of them to be hanged, prompting even so unpolitical a soul as Anne Bradstreet, the "tenth muse lately sprung up in America," to register her shock at the sight of the colony "filled with blasphemy, and sectaries, and some who have been accounted sincere Christians . . . carried away with them." Indeed, Bradstreet was so troubled that she was compelled to ask herself, she reported, "Is there faith upon the earth?" [16] Evidently what Thomas Shepard had observed as he preached his sermons on *The Parable of the Ten Virgins* in the years immediately following the Antinomian Controversy still haunted the colony's leadership. "Many of God's servants," he had written, "lie under hard thoughts and speeches in private, not only from enemies abroad, but from inhabitants at home; men out of the church censuring and judging members; men in the church, [judging] of [one] another, especially if they take it to a side. . . ." [17] Where, in all this confusion and bitterness, was the much-vaunted strength of the New England theocracy?

In the decades before 1660 the colonies' leaders obviously faced more than just a highly visible threat from prominent individuals like Williams or Hutchinson whose Puritanism had evolved in directions similar to that of the radical sectarians in England. Contemporary accounts indicate in the population at large a considerable degree of sympathy with, if not support for, radical Puritan ideology. However strictly John Winthrop and the other patentees of the Massachusetts Bay Company had tried to select individuals fully committed to the Company's religious and economic venture, they could not eradicate the subtle but profound effects of the mystical strain that always formed a part of Calvinism and that had helped to crystalize their opposition to English episcopacy. Nor could they screen out those who, in one colonist's words, sought escape from an England in which "the straitness of the place is such as each man is fain to pluck his means, as it were, out of his neighbor's throat" and so went to New England in response to their disenchantment with their social condition. [18]

Christopher Hill and other historians of Puritanism have demonstrated

the importance of England's economic situation for the later generation
of radical ideas among the Puritan populace, but we perhaps have underestimated the significance of this motivation among those who had emigrated to New England because of their painful discovery that in their
homeland "there is such pressing and oppressing in town and country
about farms, trade, traffic, etc., so as a man can hardly any where set up a
trade but he shall pull down two of his neighbors," where "many good
men," Robert Cushman continued, "are glad to snap at a crust."[19] As
early as 1620, for example, as the Leyden separatists (known to posterity
as the Pilgrims) prepared to embark for America, Cushman, who was
acutely aware of economic "straitness," warned those reviewing "the
Reasons and Considerations touching the lawfulness of removing out of
England into the parts of America" that release from economic hardship
was not reason enough to join the infant colony. "The easiness, plainness
and plentifulness in living in those remote places, may quickly persuade
any man to a liking of this course," he wrote, and so "to practise a removal." For "honest, godly and industrious men," he continued, this was
fine; "but for others of dissolute and profane life, their rooms are better
than their companies."[20] By the late 1620s, when vice and "ungodliness"
were noticeably on the upswing in the colony, Cushman's fears were
confirmed: not all those who had joined the Plymouth adventurers found
under Governor Bradford's leadership the full promise of land or religious freedom they had expected from America.

The experience of the Massachusetts Puritans was similar. In his *Planters Plea* in 1630 John White stressed that for those interested in joining
the ever-increasing exodus to New England, "respect unto the advance-
ment of the Gospell" must be "predominant" so that "we may with
greater assurance depend upon Gods engagement in the worke." He
knew his countrymen's minds well enough, however, to understand that,
as conscientiously as he and others tried to restrict the colony to those
whose vision of New England agreed with his and John Winthrop's, "it
was absurd to conceive" that all the people boarding vessels in South-
ampton and elsewhere "have all one minde," and "more ridiculous to
imagine that they have all one scope." Although White maintained that
the majority of the colonists were "farre enough from projecting the
erecting of this Colony for a Nursery of *Schismatickes*," he was troubled
by his knowledge that though "Necessitie" might press some individuals
to emigrate and "Noveltie draw on others," most upsetting of all were
those settlers animated by "hopes of gain in times to come." Tired of an
England where hardship had become the rule, many who were "low in

their estates" were led into what one of the colony's English critics called a "fools paradize."[21]

As early as the spring of 1631 New England's leaders had begun to notice that there were significant numbers of people whose objectives in coming to the New World did not square with their own. Writing to Lady Bridget, the Countess of Lincoln whose husband was an important supporter of the Massachusetts Bay Company, Deputy Governor Thomas Dudley complained of colonists who in the late summer of 1630 had returned to England, "partly out of dislike of our government, which restrained and punished their excesses, and partly through fear of famine, not seeing other means than by their labor to feed themselves." Numbering close to one hundred individuals, these repatriated Englishmen quickly raised "many false and scandalous reports" against the colonial magistrates and ministers, particularly by affirming that for the most part they were "Brownists"—that is, strict separatists in religion. Dudley urged the Countess to make clear to other English Puritans who contemplated migration that "if any come hither to plant for worldly ends . . . he commits an error, of which he soon will repent." But "if any godly men, out of religious ends, will come over to help us in the good work we are about," he continued, "I think they cannot dispose of themselves . . . more to God's glory." If that were understood, Dudley concluded, Englishmen would not "fall short of their expectations when they come hither" and so cause dissension among the colonists.[22]

Dudley was particularly worried about the "poorer sort" who had ventured across the Atlantic—many as indentured servants—for he, Winthrop, and other architects of the Bay polity had "found by experience" that such had "hindered, not furthered the work." Contemporary accounts make clear that many of these people from the lower stratum of English society had come to New England with unduly heightened expectations, and as the decade of the 1630s advanced, many among them found "all things so contrary to the high reports given out" that they were ready to join with others who had little sympathy for the strictly hierarchical society about which Winthrop had preached in his "Modell of Christian Charity" and which he thereafter had sought to build on the banks of the Charles River.[23]

In the summer of 1630, Winthrop reported to his wife that even as the first settlers around Boston struggled to establish themselves, Satan seemed to be "unbending his forces" against them. He realized that in the new colony were many people "who never shewed so much wickednesse in England" as they had done there. In 1635, when some of the new arrivals to New England were granted land north of Boston in what then was called Agawam (now Ipswich), the town and church fathers decided to be more selective in how they distributed the remaining land in their community. In that year the town's minister, Nathaniel Ward, told John Winthrop the Younger that his townsmen "of late but somewhat too late have bene carefull on whom they bestowe lots, being awakened thereto by the confluence of many ill and doubtfull persons, and by their behavior since they came. . . ." Clearly, as Edward Howes had told the same Winthrop two years earlier, despite the Bay Company's attempts to recruit only those willing to work for God and the colony, too many men and women of "weake Judgments" had voyaged to the New World. Howes had gone on to warn his correspondent that "you have too many . . . amongst you on whom it were good your ministers took a little paines, that they might be rectified," but in the first five years of its settlement the colony was preoccupied with mere survival on the edge of New England's wilderness and still lacked sufficient numbers of "orthodox" ministers to discipline the population. In 1634 John Cotton complained that in the new settlement there was work "enough, and more than enough, to fill both [his and Thomas Hooker's] handes, yea and the handes of many brethren more," but, because of the colony's need for able-bodied men and women, those among the settlers whom John White had called "the very scum of the earth" of necessity were allowed to participate in the foundation work for the New Jerusalem without any serious attempt to reform their religious doctrine.[24]

Then, too, the early leaders of the Massachusetts Puritan enterprises—ministers and magistrates both—were not agreed upon what to expect from their fellow-colonists in religious belief and practice. As the late-seventeenth-century historian William Hubbard noted, with regard to their church way the early settlers in the Bay "walked something of an untrodden path" and had joined together in worship more by "some general profession of the doctrine of the Gospel" and the "honest and good intentions they had one towards another," than by any wide-ranging consent to what constituted a true church of God. Only after the Antinomian Controversy of 1636–1638 did a true ecclesiastical and, to a lesser extent, doctrinal party line emerge as ministers left the Newtown synod convinced that thereafter they had to present a unified front against certain kinds of Puritan ideas.[25] By then, the beliefs of the disaffected and dissident were too deeply entrenched to be extirpated. Driven to the north, south, and west of the Massachusetts colony, they established spiritual enclaves from which they could launch other, more subtle assaults against nonseparating congregationalism. Once experienced, the spiritist ideas that motivated such people simply could not be proscribed.

Even in the early 1630s, then, the tiny New England colonies were populated by individuals who quite clearly were not strong supporters either of the same religious mission or the emergent social ethic which, though then only partially formed in the minds of the colony's leaders, firmly grounded the New England Way. With the passing of each subsequent decade more and more of these dissidents—or, perhaps equally important—their ideas, found their way within earshot of others in Massachusetts and Connecticut who were, as John Cotton later put it, possessed by "an itching levity" and so were likely to be "taken with every wind of new Doctrine." [26]

In some cases, as with the Gortonists or the "Anabaptists," radical Puritan ideology found enough supporters so that entire groups and communities were swayed by the promise of a different—some said *easier*—way to heaven than that offered by the conservative Puritans. Others remained within congregational churches but occasionally challenged the theological or social implications of the Puritan creed. Such individuals or families exposed the community to the novelty of more radical ideas, often with a powerfully disintegrating effect upon the community's institutions. Whether brought to their radicalism through the spiritist preaching they had heard in England or their own pursuit of the ideological implications of Puritan doctrine, or swayed by a disenchantment with their economic and social positions, those in New England who defined themselves as "Puritans" of a quite different stripe from the Winthrops, Dudleys, and Shepards, shocked their neighbors into an awareness that God's plans for New England might be quite different from the organization eventually set forth in the Cambridge Platform of 1648.

In describing the variety and range of these "other" New England Puritans, historians have been hampered by the fact that the extensive scholarship on English Puritan radicalism that has been done by Christopher Hill, A. L. Morton, B. S. Capp, and others is only partially useful in categorizing religious radicalism in seventeenth-century New England. Many of the New Englanders who expressed comparable religious views had arrived in the New World prior to the turbulent period during which the Levellers, Diggers, Ranters, and Fifth Monarchy Men, for example, emerged to challenge the English church and state. [27] For the historian to speak, then, of a Leveller movement in Rhode Island or a Digger commune on the flank of Copp's Hill indicates a total misunderstanding of the complexity of Anglo-American Puritan radicalism. Because of the unique political and religious situation in England, many of the categories under which English Puritan radicals have been discussed simply are not applicable to New England; moreover, after 1640 few such English radicals left their homeland to build their worlds anew in America. It is nevertheless true in the 1650s as well as in the 1630s, there were individuals and groups whose religious radicalism developed in ways remarkably parallel to that of the English sectarians throughout this same period, a fact that can be at least partially explained by what one historian has described as the "inherent Jacobinism of Protestant theology" that produced a "revolutionary dynamic . . . irrepressibly particularistic and anti-authoritarian."[28] Puritan radicalism in America seems to have been, then, what Perry Miller described as a controlled laboratory experiment, one in which the centrifugal tendencies unleashed by Puritan ideology and the New England magistrates' attempts to harness them can be studied.

American Puritan radicalism is best identified through large ideological categories of individuals rather than by discrete religious groups of members banded together for any uniform purpose. It still is perfectly accurate to describe the people of seventeenth-century New England as "Puritans," but as Puritans who displayed varying degrees of commitment to doctrines such as the indwelling of the Spirit or the relation of sanctification to justification, or to the role of the magistracy in maintaining religious uniformity. More important, like their English brethren, New England dissenters, as Lyle Koehler recently has noted, very often "tied themselves to theologies which became sounding boards for grievances about society."[29]

In New England Puritanism can be traced the emergence of certain virile strains of religious thought that engendered particular political and social attitudes. The revolutionary dynamic within Puritanism unravelled by an internal logic of its own, whether extended against English bishops or Massachusetts theocrats. And if during this period of English history, as A. L. Morton has written in his monograph on the Ranters, "instead of religious ideas" always developing into "openly political ones," political ideas were "reclothing themselves in religious and even mystical forms," there is all the more reason to identify in the political ideology of such American groups as the Gortonists and Particular Baptists the precise grounds of their challenge to the Puritan magistrates.[30] If, as William Haller has argued, "the vitality of dogma is evinced as often in the heterodoxies it provokes as in the orthodoxies it maintains," I hope it will become clear how the emergent synthesis of religious and political ideology known as the New England Way was continuously revitalized by the challenge of radical elements.[31]

For such purposes American Puritan radicalism can conveniently be broken down into certain major categories based on fundamental tenets, each of which holds within it very different individuals with varying complaints against the nonseparating congregationalism of the moderate Puritans. One of these categories is the *separatists*, particularly the first settlers of Plymouth Colony and, more important, of Salem, where Roger Williams first preached; they threatened to expose the ecclesiastical sleight-of-hand by which the New England Puritans claimed to be true members of the church of Christ without having separated from the corrupt Church of England. Another category is the *radical spiritists*, who proclaimed with varying emphasis their utter dependence on the power of the Holy Spirit; among their numbers were not only the antinomians of the 1630s but the followers of individuals like Samuel Gorton and Randall Holden. A third group is the "Anabaptists," or, more accurately, the *General* and *Particular Baptists*, who, from the early 1640s on, broadcast their concerns about what they termed "believer's baptism" and their objections to the strict linkage of church and state. A fourth category, the *millenarians*, is perhaps the most difficult to identify because millennial ideas informed almost all varieties of Puritanism in the seventeenth century; still, they can be located with some degree of specificity in the 1650s by their increasingly shrill insistence that to be true to its original purpose, New England had to take immediate steps to initiate Christ's kingdom on earth. A final category is the *Quakers*, followers of George Fox and James Nayler, who by the mid-1650s had come to New England to convert the population to the doctrine of the inner light.[32] Members of each of these groups cross-fertilized others, but virtually every representative of radical Puritanism in New England can be placed in one of these groupings.

SEPARATISM: THE DEVIL'S

ALPHA AND *OMEGA*

ecause of Plymouth's settlement by separatists, who chose to remove themselves from membership in the Church of England
because of what they took to be the prevalence of false worship,
the separatists have always occupied a historical position out of proportion to their actual influence on the development of New England Puritanism. Even though the great majority of Plymouth's population had
cut all ties with the English church, the colony as a whole under the guidance of Governor William Bradford and his successors made no serious
attempt to promulgate its ecclesiastical doctrine in neighboring settlements. Rather, the importance of the Plymouth colonists and the groups
that spun off from them to other areas in southeastern Massachusetts and
Cape Cod, and of the separatists who settled in Salem in the late 1620s
and early 1630s, lies in how their radical position on church and state forwarded other, more heterodox ideas.

As the anonymous author of *A Blow at the Root, Or some Observations
toward a Discovery of the Subtilties and Devices of Satan* (1650) noted, "separation" was but the first step down an increasingly "sinful" path. "*Separation* is an ordinary step to *Anabaptisme*," he wrote; and "*Anabaptisme* per-
fects itself in *Seeking*, being above *Ordinances*, and *Questioning* everything
revealed in the *Scriptures*, and in high *Raptures* and *Revelations*." If this
were not enough, he continued, "This determines in *Levelling*, and

(through that) runnes compasse (with some) to that strange and fearfull *straine*" of perfect libertinism argued by the Ranters. Separatism, he concluded, was "the Devil's *Alpha* and *Omega*." As private and peaceful as Plymouth was, it thus held within its borders volatile elements, for the separatists' aspirations toward a purity of worship comparable to that enjoyed in the apostolic churches did, in fact, encourage restless souls to question the purity of *any* ordinances in this, a fallen world, and, in some cases, the very necessity of organized worship itself.[1]

Among English Puritans the separatist movement can be traced to Robert Browne. By the early 1580s Browne had concluded that, despite the prevailing disposition among Englishmen to accept the principle of national uniformity in religious belief, for those who knew that the worship practiced in the Church of England was unscriptural it was sinful to continue as members of that corrupt national body. Because he persisted in his opinion, Browne was forced to flee the Norwich area where he had gathered his own church, and with a band of his followers he settled in Middleburg, Holland, by that time a gathering place for many who sought, as Browne so memorably put it, "reformation without tarrying for any." Even though Browne's leadership of the separatists shortly thereafter passed to Henry Barrow and John Greenwood, it was under Browne's name that for the next fifty years separatists were attacked and slandered. Browne's decision to gather in exile the churches of the elect set the pattern for others who greatly influenced the separatists who eventually crossed the Atlantic.[2]

The most famous of these individuals was John Robinson, who led his congregation from Scrooby to Amsterdam in 1607 and thence to Leyden. But of equal importance were Francis Johnson, who after an abortive attempt to emigrate to North America in 1597 was forced back to England and then to Holland, and John Smyth, who emigrated to Amsterdam in 1606.[3] In the early seventeenth century these and other prominent English Puritan ministers-in-exile gradually developed a conception of the true church as one gathered from the world by the voluntary action of those who chose to live according to God's true discipline rather than by the institutions of corrupt men, as they believed the case to be with members of the Church of England. Such separatists' rejection of the ecclesiastical hierarchy of the English church and their concomitant emphasis on the discipline that became known as "congregationalism" certainly argues for their prominence in the development of the English Puritan movement. Of more importance for their contribution to radical ideology in that century, however, was the premise that, as Edmund Morgan has explained it, "a church could not be formed by governmental compulsion or by constraint of the wicked, but only by the free consent of the good."[4] It was, of course, in large measure this doctrine that contributed to the disintegration of the English church in the 1640s and 1650s.

The ecclesiastical debates among these prominent separatists-in-exile have been fully detailed by Henry Martyn Dexter, B. R. White, and others. The impact of the thought of those whose conceptions of the church bore directly on a separatist tradition in America requires further review.[5] In this light the two most important individuals were Robinson himself and Henry Jacob, a Puritan who was forced to flee to Holland in 1606 and who thereafter frequently debated with Robinson the topic of the visible church of true believers. Even though Jacob himself never directly counseled a total renunciation of the Church of England, his belief in the necessity of a public covenant of the godly that superseded the prerogatives of any national church influenced several individuals involved in the New England experiment. Both of these influential clergymen agreed that, despite their insistence on the congregation's spiritual separation from the Church of England, it was not necessary for the godly to maintain an unequivocal separation between themselves and those who would not fully accept their conception of the gathered church. Thus, Robinson and Jacob mitigated the revolutionary import of the idea of a covenanted band of saints, even as they condemned the corruptions and unscripturalness of the national church.[6]

Earlier in his career Robinson had argued for strict separation from worship in the Church of England; but by 1614, after discussions with Jacob, Robert Parker, and William Ames—all of whom were in the Netherlands at that time—he allowed members of his congregation to hold private communion (that is, private prayer, thanksgiving, psalmsinging, scripture reading, and the like) with unseparated members of the Church of England. In the early years of the seventeenth century Robinson had maintained that the ordinances administered in his church were available only to those who had renounced the national church, but by 1624 he had moderated his stand, acknowledging that it was lawful, if not overly efficacious, for separatists to hear the preaching of an Anglican minister. Such ideas won Robinson the wrath of strict separatists like John Smyth, but the Leyden minister found no scriptural warrant, as Smyth did, to support the premise that the ordinances of the Church of England never had provided saving faith for the English populace. Thus, while Robinson maintained that his band of saints had separated from the present corruptions of the national church, he sought to avoid the charge that the ecclesiastical course he counseled led irrevocably to schism.[7]

Robinson already had moderated his separatism by the time the Leyden church had begun to contemplate a move to the New World, and, as George Langdon has noted, this meant that "in America there would be no fundamental split between separating and non-separating Puritan."[8] And although Robinson never made the voyage to New England, both William Bradford and his associate Edward Winslow took pains to point out to critics of their colony that while at Leyden both Robinson and Elder William Brewster (who did come to New England to preach to the Pilgrims) encouraged frequent communion with other "true" churches, be they French, Dutch, or Scottish, and that individuals from such churches later were welcomed into communion with the Plymouth church.[9] Because of such openness, though prone to disruption by more strict separatists like Roger Williams and Ralph Smith, Plymouth maintained a generally cordial relationship with its larger neighbor to the north during its first decades. Problems arose only when it became apparent that such a relatively tolerant stance toward any who subscribed to a gathered church encouraged those in the populace who supported a more extreme separatism to criticize the Plymouth magistrates' unwillingness to close ranks on points of ecclesiology or doctrine.

The influence of Robinson's moderate separatism can be seen in Governor Bradford's implicit accommodation of the nonseparating congregationalists of the Bay Colony and also in the unproductive pastorate of the colony's first minister, the extreme separatist Ralph Smith. Jacob's effect on the separatist movement in New England was more subtle but equally far-reaching. He is regarded as one of the master-planners of nonseparating congregationalism. The church he founded in Southwark, England, however, after returning from Middleburg in 1616 resembled the separatist church organizations of Smyth and Barrow; it served as a veritable incubator for many individuals who were to have an important effect upon New England Puritan radicalism. In 1610, despite earlier misgivings, Jacob had been won over to the idea that a gathered church was the only true visible church, a position to which he probably had been brought by his association with Robinson; and by 1612, the most fruitful year for the development of his ecclesiology, he had become convinced that voluntary membership in the church also implied the parishioner's central role in the administration of church affairs, whether the election of ministers and elders or the censure of errant members for earthly or spiritual transgressions. Because Jacob understood that such authority could be held only by the visibly godly, when he came to organize the Southwark church he insisted on a definition of the visible church much like Robinson's—that is, a church in which the members had renounced the Church of England and publicly subscribed to Puritan tenets. But, again like Robinson, he admitted that his and other covenanted churches could exist side by side with other, "mixed" congregations.[10]

As Murray Tolmie has pointed out, to "the authorities in church and state" such an "independent" congregation looked "as separatist, schismatic, and illegal as any Brownist conventicle"; but, at least logically, Jacob avoided the charge that he had totally abandoned parish churches as mere appendages of the Beast of Rome.[11] Of most significance here is what happened within Jacob's "Independent" or semi-separatist church during its first thirty years: through its internal schisms and the individuals it sent to New England, the Southwark congregation offers an example of a church which, while maintaining a semblance of openness to less reformed churches, still encouraged the development of ecclesiastical positions that openly threatened the links between church and state. As in Robinson's Leyden and Bradford's Plymouth, the hidden card was the notion of the "consent" of the godly in their very act of covenanting as visible saints.

One important separatist was an individual whose ideas partook of anything but the moderation of Jacob and Robinson, and who was destined to assume a significant role in the dissemination of radical ideology in the New World. In the 1620s Roger Williams espoused the extreme separatism advocated by Browne and Smyth and promoted in the 1640s by John Canne. By the late 1620s, after the completion of his studies at Cambridge, Williams had broken from more moderate Puritans like John Cotton and Thomas Hooker on the question of the use of the Book of Common Prayer; around the same time he had adopted Henry Barrow's position that only individuals who had totally renounced their relationship to the Church of England and then had covenanted together into individual congregations were to be considered members of the visible church. It was Williams's insistence on the necessity of *complete* separation from an institution which he considered but another limb of Catholicism that prevented him from joining the church at Boston, for in that congregation John Wilson had refused to demand of his flock a complete break from other Christians still trapped in the English parish churches. A similar disgust at the illogic of nonseparatist Puritans also kept him away—at least initially—from neighboring Plymouth, where under Elder Brewster's leadership the Pilgrims had continued the accommodation of unseparated Puritans that John Robinson had counseled. When he arrived in America, Williams first travelled to Salem, for in that Puritan outpost he was most likely to find colonists sympathetic to his own ecclesiology.[12]

The tone of Salem's separatism had been set by Samuel Skelton, an East Anglian named pastor to the tiny congregation on Cape Ann in the summer of 1629. For a year Skelton restrained his separatist tendencies, probably from deference to his co-worker, Francis Higginson, the teacher of the church and a moderate Puritan. During Higginson's illness, however, and, more openly, after his death in 1630, Skelton exposed his extreme ecclesiastical views, for although the Salem church had been founded on decidedly congregational principles, how exclusionary Skelton intended them to be was not fully revealed until the arrival of Winthrop's fleet. Skelton refused to baptize one of the children born on the voyage because the infant's parents were not yet members of any particular congregational church, and on the same grounds he had the temerity to deny the Lord's Supper to Governor Winthrop and other prominent immigrants who sought the sacrament in his meeting. Later that fall, when news of these events reached John Cotton in England, the Lincolnshire minister penned a long letter to Skelton in which he criticized such exclusionary principles. Although Cotton, like Skelton, had defended the need for covenanted congregations, he reminded the Salem minister that "an explicit Covenant is rather a solemn vow to bind the members of the Church together in nearer fellowship with God and one another, than any such essential cause of a Church without which it cannot be."[13]

Historians have long debated the justness of Cotton's remarks that with regard to his ecclesiastical principles Skelton had left England "of another judgment" and that his behavior in New England had been influenced by the separatism of "the New Plymouth men." Cotton had been equally surprised by Skelton's apparent willingness to admit "one of Mr. Lathrop's congregation" to the Lord's Supper, and his child to baptism upon sight of his testimony from this Church.[14] This Lathrop was none other than the John Lathrop who had succeeded Henry Jacob in the Southwark congregation, and Skelton's acknowledgment of the legitimacy of *this* church clearly placed him on one side of a line at that time occupied by only very few English Puritans, and not yet by Cotton himself. For while the Southwark church over which Lathrop had presided since 1624 presented itself as an unseparated institution, it had many hall-

marks of more extreme Puritan organizations, including a provision that
allowed lay members to expound and apply scriptural passages to the rest
of the congregation—that is, to "prophesy." Lathrop did not hesitate to
practice communion with avowed separatists as well as with members of
the English parish churches; and because his church's membership had
included everyone from such *bona fide* separatists as Sabine Staresmore,
who had been associated with Robinson's Leyden congregation, to conservatives such as the London bookseller John Bellamie, soon to become
a prominent presbyterian, the Southwark church remained an exciting
meeting place for those who presented a wide range of Puritan alternatives to the ecclesiastical standing order.[15]

The Jacob-Lathrop church exerted an important influence on Puritan
New England, particularly in the 1630s. Some members of the congregation emulated Jacob's own example and made the Atlantic crossing. He
had emigrated to Virginia in 1622 and died there two years later without
realizing his dream for a Puritan commonwealth. In addition to the
member of Lathrop's flock so readily received in Salem, we should recall
Richard Browne, a wherryman who by 1631 had become the ruling elder
in John Phillips's church in Watertown. "A man of very violent spirit," as
Winthrop described him, Elder Browne caused considerable dissension
in the community because he was so "well versed in the discipline of the
Separation, having been a ruler in one of their churches in London." He
and Phillips, himself a strict congregationalist, maintained the seemingly
anomalous opinion "which they had published, that the churches of
Rome were true churches." The controversy over their views alarmed the
neighboring church of Boston, which sent its own officers to look into
the matter (an action Phillips thought did not fully square with congregational principles), and for the next two years, even after Phillips himself had recanted, Browne persisted in his "errors." Browne was not
at the root of all of Watertown's troubles: within a few years Phillips,
like Lathrop in his English congregation, found himself preoccupied
with other difficulties that stemmed from congregational principles—
specifically, the purported "anabaptism" (that is, the unwillingness to
baptize infants) of some of the church's members.[16]

Other members of the Jacob-Lathrop church also emigrated to the
New World. As early as 1629, the keeper of the Plymouth church records
noted that "severall Godly persons . . . some whereof had bin of Mr.
Lathrop's Church in England" had relocated in the Plymouth area, no
doubt because of their desire to join separated churches; and there is a
record of Robert Lynell, a deacon under Jacob's pastorate, who was in

A "Separatist," from Daniel
Featley's *The Dippers Dipt*
(London, 1645).

New England by 1634.[17] Perhaps most influential was Lathrop himself,
who came to Massachusetts with thirty members of his church after they
had decided that the New World's wilderness was preferable to life in England under the bishops. Lathrop and his followers had been forced to
this decision in 1632 when a majority of the church were brought before
the Court of High Commission and subsequently imprisoned on a
charge of separatist activities. Released from prison, he and many members of his flock had arrived in Boston by the early fall of 1634. There, as
Winthrop noted, this "pastor of a private congregation in London" asked
the local congregation for permission "to be present at the administration
[of the sacrament] . . . but said that he durst not desire to partake in it,
because he was not in order (being dismissed from his former congregation), and he thought it not fit to be suddenly admitted into any other." [18]
Between Winthrop's lines we should recognize not only Lathrop's willingness to worship with what in effect still was an unseparated congregation, a tendency probably derived from Jacob and Robinson, but also his
polite insistence on the necessity of being a member of a covenanted
church separated from the Church of England before partaking of the
sacrament. Yet even though Lathrop met with no persecution in the
colony, he soon enough learned that the Boston-area churches were not
for him; and, like his more radical counterpart Ralph Smith, whose extreme separatism had made him unwelcome even in Skelton's Salem, he
moved to the Plymouth patent. By late 1634 we find him settled over the
church in Scituate. Its original members supported Robinson's moderate

separatism; but, as in 1633 in the Southwark church when several of its members after release from prison left the congregation under the leadership of the strict separatist Samuel Eaton and thereupon demanded a rebaptism of the faithful, the Scituate church too soon became embroiled in difficulties over baptism.[19]

From the earliest days of the Puritan migration to New England, non-separating congregationalism was leavened by individuals newly arrived from one of the major arenas of English Puritan controversy, forcing their more moderate brethren to consider more carefully the logic of pure congregational principles. Because we will meet some of these separatists again, it also should be noted that throughout the 1630s and 1640s the original Jacob-Lathrop church continued its own centrifugal progress, throwing from its center such soon-to-be radicals as Samuel How, one of the renowned "tub-preachers" of the 1640s, and William Kiffin, who became a prominent member of the Particular Baptists. In this church (after 1637 under the leadership of Lathrop's successor, Henry Jessey) and its offshoots the question of separation gradually was superseded by that of baptism, an evolution that took place in many of the New England churches, often when the few separatists who persisted in their views began to voice their objections to the Puritan churches on quite different grounds.[20] In New England in the early 1630s, though, through individuals like Richard Browne and John Lathrop, the debates over the precise boundaries of congregational polity were extended in several important ways.

In Salem, where the Massachusetts Puritans first encountered a strong separatist movement, the questions raised by these extreme congregationalists were not resolved as quickly as in Watertown or Scituate, primarily because the radical elements were more deeply entrenched. As early as 1629, even as Skelton was beginning to consolidate his power, Ralph Smith, who sought to join Skelton as co-minister, caused the settlement considerable embarrassment because of his radical ecclesiastical principles. His views were so divisive that finally John Endecott, the leader of the colony, required him to foreswear exercising his ministerial gifts without permission, a state of affairs that led one contrite colonist to try to explain Smith's presence in the colony by admitting that this strict separatist had been allowed to join the group "before wee understood of his difference of judgment in some things from our ministers." Although he was permitted to remain within the settlement as long as he refrained from publicly expressing his differences with other members of the church—particularly the "Old Settlers" from the West Country who had arrived before Skelton and his fellow East Anglians—Smith soon enough moved to Plymouth. He became the first settled minister over the Pilgrim church.[21] The important question here is to what degree his opinions prepared the Salemites for their acceptance of Roger Williams, who arrived in that town in 1631 after he had rejected the Boston church's offer of a temporary appointment as their "teacher" while John Wilson returned on business to England, for it was Williams himself who most radicalized the Salem community.

It had not taken Williams long to realize that he could not be content in Boston, for the congregationalism that John Wilson had established was as broadly conceived as any in the colony at that time. The Boston church's willingness to consider Williams, whose ecclesiastical views could not have been a secret to them, for the post bespeaks their ecclesiastical liberality. Williams made it clear, however, that he could have no part of an "unseparated" people. At that point Skelton, no longer restrained by Higginson and eager to have as his colleague so prominent a Puritan, mustered enough votes to have his church offer a call to the new settler, only to have the General Court quickly point out to the Salem church that, given the precarious nature of the nascent Puritan enterprise, all such appointments first should be cleared with them. Sensing the kind of governmental interference he wanted none of, Williams soon thereafter moved to Plymouth where, though never formally ordained, he regularly prophesied to the church.[22]

By 1633, however, Williams understood that in their own way, and probably due to the influence of their former pastor John Robinson and of William Brewster, the majority of the Plymouth settlers were hardly more pure in their worship than the church in Boston. To judge from Governor Bradford's account, Williams, though initially well-received, soon enough began "to fall into some strange opinions, and from opinion to practice," which caused, he continued, "some controversy between the church & him." Nathaniel Morton, writing in his *New Englands Memoriall* (1669), was less generous. He maintained that from Williams's arrival he had begun "by degrees [to vent] divers of his own singular opinions" and sought "to impose them upon others" even though he found no such "concurrence as he expected." At this point, Morton relates, Elder Brewster took the initiative himself and encouraged the Plymouth church to approve Williams's request for a dismissal to Salem, even though "some were unwilling to allow it." What Brewster most feared, Morton wrote, was that Williams "would run the same course of rigid

Separation and Anabaptistry, which Mr. *John Smith* the Sebaptist at *Amersterdam* had done." Brewster was perfectly willing to let this radical return to the Bay Colony, where, "there being many able men . . . , they would better deal with him." [23]

Brewster accurately predicted the general course of Williams's spiritual pilgrimage, for by 1639 he had indeed openly adopted baptist principles; in releasing him to Salem's church the Pilgrims for a time had delayed their colony's exposure to the "Anabaptist" challenge. And for his part Williams, emboldened by the fact that Skelton, though in weak health, had maintained his hold over a majority of the Salemites, soon joined the minister in pressing for yet purer ordinances in the Salem church. Shortly after he returned to that town in the fall of 1633, Williams supported Skelton's view that women should be veiled in church meetings, a seemingly minor point in so patriarchal an age but one important to separatists who sought to recreate the purity of the apostolic churches. Winthrop and the other magistrates rejected Skelton's argument, and soon thereafter this unresolved debate was subsumed into another of more significance, over the propriety of the newly established meetings among the colony's ministers for the discussion of doctrinal and ecclesiastical questions. Williams and Skelton disapproved of such meetings because of the presbyterianism toward which they believed such "consultations" inevitably would lead. Here, too, the Salem men were in a minority, but it is clear that their persistent attempts to establish churches in the true scriptural mold annoyed others in the Bay who wished to maintain a less extreme, and more accommodating, congregationalism, like that in place at Plymouth where, for all the initial talk of separation, by 1635 the relationship of the colony's churches to the Church of England was a dead issue. For Skelton and Williams these still were burning issues, as they were to many English Puritans. [24]

The Bay Colony's difficulties with Williams soon escalated. In the late fall of 1633 the Governor and General Court met to consider a treatise in which Williams had disputed the colony's "right to the lands they possessed here, and concluded that, claiming by the king's grant, they could not have a title, nor otherwise, except they compounded with the natives." Williams subsequently apologized to the court for this highly impolitic production, but a year later, when John Endecott ordered the red cross cut from a flag because the cross was a symbol of England's relation to the Pope, the Massachusetts authorities again were infuriated. They believed Williams had instigated the action as part of his attempt to destroy all connections to the Antichrist, whether in a flag or in a corrupt

Portrait of Roger Williams at the age of thirty-eight.

monarch's willingness to claim New England for Christ's work. After Skelton's death in August 1634, the magistrates became increasingly concerned with Williams's detrimental influence in one of the colony's most important communities. The more Williams was heard, they thought, the more likely his separatist position would gather support.[25]

By the summer of 1635 the colony had had enough. First, the church in Salem had the temerity to appoint Williams as their teacher while he was under examination for his claim that a magistrate should not tender an oath to an unregenerate man because in so doing he held "communion with a wicked man in the worship of God." Then, at a meeting of the General Court in July, he was charged with other errors that displayed his radical view of the church. He had argued, for example, that "magistrates ought not to punish the breach of the first table [the first three of the Ten Commandments], otherwise than in such cases as did disturb the civil peace," and that a man should not pray with an unregenerate person—that is, one who had not given evidence of salvation—"though wife, child, etc." Condemned for such erroneous and schismatic opinions, Williams was unequivocally warned to desist from promulgating them any longer; but, quite predictably, Williams, whom Cotton remembered as very "self-full" and "self-willed," refused to halt his attempts to institute worship as pure as that outlined in the scriptures. Establishing a precedent they were to use frequently in the next two decades, the Masschusetts authorities banished him from their territory.[26]

The nature of Williams's mission in the New World—to reestablish the church in its primitive piety, an action that demanded separation from all worldly corruption—clearly illustrates the emphasis on church discipline among the early New England separatists, a fact evident as well among their English counterparts. Williams knew better than to confuse one's act of separation from a corrupt church with salvation itself—a notion that revealed blatant dependence on the doctrine of salvation by good works—but he maintained the necessity of worship in a church as purely ordered as it could be in a fallen world. Hence his growing disgust at ecclesiastical developments in Massachusetts, which led him and other separatists farther and farther down the road to religious radicalism.[27]

Williams's banishment did not extinguish the fervor he had instilled among many in the Massachusetts Bay Colony for whom the question of church discipline was far from settled. In Salem Hugh Peter, ordained the town's minister in December 1636, had made a strong effort to eliminate the separatist elements of the church by rewriting the church covenant and excommunicating those who would not subscribe to it. Even so, those among Williams's supporters who did not immediately follow him to Rhode Island continued to cause trouble in Salem. Henry Bartholomew and Charles Gott, both of whom had been deputies to the General Court, openly rejected the new document; and several women, among them Jane Verin, Margery Reeves, and Margery Holliman, refused to worship with other members of the congregation, the latter two because they denied that the churches of the Bay were true churches of Christ. Others in Salem were troubled by the fact "that some of their members, going into England, did hear the ministers there, and when they came home the churches here held communion with them." Eleven members actually separated from the church because of this "unscriptural" behavior and for two years continued to hold private meetings.[28]

Some who had come to Salem expressly because of its separatist orientation quickly left the community. William Harris, who had arrived in New England in 1635, was one of these; he followed Williams to Rhode Island. Samuel Hubbard had come over in 1633 and upon Williams's banishment moved to Connecticut; by 1648 he was in Newport, a member of John Clarke's Particular Baptist church. Francis Weston, another of Williams's staunch advocates, was still in the Salem church in 1638. He presented to Hugh Peter the following objections, clearly separatist-based: "That he was not allowed to ask questions in time of public worship, on the Lord's day, without having imputed to him pride and self-sufficiency," and that "the church communed with Mr. Lothrop's church, who commune with the Church of England, and therefore the first of these bodies was alike chargeable with such communion." Weston further embittered Peter by complaining that the minister's wife, newly arrived from Peter's old church in Rotterdam, had not been properly dismissed, and by questioning the very discipline of the Rotterdam church. Shortly after he was examined for these opinions he, too, left the Salem area for Rhode Island.[29]

It should be noted that such objections to the discipline of the Massachusetts churches were not restricted to Salem, though before 1636 that community was largely, and properly, the focus of the government's concern. As early as 1632, Stephen Batchelor, the leader of the religious group called the "Husbandmen," had organized a second congregation in Lynn, but because he had obtained a dismission from Lynn's first church with the express understanding that he would move elsewhere, the magistrates were called in to examine his overtly schismatic behavior. Batchelor thereupon was required by the General Court to "forbear exercising his gifts as pastor or teacher publicly" within the Massachusetts patent, but he ignored the injunction and continued to preach to his separated congregation, first at Saugus, then at Newbury and Hampton. In Batchelor's case, as in the cases of other of the Salem separatists, the quest for ecclesiastical purity eventually led him into the spiritist fold. Writing to Winthrop in 1644 from Hampton to clear himself of the aspersions cast upon him by the Massachusetts General Court, Batchelor admitted that he had moved to New Hampshire to be near Thomas Jenner and John Wheelwright, two of New England's more well-known antinomians: the fact that these two were "stablished in those partes" was not "a week motive to drive, or a cord to drawe me that way," Batchelor wrote.[30] In Watertown, too, where Richard Browne recently had unsettled the church with his separatist ideas, in 1632 several members left the church because of a quarrel over discipline. A day then was set aside for them to rejoin the church or risk excommunication. All returned except one John Masters, who complained, in typically separatist fashion, "that a person had been admitted to communion whom he supposed to be unworthy of the privilege," at which point Masters had turned his back on the administration of the sacrament. Masters was excommunicated for his obstinacy; two weeks later he recanted and was restored to fellowship, but only after the Watertown church had contributed significantly to the ecclesiastical bickering in the Bay Colony.[31]

Despite such examples of separatist behavior in New England in the 1630s, the question of the separatists' influence on the development of New England Puritanism remains a vexed one, primarily because of the moderate Puritans' obfuscation of the basic issues the separatists raised. At one level, for example, the mere fact of the colonists' emigration was itself, as one historian has pointed out, an extreme form of separation, "of withdrawal from the parish churches and episcopal jurisdiction of the Church of England, even if those who left England loudly proclaimed their rejection of separation in principle."[32] As much as the New England Puritans defended the Congregational Way as a reformation *within* the national church, their sharp criticism of the parish system and their unwillingness to accept into their churches any individuals who maintained the supremacy of the Church of England were *de facto* illustrations of their commitment to a solution to their religious problems that was separatist in effect, if not explictly so termed.

To many English Puritans the logical distinctions drawn by the New England apologists for nonseparating congregationalism—particularly Richard Mather, John Cotton, and Thomas Hooker—appeared at best illogical and at worst blatantly deceitful, given what they knew of New England's church system from Thomas Lechford's *Plain Dealing* (1642) and other first-hand reports from the colony.[33] Even Giles Firmin, who had spent more than a decade in New England before returning to England, and who usually was generous in his assessment of the New England churches, reminded readers of his *Separation Examined* (1652) that separatists, in New England and old, were "not all of a size." "Some separate from Ministers & Churches, and get into their private houses, owne no officers, but please themselves with their owne gifts and opinions," he noted. But others, and here he no doubt had in mind individuals he had known in Boston and Ipswich, "live in places where there are visible and reall Saints, the Ministry godly and able. . . ."[34] His point, of course, was that in the latter communities there still were people of separatist inclination whose emphasis on the establishment of a more pure religious discipline caused difficulties, if not ones as severe as those initiated by individuals who formed private conventicles.

It also is clear that as the debates between presbyterians and Independents at the Westminister Assembly, called to reform England's ecclesiastical polity, grew more heated, the presbyterians knew that their demands for a hierarchical church structure would be strengthened if they could identify English Independents with the polity of the New England churches, particularly with the doctrinal aberrations reported in the aftermath of the Antinomian Controversy. The use the presbyterians made of the Hutchinsonians' and other radicals' challenges to the New England Way more properly belongs in a future chapter, but here it is important to note that even in the 1630s the question of New England's separatist tendency often was raised in England by both the colony's supporters and its critics.[35]

Accusations like those Thomas Dudley made to the Countess of Lincoln when he commented on settlers who returned to England to raise "many false and scandalous reports against us, affirming us to be Brownists in religion, and ill affected to our State at home" only increased as the tide of the Great Migration deposited more and more dissenters in Boston. In 1631, Edward Howes told the younger John Winthrop that in England there was "a mutteringe of a too palpable separation of your people from our church government," and in 1637 Governor Winthrop heard that in England "the Judges" had begun "to mention you [New England] in theyre Charges" to the juries. In speaking of the growing problem of "Recusants," he continued, one judge had gone so far as to rank dissenters "into two sorts, some Papists and others of the separacion, and those of the seperacion were such . . . as preferred Amsterdam before London, and N. England before old"; this particular justice also charged his juries that they should take special notice "of such as inclined towards N. England" because they were the chief "causes of error and faction in Church and State." In 1644, responding to a recently published letter of John Cotton, Roger Williams made explicit what was in the minds of many Englishmen. "What is that which Mr. *Cotton* and many hundreths fearing God in New *England* walk in," he asked, "but a way of separation?"[36]

As the practice of the Plymouth separatists under Brewster, Smith, and John Rayner (Smith's successor) illustrates, the "true" separatists' ecclesiastical goals did indeed differ significantly from those of the Bay Colony, a fact that became more apparent after the Antinomian Controversy when the ministers closed ranks and, following Thomas Shepard's lead in his Newtown congregation, began to require evidence of the effect of saving grace upon an individual's soul before he or she could be admitted to full church membership. But such tests never were instituted in Plymouth nor in the various Rhode Island churches formed in the late

1630s and 1640s as more and more radical Puritans were forced to settle there, and this unwillingness to proclaim themselves "visible saints" marks an important limitation to the separatists' plans for reform of the English Church. For all the self-righteousness of their demands, particularly in the early seventeenth century, for a rejection of the national church, they always kept their focus upon the reform of *public* worship and never claimed that a singular moral perfection—that is, a "visible" sainthood like that by which the Massachusetts Puritans eventually defined the colonial enterprise—could distinguish them as a group. In this sense, the separatists rejected all notions that in a fallen world individual congregations had any direct relationship to the universal, invisible church of true believers.[37]

In the late 1630s and into the 1640s, particularly as the separatist criticism of the New England Puritan ecclesiology was subsumed into the baptists' challenge to it, the separatists insisted that the New England Way, with its subtle gradations of membership in the convenanted congregation based on experiential (and, as such, potentially suspect) forms of evidence, was as unscriptural as the hierarchy in the Church of England from which they had removed themselves. The separatists demanded only a purity of worship within the churches and a willingness on the part of church members to subscribe publicly to the doctrinal framework of Puritanism; they knew better than to think that fallen men, even with a few saints among them, could build a New Jerusalem. Thus, when Williams asked John Cotton "seriously to consider . . . if the Lord Jesus were himselfe in person in Old or New England, what Church, what Ministry, what Worship, what Government, he would set up," he and other separatists regarded the question as rhetorical.[38] Only God's free grace could save an individual, and the workings of grace, as any good Puritan knew, were mysterious and unpredictable. Seen in this light, the New England Puritans' belief in their divinely ordained mission was blatantly presumptuous. "In strivinge soe sodainely to be better," one Englishman wrote to John Winthrop the Younger, you "may prove to be starke naught."[39]

The Plymouth separatists and others in New England so inclined recognized that the Massachusetts Puritans, through their emphasis on the evidence of grace within a presumed saint, opened a veritable Pandora's box from which would emerge all sorts of doctrinal errors and rank heresies. But if by their own concentration on outward disciplne the separatists initially were saved from a comparable experience, as many among them pushed their search for pure ordinances to greater and greater lengths, moving from their questioning of the order of the Church of England to an examination of the efficacy of *any* outward worship, they, too, as the Scots presbyterian Robert Baillie had warned, came to "break among themselves in many pieces." Some found a home in the baptist churches, and others became Seekers, Levellers, or Quakers, running "so rashly that themselves know not where to stop it." In such later incarnations the separatists had their greatest effect on New England Puritanism, for, as Baillie noted, the root of their movement—"the peoples supremacy" as the idea first was broached in the notion of a separate, covenanted congregation—continued to pose a threat to all rational order. Baillie was, he admitted, "more afraid" of this notion "then [of] any other errour of the times," for he apprehended "if it did grow, it might overturn the whole State from the very foundation, and bring upon all the Land such a confusion as was inexpressible." [40] His fears were as justified for New England as for old.

RADICAL SPIRITISM:

SWEET SUGAR-CANDY

RELIGION

he separatists' influence on New England Puritan radicalism was relatively subtle and restricted in time to the earliest years of settlement, when the epithet "Brownist" was more than just a bogey by which the presbyterians attacked congregational polity. But the impact of those among the population whom I have chosen to call *radical spiritists* was both openly revolutionary and remarkably extensive. From the arrival of Stephen Batchelor and his "Familist" contingent in 1631 through the bloody years of the Quaker persecution that mercifully ended with the Restoration, New England's moderate Puritans were persistently challenged by a variety of people—condemned variously as "Antinomians," "Familists," "Seekers," "Anabaptists," or, finally, "Quakers"—who had brought to the New World a conception of the relation of God to man that the majority of the colonists, and in particular their ministers, considered profoundly threatening and disruptive. Although most students of American Puritanism can identify only the most prominent of these dissenters—Anne Hutchinson immediately comes to mind—it is crucial to understand that, as Stephen Foster has written, "representatives of most of the sectarian Puritan opinions that emerged in their extraordinary variety in Interregnum England were to be found in some form in New England."[1] To document the varieties of radical spiritism in New England, then, is to comprehend the extent to which many New Englanders were both participants in and significant contributors to the development of the radical ideology that defined the netherworld of English Puritanism.

One of the most significant factors in the formation of Puritan radicalism was what Robert Baillie identified as a belief in "the peoples supremacy," evidenced among Browne, Barrow, Jacob, and other separatist leaders in their demands for individual congregations organized by people who had covenanted to support true forms of religious worship. The same emphasis on the importance of the individual's religious experience underlay the varieties of radical spiritism, with one important difference. While among the separatists each individual soul played his role in the establishment of proper church discipline—that is, in the formation of the covenanted congregation—among the radical spiritists the emphasis fell on explicitly doctrinal matters; they were united by a belief in the radical transformation wrought when an individual received saving grace, a transformation so overwhelming that such individuals believed themselves thereafter set apart from other human beings by the fact that in some form or other the Holy Spirit dwelled in them. This notion of "free justification by grace alone," of an ecstatic and overpowering intimacy with the divine, formed the basis for a startling number of religious, social, and political ideas that thoroughly alarmed those among the Puritan population who perceived such notions as a threat to their world-view.

While the doctrine of salvation by God's free grace assuredly was one of the linchpins of the Protestant Reformation, it was even more important to the development of English Puritanism. Among the radical spiritists it assumed the form of an inordinate emphasis on the assurance an individual gained after he had recognized the presence of the Holy Spirit within him. In some cases, the radical spiritists' belief in their regeneration was so complete that they denied the necessity of many of the instituted means of salvation on which other Protestants still felt dependent; some of them went on to question the ordained ministry, organized worship, and even the rule of Scripture itself. As William K. B. Stoever has pointed out, the most important issue debated during the synod of 1637 (and implicit in all the New England Puritans' encounters with radical spiritists) had been the degree to which God, in regenerating individuals, worked through "instruments that belong to the created order" and empowered "human faculties to perform holy actions." Radical spiritists, in contradistinction to those who believed that God worked through natural and "instituted" means and allowed the use of "objective criteria, given in scripture," by which presumptive saints might recognize their justification, maintained that at the moment of conversion God overruled the natural order and endowed the saint with an overwhelming and undeniable sense of his salvation, with a "New Light" that proved beyond doubt that the Holy Spirit worked in and through him. The test of salvation thus became experiential rather than scriptural, emotional rather than logical. In the striking simile of Peter Sterry, Oliver Cromwell's captain and an intimate of Sir Henry Vane, to those radicals who defended the doctrine of "free grace," "Spiritual truths discovered by demonstration of Reason" were as incongruous as "the Mistresse in her Cook-maid's clothes."[2]

New England's first major encounter with those who, in Nathaniel Ward's words, thought that they had "discovered the Nor-west passage to Heaven" by following "a new Gospell, new Christ, new Faith, new gay-nothings," occurred during the Antinomian Controversy of 1636–38, when Anne Hutchinson used her conventicle in Boston to attack the colony's ministers—all save John Cotton—as "legal" preachers with no true knowledge of the scriptural doctrine of the Holy Spirit.[3] A fact often understated is that many New Englanders were receptive to such ideas as Hutchinson's, not only in the 1630s as the colony's ministers were striving to halt their proliferation, but for the next two decades, well after the direction of the New England Way supposedly had been established. When in the mid-1630s an English Puritan, disturbed by the increase of antinomian errors in his own country, reminded Governor Winthrop that "Liberty is sweet so it is apt (as it is with sweet meats) to allure men to excess," he had in mind not only the kind of "Liberty" the New Englanders had obtained because of the distance they had put between themselves and the English bishops but also that which manifested itself in the freedom from church ordinances counseled by the spiritists, a fact verified by many who came to New England in that decade.[4]

Thomas Clap, one of the patriarchs of Dorchester, recalled how shortly after his arrival in the colony he had been much surprised by the great clamor about "free Grace, and for the Teachings of the Spirit." Edward Johnson, Woburn's militia-captain, likewise had encountered the ideas of some "Erronists" at his first landing. When Johnson saw the "good old way of Christ rejected by them" and refused to accept "that new light, which was the common theame of every mans Discourse," he became so disturbed that he ventured out to the woods to meditate upon the "naked Christ" these sectarians had asked him to accept. Thomas Weld, too, was troubled by the support the spiritists' ideas had garnered and in his preface to Winthrop's account of the antinomian furor of 1636–38 used a telling metaphor to describe the rapid spread of the disruptive "errors." "*Some going thither from hence* [England] *full fraught with many unsound and loose opinions,*" he noted, "*after a time began to open their packs, and freely vent their wares to any that would be their customers.*" "*Multitudes of men and women,*" he continued, "*Church-members and others, having tasted of their Commodities, were eager after them, and were streight infected before they were aware, and some being tainted conveyed the infection to others.*" In the late 1630s, as Weld and others testified, New England faced a veritable epidemic—the errors soon were conveyed "into almost all parts of the country, round about"—one whose radical germs proved virulent and resistant to any quick prescription.[5]

Given the unsettled nature of English Puritanism at this time, it should come as no surprise that many people believed it perfectly scriptural to choose the "faire and easie way to Heaven" offered by the radical spiritists, particularly since debates over the proper relation of justification to sanctification were to preoccupy Puritans for several more decades. Because the doctrinal points upon which the spiritists' message was based often were abstruse, the rank-and-file who heard the messages of Batchelor, Hutchinson, Wheelwright, and the various Rhode Island radicals very likely were seduced as much by the way spiritist doctrines reinforced their notions of their spiritual and social worth as by their judgment of its theological truth. Indeed, how little the laity understood such doctrinal wrangling may be gauged by Giles Firmin's anecdote about his experience with the antinomians in Massachusetts in the 1630s. Speaking of his return to Boston at the height of the difficulties with the Hutchinsonians, Firmin approached a prominent "Zealot" with this question: "I pray thee tell me, what is *Justification*, thou art so hot only upon it?" "He answered me," Firmin continued, "*truly 'tis so great a thing, that I do not know what it is.*"[6] It is fair to speculate that what attracted many people to the spiritists' camp was not so much the clarity of their logic but their offer of a "naked Christ" that greatly simplified the requirements for and demands of sainthood. As Stoever has written, to accept the spiritists' Gospel "seemed to reduce the ambiguity of the Christian life as understood by the Puritans, with its cycle of triumph and lapse, of faith and doubt."[7] Thus, to believe in justification by God's free grace alone was to obtain some reprieve from the intolerably high level of anxiety by which ministers like Shepard and Hooker asked people to live. Conversely, it also placed an unprecedented obligation on people themselves—rather than on the ministry—to define what it meant to be a good Christian.

In many congregations the demand for proof of one's visible saint-hood, which was becoming a prerequisite to full membership in the church, implicitly encouraged the very reliance on the Holy Spirit the New England Puritans condemned among the spiritists. The Puritans' fear of the moral laxity toward which they believed the spiritists' ideas tended, is a theme that runs throughout the New England ministers' sermons. Thomas Shepard related how upon close investigation he had "found these [spiritist] opinions to be mere figg-leaves, to cover some distempers and lusts lurking in mens hearts." Almost at the same time, in the mid-1640s, Weld echoed Shepard's sentiment, claiming that the "*very reason, besides the novelty of it,*" that "*so many dance after this [antinomian] pipe*" is because "*it pleaseth nature well to have Heaven, and their lusts, too.*" As moderate Puritans understood it, then, the doctrine of "free grace" was merely an attempt on the part of its adherents to play the saint while knowingly remaining in sin. "Antinomians" and "Familists" yearned for both "drunken dreams of the world" and "golden dreams of grace," Shepard complained. "What meaneth [this] delusion of men's brains?" he went on to ask, for to him it was readily apparent that in New England "every man hath some drunken conceit that rocks him asleep." So, too, Richard Mather's response, in the early 1650s. He found it "an ill sign of a distempered soul, when the good old way of the doctrine of faith, and repentance . . . is not savoury to a mans spirit." Now, Mather lamented, men "must have new notions, and quaint & uncouth matter," or else the substance of religion would not "go down." Given the epidemic of spiritist errors in New England and old, Stephen Geree, whose *The Doctrine of the Antinomians . . . Confuted* (1644) was one of the most searing indictments of the spiritists, could only take heart from the fact that a review of the historical record allowed him to predict with some certainty their tragic end. "This soon ripe faith will be soon rotten," he proclaimed, for the antinomians "run too fast, at first, to hold out unto the end."[8] But before the radical spiritists had run their course, much fruit was harvested from their vines.

With but few exceptions, radical spiritists did not often proclaim their religious pedigree because such behavior did not square with their claims to absolute dependence on the power of the Holy Spirit. Thus, in New England we cannot point to any figures, as we can, say, among the separatists, who were the chief influences upon the radical spiritists. To complicate matters, in the sectarian turmoil of Caroline and Interregnum England specific labels had become almost meaningless; as David Hall reminds us, the best index to an individual's radicalism was not the name by which he was called but his conception of the church and ministry, and his doctrinal understanding of sanctification.[9] In seventeenth-century New England, for example (and, for that matter, in old England, too), the two epithets most commonly used against the spiritists, "Familist" and "Antinomian," were catchall categories that included a bewildering variety of figures.[10] The term "Familist," for example, applied most strictly to members of the Family of Love, a sixteenth-century group that followed the teachings of the German mystic Henrik Niclaes, the "H.N." of so many marginal comments in the heresiographies. From Niclaes's works, which by the 1580s had attracted much attention in England, we learn that the true believer enjoyed an ecstatic union with Christ that allowed him to understand, as none of the uninitiated could, the allegorical import of Scripture. But while there is evidence to suggest that through the early seventeenth century some *bona fide* disciples of Niclaes existed in parts of East Anglia and Cambridgeshire, by the late 1630s the term "Familist" was being used in a much more general sense, usually when the leader of a conventicle saw fit to condemn the learning of the established clergy in light of his own experience of the divine and thereupon opened his own interpretation of the Bible.[11]

Another such case of misnomenclature involves Robert Brearley, the curate of Grindleton in Yorkshire, the leader of the "*Grindletonian* Familists," whose teachings were known to at least one prominent New Englander. In the early seventeenth century Brearley was notorious for preaching the indwelling of the Holy Spirit and finally caused such a stir that he was brought before the High Commission in York; though acquitted, for three more decades he often was pointed to as an indigenous English familist. In 1627, for example, Stephen Denison complained of "Grindletonian" familists "in the North parts of England" who held, among other things, "that their spirit is not to be tryed by the Scriptures, but the Scriptures by their Spirit" and "that when God comes to dwell in a man, he so fills the soule, that there is no more *sinfull* lusting," charges that as late as 1645 still were repeated verbatim by Ephraim Pagitt in his *Heresiography*.[12] Moderate Puritans obviously feared the disruptive tendencies of Brearley's spiritist preaching—one of his followers, for example, claimed that "if all which Master *Brierley* had then delivered were well learned, it were not matter if the Bible were burnt." Even after his

GEORGIAN

A "Georgian," from Daniel Featley's
The Dippers Dipt (London, 1645). Fol-
lowers of David Jorus, a leader of the
mid-16th century Münster uprising,
Georgians were viewed as spiritual
ancestors of the "Antinomians" and
"Familists" of both England and New
England.

FAMILIST

A "Familist," from Ephraim Pagitt's
Heresiography (London, 1654).
Though it is unlikely that any true Familists were in New England, radicals
such as Samuel Gorton were commonly associated with this group.

personal influence had waned, moderate Puritans frequently invoked his
example to give more warrant to their condemnation of spiritist ideas.[13]

In the aftermath of New England's difficulties with the Hutchinsonians, the General Court justified its enactment of stricter immigration
laws by pointing out that the new policy was intended, among other
things, to keep away "such as members of Mr. Brierley's church, who
were expected from England." The colonists' fears, though in this case
unfounded, were not without some substance: even Thomas Shepard,
the arch-opponent of the familists, admitted to having been swayed by
Brearley's ideas. "I had heard of Grindleton," Shepard admitted in his
"Autobiography," "and I did question whether that glorious estate of perfection might not be the truth, and whether old Mr. Rogers' *Seven
Treatises* and the *Practice of Christianity*, the book which did first work
upon my heart, whether these men were not all legal men. . . ."[14]

None of Brearley's "Familist" followers seem to have appeared in New
England (though it is entirely likely that some of the colonists who had
come from the northwest of England had been exposed to his ideas), and

for our purposes "Grindletonian," like "Familist," remains a code word
for a certain set of beliefs about the preeminence of justification over
sanctification, or, put another way, of the power of the Holy Spirit over
any scriptural or ministerial injunctions. Similarly, when they used the
term "Antinomian" New Englanders had in mind very specific individuals among their Puritan contemporaries—most prominently John Eaton,
Robert Towne, and John Traske—but, again, there is very little evidence
to link these individuals to New England's spiritists.[15] Like Brearley, to
whom they often were compared, these preachers "continually beat
upon" the "one point of Justification" and were further distinguished by
"their over-confident and bold beliefe" that because Christ was "so much
theirs" they were free from the dictates of the moral law. All three of
these individuals—particularly John Traske—maintained that Christ literally dwelled in the regenerate soul and offered his own righteousness
for an individual's salvation; because of this belief their opponents, with
some degree of justice, accused them of having too little regard for man's
inherent sinfulness and thus of downplaying (or eliminating) the necessity of living a saintly life. As one critic put it, their haughty claim that
Christ was theirs "is so farre from making them obedient, that it will in
the end prove cleane contrary."[16]

In the late 1620s and 1630s Eaton, Towne, and Traske, along with John
Eachard and Tobias Crisp, were the primary targets of the attacks on
antinomianism in England and thus, as Stephen Foster has pointed out,
would have been uppermost in the minds of New Englanders when they
confronted an outbreak of spiritist ideas.[17] Moreover, a few New England ministers had had first-hand acquaintance with these troublesome
individuals. John Cotton, who was accused by Thomas Shepard of holding crypto-antinomian beliefs, defended himself by admitting that he
knew full well what "Familist" teachings were—he had learned of them
"from a Ring Leader of that sect, Mr. Townes of Notinghamshire." But
he knew equally well that his own doctrine was free from such corruption, for Towne, like Eaton, had believed that Christ's righteousness
completely removed a man's filthiness and so made him a fully righteous
being, thus obviating any reason for him to be anxious about his sins.
Shepard was correct in claiming that some of Cotton's language encouraged comparable beliefs, but in 1636 Cotton vociferously denied any
connection to those who in England had been scathingly condemned as
antinomians.[18]

Edward Norris, who joined Hugh Peter in 1640 in his attempts to clear

An "Antinomian," from Ephraim Pagitt's *Heresiography* (London, 1654).

Salem of the heresies that had persisted in that town at least since the days of Williams, had done battle with Traske, one of the most well-known of the English antinomians. Norris, at the time vicar of Tetbury, Gloucestershire, claimed that Traske's way of "understanding the Gospel, the Kingdom of Christ, the state of Grace, the signs of Faith, and sanctification it selfe" set up "a conceited new Creature, entire of himself, as free from sin as Jesus Christ, to whom nothing belongeth but joy, tranquillity, and triumph." Because Norris believed that those who adhered to Traske's theology held that "in this estate no sinne shall hurt him, neither is he to question the favour of God . . . but ever to be confident," any ministers, Norris complained, who "made use of the Law in their Teaching, or gave any signs for tryall of faith or grace; motives or meanes to duties, rules of obedience, or such like, were presently rejected as Legalists." The Salem minister believed that such ideas led to "carnall licentiousnesse," and, like Shepard and others in England who had been exposed to such seductive doctrine, upon his arrival in New England Norris adamantly maintained that one could not build the New Jerusalem on so sandy a foundation. By the mid-1640s, when supporters of Samuel Gorton, the Rhode Island radical, had surfaced in Salem, Norris redoubled his efforts to eliminate the heretics, particularly since, like Traske, Gorton's followers attempted to mask the seriousness of their doctrinal aberrations through incessant equivocation. If Norris had learned anything from his pamphlet war with Traske, it was that "under the pretence of explaining [their] Assertions," such radicals as Traske and Gorton change "the very sense of them . . . like unto a certaine fish, whose property it is, to staine the water with a black stuffe, like inke, to blind the eyes of the Fishers."[19]

When the New Englanders went "fishing" after antinomians, they had a fair notion of what they were after: people whose dependence on "free justification" and its attendant glories virtually abrogated any need to follow the outward, "legal" dispensation presented in scripture. And, if as in the case of Brearley, in New England we cannot locate any self-proclaimed disciples of Eaton, Traske, Towne, or other English Puritans whose antinomianism had been highly publicized, we do find many individuals who risked the expression of comparable views. What distinguished such spiritists from their more moderate neighbors was not so much the influence of any one antinomian preacher as their own liberating discovery of the radical potential *within* the established body of Puritan dogma. Regarded in this light, antinomianism was more a matter of emphasis within English and American Puritanism than a conscious alternative to it, and in the 1630s and 1640s it is best accounted for by the extreme volatility of Puritanism as a whole.

Moreover, the kind of private meetings for fasting and prayer that had been sharply condemned by the English prelates initially were sanctioned in New England, and, as was the case in England, it is likely that at such gatherings some of the laity first explored those arguments whose implications eventually took them into spiritist camps. This fact was explicitly acknowledged, for example, at the examination of Anne Hutchinson at the General Court in Newtown in 1637. When one of her examiners berated her for holding private meetings at which she developed heretical and seditious ideas, she sharply noted that the custom of holding such meetings for religious edification "was in practice before I came therefore I was not the first."[20] Similarly, one of the complaints levelled at Samuel Gorton when he still was living in Plymouth concerned his private preaching. His message had proved so attractive to some of the separatists that (as Gorton later recalled with a touch of vanity) the wife of Ralph Smith "and others of his family" frequented Gorton's home "usually morning and evening in the time of family exercises." Mistress Smith even went so far as to admit that at Gorton's religious meetings "her spirit was refreshed in the ordinances of god as in former dayes," for until the time she began to visit Gorton she had found Plymouth's ministry, directed by John Rayner, "much decayed and allmost worne out." [21] In New England there was frequent opportunity for people to meet privately in such groups to discuss scriptural doctrine, and it is clear that representatives of the proliferating species of "nomads" or "walkers," whom the presbyterian Richard Vines found everywhere in London— "walkers," he claimed, "will not endure to sit at the feet of a constant godly ministry" but "wander away the Sabbath by peeping in at Church-dores, and taking essay of a sentence or two, and then if there be no *scratch*" for their "*itch*," "*lambit* & *fugit*," they move to another meeting— had found their way to the American strand. [22]

Dipped from the seething cauldron of Puritan ideology in Caroline England, the radical alternatives developed by such spiritual "nomads" manifested themselves in many ways—from strident anticlericalism at one pole to quietistic "Seekerism" at the other—and to a great extent paralleled the doctrinal emphases of many English Puritan radicals. One important difference, though, was that the New England radicals never attained the same degree of institutional organization that marked such English groups as the Levellers or Diggers. Rather, because New England's socioeconomic, political, and religious situation was so different, one finds only small clusters of radicals, who, though in some cases they knew members of English spiritist groups, rarely reached out to others in neighboring communities to marshal support against the established clergy and who thus never considered themselves anything but good Puritans. Only in Rhode Island, which by the 1640s already had become what a later observer called the "Sinke into which all the rest of the Colonyes empty their Heretickes," were there entire communities organized around radical alternatives to the standing order in Massachusetts and Connecticut, but even there the categories normally used to describe English radical spiritism were only partially applicable as each settlement hammered out its polity in an environment free from the pressures that forced more sophisticated organization upon English spiritists. [23]

The basic challenge that the New England spiritists threw at the feet of more moderate Puritans concerned matters of doctrine, particularly the understanding of Christ's role in the history of redemption. Like their English counterparts, those in New England singled out as antinomians and familists held a radical view of the doctrine of conversion; in a manner comparable to Eaton, Traske, and other English spiritists, they greatly magnified what they took to be Christ's power and direction in marking the everlasting saint. One New Englander, for example, reported that among Anne Hutchinson's followers "*Free Grace, Gospel Truth, Glorious Light,* and *Holding Forth of Christ* was all their tone." Similarly, Giles Firmin recalled that, though most New England Puritans understood that "the work of inherent holinesse which maketh us new creatures is a distinct thing from Christ his person," such had not been the case with the spiritists he had known in the colony. "This was received when the errours raged there," he noted, "that Christ was the New Creature." Like Traske, who argued that regeneration was nothing less than Christ dwelling in the saint, many New England spiritists were convinced that, once a person was justified, the Son of God dictated his every action. Thus assured of their salvation, such radical Puritans acknowledged no law but Christ within them, for he provided, in Samuel Gorton's words, an absolute "fulness of freedome and liberty." "To give Christ his true forme without us," Gorton noted, "and yet to bee without the comfort and fruit of his dwelling, and being resident in us by his grace," was mere sophistry. It is as if, he continued, "a man should affirm, that the eye is of use, and onely sees for it selfe, but not for the body in which it is, nor is of that use, as to be the light of it, for the eye sees properly for the body, rather than for it selfe."[24]

Such a heightened dependence on the doctrine of the indwelling of Christ led to the kinds of errors the General Court and the Boston church examined during the furor over Anne Hutchinson and her supporters, for chief among the sources of the doctrinal aberrations with which these radicals were charged was their insistence that justification (the moment at which a sinner understands that he is redeemed by God's grace) took precedence over sanctification (the gracious disposition to saintly acts evidenced by the truly saved).[25] Thus Hutchinson and her followers condemned the "legal" preaching of those like Thomas Shepard and Peter Bulkeley who insisted that justification was only the first of many important steps in the conversion process. John Coggeshall, a wealthy silk mercer who emigrated to New England to become a deacon in Boston's church, was charged with saying that "halfe the people that were in Church-covenant in *N.E.*, were under a Covenant of Workes" (that is, believed in the efficacy of their own efforts toward salvation), a fact for which he found biblical support in the parable of the ten virgins (Math. 25:1-13). John Wheelwright, Hutchinson's brother-in-law, went even further and condemned all but a handful of New Englanders for their misguided notions of what it meant to be a good Christian. "If men think to be saved," he argued in his famous "Fast-Day Sermon" of 1637, "because they see some worke of sanctification in them, as hungring and

thirsting and the like: if they be saved, they are saved without the Gospell." "No, no," he continued, "this is a covenant of works, for in the
covenant of grace, nothing is revealed but Christ for our righteousness." [26]

Among such highly trained ministers as Wheelwright or, for that matter, Cotton, the relation between justification and sanctification always
was kept in balance; such men never proposed that Christ literally
dwelled in the saint. But, though Wheelwright warned his supporters
"to have a care that we give not occasion to others to say we are libertines
or Antinomians, but Christians," others who overindulged in the heady
wine offered by lay prophesiers like Hutchinson and Gorton often fell
into genuine doctrinal (and moral) confusion. One distraught inhabitant
of Weymouth, for example, a town with a history of antinomian difficulties, was so troubled by all the talk of justification and sanctification
that he "fell into some trouble of mind, and in the night cried out, 'Art
thou come, Lord Jesus?'" Intent on having his query answered he then
leaped from "a high window into the snow, and ran about seven miles
off, and being traced in the snow, was found dead the next morning." To
make perfectly clear what the man so earnestly sought, Governor Winthrop closed this sad account by noting that in the snow this confused
soul had "kneeled down to pray in divers places." Later that same year
the governor told a similar melancholy tale. A young woman in the Boston church, "having been in much trouble of mind about her spiritual
estate, at length grew into utter desperation." Unable to be comforted by
friends or clergy, and hopelessly confused about whether or not she was
saved, "one day she took her little infant and threw it into a well, and then
came into the house and said, now she was sure she would be damned." [27]

More typical than such cases of extreme religious distress were those in
which individuals who contemplated spiritist ideas adopted the notion,
easily enough derived from the doctrine of "free grace," that because
Christ dwelled in the saint he offered him immediate revelations of his
Father's will. This belief in continuing revelation sealed Anne Hutchinson's fate at her examination by the General Court in 1637, for when
Deputy Governor Thomas Dudley pressed her to explain how she knew
which of the colony's ministers were under a covenant of works, she finally exclaimed: "by an immediate revelation," that is, by "the voice of
[God's] own spirit to my soul." Further, as others were quick to testify, in
her case such behavior was not new. Since coming to New England she
often had been "very inquisitive after revelations" and earlier, in England, had admitted that "she had never had any great thing done about
her but it was revealed to her beforehand." Even after her banishment she

refused to acknowledge the error of her ways. In 1639 Winthrop noted that when an earthquake struck Rhode Island while Hutchinson and some of her adherents were at prayer, "they were persuaded, (and boasted of it,) that the Holy Ghost did shake it [the earth] in coming down upon them, as he did upon the apostles."[28]

Hutchinson's experience with divine revelations is only the most notable of many. A letter of Shepard to Cotton in 1636, tells how "after his marriage" Cotton's servant no longer would go to hear his master preach "because the spirit moved him not." Trying to explain the man's behavior, the Newtown minister offered Cotton some consolation. "It was not likely out of any contempt to the woord" that the man avoided going to his meeting, Shepard told Cotton, "but Because he might happily account your selfe a legall preacher," an explanation probably laced with irony, since Cotton was the only minister whom the Hutchinsonians claimed was *not* a legalist! Nor were such opinions restricted to the immediate years of the Antinomian Controversy. In 1643 Randall Holden, one of the more articulate Gortonists, answered a letter from the Massachusetts Bay Colony by reminding the Bay Puritans that though "we are your owne Countrymen," God "hath taught us a language you never spoake, neither can you heare it, and that is the cause of your alienation from us." Another Gortonist, Edward Johnson reported, claimed that "she was a Prophetesse, and [that] it was revealed unto her, that she must prophecy unto the People in the same words that the Prophet Ezekiel did." And Gorton, a self-proclaimed "Professor of the Mysteries of Christ," in an admission that illustrates how closely his doctrine prefigured that of the Quakers, claimed that "By *new heavens* and *new earth* . . . we understand the state of [being in] Christ, or of that *holy unction* or *Christianity*, that as the visible heavens & earth . . . make a *compleat* and *fruitfull world*, even so do God & man in Christ make one durable and fruitfull *condition, wherein righteousness dwells*." For this spiritist the experience of Christ was nothing less than apocalypse itself.[29]

If the radicals' emphasis on the indwelling of Christ easily led to self-righteous pronouncements about the saint's ability to speak with divine sanction, we also do well to consider how a belief in the actual presence of God within one could lead to the idea, often associated in England with those termed the "Ranters," that God literally existed not only in man but in *all* created objects. As A. L. Morton, the most assiduous student of this unusual sect, has noted, among many of its members such pantheism was linked to the antinomian conviction that " 'the moral law' was no longer binding upon true believers." In New England there was nothing comparable to the vulgarity and exhibitionism that characterized the English Ranters—one critic of the group who had been admitted to a Ranter conventicle in England reported that at one point in their "service" a Ranter "let a great Fart, and as it gave report uttered these words, *Let every thing that hath breath praise the Lord.*" Still there are indications that some of the New Englanders' spiritist beliefs evolved in a parallel way.[30]

Nicholas Easton, a Newbury tanner whose radical ideas had been discovered about the time of the difficulties with the New England antinomians, quickly followed Anne Hutchinson to Aquidneck after her banishment from the Bay Colony and by late 1638 had attracted enough attention in his own right for Winthrop to note his erroneous belief that "every one of the elect [has] the Holy Ghost and also the devil indwelling." By 1641 Easton had advanced even farther in his radicalism. Disenchanted with Hutchinson's group, he moved to nearby Newport, where William Coddington and John Coggeshall, prominent antinomians who also had abandoned Hutchinson, had settled and where Easton began a career as a lay preacher. In Newport he advocated what clearly was allied to the Ranters' quasi-pantheistic beliefs, for he claimed not only that "man hath no power or will in himself, but as he is acted by God" but also that "God filled all things, nothing could be or move but by him."[31]

Easton's presence in the Rhode Island settlements among individuals who by the late 1650s became the earliest New England converts to Quakerism—and, indeed, his preaching proto-Quaker ideas to them—assumes even more significance when we realize that Gorton, one of New England's most advanced radicals, expressed similar views, specifically in his *Incorruptible Key* (1647), a tract most likely completed before his return to England in 1644. In that book, in addition to arguing that "God is *all in all* in every one of the Saints," Gorton (no doubt knowingly) misstated a famous biblical injunction and urged people to "*goe and preach the Gospell in* [sic] *every creature,* that is in every creature, as the life and spirit of it centereth in man," just as the "scope, drift, life and spirit of man, onely centereth in God." The similarity of this sentiment to some of the pronouncements of the Ranters is striking. Joseph Salmon claimed that "this [spiritual] power (which is God) comes forth and offers itself in a diversity of appearance, and still (by a divine progresse in the affairs of the earth) moves from one to another."[32] By the mid-1640s the Rhode Island settlements had been exposed to the kind of radical spiritism that in England prepared the way for James Nayler and George Fox, a fact that goes far toward explaining why of the New England colonies Rhode Island proved most receptive to the Quaker emissaries who arrived in the late 1650s.

By the late 1630s Rhode Island, which the Massachusetts Puritans had taken to calling "Rogue Island" because of its heterodox population, had become the most popular haven for the radical spiritists. But other communities in New England were not free from challenge to the emergent doctrinal consensus. As early as the spring of 1636, Richard Mather attempted to gather a new church in Dorchester after a majority of the original settlers had departed for the Connecticut River valley, but the proceedings were halted when a council of elders from other churches decided that some of the prospective church members were describing their conversion experiences in patently unscriptural terms. As Winthrop noted in his account of the events, most of the candidates "had builded their comfort of salvation upon unsound grounds," particularly those who claimed knowledge of their sainthood through "dreams and ravishes of spirit by fits." Writing to Mather to explain the council's advice to delay the foundation work, Shepard reminded his co-worker in Christ's American vineyard that "we came here not to find gracious hearts, but to see them too," and added that "it is not faith but visible faith, that must make a visible church."[33]

Soon thereafter Mather corrected the misconceptions of those in his flock inclined to such erroneous views and obtained approval for the church's formation, but Dorchester continued to be plagued by doctrinal problems. In February 1641, after the community had called "one Mr. Burr" to assist Mather, some members of the church, including Mather, were troubled when the new minister "delivered of some points savoring of Familism." Burr and Mather were unable to resolve their doctrinal differences, and the problem grew to such "heat and alienation" that the church had to seek advice from the neighboring churches and the General Court. Burr finally was chastised for his "doubtful and unsafe expressions" and thereupon recanted, but the course of events in the community, coming as it did upon the heels of the Antinomian Controversy, only fueled the General Court's concern with the spread of spiritist views.[34]

In 1639 the town of Weymouth encountered similar difficulties when it invited Robert Lenthall to be its minister. "Though of good report in England," Lenthall "was found to have drank in some of Mrs. Hutchinson's opinions, as of justification before faith, etc." After a "conference" with John Cotton, Lenthall was disabused of this "Antinomian" error, but he

Woodcut of Richard Mather, by John Foster, frontispiece to *The Life and Death of . . . Richard Mather*, by Increase Mather (Cambridge, Massachusetts Bay Colony, 1671). In 1636 many of his townspeople in Dorchester supposedly held erroneous religious views, some of which linked them to spiritist ideology.

continued to oppose the way the Massachusetts Puritans gathered their churches, particularly their admitting as members only those who were "visible saints"; as Winthrop noted, Lenthall "stuck close" to the opinion that "only baptism was the door of entrance into the church." Before too long the "common sort of people did eagerly embrace his opinions" and then attempted to form a baptist church in the town. The General Court was far from eager to see this occur, and by 1640 Lenthall had fallen into a by-then familiar pattern for radicals: he moved to Rhode Island, where for two years he served as John Clarke's assistant in the Newport baptist church. Even after he had left Weymouth, his influence continued to be felt. James Brittane, who had "abett[ed] the course of Lenthall," was charged with "speaking reproachfully of some elders," presumably those who opposed the establishment of the new congregation; and Thomas Makepeace was informed by the General Court that "his novel disposition" had made them "very weary of him, unless he reform." Another townsman, Ambrose Martin, was fined £10 and sent to Mather for instruction because he had persisted in "expressing his strong dislike to the exercise of ecclesiastical rule." [35]

Another problematic spiritist minister was Hanserd Knollys, who became a prominent baptist after his return to England during the civil wars. Knollys arrived in Boston in 1638, not the most opportune time for someone who held "Antinomian" opinions, and shortly thereafter moved to Dover, in present-day New Hampshire, where "some few of the looser sort of persons" (including the notorious Captain John Underhill) had settled and then called him to be their pastor. Although at first Hugh Peter tried to convince Winthrop and others that Knollys might be "usefull" because in that area of the "Piscataqua" "they grone for Government and Gospel," the new arrival soon eliminated any opportunity he had to establish himself in the good graces of the magistrates. In a letter to an English friend he claimed that he had found the New England government "worse than the high commission," for "here was nothing but oppression, etc., and not so much as the face of religion"; he made the error of entrusting this missive to someone who subsequently showed it to Winthrop. [36]

Shortly thereafter the governor received another report that soured his opinion of the minister even more. Thomas Larkham, who recently had settled near Dover and had begun to assist Knollys in his preaching, complained that though he and Knollys "went one [that is, "on"] together lovingly A While," his "poore brother" soon began "to ball about that prime evidence, etc. and under the name of Legalists to fire the comfort and shake the faith" of the "poore weake ones" in the congregation. Larkham reminded Winthrop that "the controversie is not new, you know," and soon added more of the kinds of facts at which the governor must have shuddered. Fortunately, by 1642 Knollys decided to return to England, where he reestablished his contacts with such radicals as William Kiffin and (probably through Kiffin's prompting) joined the Jacob-Lathrop church, then under Henry Jessey's ministry, and within a few years assumed a role as one of the leading baptist preachers. And like many of that group, he continued to be attacked for his antinomian views, which in his case he genuinely held; they had contributed to the spiritual unrest that marked the northern borders of Puritan settlement in New England.[37]

As late as 1650 the Massachusetts Puritans still were troubled by members of their own ministry who broached spiritist doctrine. In that year Marmaduke Matthews, who had arrived in Boston in 1638 from Swansea, Wales, was settled as the minister in Malden, but shortly thereafter some of the parishioners questioned the soundness of his doctrine. Two of them, John Hathorne and Thomas Lynde, were particularly disturbed by a sermon on Zechariah 3:9 in which Matthews touched on the matter of "the foundation of justifying faith"; therein he had publicly maintained, among other things, that "To think we can have any conviction before we have Christ is a very delusion." The community soon became enough unsettled by the ensuing charges and countercharges for the General Court to call Matthews for an examination of his views, and at that interview they uncovered more erroneous points of doctrine. At its May 1651 session the court charged Matthews with maintaining that "the gospel of grace and the sacred scriptures are a false foundation of faith to build our justification upon" and for saying that "'Tis foolishness if you think Christ doth not come but in a conditional promise." As in the case of Knollys, the authorities were not pleased to discover doctrine that two decades earlier had caused such problems and went so far as to censure the Malden church for settling Matthews without taking the care to certify his orthodoxy.[38]

Like Lenthall and Knollys, Matthews, too, eventually left Massachusetts when he no longer could stomach the New England Puritans' intolerance, but by the time he and others had departed—for Rhode Island or back across the Atlantic (after moving to Yarmouth on Cape Cod Matthews returned to Wales)—they had done their work: throughout New England radical spiritist doctrine had garnered strong lay support. Edward Johnson, for example, wrote of one William Dinley, a "barber-surgeon" who was so taken by antinomian ideas that "So soone as any [people] were set downe in his chair, he would commonly be cutting of their haire and the truth together." Thomas Marshall, the ferry-man who worked between Boston and Charlestown and who, because his occupation put him in frequent contact with both the "Opinionists" and their detractors, was so "agitated by the *Counterbuffs* of Divinitie, which the respective passengers vented" that he himself became "inflamed" with antinomianism. Stephen Greensmith dared to affirm "that all the ministers (except Mr. Cotton, Mr. Wheelwright, & he thought Mr. Hooker) did teach a convenant of works," and was fined £40 for his opinions; one Ralph Mousall was dismissed from his post in the House of Deputies for approving of Wheelwright's doctrine and conduct. By 1640 even Connecticut, settled but a few years before, had its spiritists. In the late summer of that year Winthrop noted that a "Mr. Collins" who had been hired to teach school in Hartford was "taken" with Hutchinson's heresies; and a few months later, probably prompted by Collins's activities, Hooker wrote to Shepard that he was "marvelous apprehensive of hazards" from antinomians at Hartford and New Haven. "Myself and my brother Stone," he continued, "are making out what forces we may agaynst it, for we feare a suddayen alarum; and ergo we should have our people have ther weapons in a readinesse . . . to outface these delusions."[39]

The spiritist doctrine of the indwelling of the Holy Spirit and the numerous corollaries commonly derived from it appeared in many New England areas during the years before the Restoration. But because the points of doctrine were so liable to obfuscation and those who held them frequently willing to admit to "misunderstandings" to avoid punishment, the numbers of those examined and/or chastised for spiritist beliefs cannot be taken as an accurate indication of their presence. Equally revealing are the much more common cases of those who challenged the moderate Puritans on ecclesiastical points derived from radical spiritist ideology—that is, what we might term the *institutional* ramifications of radical spiritism.

Chief among these were the remarkably common attacks on the ministry itself. Despite the fact that most historians of colonial New England have emphasized the respect in which the clergy were held, settlers questioned not only the justness of the doctrine their ministers preached but the very legitimacy of their office: as Shepard put it, "we lie under slander of many, . . . as if elders in churches were but only ciphers." A suspicion—indeed, often a condemnation—of the prerogatives of a specially trained ministry had marked English radical thought at least since the time of the true familists, and between 1630 and 1650 anticlerical views of one form or another were held by the whole spectrum of left-wing Protestants, from the antinomians to the early Quakers.[40] As were the spiritists' beliefs in continuing revelation and the Ranters' more extreme pantheistic views, anticlericalism was easily derived from the basic spiritist doctrine of the indwelling of Christ. It was not that great a conceptual leap for those who felt threatened by "legal" preaching to extend their condemnation to any preaching by a regular ministry, under the assumption that he who was saved by God's free grace had within him a testimony more valid than that anyone else could provide.

As with so many other radical ideas in colonial New England, the legitimacy of the ministry was first raised during the arraignment of Anne Hutchinson. By her actions she had implicitly arrogated to herself some of the authority of the ordained ministry, particularly by her reinterpretation of the Reverend Mr. Cotton's sermons and her willingness to judge the doctrinal orthodoxy of the rest of the New England clergy. Errors "fifty-three" and "fifty-four" from the lengthy list condemned by the assembly of churches in Newtown in 1637 make this explicit, for among the "erroneous opinions as were found to have been brought into *New-England* and spread under-hand there" were these, that "No minister can teach one that is annoynted by the Spirit of Christ, more then he knowes already . . ." and that "No minister can bee an instrument to convey more of Christ, then hee by his owne experience hath come unto."[41] Further, though Hutchinson herself never counseled outright abolition of the ministry, there is ample evidence to suggest that other New Englanders influenced by spiritist ideas moved toward just this extreme position.

In the spring of 1639, Ambrose Martin of Weymouth added to his list of offenses by "calling the church covenant a stinking carryon & a humane invention, & saying he wondered at Gods patience, feared it would end in the sharpe, & said the ministers did dethrone Christ, & set up themselves"; he was fined £10 and "counseled to go to Mr Mather to bee instructed by him." If Martin's case is any indication, what Thomas Weld noted in his preface to Winthrop's *Short Story* (1644) was hardly exaggerated. During and after the Antinomian Controversy, he wrote, "*after our Sermons were ended at our publike lectures, you might have seen halfe a dozen Pistols discharged at the face of the Preacher, (I meane) so many objections made by the opinionists in the open Assembly against our doctrine delivered, if it suited not their fancies.*" As late as 1641, the Boston church still encountered such criticism. In that year Francis Hutchinson, who as Anne's son never had

had any difficulty in understanding the implications of her doctrine, was fined, imprisoned, and finally banished for "calling the church of Boston," under John Wilson's ministry, "a whoare, a strumpet, & [for holding] other corrupt tenets."[42]

Such behavior was not restricted to the Boston church. In Salem in 1642 William Gault was tried before the quarterly court for "reproachful and unseemly speeches against the rule of the Church," and two years later John Stone of Gloucester was arraigned for "scandalizing" the town's minister, Richard Blinman, by "charging him with a false interpretation of Scripture, [and] also saying, that if an angel from heaven should preach the same, he would not believe it." Stone also made it clear, as the court record reveals, that in his community "there were others of his mind." Ten years later the issue still was not dead: a Mrs. Holgrave was presented to the Essex Court for saying "that if it were not for the Law she would never come to the meeting, the Teacher was soe dead." She was so disgusted by what she heard from this clergyman that she "persuaded Gudwife Vincent to come to her house on the Sabbath daye and reade good bookes, affirming that the Teacher was fitter to be a Ladye's chamberman than to be in the pulpit." Similarly, in 1649 in Watertown, Samuel Straiton and his wife were fined for "speaking against ministers, church members, and magistrates"; and in 1642 George Willerd of Plymouth was brought before the colony's General Court for announcing that those who contributed to the minister's salary were no more than "fooles, and knaves and gulls." In Sudbury in 1650 John Ruddock stood up in town meeting and told Edmund Brown, the minister, that "Setting aside your office, I regard you no more than another man." And Gorton, speaking to some "praying Indians" who had wandered into his colony in Rhode Island, was quick to tell them that, while New England Puritans "teach that you must have Ministers," these church officers "cannot change men's hearts, God must do that, and therefore there is no need of Ministers."[43]

Closely linked to such arguments against the clergy's doctrine was the radicals' condemnation of their claims to special privilege through their training and education; some radicals, that is, heartily endorsed preaching per se, as long as it was done by people uncorrupted by the pride that often accompanied human learning. Hence, for example, Gorton's complaint that "in these our dayes, the immediate inspiration and revelation of the Spirit, is abhorred both in prayer and prophesie; but all must be hewed out by study [,] and so kept in schools of humane learning, Libraries, and in men who have most means and time to exercise themselves in such things. . . ." One of the things that most troubled Gorton about the Puritan ministry was its reliance on a book learning that masked a deeper spiritual emptiness. "That ministry," he continued, "that spends its time, study, and care in seeking and hoping for the trans-fusing of the Spirit of Christ into such hearts where the seed of God is not," was merely futile. It "is of like wisdome," he concluded, "and will have like success, as if a man should spend his time and study to teach a dog the art of arithmetick, Astrology, or navigation." For his part, as Gorton later put it in a letter defending himself from the calumnies printed in Nathaniel Morton's *New Englands Memoriall*, he was proud that he had not "bin drowned in pride and ignorance through Aristotle's principles and other heathen philosophers, as millions are and have bin, who ground the preaching of the Gospell upon humane principles to the falsifying of the word of God."[44]

Giles Firmin, who after his return to England commonly sprinkled his treatises with revealing anecdotes from his New England years, suggests that in other cases besides Gorton's the laity's challenge to the ministry centered on their haughty claims to privilege through education. "One of *Mrs. Hutchinsons* followers," he noted in his *Separation Examined*, "on a Lords Day stood up in the Congregation, and would defend it [the anti-nomian doctrine of justification] against the learned and reverend Teacher, and told him the text was read so in the original." Some like Gorton among the laity did read Hebrew and Greek, but in this case Fir-min strongly doubted the parishioner's qualifications to make such a claim. "What can these men," Firmin asked, "say to this that know not the Originall, nor Grammar, both which a man must know to answer this?" Edward Winslow's complaint against the Gortonists was similar; he had found them "unlearned men, the ablest of them could not write true English, no not in common words." Yet these unlettered souls, he continued, "would take upon them to interpret the most difficult places of Scripture" and with a predictable conclusion: to "wrest them any way to serve their owne turne."[45]

Another of Firmin's reports amusingly supports such ostensibly ar-rogant judgments. Speaking of lay preachers in some New England towns who "were highly conceited of themselves, and must be Exercis-ing (Mr. Ward called it Exorcising) their gift," Firmin gave as an example "a bog fellow, forward to put forth himself," to whom God finally "gave a check." "This gifted Brother in his Preaching," Firmin related, "I think the place he quoted, was, *Let thy Saints shout for joy*, Psal. 132.9." "I am sure *Shout* was the word he would have said," Firmin continued, "but in stead thereof, he said, *Let the Saints shite for joy*." To Firmin, who upon his return to England took the trouble to get himself ordained (though, as Thomas Edwards pointed out, upon his first arrival in London he kept a "Lecture," though he was not then "in Orders, nor ever [had] Preached"), the lesson was obvious. "This was a foul mistake, for a gifted Brother, the Holy one might do it, to make him ridiculous, who could meddle with his Holy things, with such a proud frame."[46]

As with the doctrinal ramifications of spiritist ideas, the radicals' criticism of the ministry sometimes led to beliefs that anticipated those of the Quakers, particularly in the late 1640s and early 1650s as New Englanders became more aware of the anticlericalism spreading in England. In 1654, for example, Edward Johnson complained that "many pamphlets have come from our Countrymen of late, to this purpose, namely, squirrillously to deride all kinds of Scholarship, Presbytery, and Synods"; and it is very likely that foremost in his mind were the works of William Dell, who in such sermons as *The Tryal of Spirits* (1653) led the attack against ministerial prerogatives.[47] And in the same year that Johnson published his *Wonder-Working Providence*, Roger Williams told the younger John Winthrop, then in Connecticut, that "two of Mr. Dell's books were lately burnt at the Massachusetts" because they contained "some sharp things againt the Presbyterians and Academians." Williams, himself no moderate Puritan, admitted that he personally had brought from his last trip to England a copy of Dell's *Tryal*. A year later Charles Chauncy, minister to Scituate, already considered Dell's anticlericalism serious enough to devote a major sermon, *God's Mercy*, to a rebuttal of his arguments against the necessity of "school-learning" among the clergy. "Some go so far," he noted, "as to account these blessings to be curses, so as to say that our ministyres are antichristian, and schools of learning popish, and the seminaryes of wickedness, & looseness. . . ." Chauncy admitted the failings of some of his colleagues; but, he pleaded, "let not whole societyes or professions be charged or blemished for the faylings or scandalous carriages of some." Further, throughout the sermon Chauncy maintained that "whatever he [Dell] saith, ye must expect no reason from him," for "ye must take all from him as dictates of the Spirit."[48] Better an over-educated university man, Chauncy believed, than an unlettered radical guided only by his own delusions.

The kind of radical spiritism Dell represented, in which anticlericalism played so important a part, was in fact a half-way house to Quakerism. At many points his ideas bear comparison to those of some of New England's more advanced radicals, particularly the Gortonists, themselves highly sympathetic to the Friends. Like Dell, William Erbury, and others of this circle, Samuel Gorton insisted that ministers should "present Christ Jesus unto the world, as in a figure by all things contained therein," and derided an overly educated clergy as similar to "the Ostrich, of whom it is said, she can digest Iron" and so "falls upon" feeding herself "with the dish or platter in which the food is brought" rather than on the "bread of life" the vessel contains. Gorton and his followers found "the Ministry of the Word so *monopolized*" by men of university education who had "hewen out" their clerical position "*by the art, wisdome, and will of man, prostrating themelves thereunto*," that he despaired of ever hearing the true Word spoken in the Puritans' churches. Like Dell and others, he called for an unction of the spirit in him who preached and so encouraged—as did many English radicals—"prophesying" by any member of the congregation. The spirit, he noted, "uttereth it selfe freely without respect of Persons in all the Congregations and Assemblies of Saints." "Onely listen unto the Oracle of God by whom hee is pleased to utter it," he pleaded, "for ye may all prophecy one by one for the edification of the Church." [49]

Anticlericalism in such varied forms was only one of several kinds of challenges to the institutional structure of New England Puritanism. As early as the 1640s there were in the colonies those willing to eliminate virtually all vestiges of the outward church in their quest for spiritual purity. At the same time that he berated the church of Boston as a "strumpet," Francis Hutchinson was charged with having denied "that Christ gave any power to pastours or teachers to baptize" and "that there is or can be any presbytery without apostles or evangelists." His friend "Mr. Collins," who had been driven from the Barbadoes for his "Familist" preaching, similarly maintained "that there were no gentile churches (as he termed them) since the apostles' times, and that none now could ordain ministers." A few years later, when the Gortonists had been captured and brought to Boston for trial, after one of John Cotton's sermons Gorton himself was heard to say "That in the Church now there was nothing but Christ, so that all our [that is, the Puritans'] Ordinances, Ministers, and Sacraments, &c. were but mens inventions, for shew and pomp." In New Haven a "Mistresse Moore" rejected the ordained clergy, claiming that Christ once had appointed ministers, but now "pastors & teachers are but the inventions of men." In the 1650s such notions became even more common. Nicholas Upshall, who later became a Quaker, and Ann Burden of the Boston church were excommunicated for "neglecting and denying Gospel ordinances," and in the town of Sandwich, William Leverich complained that many of his parishioners were "transported with their . . . Fancies, to the rejecting of all Churches and Ordinances, by a new cunning." Three years later, after Leverich had left the town for a new church on Long Island, Peter Gaunt was one of several people charged with neglecting public worship; he claimed that "hee knew noe publike vizable worship now in the world."[50]

These individuals and others, as their contemporaries pointed out, expressed views associated with the English radical group called the "Seekers," those who, as Robert Baillie noted when he described the beliefs of New England's own preeminent member of this sect, Roger Williams, argued that "there is no church, no sacraments, no pastors, no church-officers, or ordinances in the world, nor has been since a few years after the Apostles."[51] Although many English radicals passed through a Seeker phase—in 1646 Thomas Edwards observed that "the sect of Seekers growes very much, and all sorts of Sectaries turn Seekers"—it is clear that Williams was instrumental in bringing to wide public attention the tenets of this loosely organized sect. In 1644 Baillie reported that "one Mr. Williams has drawn a great number [in England] after him . . . , denying any true church in the world, and will have every man to serve God by him selfe alone, without any church at all," a significant fact since Williams had arrived at his beliefs a few years earlier, after he had spent a short time as a baptist, in New England. This movement among radical spiritists, at least in its earlier years, had a particularly American flavor.[52]

Although at one time or another many Seekers, like Williams, numbered themselves in the ranks of other groups of radicals, their rejection of the outward church in all its forms was based not so much on the assumption that only those who had experienced the work of the Spirit could establish a visible church but rather on the belief that true churches could be formed only by ministers commissioned *directly by Christ*, as the Apostles had been. Seekers believed that because shortly after the apostolic age the Church had fallen into profound corruption and the true apostolic succession had been broken, for centuries Christians had had no way to band together in true Gospel churches. Those in each age who had been spiritually awakened could only bear testimony against the Antichrist and await the time when Christ would reappear on earth to reestablish his apostolic church, hence "Seekers" or "Expecters" who anticipated a time when "Christ shall send forth new Apostles to plant Churches anew" and so reform "the Apostasie of Antichrist [that] hath so farre corrupted all."[53]

In some cases such beliefs led only to further condemnation of the

An "Adamite," from Daniel Featley's *The Dippers Dipt* (London, 1645). Adamites, often linked to Seekers, awaited the new dispensation of Christ in the nakedness Adam lived in before the Fall. The colony of Connecticut included this group in laws it passed against religious dissenters.

A "Seeker," from Ephraim Pagitt's *Heresiography* (London, 1654).

ordained ministry and their adminstration of the sacraments, with individuals forming separate congregations on the basis of such protestations. When asked "why they spake against the Ordinances of the Ministry," the Gortonists answered that "they were ordained onely for the time of the Nonage, but after the Revelation was written, they were to cease," a fact that did not prevent them from establishing churches of their own. In the case of people like Williams, however, it meant something more extreme: eventually Williams himself "refused communion with all, save his own wife," and began to "preach and pray with all comers," since no form of worship—be it congregational, baptist, or Gortonist—could be more true than any other.[54] For Williams, the English radical Lawrence Clarkson, and others, Seekerism formed an important link in the chain of arguments for religious toleration.

It was precisely this openness to all forms of worship that disturbed many in New England and old who had watched the evolution of Williams's religious thought; their fears were amply confirmed in 1644 when he published his radical tolerationist tract, *The Bloudy Tenent of Persecution*. Perhaps equally upsetting to New Englanders was his and other Seekers' understanding of church history and its relation to the millennial promise. The Seekers whom Nathaniel Ward lampooned as "young Spaniels, questing at every bird that rises" and "at a dead stand, not knowing what to doe or say . . . , looking for new Nuntios from Christ," questioned the whole notion of the church covenant on which the New England Way was based.[55] Their search for purity in church worship had nothing to do with the grandiose drama of a city on a hill; for they believed that, like all other such experiments organized to reinstate the proper form of the universal Church, the New England Puritans' system was doomed to failure. Only Christ's second coming would restore the Church from the ruins of antichristian apostasy, and to think otherwise was mere antichristian fancy.

Because of the nature of the Seekers' criticism of the Puritan churches—as Williams's later career in America illustrates, its main thrust was quietistic—the group's influence in New England was subtle and is difficult to assess. But one fact is clear. Like their English counterparts, whom Thomas Edwards saw as contributors to the further "issue" of "Sects and Schismes," in America the Seekers were a transitional group whose importance lay in how their ideology served to wedge open the way to other, more radical ideas, particularly among the inhabitants of Rhode Island, who by the late 1640s had emerged as the New World representatives of the most advanced Puritan radicalism.[56]

In the late 1630s, some of Anne Hutchinson's followers already had moved to separate the civil and religious spheres, a position which followed logically from the Seekers' assumption that in such degenerate times no religion could be considered more true than another and so none should be given state support. In his *Anabaptism, the True Fountaine of Independency* (1647) Robert Baillie reported that by Williams himself he had been informed "*that* Mistresse *Hutchinson in the first place she settled with her company after her banishment* [in Aquidneck in 1638], *did perswade her husband to lay down the office of the Magistrate, as that which was unlawfull for Christians to bear*," and in his *Dissuasive from the Errours of the Time* Baillie alluded to another of Williams's reports, from which he learned that among the Rhode Island radicals some maintained "That the Saints are not to submit to the powers of the world or worldly powers, and that the powers and governments of the world have nothing to doe with them for civill misdemeanors." For the civil magistrate to support one form of religion over another, these colonists argued, was for him to claim a priority for the chosen form that simply could not be maintained. Seekers believed that only after the new dispensation would Christians be able to discern the true form of Christ's universal church; thus for a Christian to lend support—as an officer or even a voter—to civil magistracy implied an insufficient understanding of the distinction between the things of Caesar and those of God.[57]

Against this background, John Eliot's account of a conversation between some of his Indian converts and Gorton when the former had stopped in Shawomet to discuss what the Bay Puritans had taught them takes on particular significance, for it is clear that, though Williams has received most of the credit for advancing the notion of the separation of church and state during this period in New England, Gorton contributed significantly to debate over this idea. When Eliot asked what the Indians had talked about with Gorton, for example, one of his informants recalled Gorton's very words: "*They teach you that you must have Magistrates,*" he said, "*but that is needlesse, nor ought to be.*" When the natives then asked Gorton to elaborate, he replied that "*when a man sinneth, he does not sinne against Magistrates, and therefore why should they punish them? but they sinne against God and therefore we must leave them to God to punish them.*" In his published works Gorton elaborated this position. "Let no man think," he wrote in *An Antidote against the Common Plague of the World* (1656), "that we hold government useless and unlawful, but only desire that all things were considered according to their nature, and exercised and kept within their proper confines and cercuits." Or, as he had put it in *An Incorruptible Key* (1647), "the office of the Magistracie" had to be kept "within the compasse of civill things, that is to have relation to what ever concernes the relation between the creature and creature simply as they stand in reference to one another, in that respect," and was not to meddle in affairs of the spirit. Gorton believed that the intolerance of the New England churches, which labored "in the field of their home-made covenants and performances," had to be exposed for what it was— presumptuous usurpation of the "power and dominion" that belonged only "unto the Son of God" and evidence of a severely limited understanding of the absolute distance between the heavenly and earthly spheres.[58]

One of the most unexplored aspects of radical Puritan ideology in New England is closely related to the thrust of Gorton's comments on the relationship of church and state, for implicit in his arguments, as it was in the spiritism of Hutchinson, Williams, and the baptists, was the priority of the Spirit over the demands and restrictions of human law. Moderate Puritans rightly believed this notion would open the way to civil as well as ecclesiastical anarchy. There has been little recognition among historians, apart from a few remarks on the disarming of the Hutchinsonians, of the effect of radical spiritist ideas upon political ideology in New England, shown not only in criticisms of the civil magistrate's interference in religious matters, but also in a radically egalitarian view of society rooted in the belief that the indwelling of Christ obliterates all artificial distinctions among men. Considering the upheaval in England over the demands of the Levellers and Diggers, we should be more alert.

The New England Puritans' profoundly conservative social vision, epitomized in Winthrop's eloquent defense of a hierarchical society in his "Modell of Christian Charity," is often cited. Yet within five years of the arrival of Winthrop's fleet, despite the strong emphasis in Puritan promotional literature on the need for order and discipline—John White, for example, reminded prospective settlers that they should be "willing, constant, industrious, obedient, [and] frugall, lovers of the common good"—many who came to New England from England to escape "a low condition as is little better than beggery" found it possible to change radically their economic and social status.[59] If such a change was not possible for all who sought it, enough people had seen their neighbors succeed at changing their stations to call into question the final justness of Winthrop's conception of a society in which "some must be rich[,] some poore, some high and eminent in power and dignitie, others mean and in subjeccion." Not that in New England there developed anything comparable to the widespread political challenge of the Levellers, who attained their prominence through exploitation of Caroline England's complex socio-political situation. Yet, in New as well as old England, many dissatisfied with their lot as social underlings found religious doctrine that encouraged the belief that society might be reconstituted on more egalitarian premises.

Such doctrine first became evident in New England during the difficulties with Anne Hutchinson. The antinomians' claims for the preeminence of justification led to a belief that "the Spirit giveth such full and cleare evidence of a person's estate" that he had "no need" to be tried by obedience to outward law. However, the notion of the indwelling of Christ could be used to separate socially as well as religiously those who were truly valuable members of society from those who were not, without regard for claims to distinction through birth, wealth, or education, and cause some of insignificant status to take new risks.[60] Richard Gridley, "an honest poore man," was censured by the General Court during the Antinomian Controversy because he was "very apt to meddle in publike affairs, beyond his calling of skill (which indeed was the fault of them all, and of many others in the Country)." As Emery Battis has pointed out in his sociological analysis of the Hutchinsonian faction, the "core" and chief "support" groups of the antinomians were well-established socially and economically, but the "peripheral" group, no fewer than seventy-nine of whom left Massachusetts with either John Wheelwright or Hutchinson, very often were marginal members of society like Gridley, who, once "caught up in the centrifugal force of the Hutchinsonian movement," used spiritist doctrine to "confirm" their "self-evaluation" and "to offer psychological compensation for an inferior status in the community."[61]

By the early 1640s the Massachusetts authorities were confident that they had rid themselves of the most dangerous antinomians. Still, the political implications of spiritist doctrine had taken hold. In the summer of 1640, Lord Say and Sele, one of the colony's strongest supporters, wrote Winthrop that he had decided to shift his support to the colonization of the West Indies, where the climate and soil were better than New England's. He had become increasingly disturbed by the movement toward more democratic government in Massachusetts, a change brought on by a rapidly intensifying labor shortage and the consequent benefit to the lower classes, who began to press for more power in the House of Deputies. "Noe wise man," Lord Say and Sele wrote the Governor, "shoud be soe folish as to live whear every man is master, and masters must not correct theyr servants." Winthrop himself had always staunchly defended the magistrates' prerogative of a "negative voice" over the deputies; he warned that its elimination would bring the government "from a mixt Aristocracie to a meere Democracie . . . , the meanest & worst of all formes of Government."[62]

In 1641, Thomas Shepard, whose works reveal his acute sensitivity to a challenge from the lower classes, noted that because reports were abroad that "no men of worth are respected," the country was increasingly "neglected" by those like Lord Say and Sele who had offered the colony considerable political and financial support. "I confess," Shepard continued, "if under heathen masters, then desire liberty rather; but when men will live as they list, without any over them, and unfit to rule themselves, I much doubt whether this be according to God." Part of the problem, he said, was that masters and servants both were increasingly "eaten up with the world." Also, too many people believed that "the estate of the church" was "democraticall and popular" but forgot that "the government of it under Christ . . . is aristocratical," to be administered "by some chief, gifted by Christ, chosen by people to rule over them in the name of Christ, who are unable and unfit to be all rulers themselves."[63] The antiauthoritarianism fomented by the Hutchinsonians had become deeply rooted, and by the mid-1640s not only the clergy but all other men of privilege were under attack.

The Rhode Island settlements witnessed the most intense efforts to democratize church and state in response to the egalitarian promise of the Holy Spirit. The situation was epitomized in the words of an Aquidneck townsman, one Job Tyler, who, summoned by the local sergeant-at-arms to appear in court, haughtily replied that "he car'd not a fart [nor] turd for all their warrants." Such an insulting breach of authority—and decorum—was not isolated; it found its theological defense in the writings of Rhode Island groups like the Gortonists and, later, the baptists. Indeed, when Gorton and his followers were brought to trial in Boston in 1643, a principal charge against them pertained to the insolence with which they treated any summons to appear before a civil authority.[64]

The most revealing description of the Gortonists' unwillingness to defer to their supposed superiors appears in *Hypocrisie Unmasked* (1646), a tract prepared by Edward Winslow at the request of the Massachusetts government. Winslow noted that to Gorton the equality of all men was so literal a fact that any deference to a hierarchical system—be it civil or religious—seemed to him to deny the true priesthood of all believers. Thus Gorton criticized the Massachusetts Puritans, he continued, because they insisted that leaders "be honorable, learned, wise, experienced, and of good report" and did not realize that, to be judged fairly, a man had to be tried by his spiritual peers. Winslow admitted that the Gortonists "seem to acknowledge some way of ministring Justice, but the mysterie," he added, "lies in that word *Office*, [for] they would have no man set up in the Office of Magistracy, distinguished from other men, but would have such a common power to the Brethren, so that a man may judge as a Brother, but not as an Officer."[65]

Gorton justified his contempt of authority by claiming, as did many other radical spiritists, that the administration of justice "belongs only to the Lord" and that "men make themselves Gods . . . by ruling over the bodies and estates of men." Winslow, who wrote *Hypocrisie Unmasked* when he was living in London as the colony's agent and thus was highly sensitive to the uses to which such ideas were put by English radicals, objected to Gorton's implicit apology for what he considered an inconceivable political liberty. Winslow feared that if "the administration of Justice and judgement belongs to no officer, but to man as a Brother, then to every Brother, and if to every Brother, whether rich or poore, ignorant or learned, then every Christian in a Common-wealth must bee King, and Judge, and Sheriffe, and Captaine, and Parliament-man, and Ruler . . . ," a situation that inevitably would lead to "the establishment of all confusions, and the setting up of Anarchy worse then the greatest Tyranny." But Winslow had read Gorton's words rightly; the Rhode Island radical had declared that "to be a Brother, and consequently a coheire in Christ, is a higher sphere then to be a civill Officer." Similarly, his associate Randall Holden had told the Massachusetts authorities that he and others in Shawomet did not "thinke the better of any man for being invested into places or things that will in time waxe old as doth a garment," nor did they judge "the worse of any man for the want of them." If such doctrine led, as Winslow knew it would, to a challenge in New England similar to that of the Levellers in England, so be it. To the Gortonists the rebirth of man in Christ offered nothing less than full fraternal equality.[66]

Gorton's arguments were even more dangerous because he applied them not only to the political or civil sphere but to the domestic as well. Winslow noted that in one of Gorton's replies "to a prudent man in this Country [that is, in England], and one of the chiefe, and most understanding of this peculiar fellowship," he had "stoutly" maintained that, just as "there are no relations in the Commonwealth between rulers and subjects, nor in the Church between officers and brethren," so there were to be none "in the families between husband and wife, master and servant, father and sonne." Nor were such ideas unique to the Gortonists. Immediately after the Antinomian Controversy, Shepard inquired into the reason why "there is so much discontent [in families], that servants are weary of their masters, masters of their servants? and there are such complaints one of another, with little respect one of another?" He placed the blame in "a want of holiness, power, and life of godliness" in the people, but the root of such difficulties lay in doctrine that encouraged such insubordination under the pretense of spiritual equality. By the mid-1640s, in Rhode Island as well as in England, some individuals were willing even to sanction divorce, on the grounds that one partner was not yet, nor showed any evidence ever of becoming, the spiritual equal of the other. Robert Baillie noted that "M. *Gorting* and his Company" main-

tained that it was "lawfull for every woman to desert her husband when
he is not willing to follow her in her Church-Way," for a woman who
saw into "the mystery of Christ" and thereupon entered "the Lords
House" had every right to abandon a spouse who had not been given the
same invitation. If, as Shepard observed in 1641, "either men have rules
to walk by, or their own wills and apprehensions are to be rules," some
New Englanders had indeed taken Christ to themselves in such ways that
deference—in the political, social, or moral spheres—never again could
be palatable.[67]

Such ideas in England, as noted, found their clearest expression in the
Leveller and Digger movements, but New England lacked the political
ingredients—most obviously the parliamentary crisis and the civil war—
that so closely focused English radicals' attention on a broad political
program. It is worth noting that during this period the New England
magistrates were remarkably sensitive to political developments in England and thus had an immediate frame of reference in which to place
political threats like Gorton's. In 1648 Thomas Harrison apprised Winthrop of the rapidly increasing power of the Levellers in the Army, describing their program—"to bringe allmost a parity upon all persons in
the Kingdome, none to exceed 400 *lbs.* per annum: noe freman, to be
without 10 *lbs.* yearly rents, &c."—and the "Bookes entitled Appeales to
the people . . . put forth by Lilburne and others," whose purpose was to
persuade the people "that all power and soveraignty is devolvd & come
backe to its first subject, viz. themselves." A year later Roger Williams,
an indefatigable importer of radical ideology, told the younger John
Winthrop that he had heard "of a book from England importing another
high case on foot touching a more equal division of lands among brethren, and provision for younger brethren." The book might very well
have been a Digger tract.[68] Although New England experienced nothing
like the threats posed by English groups who sought the total reorganization of society, the magistrates' and ministers' apprehensiveness at the
democratic longings of many of their fellow-colonists must be placed in
this wider frame of reference. Peter Bulkeley's words to John Cotton reflect the frustration felt by the early 1650s by the colonies' leaders in the
face of such serious challenges to their authority: "Shall I tell you what I
think to be the ground of all this insolency which discovers itself in the
speach of men?" "Truly I cannot ascribe it so much to any outward
things, as to the putting of too much liberty and power in the hands of
the multitude, which they are too weak to manage. . . ." "The heady or

headless multitude have gotten the power into their hands," he concluded. And all had become "confusion." [69]

Adherents of radical spiritism were also willing to consider and accept points of doctrine that encouraged behavior that overturned the moral expectations of seventeenth-century society. Critics of spiritist beliefs always had claimed that such views encouraged general moral laxity, and in New England this tendency was bolstered by some of the colonists' adoption of religious ideas that threatened the support-systems that had been instituted to provide the most basic kinds of social order. Such ideas—in particular a belief in full freedom from sin and a denial of the physical reality of heaven and hell, and a belief in the mortality of the soul—were among those the Massachusetts Puritans found most reprehensible. No other Christian heresies seemed to place the city on a hill in such utter jeopardy.

As Christopher Hill, A. L. Morton, and others have shown, by the late 1640s and early 1650s such heresies evolving from more common spiritist doctrines were congenial to a wide variety of English Puritan radicals. [70] The belief that in this life man can become wholly free from the bondage of sin was rooted in the claims of familists and Grindletonians that unerring obedience to the Spirit put a divine perfection within man's reach. Moreover, by the 1630s preachers like John Eaton and Tobias Crisp, who had emphasized the birth of a "New Creature" with the coming of Christ to one's soul, began to distinguish, in William K. B. Stoever's words, between "the divine life of Christ dwelling in the regenerate and the corrupt life of the old man dwelling side by side with it" and claimed that the former provided the full righteousness necessary for salvation. An individual's "lusts" were of no consequence when God accepted Christ's perfect obedience as restitution for the sins of the old, fallen man. Among General Baptists like Henry Denne and Thomas Lamb, both of whom were known to the Gortonists, such ideas also were linked to a belief in the general redemption of humanity, ensured by the scriptural promise that Christ died for the sins of *all* men. Here, too, was reason for discounting the final importance of man's sinfulness. [71]

In *Theses Sabbaticae* (1649), a treatise prepared as the ideas of John Saltmarsh and other prominent English radicals had begun to infiltrate the colony, Shepard noted that in such degenerate times "Some think that there is no sin but unbelief, . . . and therefore, there being no sin against any law (Christ having by his death abolished all of them), the law cannot be a rule to them." In 1650 the colony became incensed over the case of Marmaduke Matthews, who claimed, among other things, that "for my part I do reprove no sin in persons under the gospel, but unbelief, because all sins are included in unbelief, nor persuade to any duty but to faith, because he that will believe, will obey." In *Theses Sabbaticae* Shepard had articulated the moderate Puritans' response to such ideas in the sharpest rhetoric: "Are drunkenness, whoredom, lying, cheating, witchcraft, oppression, theft, buggery, no sins," and "consequently not to be repented of, nor watched against, but only unbelief?" Shepard's dismay at such fallacious reasoning was shared by his friend Peter Bulkeley, thoroughly disgusted by colonists who believed that "you shall be saved and yet live in your sinnes," for this was to "take hold of the Devils Covenant instead of Gods." How could anyone believe, he asked, that God "would forgive us our sins and save us, yet suffer us to walke in our wayes, fulfilling the will of the flesh and of the minde?"[72] The answer simply lay in how radically one understood the doctrine of the indwelling of Christ.

Some New Englanders were not loath to voice other, more tangled rationalizations for what critics termed their "libertinism." Shepard observed that some colonists had begun to argue that because "all things good and evil come from God's will, and all things that are done are wrought by him, and all that he doth is good," therefore "all sinful actions are good, because God works them." Evidently this "most subtle and pernicious practice" of "wash[ing] all [sin] off from themselves, and lay[ing] the blame . . . upon God himself," was increasingly common, and Shepard's answer to such folly was unequivocal and firm. "What have we to do to take the measure of our ways by his [that is, God's] working will?" Shepard asked sarcastically. "God's will is his own rule to work with, not our rule to work by," he continued; thus "Our actions may be most sinful, when his working in and about these may be most just and holy." The case of Hugh Bewett, arraigned by the Bay Colony in 1640 because he publicly maintained that "he was free from original sin and from actual also for half a year before, and that all true Christians after [blank] are enabled to live without committing sin," offered a clear test of the colony's resolve in such matters. The jury found him guilty of heresy and because "his person & errors" were "dangeros for infection of others" banished him under pain of death.[73]

Faced with such an alternative, Bewett did what any serious radical in the New World would do: he moved to Rhode Island, beyond the reach of the Massachusetts Puritans, where the inhabitants tolerated almost any

THE
BLOVDY TENENT,
of PERSECUTION, for caufe of
CONSCIENCE, difcuffed, in

A Conference *betweene*
TRVTH and PEACE.

VVHO,
In all tender Affection, prefent to the High
Court of *Parliament*, (as the *Refult* of
their *Difcourfe*) thefe, (amongft other
Paffages) of *higheft confideration.*

Printed in the Year. 1644.

Title page of *The Bloudy Tenent of Persecution, for cause of Conscience*, by Roger Williams (London, 1644).

idea that did not directly threaten civil peace. In Shawomet, where the majority of the Gortonists had settled, Bewett found the settlers untroubled by his understanding of sin. Indeed, Gorton, their leader, questioned the existence of sin in yet another way, suggesting that the privileged classes had invented the notion the better to control the lower orders of society. In *An Antidote*, for example, in the course of condemning the established ministry for their reliance on education, Gorton linked such ministers to an elaborate conspiracy "to set up men in temporary authority, to praise the able and wealthy, and to press the poorer sort

A "Libertine," from Daniel Featley's *The Dippers Dipt* (London, 1645). Libertines supposedly argued for both religious and moral freedom and often were associated with English antinomians.

with burdens of sins, and such abundance of servile obedience, as to make them slaves to themselves and others." Like Gerrard Winstanley, the Digger who believed most theological doctrine the tool of the privileged classes—he claimed, for example, that "kingly government . . . hath made the election and rejection of brethren from their birth to their death, or from eternity to eternity"—Gorton condemned as oppressive the common understanding of sin and argued that the joyful mystery of Christ's presence in the saint freed him from arbitrary enslavement to those who had invented such concepts to perpetuate an unjust social order.[74]

In some ways New England's radical spiritists played directly into the hands of their critics by providing many instances of immoral behavior that could easily be linked to their unorthodox understanding of sin and guilt. When in 1640, for example, the inhabitants of Providence had had their fill of the Gortonists and complained to the governor of Massachusetts of their "licentious lust," they particularly noted the group's apparent disregard for the visible consequences of their theological radicalism. They acted like "savage brute beasts," the Providence men declared, "who put no manner of difference between houses, goods, lands, wives, lives, blood, nor any thing will be precious in their eyes," behavior that in some respects anticipated the Christian communism of the Diggers but also, more importantly, implied the kind of freedom from inhibitions, social and sexual, advocated by the Ranters.[75]

Other contemporary reports verify the popular perception of Rhode Island's "licentiousness." Gregory Dexter, the English radical printer who recently had emigrated to Providence, claimed that in the settlements throughout this region "a sweete cup hath rendered many of us wanton and too active." Another Rhode Islander, William Arnold, who had instigated Gorton's capture by a contingent of militia from the Bay Colony, gives credence to Dexter's comment, with special reference to the Gortonists, who were "rather like beasts in the shape of men [,] to doe what they shall thinke fit in their owne eyes."[76] Men were brought to such base conditions, Arnold and others claimed, when they refused to be accountable for the evil in their hearts.

As late as 1702 Cotton Mather still described Rhode Island as a den of "*Antinomians, Familists, Anabaptists, Anti-sabbatarians, Arminians, Socinians, Quakers, Ranters*, every thing in the world but *Roman Catholicks*, and *Real Christians*." Still, not all the improprieties in the Rhode Island communities could be considered the direct consequence of doctrinal heresies. The John Bradstreet whom Robert Muzye described as having "had dealings with the maids at Rhode Island, set them on their heads, took them by the gingoes [that is, by their maidenhair]," and as having fathered several illegitimate children, may simply have been an individual with a hearty sexual appetite. But there is no denying that by the 1650s the colonies were worried about the spread of doctrines more heretical than any they yet had seen, and with moral tendencies at least as pernicious.[77]

Among Gorton's followers was one John Weeks, who had met Gorton in Plymouth in 1637 and followed him to Rhode Island two years later. Describing Weeks and his wife in his *New Englands Memoriall*, Morton recalled that soon after this couple had been influenced by Gorton they "became very Atheists, looking for no more happiness than this world affords, not only in practice such, but also in opinion."[78] The Weekses were voicing what in England had become an increasingly common notion, that hell, like sin, was not to be taken seriously by the spiritually enlightened but rather was to be understood allegorically. Often brought to such consoling beliefs after an experience of profound religious melancholy or despair, various English radicals—most prominently William Walwyn and Gerrard Winstanley—argued that God would not punish man eternally for sins committed in a temporal world and, further, that the fact of all men's eventual salvation proved the existence of hell a mere fiction. In some radical circles the threat of eternal damnation came to be viewed, like the notion of sin, as but another tool used by the privileged classes to maintain their social position. Certainly Morton, for example,

Woodcut from *The Ranters Ranting*, by John Reading (London, 1650), illustrating popular conceptions of the Ranters' lewdness.

was outraged at the Weekses' beliefs because he, like William Bradford before him, felt it his personal duty to maintain Plymouth society upon a profoundly deferential basis.[79]

In this framework we can assess John Eliot's report, again provided by some of his "praying Indians," that among the Gortonists' basic tenets was a denial of any punishment (or, for that matter, of any reward) in the afterlife. The Warwick settlers, one native told Eliot, had said that the Massachusetts Puritans "*teach you that there is a Heaven and Hell, but there is no such matter.*" When asked to elaborate, one of the Gortonists—very likely the leader himself—said that "*there is no other Heaven, then what is in the hearts of good men; nor no other Hell then what is in the hearts of bad men,*" a startling analogue to Walwyn's belief that hell was nothing but the guilty conscience of those who had evil in their hearts.[80]

Earlier, when Gorton had been charged by the Massachusetts authorities with rejecting the word "eternal" as it applied to punishment, he had defended himself by claiming that once the soul was touched by the

Spirit of God it *already* was in eternity; righteousness was in itself life eternal, and sin eternal death and punishment. A penalty, therefore, was not assessed arbitrarily at some future time but was rather the natural and inevitable result of evil actions. Such doctrine, Gorton declared, "as sets forth a time to come, of more worth, and glory, than either is, or hath been, keeps the manna til tomorrow, to the breeding of worms in it." To the Gortonists heaven was a condition of the soul *on earth*, and the divine spark of regeneration implied the immediate and eternal destruction of evil as well as the salvation of good, opening the way for man's final perfection in this life. "The righteousness of God is of eternal worth and duration," he maintained, "but the one and the other [the good and evil courses of life] being wrought into a change at one and the same time, thence comes the capacity of an eternall life and eternall destruction." Among Gorton and his followers heaven and hell came to be regarded as psychological conditions, and conventional morality was to be upheld only if it made one feel spiritually healthy.[81]

Like many other seventeenth-century historians, Morton sought to display such beliefs in as unflattering a light as possible and thus oversimplified some of Gorton's rather sophisticated arguments. When, for example, he reported that the Rhode Island radical "hath not shunned to say and affirm, That all the felicity we are like to have, we must expect in this life, and no more," he added, perhaps salaciously, that soon thereafter Gorton had "advised one with whom he had some speech, to *make much of her self for she must expect no more but what she could enjoy in this life*."[82] This suggestion of Gorton's sexual license certainly would have jarred the memories of some in the colonies who had been present in 1638 when John Underhill, one of the most blatant (and colorful) antinomians, was charged by a young woman whom he had "seduced" and "drawn to his opinions" with having thus described his "assurance" and its consequences: "He had lain under a spirit of bondage and a legal way five years, and could get no assurance, till at length, as he was taking a pipe of tobacco, the Spirit set home an absolute promise of free grace with such assurance and joy, as he never since doubted of his good estate, neither should he, though he should fall into sin." Whether this particular "seduction" was spiritual or sexual remains unclear, but in the course of Underhill's subsequent examination the low tone of his moral behavior became evident to all.[83] Like Gorton, who presumably would sin because he had internalized heaven and hell, Underhill's complete confidence in his salvation, no matter how much he sinned, could only further rend New England's fraying social fabric.

Detail from John Reading's *The Ranters Ranting* (London, 1650), showing promiscuous, naked dancing at one of the Ranters' "love feasts."

The radical spiritists' internalization or "spiritualization" of the afterlife led to one further heresy, a denial of the immortality of the individual soul, an idea often linked to their conjectures about the soul's final absorption into the Godhead.[84] During the winter of 1637–1638, for example, when the General Court was hearing the case against the antinomians, Winthrop noted that in some of the congregations swept by antinomian doctrine, "divers other foul errors were discovered." In addition to unearthing some relatively conventional spiritist ideas—"That we are not bound to the law, not as a rule," for example—the magistrates and clergy charged with the investigation of these "growing evils" discovered some decidedly startling opinions, not only "that the Sabbath is as other days," linked to the spiritist belief that the saints were free from the necessity of observing an outward sabbath because of their continual communions with God, but also "That there is no resurrection of the body" and "That the soul is mortal, till it be united to Christ, and then it is annihilated, and the body also, and a new given by Christ." The "mortalist" heresy had appeared in New England.[85]

As J. F. Maclear has recently pointed out, the mortalist issue became a serious point of discussion in Anne Hutchinson's church trial in March 1638. The first of four opinions attributed to her by Shepard, who had conferred with her through the winter, concerned her highly unorthodox understanding of the resurrection: he charged her with, among other things, maintaining "That the Resurrection mentioned 1 Corinthians 15 is not of our Resurrection at the Last Day, but of our Union to Christ Jesus." In her defense Hutchinson asked her inquisitors to consider that "*The Spirit is immortal indeed but prove that the Soule is*," but this nice theological distinction did not prevent the assembly from perceiving the link between her understanding of immortality and other of her antinomian tenets and so finally concurring with John Wilson's sharp condemnation of her opinions as "*dayngerous and damnable*." Further, the Boston pastor reminded the church of the intellectual pedigree of such ideas. Hutchinson's understanding of the soul's immortality, he noted sharply, was "*no less than Sadducisme and Athiisme and therefore to be detested*." Although Hutchinson's eventual excommunication was based on more charges than these, clearly the ministers feared the potentially disruptive implications of her mortalism. Wilson spoke for them all when he noted that "if we deny the Resurrection of the Body than let us turn Epicures. Let us eate and drinke and doe any thinge, to morrow we shall dye."[86]

The reason some of the antinomians who followed Anne Hutchinson to Rhode Island later joined with Gorton, Williams, or William Coddington and the early New England Quakers was that these individuals had extended and developed many of the spiritist ideas to which Hutchinson's followers had been exposed. As Maclear has observed, the Quakers, like some antinomians, often spoke of resurrection "as deliverance by Christ from the grave of sin" and taught "that Christ's kingdom was even now established in his saints."[87] More important, the spiritualization or, as the Puritans often put it when describing the theology of such heretics as Gorton, the "allegorizing" of heaven and hell, and of the soul's immortality, a tendency evident in Hutchinson herself, implicitly challenged the eschatological premise on which the New England experiment was based. When Cotton told his intransigent parishioner that "in denyinge the Resurrection of thease very Bodies you doe the uttermost to rase the very foundation of Religion to the Ground and to destroy our fayth," and added that "if there be no Resurrection than all is in vayne and we of all people are most miserable," he had foremost in mind the Puritans' very purpose in founding New England.[88] If there was to be no literal Last Judgment, that is, if Christ already had come in the hearts of his saints, why should Cotton, Shepard, Hooker, and their ministerial colleagues struggle to establish and maintain a Bible Commonwealth? This sobering question exposed the full challenge of the radical spiritists in Puritan New England, a challenge that had been set as early as the 1630s.

In varying ways and to various degrees, then, the radical spiritists posed a serious threat to the New England Puritans' plans to establish the New Jerusalem, and through the 1640s and 1650s the steps the magistrates and ministers took to protect their vision of Christ's kingdom on earth grew increasingly severe, culminating in 1656 in their ignominious response to the Quakers when four of this sect were hanged on the Boston Common. The arrival of the Quakers and the subsequent willingness of many New Englanders to accept their beliefs was only the most memorable of a long series of encounters with radical spiritist ideology, ones that indicate how closely the development of English Puritan radicalism was replicated in the New World. The uniqueness of the New England population is undeniable; as historians are fond of pointing out, the congregationalists or "Independents" who before the Restoration were in England at best a troublesome minority solidly controlled most of New England. And complex constitutional issues that did not directly affect the colonists helped mold English radical ideology. Nevertheless, what happened doctrinally, institutionally, and politically to English Puritanism occurred in its American form as well, as though by the unravelling of an interior logic.

There is, however, another way of thinking about the effect of the various forms of radical spiritism on colonial New England. If on one level these individuals and groups display the remarkable continuities between English and American Puritanism, they can illuminate something quite different—the influence of radical spiritist ideology on the development of congregational doctrine and polity in a region where neither presbyterianism nor Anglicanism prevailed, as one or the other did in England in these same years. Just as the debate over separatism in New England assumed new and different forms because of the special nature of the population, so too did the ideas of the radical spiritists. Though never (except in some parts of Rhode Island) the dominant force in New England's religious history, in part because of their admittedly ill-defined goals and their inherently anti-institutional bias, the radical spiritists undeniably helped to shape the ideological synthesis called "New England Puritanism."

THE QUICKSANDS OF
ANABAPTISTRY:
GENERAL AND PARTICULAR
BAPTISTS

hose in New England who questioned the propriety of infant baptism, or, for that matter, even the manner of its administration, risked being lumped with the many types of radical spiritists and even acquired an epithet—"Anabaptist"—that resonated as profoundly as "Antinomian" or "Familist." Indeed, as late as 1652, even after the differences between the English baptists and Continental anabaptists were clearly discernible, in a discussion of the impending fall of Antichrist, New England's Edward Johnson indiscriminately linked New England's "Familists, Seekers, Antinomians, and Anabaptists" as preeminent opponents of the rule of the saints and counted on his audience to know what traits they shared.

To Johnson, as to most of his contemporaries, "Anabaptism" conjured up the horrible anarchy in the city of Münster under the rule of John of Leyden. In addition to rejecting paedobaptism (the baptism of infants), the "Anabaptists" purportedly cultivated a dangerous and unprincipled mysticism, which, coupled with their strict separatism and antiauthoritarianism, threatened a reign of terror in those communities that failed to crush their doctrines. If allowed to go unchecked, moderate Puritans believed, these shock troops of the Antichrist's army promised to overturn, as they had in Germany, the civil and moral order on which Christian society rested. Daniel Featley, the Anglican controversialist who castigated the baptists in his popular *The Dippers Dipt* (1645), spoke for the majority of Englishmen when he noted that "in one Anabaptist you have many Heretiques, and in this one Sect as it were one stock, many erroneous and schismaticall positions and practises *ingraffed*." [1]

Like their English brethren, the New England baptists had little to do with the Continental anabaptist tradition, though the General Baptist sect could trace some of their roots to Dutch anabaptism. [2] As in the case of the radical spiritists who opposed the predominant Puritan position on the indwelling of the Holy Spirit, the English and American baptists who challenged the Puritans' view of paedobaptism arrived at their views primarily by reexamining the logic of Puritan doctrine. They did not reject outright the Puritan platform for the reformation of the English church but critically reexamined certain basic Puritan assumptions. Put most simply, the baptists asked their critics to accept what they found an unalterable fact: infant baptism had no scriptural warrant. Because they found no express Biblical injunction for paedobaptism, baptists insisted that the ordinance was reserved for adults who wished to affirm their membership in the reformed church. These, then, were no Münster anabaptists inveighing against the total corruption of all magistrates and refusing to obey any law but that of the spirit within them; seventeenth-century English baptists asked only that the Puritans reconsider how they brought people into church fellowship. [3]

There is, however, much hidden beneath this simple demand, for even if the individuals the Puritans so labeled were not true anabaptists, their insistence on adult baptism in several ways seriously challenged the order of the Puritan churches, particularly those of the "Independents" or non-separating congregationalists. Consider, for example, the most frequent rebuttal to the baptists' demand for scriptural proof of infant baptism: the analogy to the Jewish rite of circumcision, the seal of God's covenant with his chosen people, first administered by Abraham. As Murray Tolmie has noted, for many Puritans infant baptism so regarded "became the binding symbol of the unity of church and state as dual aspects of an integral Christian commonwealth in which every member, irrespective of his individual inner spiritual life, had outward responsibilities as a

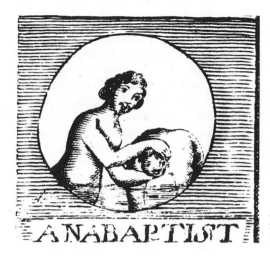

An "Anabaptist," from Ephraim Pagitt's *Heresiography*
(London, 1654).

Christian and as a citizen."[4] To the New England Puritans the Abrahamic
covenant was the cornerstone of the ecclesiastical edifice that housed
God's visible saints; but the baptists contended that, rather than forming
a solid foundation for the New Jerusalem, dependence on infant baptism
was building one's church on quicksand. The baptists believed that an
individual who closed with Christ made an entirely new covenant with
God, one that both superseded Abraham's and demanded that he who
covenanted had the requisite maturity to choose whether or not to accept
Christ as his savior. If the baptists had their way, the intricate genetics of
salvation on which the New England Puritans believed the continuity of
their churches depended, with the children of church members guaranteed the right to baptism by their virtue as the "seed" of believers and so
placed under the spiritual watch and care of the church, would simply
crumble.[5]

Then, too, most baptists were strict separatists and their ecclesiology
appealed to some Puritans, particularly the inhabitants of the Plymouth
colony and the small but significant groups of separatists in Massachusetts towns like Salem and Lynn, who rejected the tenuous logic of nonseparating congregationalism. It was no accident that in Providence in
1639 Roger Williams was "emboldened" by Katherine Scott (none other
than Anne Hutchinson's sister) "to make open profession" of "Anabaptistry" and thereupon consented to be rebaptized by Ezekiel Holliman of
Salem; many baptist converts were won from the separatist ranks after

the latter had been asked to explain why, if they had indeed separated from the Church of England's corruption, they still affirmed the baptism they had received in its bosom. One's rebaptism and entry into new church fellowship with those who likewise had rejected the Church of England seemed to go hand-in-hand, and to many Puritans who were dissatisfied with the equivocation of nonseparating congregationalism marked a logical extension of the separatist position.[6]

In some cases the baptists' rejection of a belief in the efficacy of a sacrament administered by officers of a corrupt national church led to views commonly associated with the Seekers: if one denied the validity of the baptism administered by Anglican clergy, there remained the problem of how *anyone* who baptized another had obtained his commission to dispense this divine ordinance. Again Williams offers the most famous example in New England. A short time after his rebaptism he adopted the Seekers' position regarding the ministry. Eight years later Robert Baillie reported that in England such action had become a common trend. "Very many of the Anabaptists are now turned Seekers," he noted, "denying the truth of any Church upon earth for many ages past, denying that there are any Pastors now on the earth, that there may be any preaching of the word, and joyning in prayer, any celebration of Baptism or the Lords Supper," until "God from heaven send Apostles to work miracles and set up Churches. . . ."[7]

Although some New England Puritans rejected the baptists' position because it so easily led to such conclusions, still others were swayed by their argument that the discipline of the New England churches, particularly the Puritan ministers' emphasis on the doctrine of preparation for salvation, encouraged the kinds of formalism the colonists had sought to leave behind in England. In a sense, by their claim to establish churches more pure than those already formed in New England and their highly subjective emphasis on the conversion experience, the baptists implied that nonseparating congregationalists, no matter how good their intentions, simply were not holy enough, and that their reliance on institutionalized forms rather than on the free grace of God only undermined the basis of a Christian commonwealth. The memory of the Antinomian Controversy still fresh in mind, the New England Puritans reacted predictably to this criticism. They excoriated the baptists for pretending to divine "revelations" and sharply criticized their unwillingness to assent to the collective theological wisdom of such renowned divines as Hooker and Shepard. The Cambridge minister spoke for the clerical majority in his colony when in 1645, in his preface to an anti-baptist tract published by George Phillips of Watertown, he censured the baptists for just this "perfectionism." They "condemn all the best reformed churches," Shepard complained, "forsake all Gods faithfull Ministers . . . , confusedly gather into private churches, [and] set up and commend an unlearned ministry." "It may be," he concluded, that "they like [no churches] at all, because they can edifie themselves best by promiscuous prophesie."[8]

In this last phrase Shepard referred to one further baptist threat to the Puritans' city on a hill, for what frequently accompanied the baptists' subjective and emotional definition of religious experience was their encouragement of a much greater lay participation in their churches than the Puritans permitted in theirs. This sect offered those who had not become visible saints in New England Puritan congregations the opportunity not only to become members of a religious community without passing the rigorous trials of preparation but also themselves to be preachers or lay exhorters. A passage from Edward Barber's *Anabaptists Catechisme* (1645), though pertaining specifically to the English General Baptists, reveals the group's pride in the humble origin of its ministers. When asked to explain "*the rule by which you walke*," Barber replied that "We are a free-born people, and have privilege above all in rule"; pressed to name the well-known preachers in the Baptist churches, in addition to "Mr. [Hanserd] *Knowles*, a learned Scholler," he noted the following: "Mr. *Patience*, an honest Glover," "Mr. *Griffin*, a reverend Taylor," "Mr. *Spilsbey* [that is, Spilsbury], a renowned Cobler," and himself, "a Buttonmaker."[9] By such anticlericalism and a concomitant democratization of the church offices, and particularly by an insistence on the primary importance of the lay exhorter's message, the baptists proved another of those sects whose meetings served as birthing stations for many who eventually joined the Quaker ranks. As Geoffrey Nuttall has observed, many English radicals "passed through a Baptist period before finally coming to rest among the Quakers," a fact the nineteenth-century historian Peter Oliver had noted among New England dissenters as well. "Anabaptism was very nearly allied to Quakerism," Oliver observed, "and, to some extent, prepared the way for it in Massachusetts Bay." "The first steps in this fanatic ladder were short," he continued, and, particularly in Rhode Island, "the medley inhabitants were continually ascending and descending upon them, imagining themselves the saints of the Most High."[10]

There has been some misunderstanding of the history of the baptists in New England, primarily because so many of them were associated with the "medley inhabitants" of Rhode Island and often were confused with

some of them, a situation that has prevented most historians from recog-
nizing the importance of the fact that for a time the baptists in the New
World were divided, as they were in England, into two distinct groups.
What adds to this confusion is that, though by 1644, with the publication
in London of the *Confession of Faith* of seven of the most prominent "Particular" baptist churches, there was no good reason for their opponents
to conflate this group with the "General" Baptists, they continued to do
so for rhetorical purposes. Through the 1650s in old England and New
the opprobrious term "Anabaptist" remained the most common way of
identifying members of either group, while in truth it only served to
confuse both their means and ends in church reformation. A review of
the differences between the General and Particular wings of this group is
essential to enable us to understand that, though the General Baptists'
final impact on America's religious development was less extensive and
dramatic, during the period before the Restoration their specter loomed
as ominously over New England as that of their doctrinally more conservative brethren in the Particular Baptist churches.

The roots of the General Baptist congregations in New England are
found in the history of the English Puritan separatists during the Elizabethan period, in particular in the church of John Smyth, pastor of a separatist group in Gainsborough, who with his congregation emigrated to
Amsterdam in 1608.[11] Shortly after their arrival in the Low Countries
many members of Smyth's church, including the pastor himself, began
to doubt the validity of their baptism in the Church of England and, with
the advice of the Waterlander Mennonite church (which in many ways
qualified as a genuine "Anabaptist" institution), decided to rebaptize
themselves. From the Waterlander church Smyth drew other arguments
to buttress his separatist views, most notably to support his belief that the
true church was not a national church but a covenanted band of saints,
and that because there was to be a full separation between the civil and
religious spheres, any sort of enforced state religion was anathema.
Smyth's group also adopted the Mennonite doctrine of a general redemption for all mankind. Rejecting the Calvinist doctrine of strict predestination, Smyth and his so-called "Se-baptists" asserted that Christ had indeed died for all—that is, for all who repented, accepted the offer of his
grace, and thereupon were baptized. Thus Smyth and his congregation,
again following the Mennonites' lead, gave a significant emphasis to
man's personal responsibility for his salvation; it was up to each individual to accept the offer of Christ's atonement and so to become a true
Christian.[12]

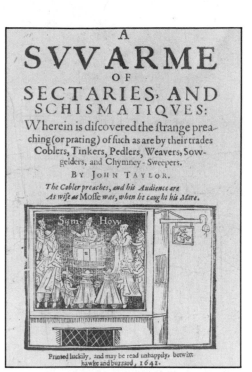

Title page of *A Swarme of Sectaries and Schismatiques* (London, 1641), John Taylor's diatribe against Samuel How and other "tub preachers," who preached in General Baptist conventicles in the 1640's.

Title page of *A Reply as True as Steele, To a Rusty, Rayling, Ridiculous, Lying, Libell* (London, 1641), John Taylor's rebuttal to an attack on his *Swarme of Sectaries*, illustrating how vitriolic heresiographers could be.

Smyth, however, soon made plans to merge his church entirely with that of the Waterlander Mennonites, and at this point one of the leaders of his congregation, Thomas Helwys, mobilized significant opposition. Though Helwys, too, had accepted the necessity of rebaptism and a belief in general redemption, he could not adopt other of the Mennonite beliefs, which, influenced as they were by the Continental anabaptist tradition, included a full and unequivocal condemnation of the civil magistracy. Unable to reach a compromise with Smyth, in 1612 Helwys and his supportrs separated from Smyth's church and, after concluding that their emigration to Amsterdam had in fact been an unjustifiable flight from persecution, returned to England, where they thus became the first "General" or "Arminian" Baptist church. Upon Helwys's death in 1616 John Murton, a Gainsborough furrier who had been a member of Smyth's church in Amsterdam, assumed leadership over the group; by 1625 there were at least five General Baptist meetings in England, the most prominent of which remained Murton's London congregation.[13]

These, then, were the "Anabaptisticall Wolves" whom Stephen Denison noted in 1627, individuals who "jumpe with the Arminians to conditional election upon foreseene faith or workes, in denying the doctrine of reprobation in the true sense thereof, in maintaining of universall redemption."[14] And although not inclined to codify their doctrines in any systematic fashion, a fact that made their congregations a haven for a wide variety of radical Puritans, throughout the 1640s and '50s the General Baptists were clearly identifiable as a separate and influential group in England's radical circles. Like the radical spiritists with whom they often crossed paths, they emphasized an individual's apprehension of the glorious truth of Christ's sacrifice and sought to unite in loving fellowship all those who shared this experience; this, rather than any creedal statement, most frequently united them in their worship. Moreover, they were further distinguished from other baptists because, as Tolmie has observed, it was a vigorous argument about "Christ's dying for all"—the doctrine of general redemption—rather than a defense of believer's baptism that most often distinguished their publications from those of other radicals. Though rebaptism, often supplemented by "love-feasts" at which they washed each other's feet, imposed hands on the new convert, and then offered a "kiss of charity," remained an important part of their worship, the General Baptists most often were attacked for their open Arminianism and the claims to perfection that followed hard upon it, rather than for any insistence on "dipping."[15]

If the beginnings of these "Generalists" lie in the strict separatist con-

The WOLFE in a
ſheepes skinne.

The WOLFE in his
owne skinne.

Woodcuts from *The White Wolfe*, by Stephen Denison (London, 1627), which warned of the proliferation of "Mysticall" and "Anabaptisticall" "Wolves" who hid in sheep's clothing.

gregations, the early history of the "Particular" Baptist churches in England returns us to yet another type of Puritan institution, the important Jacob-Lathrop semi-separatist congregation so important in New England's history; several individuals who became the leaders of this wing of the baptist movement came from the various schisms within this church that occurred in the 1630s and 1640s. In 1633, for example, after the release from prison of a large number of the church (including Lathrop himself), Samuel How, Mark Lucar, and others joined a strict separatist congregation, and a year later Samuel Eaton also parted company with Lathrop to serve as their pastor. The extant records indicate that, in addition to seeking closer ties to other, more radical separatist congregations, these individuals, led by How, received a "further baptism" when they merged with the new group. After Lathrop and thirty others emigrated to New England in 1634, the Southwark church was left without a leader until 1637, when Henry Jessey, an acquaintance of Governor Winthrop who himself had considered moving to the New World, was appointed pastor and quickly discovered that the question of baptism that bothered so many separatist and semi-separatist Puritans remained an equally thorny issue among his flock. Jessey held the church together for a year, but in 1638 another serious defection occurred as several members joined the church of John Spilsbury, who openly advocated believers' baptism. Four years later William Kiffin, though still a member of the Southwark church, also was rebaptized and soon thereafter, like How and Spilsbury, emerged as a major baptist spokesman. By 1644 Jessey became convinced that baptism had to be restricted to believers and a year later decided to be rebaptized, by none other than Hanserd Knollys, who had joined the Southwark congregation after his return from New England in 1641 and thus had wandered from the "Antinomian" camp to that of the "Anabaptists." [16]

By 1644, then, there had emerged from London's most prominent separatist church a significant number of individuals who had arrived at a defense of adult baptism not through any contact with the Dutch Arminians who had influenced the Smyth-Helwys church, but independently, by remaining within the strict Calvinist system that the Jacob-Lathrop church always had represented. Because this group did not maintain the "general" redemption of mankind, but rather, like the good Calvinists they were, believed in the limited atonement of Christ for a preordained number of saints, they were termed "Particular Baptists" and quickly became a distinct and potent force among London's Puritans.

They grew even more prominent after an important meeting in the spring of 1644, to which they had invited Independents like Thomas Goodwin and Philip Nye as well as the separatists Sabine Staresmore and Praise-God Barbone. Assured by the representatives of the other groups that their churches would remain "in communion" with those committed to believers' baptism, Kiffin and the leaders of six other Particular Baptist churches shortly thereafter issued *The Confession of Faith of those Churches which are commonly (though falsely) called Anabaptists*, a detailed statement of their ecclesiastical position. They were accused of swelling the "Anabaptist" ranks through this action—Stephen Marshall, a Puritan minister thoroughly unsympathetic to their cause, accused them of "spreading Opinions of Anabaptism and Antinomianism with such Turbulency, that it tends to a Division amongst them that join in the Owning of this great Cause." In their *Confession*, however, the seven churches only reasserted basic separatist principles, with the additional provisos that the church was to be gathered from the world by believers' baptism and that toleration of other Christian opinions would be a cardinal principle for both church and state. As with the Helwys-Murton group, then, these were not true anabaptists but conscientious Puritans who differed from some of their brethren about how the saints of God's true churches could identify themselves.[17]

It should be apparent that to speak of "Anabaptism" in the 1640s was in effect to refer to a tangled skein of arguments and relationships among Puritans who themselves often were of very different stripes. As in the case of the doctrine of the radical spiritists, many of those in New England who adopted the principle of adult baptism, though encouraged at certain points by emigrants from the London baptist churches, arrived at their beliefs in essentially the same way their English brethren did— through a reexamination of Puritan doctrine. They came to accept, indeed to add strands to, both the General and Particular Baptists' positions regarding proper church discipline.[18] The New England baptists should not be viewed simply as impassioned sponsors of the idea of religious liberty. Their relationship to the whole spectrum of radical Puritan thought, in England as well as in the colonies, needs to be examined, for, though consistently eclipsed by Williams and his efforts to win support for religious toleration, other New Englanders, little celebrated, who passed into or through baptist churches contributed significantly to the development of radical Puritan ideology.

Though most historians date the beginning of the baptist movement in New England with Williams's own rebaptism in 1639, there is evidence of agitation for adult baptism before that year. In the Plymouth church records, for example, in 1638 there is mention of one John Cooke, formerly a deacon of the church, who "fell into the error of Anabaptistry" and then joined with others who "carried on the Schismaticall delusion," all this occurring not long after the "business about Gorton." Gorton had been in Plymouth in 1638, but by 1639 he had moved on to Aquidneck, after the Plymouth government had tried him for insubordination and heresy. It is possible that Cooke had absorbed some of his ideas from this flamboyant radical, who by the mid-1640s was preaching in some of the most famous General Baptist conventicles in London. When we add to this admittedly meager evidence the fact that in Plymouth Gorton had been specifically charged with preaching, among other things, "no more happiness than this world affords," there is more reason to believe that in disciplining Cooke, as in banishing Gorton, the Plymouth authorities were reacting to doctrine later associated with the General Baptist "tub preachers" or even more radical Puritans who often frequented their meetings. Separatists themselves, the Plymouth townspeople were ripe for the kinds of arguments put forth by those who demanded a more complete break with the Church of England, and their magistrates' quick response to these two individuals suggests that they knew just how seductive "Anabaptist" ideas could be.[19]

The possibility that the earliest baptists in New England were "Generalists" is strengthened by another entry in the Plymouth church records, one that immediately follows the details of the disciplinary action taken against Cooke. "Not very longe after this," Samuell Hickes "began to be unsettled about severall of the ordinances of Jesus Christ," particularly about the propriety of baptizing infants and singing psalms at meeting, a situation serious enough to elicit a thorough rejoinder by the Plymouth church. We should not be surprised to find questions about baptism in Plymouth at this time. Between 1638 and 1641, for example, Charles Chauncy, who advocated the baptism of infants by dipping rather than by sprinkling, served as John Rayner's assistant in the Plymouth pulpit and stirred a good deal of controversy. But although the proper mode of baptism was an issue among some Particular Baptists in England and Chauncy was later to cause more trouble over this point when he assumed the pulpit in Scituate after Lathrop had left that church, Hickes's arguments against the discipline of the Plymouth church clearly were of a different order.[20] He need not necessarily have been influenced by Gorton, but there is little doubt that by the late 1630s Hickes's views were even more radical than those of Williams.

Like many radicals of the 1630s and early 1640s, Hickes drew his ideas from a wide range of radical Puritan opinions that circulated in the conventicles and then mixed his own peculiar concoction from them. His questions to the church concerned not only the scripturalness of psalmsinging but also the necessity of keeping the Sabbath a holy day, two implicit criticisms against the formalism of church worship often leveled by antinomians, who proclaimed a perpetual "internal" Sabbath for those who had Christ within them. To be sure, Hickes's seventh query was a request for scriptural evidence for the baptism of infants, which Plymouth defended with the usual references to the seventeenth chapter of Genesis, where to seal His convenant with Abraham God asked that every male child be circumsized; but even more interesting are other of his questions, some of which displayed him well on his way through "Anabaptism" to Seekerism, a passage characteristic of many English General Baptists. Hickes questioned, among other things, the apostolic succession by which ministers claimed the powers of their office and suggested that, because the true succession had been interrupted for centuries, ordination now was "a bare Impty thing." He doubted that any could "sett up a visible Church and ordinances without a minnestry sent from God to fitt them and call them to that worke" and asked the Plymouth men to show him a "scripture to prove that the world should be compelled to maintaine the Church officers." The Plymouth church offered lengthy answers to these and other questions and finally admitted that their problems with him had "occasioned some good, for hereby the orthodox were put upon more strict enquiry" into church discipline.[21]

But while the church's response ostensibly contributed to "the silencing of such Cabills as did about those times arise from him and others" of similar opinions, "poor unsettled" Hickes himself could not be saved. Despite all attempts to show him the error of his ways, he "fell yet further and further, and at last became a quaker." Few Particular Baptists ever raised the kinds of questions he had, and, equally significant, his later "descent" into Quakerism reflects a pattern common among many radicals who earlier in their careers had moved in General Baptist circles. The presence of Gorton and Hickes in separatist Plymouth at this early date suggests the possibility of a strong General Baptist influence on the religious radicalism that later developed in southeastern New England, especially on Cape Cod and in Rhode Island.[22]

Other early records, particularly those from the Bay Colony proper, reveal the presence of members of the Particular Baptist wing at about this same time. In Salem in 1639, William Wickenden and William Walcott were charged with anabaptism and thereafter moved to Providence where Chad Brown and other Particular Baptists earlier associated with Williams had settled. And at about the same time, in Charlestown, Seth Sweetser, who later joined Thomas Goold's Particular Baptist church in Charlestown after its foundation in 1665, was denied his share of the common lands and other freeman's privileges because he openly expressed his baptist views. By 1639 the presence of these and other "Anabaptisticall Spiritts" in the Bay Colony had so unnerved Ezekiel Rogers of Rowley that at his ordination he "tooke occasion" to "speake somewhat earnestly about Catechizing" against them. Though he may have intended the term "Anabaptist" to include antinomians left over from the difficulties in the Boston church, there is little doubt that by 1640 the New England Puritan churches, both separatist and nonseparating congregational, were beginning to confront the same baptist challenge that preoccupied so many of their English brethren.[23]

The cases of Cooke, Hickes, and others were only a prelude to a great outburst of baptist agitation in the 1640s, for if the New England Puritans' struggle with the Hutchinsonians most seriously marked their first decade in the New World, their second was consistently punctuated by difficulties with this very different group, whose two-pronged attack forced them to close ranks around anyone who smacked of "Anabaptism" without bothering to ascertain whether they were "Generalists" or "Particularists." The first major test of their resolve occurred in Lathrop's Scituate church, where the question of baptism and its proper administration was no more settled than it had been in the Southwark congregation he had left behind. Those among Lathrop's parishioners who had argued for "dipping" infants evidently found some of the town's original settlers similarly inclined, and the church became so torn by bickering over this issue that in 1639 Lathrop moved to the new settlement of Barnstable on Cape Cod. The individual whom the town eventually chose as Lathrop's replacement, however, only increased their difficulties, for Charles Chauncy, Rayner's assistant at Plymouth before that town had voted not to install him permanently, was notorious as a "dipper."[24]

By the time Chauncy came to Scituate his defense of baptism by immersion was no secret; indeed, it was partially for this reason that he had not been approved as Rayner's co-worker in Plymouth. His position on "dipping," however, was linked, as it sometimes was among other Particular Baptists, to other, equally important issues, especially the nature of his separatism, which was more extreme than that of Plymouth's leaders. It is very likely that the resistance he met in that colony's chief town had much to do with the magistrates' fear that his radical understanding of church fellowship was incompatible with the moderate position worked out by John Robinson and Elder Brewster. In 1640, after the Plymouth church had voted against Chauncy's installation, a motion was made by some of his supporters to allow him to settle at "Jones river, some three miles from Plimouth," where they hoped to see him "lay the foundacion of an Academy & reade the arts to some that are fitt for that purpose, that so they may also have use of his gifts." Though this plan evidently had the approval of Bradford and Rayner, Edward Winslow vigorously opposed it and told the Governor that if Chauncy were allowed to settle so near to Plymouth, the colonists "must still retaine his errors etc. with his gifts, which were like to weaken if not destroy both Congregacions of Plimouth and Duxborrow," particularly since Chauncy's judgment was "more rigid then any Separatists" Winslow had "ever read or knew." By way of example he cited Chauncy's publicly expressed belief that it was "lawfull . . . to censure any that shall oppose the major part of the Church," a point of discipline alien to the Plymouth church but maintained by more strict separatists, like some of those at Salem. To keep Chauncy nearby would be to tolerate a man who, as Hooker described him, was "so adventurous and pertinaceous" in his beliefs that he would "vent what he list and maintain what he vents," even if it were doctrine that tended further to divide the towns in the colony.[25]

Chauncy, then, was not a man easily molded by "advice" from other ministers. "He openly professed," for example, that "he did verily believe the truth of his opinions, as that there was a God in heaven, and that he was settled in [them] as the earth was upon the center." Winslow obviously feared that should Chauncy gain his own pulpit he would "vent" views even more unsettling than those concerning the baptism of infants by immersion, a hunch suported by Hooker's report that after Chauncy was rejected by Plymouth he had been invited to settle in Providence, an area "most meet for his opinions and practise." Instead Chauncy moved to Scituate, where he promptly exacerbated the controversy begun during Lathrop's pastorate. For the next few years the community was split into two separate churches, each claiming that the other had been improperly constituted, and so severe was the animosity that both sides appealed to prominent clergy in Massachusetts and Plymouth to help settle their claims. The town's difficulties preoccupied both colonies for a number of years and were a decided impediment to the peace of the churches in the area. Only in 1654, when Chauncy left to assume the presidency of another "academy," Harvard College, a position offered to him with the charitable (and perhaps naive) agreement that he would no longer broach his unorthodox opinions, did Scituate experience any degree of calm. By that time, too, in comparison to other "Anabaptist" views the Puritans had to counter, Chauncy's advocacy of baptism by immersion had become a relatively minor matter.[26]

The Puritans' experience with Chauncy in Scituate offers a good illustration of how questions over even the administration of baptism to infants could seriously unsettle the colonies' ecclesiastical harmony. As the decade unfolded such disruptions by both General and Particular Baptists reached what the Puritans considered epidemic proportions. In addition to the group of baptists in Providence, for example, John Clarke, one of those disarmed during the Antinomian Controversy, by 1639 had formed a separatist church in Newport and five years later openly practiced adult baptism, perhaps at the encouragement of Mark Lucar, one of those who in 1633 had left Lathrop's Southwark church to join with John Spilsbury. In 1641, following Spilsbury's lead, Lucar was rebaptized and soon thereafter moved to Rhode Island, where he became a ruling elder in Clarke's church. By all reports, at this time Clarke was a Particular Baptist. He maintained the "doctrine of efficacious grace" and even penned a lengthy manuscript "containing his judgment and the judgment of the Church respecting that soul supporting doctrine of personal election." So, too, was Thomas Patience, who had become convinced of the propriety of believer's baptism "in the woods in that wilderness" of New England, where "for three days one after another" the Lord had revealed to him the scriptural proofs for the sacrament's proper subjects and administration. Patience then reversed Lucar's example and returned to England in 1644, in time to add his name (as Kiffin's associate, no less) to the famous *Confession of Faith*.[27]

In Massachusetts, too, more baptists began to make known their beliefs. As early as 1639 in Lynn the Lady Deborah Moody, a cousin to Sir Henry Vane the Younger, criticized the church members for their "high conceite" and "bickering," which "did eate out Christian society"; four years later in Salem she was "taken with the error of denying baptism to infants." In 1644 another Essex County resident, Joseph Redknap, a wine cooper from London, was charged with "not suffering his child to be baptized," as was Thomas Painter of Hingham, who declared that "our baptism was anti-christian." Painter was whipped for his insubordination; a year later he joined Clarke's church in Newport. Christopher Goodwine of Charlestown evidenced similarly uncivil behavior, "throw-

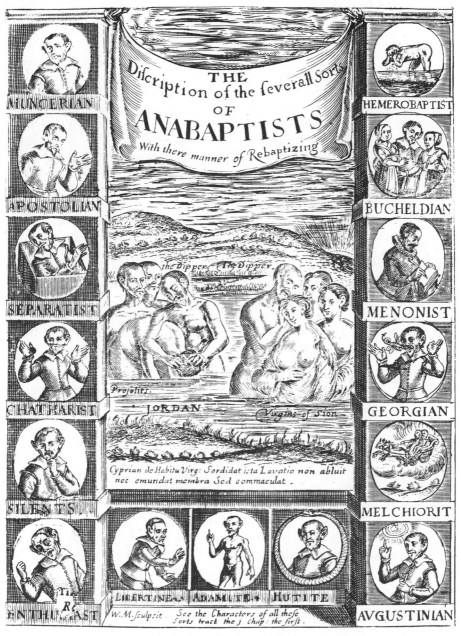

Frontispiece to *The Dippers Dipt*, by Daniel Featley (London, 1645), showing the different groups of "Anabaptists" whom Featley condemned.

ing done [down] the Basin of Water in the meeting house & strikeing the constable" who sought to apprehend him. Like Painter, too, he expressed "High contempt for the Holy ordinance" when he was examined in court. In 1646 in Essex County, two witnesses testified that one "Witter" had said that "they who stayed at the baptising of a child did take the name of the Father, Sonn, and Holly Ghost in vain, and broke the Sabbath." So it went through the middle of that decade, with many others censured for turning their backs or leaving the meeting at the administration of the sacrament, all giving testimony to their dissatisfaction with the baptism of infants.[28]

Except for Clarke and Patience there is very little evidence whether these and other individuals were General or Particular Baptists, and this makes all the more important the case in the mid-1640s that suggests very strongly that at this time adherents of both groups were active in the Bay Colony. In the spring of 1643 in Watertown, which a decade earlier had had its difficulties with separatism, Nathaniel Briscoe questioned the validity of infant baptism and protested the support of the ministry by taxation of all townspeople, regardless of whether they were church members. Thus far Briscoe's behavior resembled that of others in the colony during that decade, but the dissenter then approached the town's minister, George Phillips, to speak further with him about "the Churches constitution" and "Infant Baptisme," with a decidedly unusual result. By Phillips's own account, Briscoe thereupon "desired that I would pen down those arguments that had passed betwixt us on my part," and, after transcribing the paper, "communicated it to some that were contrary to my apprehension in these points, and either himself, or some others by his means, sent them to England." Imagine Phillips's surprise when later that year he discovered not only that Briscoe had answered in manuscript his defense of infant baptism, but that another of his parishioners, one "Prescod [Prescott]," had in hand Thomas Lamb's 1643 *A Confutation of Infant Baptism*, purportedly addressed to Phillips's text! "It put me into a kinde of wonderment," Phillips wrote, "to see my name set forth in print, and as an Author of a Treatise, who never writ any such Treatise."[29]

How Lamb had acquired Briscoe's transcription is as mysterious as why this prominent leader of the General Baptists decided to write his first substantial defense of adult baptism against the words, not even published, of a New England congregationalist. By 1643 Lamb, who made his living as a soapboiler in London, had organized a church in Bell Alley, Coleman Street, and opened his doors to all kinds of religious radicals, particularly to those who preached "universal Grace" and "Arminian tenets." In addition to officiating at a meeting where General Baptists commonly met with Seekers and Ranters, and where lay prophesying (even by women) was common, he organized extensive evangelical tours through the south of England, traveling with such other notorious radicals, then in their baptist phase, as Henry Denne and Samuel Oates, both of whom had been baptized by Lamb himself. Whether or not Briscoe knew Lamb personally, then, when *A Confutation of Infant Baptism* was brought to him in Watertown he had before him the arguments of one of England's most important General Baptist spokesmen. Moreover, even if the two were not acquainted, some of Briscoe's ideas clearly were related to the Generalists'. His own answer to Phillips, for example, "was fuller of teeth to bite and reproach the ministers of the country," one seventeenth-century historian wrote, "than [of] arguments to convince the readers," and this anticlericalism, as well as his antiauthoritarianism, was much more indicative of Lamb's wing of the baptists than of Spilsbury's and kept Briscoe in the baptist fold even after he had been heavily fined for "publishing" his opinions without consulting the magistrates.[30]

After Phillips's surprise at seeing his name in print had worn off, he responded to Lamb in 1645 in *A Reply to a Confutation of some grounds for baptisme . . . put forth against mee by one Thomas Lamb*, the first of several defenses of infant baptism published by New Englanders in the next several years. The *Reply* is particularly significant because it was composed at the height of the Bay Colony's difficulties with others inclined toward General Baptist ideas. The same year that Briscoe was causing trouble in Watertown, the Massachusetts authorities were pressing their case against Samuel Gorton and his followers, then on trial in Boston for heresy. Though the literature about Gorton is replete with the term "Familist," there is little doubt that he shared many of his opinions with the General Baptists, particularly in light of his later association in London with Lamb himself, as well as John Eliot's report that the Gortonists often spoke "*of Baptism*, and said, *that they* [the Puritans] *teach you that infants must be baptized, but that is a very foolish thing . . . because infants neither know God or Baptism*. Given such facts, as well as the similarity of his radical ideology to that of others among the Generalists, we have every reason to believe that in New England Gorton was the foremost proponent of the General Baptist position.[31]

When in 1669 Gorton responded to Nathaniel Morton's attack on his beliefs, he sidestepped the charge that he preached "general redemption" and only refuted the claim that such a belief encouraged hedonism. He stoutly maintained that there was "not a man woman or childe upon the face of the earth that will come forth and say that ever they heard any such word come out of my mouth." On the contrary, he was "farre from understanding" John's message that Christ died for the sins of all the world in the "sense of the generallists," who "extirpate and root out" Christ's role in the work of redemption. They denied any more "Divine or Eternall nature th[a]n is in the elements or beginnings of all earthly and transitory things," Gorton noted, and, because of this incipient pantheism, were prevented from being witness to an "eternall power manifest in that which in it selfe is temporary," that is, the power of the Holy Spirit. Only by accepting this last premise was a man saved, and the responsibility to so believe rested with every individual.[32]

It is tempting to recall that in the late fall of 1643 William Waddle, one of the Gortonists tried and convicted in Boston, was put to hard labor in Watertown at the height of the commotion about Lamb, and so to speculate that it was through him that Gorton first heard of "Lams church"; but it also is possible that while living in London before his emigration in 1637, Gorton may have encountered, if not Lamb himself, other General Baptists who had spun off from the Helwys-Murton church. Of equal importance for the subsequent history of the Generalists in New England, though, upon his return from England in 1644 after four years in the center of London's radical underground, Gorton was content to resettle in Warwick and so ceased to challenge the Bay Colony with his views. Through the next decade he continued to draw disgruntled Puritans to his side; the year he returned, for example, Ezekiel Holliman joined him in Warwick. And there is evidence that some Massachusetts residents still sympathized with his ideas. But for the most part Gorton chose to forward his views primarily through the tracts he published in London.[33] His acquiescence in the face of the large Puritan colonies to the north and west may have been purely pragmatic or perhaps indicative of a willingness on his part to consolidate his gains in Rhode Island. In any event, by the 1650s in the larger Puritan colonies the voice of the General Baptists' most outspoken leader had been drowned out by countless others, most of whom represented the Particular Baptist position and whose criticism of the Calvinist churches of Massachusetts and Connecticut was of a very different order.

Through the 1650s in Rhode Island, the choice to become a General or Particular Baptist remained a very real one. In Providence in 1652 the church split over the adoption of the so-called "Sixth Principle" (Hebrews 6:1–2), the laying on of hands on all baptized believers before they were admitted to the Lord's Supper, a practice which by the mid-1640s had been regularly instituted by Edward Barber and other English General Baptists, though resisted by Lamb himself.[34] In Providence, the Arminian Six-Principle faction eventually prevailed and eclipsed the Calvinist Baptists. A similar rift occurred in Newport a few years later, after Clarke had left for England with Williams to try to secure a charter for his settlement. During his absence, Rhode Island's first historian wrote, "some of the brethren embraced the opinion of the laying on of hands, as necessary to all baptised persons," and by 1656 they not only claimed that such a ceremony "was necessary to church communion and fellowship" but openly advocated "the doctrine of grace and free-will." Unable to resolve their differences, the two groups split into separate congregations, the Generalists led by "Mr. Wm. Vahan [Vaughn]." In Newport, Clarke's church remained the more prominent institution, and like Gorton's in Warwick it soon proved important for the reception its members gave the first Quaker emissaries to that area.[35]

In Massachusetts, the principal difficulty lay with those individuals who, though remaining strict Calvinists, questioned the wisdom of administering a sacrament to infants, who obviously could not yet consider or accept the great truths of Christianity. Though their willingness to accept the remainder of New England church discipline often made these dissenters difficult to identify, once they revealed their antipaedobaptist sentiments they quickly were censured. One indication of how serious the Puritans considered the baptists' threat to the establishment and perpetuation of a corporate identity for the colony was the amount of energy their ministers expended in answering the numerous baptist tracts that had been brought from England. In 1644, at the same time that he was preparing his famous *Survey of the Summe of Church Discipline*, Hartford's Thomas Hooker preached a set of sermons, eventually published in 1649 as *The Covenant of Grace Opened*, in answer to John Spilsbury's *A Treatise Concerning the Lawfull Subject of Baptisme*, an important Particular Baptist pamphlet, published in 1643, also attacked by Richard Mather in an "Answer to Nine Reasons of John Spilsbury to Prove Infants Ought Not to Be Baptized" (c. 1646).[36]

At about the same time Cotton ran into difficulties with none other than Nathaniel Briscoe, whom he described as having fallen "into acquaintence with some who stood aloofe to the Baptisme of Children" and who had provided to him some books "against the same." At the suggestion of Phillips, Briscoe had begun to visit other clergymen in the colony to try to resolve his doubts about infant baptism; but, as Cotton indicated, the Watertown resident could not be convinced of the propriety of administering that sacrament to children because of the "scruples he had, which were all comprised in a printed book" by "one of the chiefest of note that way, for moderation and freedom, from the leaven of other corrupt opinions, which are wont to accompany the denyall of Infants Baptisme." Cotton forebore to name the author of this tract, though his description of its author suggests that it was more likely a Particular Baptist such as Spilsbury than a Generalist like Lamb. When Benjamin Woodbridge, a young scholar to whom Cotton had entrusted the job of answering the book, prepared a text Briscoe found "so full of scholarship and termes of art, that he could not well understand it," Cotton wrote *The Grounds and Ends of Baptisme of the Children of the Faithful*, published in 1647.[37]

Dissatisfied colonists like Briscoe obviously welcomed any tracts, whether by General or Particular Baptists, that supported their wide-ranging criticisms of paedobaptism and the New England Way, forcing New England Puritan apologists to aim their counterarguments at a wide range of targets. By 1648, in his *Just Vindication of the Covenant and Church Estate of Children of Members As Also of Their Right to Baptisme*, Thomas Cobbet of Lynn addressed his pages to the arguments of so motley a crew of "Anabaptists" as Spilsbury and Christopher Blackwood, both Particular Baptists, and Henry Denne, one of Lamb's well-known associates and a frequenter of many radical conventicles. Like Cotton, Hooker, and Phillips, Cobbet justified the baptism of infants by an appeal to the Old Testament rite of circumcision and proceeded to defend the Puritans' notion of their federal covenant with God, which they believed to have been ratified by their willingness to undertake the hardships of settlement in New England to preserve the churches in their Gospel purity, a defense aimed at both Particular and General Baptist criticism of the New England theocracy.[38]

Thomas Shepard, in his *The Church Membership of Children* (1663), another tract prepared during this decade but not published until the controversy over the church membership of children of baptized but unconverted parents was resolved in the Half-Way Covenant (which allowed such children later to present their offspring for baptism), went to even greater lengths to defend the New England Way. Shepard was particularly disturbed by the baptists' increasingly serious attacks on the Puritans' decision to baptize only the children of "visible" saints, under the assumption that at maturity these individuals would themselves show the signs of grace requisite to full church membership and so transfer to their own "seed" the same promise they had fulfilled. Against the baptists' claims that by defending such an elaborate system of genealogical preference the Puritans fell into a morass of hopeless formalism, the Cambridge minister staunchly maintained that the only ground of admission to church membership was "federal holyness, whether externally professed as in grown persons, or graciously promised in their seed," not, as the baptists thought, the mere decision to accept Christ as one's savior and so to be baptized.[39]

As Shepard's arguments indicate, by the mid-1640s the baptists had brought the New England Puritans to a line of defense they would continue to reinforce until the intricacies of federal baptism were officially codified at the synod of 1662 with the ratification of the Half-Way Covenant. Further complicating and intensifying the Puritans' response to the baptists during this decade, though, and thus influencing their justification of the baptism of the children (and eventually the grandchildren) of visible saints, prominent English baptists directly intervened in the affairs of their New English brethren after the Bay Colony passed a stern law against those who openly expressed antipaedobaptist views. With the institution in the summer of 1644 of this ordinance, which threatened banishment for any "Anabaptists" who did not see the error of their ways, New England baptists ironically were given a powerful new weapon with which to attack the Puritan polity; persecution (and the martyrdom it implied) provided a compelling way to focus the attention of an increasingly tolerant English Puritan population on the New Englanders' unwillingness to tolerate any but those who accepted the premises of the New England Way.[40]

The anti-baptist ordinance itself is worth a brief examination, for its language suggests why Particular Baptists in England, who had gone to such lengths to differentiate themselves from both Continental anabaptists and their own General Baptist countrymen, were troubled by the New England Puritans' unwillingness to accept a distinction with which the more enlightened English Independents by then were quite willing to live. In the preface to the law, the Massachusetts General Court invoked the specter of Münster, described the "Anabaptists" as "incendiaries of commonwealths," and went on to note "that they *who have held the baptizing of infants unlawful, have usually held other errors or heresies together therewith*," a more accurate description of the Generalists who gathered around Lamb, Barber, and Gorton than of the fairly disciplined and strictly Calvinist members of the Particular Baptist churches. Since the Puritans had arrived in New England, the court went on to claim, more and more individuals had appeared who "denied the ordinance of the magistracy," the "lawfulness of making war," and the "lawfulness of magistrates," positions maintained most vociferously either by the General Baptists, or, in the case of the refusal to fight secular wars, by true anabaptists. The net the Puritans had cast for the "Anabaptists," then, was a very wide one. When it became apparent that despite the Puritans' claims that by their law they were trying to extirpate more radical ideas they caught only Particular Baptists, some prominent Englishmen decided to enter the fray.[41]

The most important gesture of the English baptists toward the plight of their New England cousins came in the form of letters from Henry Jessey and John Tombes to the churches of New England. In June 1645, just days before his rebaptism by Knollys, Jessey wrote an open letter urging the elders of the Bay to be more tolerant of those who differed from them on the point of infant baptism. For several years Jessey had been the pastor of the Southwark congregation, a position that guaranteed him the respect of many New England Puritans, and he was personally acquainted with several members of the Winthrop family (particularly the younger John Winthrop), as well as with John Wilson, Thomas Weld, and George Phillips.[42] When he wrote that in England "it is reported commonly, & use is made of it in pulpits against the Gathered Churches called Independents, that in NEW-ENGLAND they will not suffer others to live with them, that differ from them about Church-affaires," he spoke as a concerned friend as well as a baptist sympathizer. He went on to warn the colonists that already the law against the "Anabaptists" was a deterrent "to some from coming to [gather] among you" and, perhaps more important, "a Tr[ial] unto some Godly Marchants here, that wish well to you, that say, this will be greatly to your damage, every way." His letter spoke directly to those in New England who had begun to worry about the colony's loss of support among prominent Englishmen.[43]

To encourage further the repeal of the law, Jessey enclosed with his letter both a manuscript copy of John Tombes's arguments against infant baptism, formulated in 1644 and published in 1645 in *An Examen of the Sermon of Mr. Stephen Marshall, About Infant-Baptism*, and a letter from Tombes himself, addressed to the New England churches through John Cotton and John Wilson. Like Jessey, Tombes had remained a Calvinist even as he moved toward antipaedobaptism and permitted within his own congregation the liberal membership practices that had marked the

Southwark church since Jacob's pastorate; he, too, was no enemy to the New England Puritans.[44] Understanding that there was "some disquiet" in the New England churches "about paedobaptisme" and having been "moved" by some "that honour you much in the Lord Jesus" to try to effect some change in the colonists' policy toward dissenters, Tombes commended his arguments to them in the hope that they would adopt a more tolerant, and politic, stance with regard to baptism. The New Englanders, of course, held fast to their ways; soon thereafter Cotton informed Tombes that he had forwarded his manuscript to Cobbet to be reviewed and answered.[45]

The letters of Jessey and Tombes were not the only appeals made to the colonists from England after the anabaptist ordinance was passed. At almost the same time that the baptists sent their messages, Thomas Goodwin, John Owen, and other Independents expressed their own reservations about the New Englanders' recent actions, no doubt worried, as Jessey's letter implied they were, that their own cause would suffer by association with the colonists', particularly because the Independents then were defending the New Englanders' ecclesiastical polity before the Westminster Assembly of divines. Like Jessey and Tombes, these men urged the New England Puritans "to suspend all corporal punishment or restraint" on persons who dissented from the New England Way and who "practise[d] the principall of their Dissent without Danger or Disturbance to the Civill peace of the place."[46] Despite the influence of these prominent Puritans, they finally could get no better results through their advice than had the London baptists.

Samuel Gorton's arrival in London that same year to present his case against the Massachusetts magistrates to the Commission for Foreign Plantations brought even more unflattering attention upon the New Englanders. Although the Gortonists' trial and punishment had occurred before the passage of the new law, this group's activities very likely had contributed to its enactment; through his fervent evangelical activity and the 1646 publication of *Simplicities Defence against Seven-Headed Policy* Gorton exacted a degree of revenge. He was instrumental in bringing to wider public attention the New England Puritans' extreme reaction to any who raised their voices in honest dissent from their church system, and by the time the colony's agent in London, Edward Winslow, rebutted Gorton's arguments, much damage clearly had been done to New England's cause. Just as the untimely publication of Winthrop's *Short Story* in 1644 had been used to brand the colonies as a den of sectaries, so

Winslow's tract only pointed more clearly to the self-righteous stubbornness of New England's leadership and so produced more sympathy for the baptist cause.[47]

This flurry of activity in England in their favor gave much needed encouragement to the New England baptists, aided significantly also by the dissatisfaction of many New Englanders themselves with the stringency of the magistrates' measures against dissenters. For a few years after its passage, the law against the anabaptists was much debated among the populace. At a meeting of the General Court in the spring of 1645, two petitions were presented, one for suspending the new law, and the other for easing the enforcement of a similar law, enacted during the Antinomian Controversy and forbidding the entertainment of any strangers without the express permission of two of the magistrates. Action on these requests was delayed, however, and a year later eighty freemen from Dorchester and Roxbury petitioned the court for *stronger* measures against dissenters, noting in their petition that the "good lawes or orders" already enacted against the anabaptists had proved "a special meanes of discouraginge multitudes of erroneous persons from cominge over into this countrie." Through the late 1640s such disagreement continued, but despite the attempts of some of the more liberal Puritans to have the laws against dissenters rescinded—and the moral victory won earlier when the court had been persuaded to commute the sentence of the Gortonists—the hard line prevailed. Through the 1640s more and more "Anabaptists" were disciplined in the churches and courts of Massachusetts, and the cries for toleration that had been raised by Williams and others, though heard and to some degree acted upon in England, in the colonies fell only on deaf ears.[48]

The most severe application of the law against baptists occurred in the summer of 1651, when John Clarke, Obadiah Holmes, and John Crandall, all members of the Newport Baptist church, were apprehended in Lynn and charged with the open promulgation of antipaedobaptism. Clarke had been troubling the Massachusetts authorities for at least two years before his arrest, for he and Mark Lucar, who had come to New England from Spilsbury's congregation, had engaged in much evangelical activity in and around Seekonk (later Rehoboth) in the Plymouth colony, not far from the borders of the Bay Colony. Late in 1649, Williams had written to John Winthrop the Younger that "at Seekonk, a great many have lately concurred with Mr. John Clarke, and our Providence men, about the point of a new baptism and the manner by dipping." By then Williams had passed beyond his baptist stage but still heartily approved of Clarke's behavior; whatever Winthrop thought, Williams still believed that "their practice comes nearer to the first practice of our Great Founder, Jesus Christ, than other practices of religion do."[49]

The Massachusetts Puritans could not have disagreed more and showed their alarm at events in Seekonk, where fourteen colonists had been rebaptized within a week, by formally expressing their concern to the Plymouth General Court. The Bay Colony never had been comfortable with the fact that Plymouth was more tolerant of dissent than it was; "and now," the Massachusetts authorities wrote, "to our great grief, we are credibly informed that your patient bearing with such men has produced another effect: namely, the multiplying and increasing of the same errors." Not hearing of "any effectual restriction" on the new baptists, the Bay Colony asked Plymouth to consider their neighbor's "interests," for the "infection of such diseases, being so near us," they complained, "are [sic] likely to spread into our jurisdiction."[50] But the Plymouth men let matters rest as they were, and, as had been the case with Gorton, Massachusetts had to wait to catch the troublemakers within their own borders.

Their opportunity came in July 1651 when Clarke and two others from his church visited Lynn at the request of William Witter, who had been rebaptized in the Newport church but had continued to reside north of Boston, and who presumably had made some new converts whom he wanted Clarke to "dip." The three visitors were arrested at Witter's home after holding a private service on the Sabbath and were forced to attend Cobbet's church meeting, after which Clarke rebuked the congregation for upholding infant baptism. The next day, without the constable's knowledge, the three baptists held another service, at which Holmes rebaptized three persons, including one member of the Salem church. By then the Lynn authorities had had enough. The three Rhode Islanders were taken to Boston and imprisoned, and a week later tried and found guilty of, among other things, holding a private meeting on the Sabbath, disturbing the public worship, and denying the scriptural authority of infant baptism. All three were sentenced to pay large fines or else be whipped; and, though at first all three refused to pay, preferring to become martyrs for their cause, some friends finally posted bail for Crandall and Clarke. Holmes, however, refused a similar act of generosity; after keeping him imprisoned for two months, the court decided to administer thirty lashes, a sentence carried out before a large and partly sympathetic crowd.[51]

Later that year Clarke sailed for England with Williams to try to obtain a new charter for the Rhode Island settlements and lost no time in joining Kiffin's London church and publishing the following year *Ill Newes from New-England*, an account of his and his associates' ill treatment in Massachusetts. Neither did Holmes let matters rest. After he returned to Seekonk, where he had become pastor of the new church, he wrote a description of his persecution and sent it to Spilsbury, presumably with the intention of having the prominent English baptist publicize his cause against the New England Puritans. In these reports neither Holmes nor Clarke spared any details. Clarke revealed that the Puritans were not above slanderous moral arguments against their enemies, for they claimed that in Lynn Clarke had "baptized Goodwife *Bowdish* naked," whereas in fact, Clarke explained, she "had comely garments from the Crown of her head to the sole of her foot." Holmes's letter reveals a similar pettiness in the Bay authorities. He reported that while he was on the witness stand during his trial, John Wilson had become so enraged that he jumped from his chair and struck and cursed Holmes for his purported insubordination.[52] With every new report making them sound more like the intolerant Scottish and English Presbyterians—the heresiographer Thomas Edwards, for example, was fond of quoting accounts of baptists who had "faire opportunities to feed their eyes full of adultery in beholding young women naked, and in handling young women naked"—by their treatment of the baptists the New England Puritans continued to isolate themselves from those in England who should have remained closest to them. By that time, it was obvious that the New Englanders had firmly decided not to behave like English Independents and espouse the principle of religious liberty. Though they knew, as Williams put it, "what sad *complaints*, in *letters, printings, conferences,* so many of Gods people" had "poured forth against" their "persecuting," the New England Puritans' course was set. They believed that Clarke, Holmes, and Crandall, good Calvinists though they were, had gotten only what they deserved when they refused to acknowledge the principle of federal holiness on which the idea of New England was based.[53]

By the mid-1650s the New England Puritans had become preoccupied with a large number of radical spiritists, some of whom were encouraged by General Baptists in Rhode Island. But just before the arrival of the first Quakers they once again were forced to take direct action against a prominent advocate of adult baptism, this time no interloper from Rhode Island but none other than Henry Dunster, president of Harvard College. As the colonists gradually began to feel the impact of the law prohibiting baptist views, many who questioned paedobaptism resolved to hold their peace in exchange for not being censured; for, as the English Independents had urged, the Puritan magistrates, faced with more and more baptists and their fellow-travelers, allowed their countrymen to hold dissenting views as long as they did not seek either to convert others to their ways or to leave the watch and care of the congregational churches. But as a prominent public figure who had openly declared his dissent from infant baptism, Dunster, like Clarke and his associates, could not be allowed to go unpunished.[54]

In 1653 Dunster had shocked the colony by refusing to baptize his newborn child, though he had had the rite administered to his three older children. Because of his position as president of the colony's only seminary of higher learning, Dunster quickly was summoned before the magistrates for an examination of his beliefs. For two days early in 1654 he debated with nine of the colony's leading ministers, including the intemperate John Wilson, the thesis, "Visible believers only should be baptized," and his defense of the affirmative proved every bit as rigorous as any found in the apologies of the English Particular Baptists. When Dunster maintained that "if we be engrafted into Christ by personal faith, then not by parental," his opponents countered by arguing that "an infant makes his covenant in his public person," and, further, that "an immediate parent is a public person in regard to his children." At this point in the proceedings Dunster magisterially undercut the whole notion of a federal covenant by reminding the ministers that "There is no further person but Christ for us to stand in." A letter of Dunster's from this same period further clarifies the position he defended at his public examination. "The baptism of infants," he wrote, "forcibly deprives spiritual babes . . . of their due consolation from Christ, viz.: the remission of sin, &c., and dutiful obligation to Christ, viz.: to believe in him, die with him to sin, and rise to newness of life." "Without visible faith and repentance," which for infants were impossible, Dunster argued, there could be no true baptism.[55]

The ministerial conference did nothing to change Dunster's mind, and to save Harvard from the "Anabaptists," in May 1654 the General Court passed a law prohibiting anyone "unsound in the faith" from teaching at the college or in the colony's public schools. To test the magistrates' resolve in this matter, in July Dunster interrupted a baptismal service in Jonathan Mitchel's Cambridge meetinghouse and reaffirmed his anti-paedobaptist views. Whereupon the court demanded his resignation from Harvard, effective that fall, and again summoned him for an examination of his beliefs. At this public meeting, in April 1655, Dunster showed no signs of acquiescing to the court's demands. He affirmed that "the subjects of Baptisme were visible penitent believers" and claimed, as had many other New England baptists, that "the Covenant of Abraham [was] not a ground for Baptisme." Further, he revealed his opposition to the increasing support for what later became the measures of the Half-Way Covenant by warning magistrates that the "corruptions" then "stealing into the Churches" demanded that "any faithful Christian . . . beare witness" against them. Surprisingly, for such comments, as well as for his behavior in the Cambridge meeting, Dunster escaped with only a public censure; evidently the magistrates felt that he was no Obadiah Holmes. But Dunster had had enough and soon moved to Scituate, which was out of the bounds of the Bay Colony and where there were many people inclined toward his views.[56]

By making what in retrospect seems the anomalous trade of Chauncy for Dunster as Harvard's president, the colony in fact did put the college in better hands, but the magistrates were not able fully to eliminate Dunster's influence upon others of the baptist persuasion. It is important to recall that in 1640 he had arrived in Charlestown with Thomas Goold and John Russell, two men whose struggles against the Puritan oligarchy ended triumphantly with the establishment of the first baptist church in the colony, in Charlestown in 1665, and over whom Dunster presumably exerted some influence.[57] In 1653, for example, Russell had authored the Woburn "memorial for Christian liberty," signed by twenty-nine inhabitants who requested the General Court to rescind their order that "no person within this jurisdiction shall undertake any constant course of public preaching or prophesying without the approbation of the elders of four of the next churches, or of the county court." If this petition is any indication, there was considerable support in some of the colony's towns for the separation of church and state, even if it was not expressed in openly baptist terms. Couched in the traditional rhetoric of congregational polity, Russell's argument reaffirmed the prerogatives of each church within a congregational system and implied that the new law gave the magistrates a "supremacy where Christ gives none." If the magistrates, who refused to act on the petition, did not then know of Russell's baptist sentiments, they certainly were aware of them by 1666, when he turned his back on the administration of the sacrament in the Woburn church. Three years later he joined the baptist church that had been founded in Charlestown.[58]

Dunster's influence on Thomas Goold, the founder of this Baptist church, was more direct. A tenant on the younger John Winthrop's land in Charlestown, Goold realized sometime between 1652 and 1655 that he had some scruples about infant baptism; he later recalled how shortly thereafter "God was pleased at last to make it clear" to him that "by the rule of the Gospel" children "were not capable or fit subjects for such an ordinance." When in 1655 he refused to have his young daughter baptized, Charlestown's minister, Zechariah Symmes, summoned him to a church meeting to discuss his objections, whereupon with the advice of "Master Dunstans [that is, Dunster]" he complied and publicly defended his baptist beliefs. Dunster and he had kept in close contact over the years. Goold's narrative of the founding of the first baptist church reveals that at the time he tendered his advice, the deposed Harvard president was paying Goold a visit in Charlestown. Two years later, when Dunster again was in court for his refusal to have yet another child baptized, Goold appeared at the same session to answer the same charge.[59]

As his move to Scituate indicates, Dunster had no stomach to challenge the Bay regarding his position at Harvard; as he later put it so clearly in a letter to a minister at Bury in Lancashire, "Controversyes I am unwilling to launch into." He also had no desire to minister to a baptist congregation of his own and in 1656 refused a request to join a prominent baptist congregation in Dublin, an offer supported by none other than Henry Cromwell.[60] In the mid-1650s, the leadership of the Particular Baptists in Massachusetts passed to Goold, who, after being censured by the Charlestown church in 1657 and deprived of the privilege of taking communion, began to take steps down the path that led to the organization of the colony's first Particular Baptist church. In November 1663, at the encouragement of some baptists newly arrived from Kiffin's London church, he began to hold private meetings in his home, for which the church again censured him. And by 1665, having failed to convince the Puritans that one could disagree with the congregationalists' position on infant baptism and yet remain within their churches, a nonseparatist stance maintained, as William McLoughlin has noted, by Jessey and other English Particular Baptists, Goold finally took the step of forming his own covenanted congregation.[61]

Goold's story illustrates an important fact. Before 1660 the baptist movement in New England (including Rhode Island), remained relatively unfocused, even as more and more people were swayed by the logic of its more articulate spokesmen. While some historians explain this situation by noting that throughout the first thirty years of New England's history the baptists lacked strong and consistent leadership, it is just as likely that the very nature of their challenge, especially in the case of the Particular Baptists, prevented them from emerging from these decades in as strong a position as their English counterparts, who by 1660 had so entrenched themselves that even the rigorous application of the Clarendon Code could not crush them. For unlike the radical spiritists, whose rancorous debates with the New England Puritans were focused on points of doctrine, the baptists most often quarreled with the New England majority over matters of discipline. Most "Anabaptists," for all the Puritans' attempts to associate them with other radicals, advocated reform only of particular ecclesiastical measures; the historical record indicates that more often than not they remained within the Puritan congregations, even as they objected to the administration of baptism to infants.[62]

Because the baptist challenge was conducted almost exclusively within the theological framework of New England Puritanism, the disciplinary measures utilized against this group remained, on the whole, fairly moderate and primarily correctional: the John Clarkes and Obadiah Holmeses who received severe treatment were mercifully few. As long as a parishioner's main offense was restricted to turning his back on the administration of the sacrament, he was dealt with by way of counsel and advice. Because such individuals accepted the validity of the remainder of Puritan theology and knew that a refusal to listen to the ministers' "reason" eventually could lead to banishment, as often as not they would stand "corrected" and remain within the Puritan church. Only as the Puritans' logic was turned more and more to a defense of the Half-Way Covenant did the issue of baptism forcefully rock the foundation of the church system, freeing some members of the colony to build baptist churches in the wake of the schism that followed the Synod of 1662.[63]

I have been speaking here primarily of Particular Baptists, for, like their English counterparts, the Generalists often challenged the Puritans on explicitly doctrinal matters and joined with radical spiritists in providing support (and sometimes converts) for the incipient Quaker movement in Rhode Island, Massachusetts, and Plymouth.[64] Despite the fragmented nature of their churches, however, throughout these years both the Particular and General Baptists argued two important points: first, that the close relationship between church and state that had marked the New England Way from the first settlement was an impediment to the flowering of true Gospel piety (see Chapter 7); and, second, that the institutionalization of "grace" that increasingly marked the discipline of the

Puritan churches did not necessarily validate the Puritans' progressivist view of history.

On the question of the institutionalizing of "grace," the baptists challenged the Puritans' understanding of how God works in human history. By denying the application of the Abrahamic covenant to New England—and particularly the doctrine of preparation for salvation derived from it—General and Particular Baptists questioned the Puritans' linear view of history and, by implication, New England's special place in history. They saw no reason to believe that the history of the work of redemption unfolded with special reference to the covenanted society. Rather, they expected that the growth of Christ's true, invisible Church would be nurtured through frequent showers of grace, and rather than building their faith upon the destiny of a federated colony composed of "visible" saints, they accepted into their congregations any and all individuals who had understood the necessity of Christ as their savior and had been rebaptized to prove it. Thus, from their quarrel with the Puritans the baptists emerged willing to respect—indeed, to accept—any Christian church founded on true Gospel piety.[65]

The Puritans had good reason to fear the effects of "Anabaptist" ideas, for, despite the fact that before 1660 the baptists were not well organized, the inner logic of their criticism of infant baptism ran counter to one of the deepest streams of New England Puritan ideology. To understand the various laws passed against them—even if the full force of such ordinances was very rarely applied—one need only recall how all too often the Puritan clergy discovered in their communities what in 1645 Shepard called "the unsettlednesse and ungroundednesse of so many godly Christians." To such people the baptists pointed out both the inconsistencies in and the presumption of the New England churches. If, as Richard Mather noted in 1650, "it is but too manifest that many of al sorts are now a daies hankering and leaning that [Anabaptist] way," the baptists' message that Christ comes only to him who stands alone in his faith could be as profoundly disintegrating as the doctrine of any radical spiritist. It is hardly surprising that both Quakers and Fifth Monarchy Men often emerged from the baptist ranks, or that when such individuals emerged they bore out the justness of Daniel Featley's warning that "if this Secte prevaile, we shall have no Monarchie in the State, nor Hierarchie in the Church, but an Anarchie in both." With regard to some communities in New England, his was a frighteningly prescient observation.[66]

CHRIST'S SECOND COMING: MILLENARIANS AND QUAKERS

Through radical Puritans thus far examined all shared the seventeenth century's widespread interest in eschatology, but two other groups, the millenarians and the Quakers, warrant separate treatment because of their heightened concern with Christ's imminent reign on earth. The radical millenarians, represented most memorably by those in England known as the Fifth Monarchy Men, and the Religious Society of Friends, as the Quakers properly are termed, admittedly differed in their understanding of how the world was to be made ready for Christ: the former urged swift and, if necessary, violent action to initiate the thousand-year rule of the saints that would precede the Last Judgment, while the latter counseled virtual acquiescence in the face of persecution to witness the saving power of Christ's truth. One group expected the establishment of Mosaic law that would mark the Fifth Monarchy described in the Book of Daniel; members of the other group shared an understanding that the second coming of Christ was to be realized internally, in the heart of each saint. Yet both groups drew members from the ranks of disaffected radical spiritists and baptists by their insistence that recent events in English history, of which the settlement of

New England was among the most significant, indicated that a new dispensation was at hand. By the mid-1650s New England Puritans, like their English brethren, found more and more of their time devoted to representatives of these groups, who in their different ways sharply challenged the ideology of the New England Way.[1]

As J. F. Maclear has shown, a belief in the literal second coming of Christ pervaded New England Puritan culture (as it did England's) and contributed significantly to the New Englanders' understanding of their role in the history of redemption. Certain New Englanders might be termed *radical millenarians*: their enthusiasm for the immediate institution of a Christian commonwealth administered by the saints moved them to theological and political positions more extreme than those held by the majority of the populace, particularly the ministers and magistrates, who, as Maclear points out, because of their moderation and pragmatism, as well as their deep respect for the tradition of English law, were unwilling to ground the colony exclusively in laws derived from Deuteronomy.[2] Although in New England the agitation for the establishment of the Fifth Monarchy was not comparable to what London experienced in the aftermath of the execution of King Charles, through the first thirty years of settlement there were several important, if unsuccessful, attempts to urge upon the colony a more rapid and thorough reformation of society than most New Englanders were ready to accept, one that would replace for all time the imperfect laws of men with those of God.

In New England the radical millenarians had a particularly strong base on which to build, for the belief in an age of glory that preceded the Last Judgment, an idea popularized among English Puritans in the millennial speculations of Thomas Brightman, Joseph Mede, and others, had given added meaning to the emigration to America. With the increasing corruption of and persecution by the prelates in the Church of England, many conscientious Puritans felt that their country had become but another appendage of the Antichrist; and as more and more of them decided to leave England—in Thomas Hooker's words, because "England hath seen her best days, and the reward of sin is coming on apace"—they transferred to the American strand their hopes for a New Jerusalem over which Christ soon would reign.[3] Further, among English Independents in particular there was a widespread belief not only that recent political events in England proved that the glory foretold in the Book of Revelation would be known by the present generation but also that the gathering of the churches in a congregational manner necessarily preceded it. As it became apparent that the Westminster Assembly was controlled by presbyterians, New England, where most of the churches already were modeled on the congregational pattern, assumed even greater importance. To emigrate to the New World, then, signaled, among other things, one's willingness to prepare for the final battle with the Antichrist.[4]

Because such a heightened excitement about the last days could readily degenerate into violence against those unwilling to accept an immediate rule by the saints, Massachusetts's magistrates and ministers were careful to control such beliefs, particularly so that the colony would not become another Münster, where a century earlier government by another group of "saints" had resulted in ecclesiastical and moral anarchy.[5] The colony's leaders partially accomplished this task through an insistence that, while the settlers had reason to expect the day when Christ ruled the earth through his saints, they could not presume that such a rule had begun. Rather, New England congregationalists, like English Independents, were to continue to gather into covenanted churches because the very act of convenanting, by which each new church was established, marked another significant step to the final days. Clustered together in what they regarded as true apostolic churches while all around them Babylon fell, the visible saints were to nurture each other and await the descent of Christ. What they did in the present thus held immense significance for their future glory, but always they were reminded that their immediate actions were simply preparatory.

In New England and old some radical millenarians, rejecting this course, counseled the immediate arrogation of civil and ecclesiastical power to the saints themselves, who would rule by the Mosaic code. The radicals' desire to establish society directly upon the pattern of scriptural law, a desire rooted in a biblicism even more scrupulous than that of most Puritan clergy, bespoke a sharp disenchantment with the course these ministers had charted for reform of the English church. Tired of waiting for the overthrow of the Great Beast, they assumed personal responsibility for this momentous task. It should come as no surprise, then, that in New England, where since the 1630s millennial excitement had run high and the congregational order was firmly established, some of the settlers attempted to expedite the fulfillment of prophecy.

The first indication in New England of the presence of a millennial eschatology more radical than that which the clerical majority were willing to tolerate came during the Antinomian Controversy, when in the fall of 1637, at Anne Hutchinson's examination by the General Court in Newtown, William Bartholomew, a deputy from Ipswich who had known the defendant in London, reported that he always had found Mistress Hutchinson "very inquisitive after revelations." Batholomew also recalled that though Hutchinson "liked not" Thomas Hooker's "spirit," she admired his famous sermon, *The Danger of Desertion*, because she believed that its message about England's progressive apostasy had been vouchsafed to her directly by the Holy Spirit. "It was revealed to me," Hutchinson plainly put it, "that England should be destroyed" as part of the Antichrist's fall.[6] As the court well knew, much of her errant behavior could be explained by just such beliefs, for Hutchinson was convinced that she lived during the final days and so had to bear personal witness against New England's purported corruption. She defended her role as an explicator of Reverend Cotton's sermons because she felt it her duty to expose the hypocrisy of the majority of the Bay's ministers. To her mind, only Cotton properly prepared his parishioners for Armageddon.

It was Cotton, too, who more than any other New England minister encouraged millennial speculation among his fellow colonists, and this fact only added to his embarrassment when the colony took to task Hutchinson and other members of his church for heretical and seditious ideas they did not hesitate to lay at his door. Even before his arrival in the colony in 1633 he had established a reputation as a student of the prophetic books, particularly by his series of lectures on Canticles at St. Botolph's, published in 1642 as *A Brief Exposition of the Book of Canticles*; his taste for eschatological prediction was further whetted by his early experience in Boston, where just before his difficulties with the antinomians he had nurtured a significant religious revival.[7]

After his chastening experience with the Hutchinsonians, Cotton increased his study of the prophecies. In the late 1630s he initiated a major sermon cycle on Revelation, delivered at the Thursday lectures in Boston, in which he continued to speculate on the precise time of the Antichrist's fall. These sermons, published in part in *The Powring Out of the Seven Vialls* (1642), *The Churches Resurrection* (1642), and *An Exposition upon the Thirteenth Chapter of the Revelation* (1655), and in which, as Edward Johnson noted, Cotton predicted "some sudden blow to be given to this blood-thirsty monster [the Antichrist]," very likely were Cotton's way of maintaining the heightened piety of the colonists in the aftermath of the antinomians' banishment.[8] By redirecting the colonists' fervor from the intensely personal definition of religious experience maintained by this group toward a more *communal* ideal, Cotton maintained his position as one of the colony's most respected clergymen. In 1641, he warned his fellow New Englanders that "If we do not strike a fast covenant with our

God to be his people, . . . then we and ours will be of this dead-hearted frame a thousand years."⁹ Partly irenical in intent, his eschatological writings not only united New Englanders against a much larger and more significant enemy than the Hutchinsonians but also displayed the tenacity through which he remained a leader of those among the populace who refused to allow New England to relinquish its central role in the Reformation.

As we have seen in the case of Hutchinson, the effects of Cotton's preaching were contagious but not always salutary. Another of those interested in his explication of the prophecies was Thomas Lechford, an attorney who had frequented Hugh Peter's church in London before Peter's flight to Amsterdam in 1629 and who shortly after his arrival in New England in 1638 became embroiled in controversy over a book-length manuscript, "Of Prophesie," which he had brought to Cotton for comment.¹⁰ At first the Boston minister "had not the leisure to read it," Lechford recalled, but after Deputy-Governor Thomas Dudley had perused it (at Lechford's request), Cotton was drawn into the stir Lechford's "errors" caused. In December 1638, Dudley apprised Governor Winthrop that he had found the "scope" of Lechford's writings "erroneous and dangerous, if not hereticall." The Antinomian Controversy fresh in his mind, he warned the Governor that "It is easyer stopping a breach when it begins, then afterward." "We saw our error," he continued, "in suffering Mrs. Hutchinson too long."¹¹

One of Lechford's "erroneous and dangerous" opinions directly related to New England's church polity: he argued that "the Apostolic function [was] not yet ceased" and that "there still ought to be such, who would by their transcendent Authority govern all churches." From his manuscript it was clear that he had arrived at his defense of the "office of Apostleship" through a study of the prophetic books. He claimed that "the Antichrist described in Revelation was not yet come, nor any part of that Prophecy yet fulfilled from the 4th chapter to the end," an opinion that flatly contradicted the preaching of Cotton and others on Revelation and that called into question the New Englanders' de facto separation from the Church of England, which they considered corrupted by the Antichrist's soldiers. Complicating Lechford's position even more, Dudley had learned that in other of his theological opinions Lechford "favoureth Mr. Lenthall," the Weymouth minister then being scrutinized for his antinomian beliefs. Anticipating another outburst of radical spiritism, the deputy-governor urged Winthrop to move quickly against the attorney, a plea he repeated even more urgently two weeks later when his great fear was confirmed. "The worst opynion in his book," Dudley wrote, "is taken upp by others." [12]

Dudley thereupon suggested that instead of being printed, as the author wished, Lechford's manuscript should "rather be putt into the fire." Winthrop, always the more moderate man, chose to proceed more slowly; it was apparent that the attorney was not the charismatic leader that Anne Hutchinson was. By January 1639, however, "Of Prophesie" had caused enough controversy to warrant its author's examination by some of the elders, who asked to see other writings of Lechford's, in particular a treatise that dealt explicitly with the millennial promise of Revelation. In a letter to Hugh Peter, then in Salem, Lechford requested that—in addition to John Norton and George Phillips—Peter himself, Nathaniel Ward of Ipswich, and Thomas Parker of Newbury be named to the council charged with an evaluation of his work so that the council's decision would be reached with "all legal favour" to the author. Lechford's request was granted, but the council nevertheless refused to accept the validity of his defense, especially his belief that such ideas as his might be held, as he put it, "*salva fide*" and without harm to those in the church who interpreted scriptural prophecies differently. As an indication of how serious the General Court considered his errors, Lechford thereafter was excluded from fellowship in the Boston church and also stripped of freeman's privileges. [13]

Lechford remained in the colony for two more years, perhaps attending Cotton's famous sermons on Revelation even though he himself would disagree with Cotton's belief that the fifth vial already had been poured; as Lechford put it, "it is probable there shall come yet a greater Antichrist then ever hath bin." But because of his increasingly pointed criticism of the congregational church order, by the early fall of 1640 his differences with the Bay's ministers had intensified; the next summer found him in England, where he published his *Plain Dealing; or, News from New-England* (1645), a sharply worded but astute assessment of the New England experiment. True to his reading of Scripture, he defended the validity of episcopal ordination and rejoined the Church of England, even as its bishops were being severely challenged by the Long Parliament. [14]

The reforms of this parliament, which gave the lie to Lechford's notions of the Antichrist, only strengthened the New England ministers in their own millennial predictions: as Lechford reported to a friend in England in 1640, in New England "some cry out of nothing but Antichrist and the Man of Sin." [15] When Lechford requested Thomas Parker's inclusion on the council named to examine his work, he chose one whom he hoped was a kindred spirit. Parker's interest in the prophetic books, for example, later culminated in his *Visions and Prophecies of Daniel Expounded*, published in 1645. Lechford no doubt believed that Parker's open presbyterianism would make him sympathetic to his own belief in the importance of the episcopacy in Christ's plans to redeem the world from antichristian apostasy.[16] Lechford's attempts to unravel the prophecies were not unusual; it was his condemnation of New England's government in light of his reading of the prophetic books that so upset the colonial government. If nothing else, Lechford's millennial writings warned the magistrates to be on their guard against interpretations of Daniel and Revelation that might wreak havoc with their carefully constructed ecclesiastical system.

Speculation on the precise time of the millennium was not restricted to Massachusetts. In the early 1640s in the Connecticut Valley, Ephraim Huit of Windsor preached the sermons published in 1644 as *The Whole Prophecie of Daniel explained*, and four years later from neighboring Hartford Thomas Hooker offered his *Survey of the Summe of Church Discipline* as a model for the constitution of the churches over which Christ would reign upon his return to earth.[17]

Nicholas Easton, whose radical ideas about the indwelling of the Spirit brought him close to Ranterism, reportedly taught that "gifts and graces were that antichrist mentioned [in] Thess[alonians 2 : 3−6], and that which withheld, etc., was the preaching of the law," an idea that John Wheelwright earlier had explored in his infamous "Fast-Day Sermon" of 1637 and that had encouraged some colonists to reject the doctrine of preparation espoused by Shepard and other ministers.[18] In Aquidneck (later Portsmouth), a group of antinomians attempted to establish a new colony explicitly upon the primitive church order. Before they left Boston as outcasts they had formed a new covenant, incorporating themselves "into a Bodie Politick" and submitting their "persons [,] lives [,] and estates unto [their] Lord Jesus Christ, the King of Kings and Lord of Lords and to all those perfect and most absolute lawes of his given us in his holy word of truth, to be guided and judged thereby." Within a year their theocratic experiment came to nought when William Coddington, the "Judge" of the infant colony, was ousted from his position. The experiment at Aquidneck, however, was a genuine attempt to live exclusively by biblical injunction through a rule of the saints. Probably undermined by the radical spiritism of some of its members, who in their eagerness to obey the promptings of the Spirit rejected any outward laws, the settlement was irrevocably splintered into several factions, some of whom moved away to form other radical Puritan communities.[19]

The majority of the Aquidneck settlers had come from Cotton's church in Boston; this is not surprising when it is recalled that in 1636 Cotton had been named to a committee charged with framing an inclusive set of laws for the colony. That charge resulted in *Moses His Judicials*, a strict theocratic formulation of civil and ecclesiastical laws, which, though never formally adopted by the General Court, displayed how Cotton's millennial enthusiasm spilled over into the overtly political arena: if the days of the Antichrist were indeed numbered, as he thought they were, he felt perfectly justified in searching scripture to provide a model for the government over which Christ would reign. *Moses His Judicials* was published in 1641 (under the title of *An Abstract, or The Lawes of New England*), but more significant was the code's reprinting in 1655 by William Aspinwall, a New Englander who had returned to England to become a prominent Fifth Monarchist. Aspinwall, who was part of the Aquidneck experiment, evidently believed that, though the center of action in the Protestant world had shifted back to England, his countrymen had no better guide for further reformation of the English state than that assembled by the eminent Cotton.[20]

Cotton's disappointment with the colony's refusal to accept *Moses His Judicials* as the basis for its legal system might have been one of the factors that made him consider moving to the colony of New Haven, where his friend John Davenport had settled. He even provided some suggestions for the establishment of a strictly theocratic government in New Haven. But he finally decided to remain in Massachusetts, where he could help chart that larger colony's journey to the promised land. It soon became apparent that, despite recent events in England, God still had predestined Massachusetts for a major role in the establishment of Christ's kingdom, a belief confirmed for the Puritans by the increasing successes of evangelists like Henry Whitefield, Jonathan Mayhew, and John Eliot in bringing the native Americans to Christianity.

The colonists believed that the conversion of the "heathen" was of major significance because the New Testament promised that before the Last Judgment the entire world would be brought to the Gospel; further, during the decade of the 1650s it assumed even more importance as more and more Puritans became convinced that the native Americans were the descendants of the Ten Lost Tribes of Israel whose conversion would immediately precede Christ's second coming.[21] The New England Puritans had always felt a special obligation to convert the Indians to Christianity; a desire to bring the Gospel to the "unsettled" wilderness of the New World had marked Puritan propaganda literature from its earliest stages. But after 1650 the colonists' efforts toward the Indians grew in importance because of the publication of Thomas Thorowgood's *Jewes in America*, in which he reported John Durie's story that in the depths of the Andes was a tribe of Indians who had been observed practicing Jewish ceremonial rites and who, after questioning by white explorers, had claimed to be descendants of such Jewish patriarchs as Abraham.[22] In New England such strong "proof" of the Indians' relationship to the Lost Tribes gave further impetus to the translation of Scripture into the Indian tongues, and with every new Indian convert the Puritans found more evidence that the Jews were indeed being "called in" to the fold. By the mid-1650s, when Oliver Cromwell began to negotiate for the reentry of the Jews into England, many Puritans in both New England and old awaited with eagerness the institution of the Fifth Monarchy.[23]

Of the New England Puritan ministers who worked most actively with the native Americans, John Eliot, the famed "Apostle to the Indians," took the lead in trying to establish the identity of the native Americans as the Lost Tribes. In one of the "Eliot Tracts" through which he communicated news of his and other evangelists' efforts with the natives, Eliot added to the growing evidence for the Indians' Jewish ancestry a story he had heard from Thomas Dudley, who had been told by one "Captaine *Cromwell*" that he had seen "many Indians to the Southward Circumsized, and . . . was undoubtedly certaine of it."[24] In addition to his compulsive attempts to understand his Gospel labors in relation to the prophetic books, Eliot attempted to establish among the tribes he converted a form of government based exclusively on scriptural law, a fact that distinguished his evangelical labors from those of his co-workers in the native American vineyards. Because, as he put it, he had found the Indians without any "wisdome of their owne (I meane as other Nations have) wherein to stick," he believed that they would "readily yeeld to any direction from the Lord, so that there will be no such opposition against the rising Kingdome of Jesus Christ among them."[25]

But Eliot's instructions to the Indians to "fly to the Scriptures, for every Law, Rule, Direction, Form, or whatever we do," were aimed at more than the immediate conversion of the Massachusetts tribes. Caught up in his study of prophecy, he sought to extend the government described in Exodus and Deuteronomy to the saints throughout the world, including his native England, where, though many already were nominally "Puritans," in the aftermath of Charles's execution there still was chaos in the political and religious spheres. Because Eliot maintained that "when every thing both Civil & Spiritual are [sic] done by the direction of the word of Christ, then doth Christ reign, and the great Kingdome of Jesus Christ which we weight [sic] for, is even this that I do now mention," he hoped that his accomplishments with the unlettered Indians in Natick would provide the beacon for another, greater city on a hill. Humble as it seemed, his experiment with the "praying Indians" announced to "all Kingdomes and Nations" that by following scriptural injunctions for the proper organization of their governments they, too, could become "the Kingdomes of Christ." "Oh the blessed day in *England*," Eliot exclaimed, "when the Word of God shall be their *Magna Charta* and chief Law Book," as it already had become in the outpost of the Gospel carved from the western edge of Massachusetts.[26]

Eliot's modest success in christianizing the Indians led to his most controversial work, *The Christian Commonwealth*, which, though composed in 1651, through circumstances now inexplicable was not published until the height of the Fifth Monarchy agitation in London in 1659. Its optimistic tone clearly reflects its origin a decade earlier when Eliot had brought "a people without any forme of Government" to "deduce all their Laws from the holy Scriptures." In 1650, with its monarch beheaded and with radical Puritans assuming more and more power, England itself seemed to Eliot in a state analogous to that of the Indian tribes with whom he worked; like the natives, his countrymen were "in a capacity to chuse into themselves a new Government." Just as a decade earlier Richard Mather, John Cotton, and other New England ministers had offered from their American experience models for the proper ecclesiastical reorganization of England, so now Eliot sought to calm the frenzy of England's political debate with the "counsel of the Lord" he had gained from his New England years. With that in mind, in the preface to *The Christian Commonwealth* he excitedly urged his fellow Puritans in England to seize the moment to "set the Crown of *England* upon the head of Christ." "Let him be your *JUDGE*," Eliot urged; "Let him be your *LAW-GIVER*, Let him be your *KING!*"[27]

Eliot's enthusiastic preface was followed by a straightforward, Hebraic "Platform of Government" that quickly won him a following among England's most fervent Fifth Monarchists. Like Cotton's set of laws, also championed by the English radical millenarians after its republication in 1655, *The Christian Commonwealth* epitomizes the millennial excitement felt by many colonists who objected to the Massachusetts leaders' unwillingness to replace their heritage of English law with a more radical form of government. Such individuals always were in the minority, for in New England there were many more who, though equally moved by millennial prophecy, believed that the theocracy established in New England closely approximated the divine plan for civil governments. They saw no reason to renovate the legal system along the lines Eliot suggested, a fact vividly illustrated by a rhetorical query to Governor Winthrop: "Is not government in church and Common weale (according to gods own rules)," Samuel Symonds asked in 1647, "that new heaven and earth promised, in the fullnes accomplished when the Jewes come in; and the first fruites begun in this poore New Eng[land]?" Such colonists as Symonds found Eliot's plans for a Christian commonwealth suitable enough for the native Americans before they had developed a more complex society but not relevant to what they regarded as the New England Puritans' relatively successful reformation of church and state, the substance of which they sought to return to England.[28]

Eliot paid deeply for his manuscript, for it finally was published when New England's leaders were attempting to reach an accommodation with the new monarchy; as the late seventeenth-century historian William Hubbard tersely noted, around 1660 "an odd kind of book was unhappily printed by one of the ministers of New England . . . that gave great distaste to the General Court, as savouring too much of a Fifth Monarchy spirit." Because the book contained "sundry expressions . . . offensive to the Kingly government of England," Eliot was called before the court and censured for what had become, ten years after its composition, a serious embarrassment to the colony.[29] But taken in its proper context *The Christian Commonwealth* was hardly an indiscretion. As much as any of Cotton's writings, it testified to the heightened expectation of the Last Days that so animated many New Englanders during those heady years when New England still seemed assured of its central role in Protestant history.

Eliot never sought to impose his plan directly upon Massachusetts. He maintained general confidence in the colony's lay and clerical leadership. It was, after all, they who had founded and supported the enterprise that made possible his own evangelical labors. Others were less convinced of the propriety of supporting the New England theocracy. Disappointed in what they had seen of New England's government and stimulated by the exciting news of Puritan reform in Interregnum England, they returned across the Atlantic to contribute to what they came to regard as more important tasks than the conversion of a handful of Indians.

Among the many who went back to England in the early 1650s, when the Little Parliament promised a central role in the reformation of church and state, only a few made enough of a mark to warrant mention in contemporary accounts. Their contributions to radical millenarianism, however, are well worth noting. Some, like Hanserd Knollys, accused of antinomian tendencies in New England, and upon his return to England the leader of a Particular Baptist congregation, were swept into Fifth Monarchist activity almost as an extension of their membership in radical congregations. Knollys's signature, along with those of William Kiffin, Henry Jessey, and other baptists, frequently appeared on petitions criticizing Oliver Cromwell's regime and calling for further reformation. And, like New England's Hugh Peter, Knollys often was singled out as one of the main troublemakers among the radical sectarians, even though he never participated in any of the violence initiated by more extreme Fifth Monarchists.[30]

The career of the apothecary Thomas Tillam followed a similar pattern. After a brief stay in New England, he returned to England, was associated briefly with Knollys's congregation, and in 1655 became pastor of a Particular Baptist church in Hexham. As early as 1651, in *The Two Witnesses*, he had made clear his millenarian sentiments, agreeing with prominent Fifth Monarchists like John Rogers that the literal reappearance of Christ on earth was imminent. And Tillam, like Anne Hutchinson, who had based her criticism of New England on God's personal revelations to her, grounded his faith in an extreme spiritism. He admitted to believing that those whom God had singled out to preach the Gospel had had their missions vouchsafed them in "Visions, Dreams, Revelations," and calls "immediately from Heaven." By 1652 Tillam had become a Seventh-Day Baptist and in 1657 he published *The Seventh-Day Sabbath sought out and celebrated*, a reply to a pamphlet by Aspinwall in which Tillam maintained that "the signs of his second coming who is the Lord of the Sabbath are so fairly visible that, although the day and hour be not known, yet doubtless this generation shall not pass, till new Jerusalem's glory shall crown obedient Saints with everlasting Rest."[31] Another baptist, John Clarke of Newport, in England for several years to negotiate a new charter for the colonies in Rhode Island, signed a 1654 Fifth Monarchist document that originated in Jessey's church. As an itinerant preacher in the English countryside always ready to "dispute the points of freewill, and universal redemption, and spiritual baptism, and seeking," he often shared with his listeners his eagerness for the immediate establishment of Christ's earthly kingdom.[32]

Many of those who actively joined the ranks of the radical millenarians came from baptist congregations; their emphasis on purity of worship, always a major concern, easily found expression in the civil sphere. As B. S. Capp and J. F. Maclear have noted, however, the Fifth Monarchists did not draw their membership exclusively from one sect, nor should they themselves be so regarded; theirs was a genuine attempt to unite under Christ's own standard Puritans of all stripes who had become disillusioned with the government's efforts at political and religious reform. The movement attracted not only dissatisfied Seekers like Raphael Swinfield, who joined the Fifth Monarchists after his return from New England because he had himself been "walking *alone*, and very desolate for want of such a society as this," but also committed ministers like Knollys or Kiffin whose rage for ecclesiastical purity carried over into the political arena. Even more telling for our purposes, however, are two New England Puritans, William Aspinwall and Thomas Venner, both of whom, after disenchantment with the New England Puritans' search for a new Gospel order, emerged in London as vociferous spokesmen for the immediate rule of the saints. In addition to illustrating the close connection between New England Puritan ideology and a more radical reading of the prophecies, Aspinwall and Venner demonstrate how dramatically the experience of moving to New England to establish the New Jerusalem influenced their decisions to risk reputation and, in Venner's case, life and limb, for Christ's kingdom.[33]

Aspinwall became one of the most important Fifth Monarchist pamphleteers in London after his return from Boston in 1653. He had been implicated in the Antinomian Controversy and was among those banished to Rhode Island—in his case for his strong defense of John Wheelwright when Wheelwright was tried for sedition on the basis of comments made in his "Fast-Day Sermon." Sealing the testament to his radical credentials, Aspinwall also signed the social covenant composed just prior to the antinomians' exile. For several years afterward he lived at Aquidneck, but there he, like Coddington, who eventually was ousted from the settlement, met with considerable disfavor. He returned to Boston, expeditiously renounced his previous actions, and resumed positions of considerable responsibility. When he found the New England Puritan leaders less interested in church reformation than in the maintenance of their own authority, he returned to Interregnum England.[34]

A Brief Description
OF THE
Fifth Monarchy,
OR
KINGDOME,
That fhortly is to come into the World.

The Monarch, Subjects, Officers, and Lawes thereof, and the furpaffing Glory, Amplitude, Unity, and Peace of that *Kingdome.*

When the Kingdome and Dominion, and the greatneffe of the Kingdome under the whole Heaven fhall be given to the people, the Saints of the Moft high, whofe Kingdome is an everlafting Kingdome, and all Soveraignes fhall ferve and obey him.

And in the Conclufion there is added a Prognoftick of the time when this fifth Kingdome fhall begin.

By WILLIAM ASPINWALL, N. E.

2 Pet. 3. 13. *Neverthelefſe, we according to his promife, look for New Heavens, and a new Earth, wherein dwels righteoufneſſe.*

Pfal. 2. 10, 11, 12. *Be wife therefore O yee Kings : be inſtruᵭed yee Judges of the Earth. Serve the Lord with feare, and rejoyce with trembling. Kiffe the Son leaſt he be angry, and yee perifh from the way, when his wrath is kindled but a little.*

Pfal. 76. 12. *For, he will cut off the Spirit of Princes ; he is terrible to the Kings of the Earth.*

Job 12. 21. *He poureth contempt upon Princes : he is terrible to the Kings of the Earth.* *August y 1ˢᵗ*

LONDON:
Printed by *M. Simmons,* and are to be fold by *Livewell Chapman* at the *Crown* in *Popeshead-Alley.* 1653.

Title page of *A Brief Description of the Fifth Monarchy or Kingdom,* by William Aspinwall (London, 1653). The author had been implicated in the Antinomian Controversy in New England. In this tract he explains and defends his views of scriptural prophecy.

There he wasted little time in promulgating views that he must have kept repressed in Boston for a decade. Within a few months of his arrival in London, he published *A Brief Description of the Fifth Monarchy*, in which he argued that the only laws binding the saints were those legislated by God and recorded in the Bible. He urged earthly rulers—who were to be chosen by all the people from those who were full church members—not to administer laws that mixed earthly expediency with divine wisdom but simply to institute and enforce the divine standards available in Scripture. Drawing on his experience in Massachusetts, where civil rulers were popularly elected from the visibly elect, Aspinwall published within the next three years four more tracts that defined his vision of the Fifth Monarchy. In *Thunder from Heaven* in 1657, he took a moment to address his New England friends directly, reminding them that "if old England Christians who walk in holy fellowship together had had the opportunity which you have had, and still have, they would ere this have set up Jesus Christ as King, not only in their churches but in the commonwealth also." He soon made clear the point of his reminder as well as his reason for leaving Boston. Though God had done "great things" for the colony, now the New Englanders were openly "dishonour[ing] his Son by withdrawing [their] necks from under his Yoak."[35] In Massachusetts Aspinwall had witnessed only a partial rule of the saints; in the political flux of revolutionary England he saw the opportunity to use what he had learned in New England to establish that rule more completely.

In the same pamphlet he paid a debt to an old teacher by chastising the colonists for not having adopted *Moses His Judicials*, which Aspinwall had gotten republished in 1655 by the Fifth Monarchist printer Livewell Chapman. Cotton, Aspinwall reminded his readers, had "collected a whole Sisteme, or body of Laws . . . out of the word of God," all "with a divine stamp upon them," but the stubborn magistrates had refused to acknowledge the imperfection of their own laws and so had rejected his compilation. Aspinwall still believed that the institution of the Fifth Monarchy depended in part on the success of the colonists' venture in New England. He beseeched New Englanders "again to revise what was commended" to them "by that faithful servant of Christ" Mr. Cotton and so to be "persuaded in the Lord to take his Laws" for their own and to make them their "Magna carta," a phrase resonant of Eliot's own advice to England.[36] Having by his own calculation spent "upwards of 22 years" in New England, and writing as one who "still cordially affects the peace of your Jerusalem," Aspinwall urged New Englanders to recall that it still was within their power to become a "Beacon set on a Hil,"

Woodcut, circa 1661, of Thomas Venner, the New England wine cooper who later led Fifth Monarchy uprisings in London.

particularly when such darkness had settled over England in the person and through the policies of Cromwell. In such works as *An Expectation and Application of the Seventh Chapter of Daniel* (1653), *The Work of the Age; or, The Sealed Prophecies of Daniel opened and applied* (1655), and *The Legislative Power is Christs Peculiar Prerogative* (1656), Aspinwall continued to press upon his countrymen a government of the saints and, along with John Rogers and Christopher Feake, eventually emerged as one of the most important theoreticians for those who in the late 1650s could wait no longer to bring God's laws to all men, whether or not they wanted them.[37]

In 1661 one of the most impatient of these "saints," New England's Thomas Venner, led the famous Fifth Monarchist uprising against the restoration of the monarchy. Admitted in 1637 to the church in Salem, where he came into contact with many of Williams's sympathizers, Venner had by 1644 moved to Boston, though retaining his original membership in the Salem church. By the fall of 1651 he found the lure of the English Puritan revolution too difficult to resist; as the Massachusetts General Court later put it, he "went out from us because he was not of us." Soon enough he proved the justness of that remark, for by 1656 he led a radical conventicle in Swan Alley, Coleman Street, in London, where his followers stockpiled arms and quickly acquired a reputation for extreme millenarian views. Venner's radicalism became progressively more violent. In 1657 he and several of his adherents were apprehended and imprisoned for two years for plotting to overthrow the government. As William Hooke, the Taunton, Massachusetts, minister then serving as Cromwell's chaplain, described the abortive conspiracy, "It was carried on by tumultuous, outrageous, disoriented men, pretending to fifth monarchy." "In this design," he continued, "one Vennour, not long since dwelling in your [that is, Winthrop's] Boston, . . . is a principle actor, who being brought before the protector, spoke and behaved himself with [as] great impudence, insolence, pride and railing as . . . you ever heard of." [38]

Upon his release Venner proved wholly incorrigible. Early in 1661 he and a ragtag band of armed followers ran through London's streets shouting "Live King Jesus," and tried vainly to enlist support for their revolution. They murdered those who stood in their way. A few days later they emerged from Cane Wood on another bloody rampage, only to be driven into a building where they finally were captured. One of their number turned out to be John Baker, who had run afoul of the authorities in Boston and, later, in the radical troublespots of Dover and Wells. Venner, too, was captured and, though severely wounded, was kept alive for a traitor's trial. Asked whether or not he was guilty, he immediately invoked his American experience; a contemporary observer noted that Venner thereupon "began an extravagant and bottomless discourse about the fifth monarchy, and his having had a testimony above twenty years in New England." It was not he but Jesus who had led the insurrection; he could not be accused of treason because the true "King was not yet crowned." The Court had little difficulty in sorting through such excuses: they sentenced him to be hanged, then drawn and quartered, and ordered that his head be placed atop one of the city's gates as a warning to others who might wish to question the legitimacy of the newly crowned king. The sentence was carried out to the letter.[39]

"We'll never deny his New England testimony," wrote the compiler of the narrative of Venner's trial, because such troublesome New Englanders had been making old England "smart for too long." Aspinwall, Baker, and Venner were but a few of the ex-colonists who at that time stung England's wounds. Though founded and nurtured by Puritans motivated by a profound millennial expectation, by the early 1650s New England looked to some of its inhabitants more and more conservative, particularly in light of the political gains of the radicals during the years of the Long Parliament. The fact that the New England clergy, though alienated from the presbyterian majority in the Westminster Assembly on questions of church polity, were closely aligned with that majority in their opposition to religious toleration was not lost upon the radicals.[40] Neither was the New Englanders' unwillingness to accept the political ramifications of their belief in the indwelling of Christ or in the equality God promised all believers. English Puritans who had staked their lives and futures on the wager that in America a true revolution of the saints would occur thus had reason to be disenchanted; and, as the decades of the 1640s and 1650s passed without the prophesied pouring out of the seventh vial, some colonists wondered whether their efforts to fulfill prophecy could not be put to better use where the government, as fragmented as it was, seemed genuinely interested in full and holy reformation.

Like other forms of radical Puritanism in New England, radical millenarianism is best understood as a matter of degree. America provided a place in which Puritans tried to hasten the course of the prophecies in Daniel and Revelation, and the over-eager among them who finally abandoned New England only returned to a much greater failure of that dream when Charles II successfully reestablished the preeminence of the Anglican church.[41] For a few decades a wide range of New England Puritans had speculated on the precise time of the Antichrist's fall and Christ's bodily descent to rule the earth, and some among them found it difficult to accept the possibility that God's timetable might well have little to do with theirs. The majority finally accepted this understanding of prophetic Scripture; others, like Venner, rebelled against it. But the larger point is that America, as much as England, harbored its share of those who lived in a faith that convinced them that they would witness the dawn of millennial glory.[42]

The New England theocrats' relative success in convincing their fellow colonists that their society was reformed along scriptural lines mitigated any serious danger from radical millenarians in their communities. Some New Englanders, in their eagerness to see Christ's reign on earth, challenged the interpretation of prophecy offered by Cotton and others, but they never posed as dangerous a threat to the social order as their counterparts in England. The most severe punishment doled out to a radical millenarian in New England was Eliot's chastisement before the General Court, to whose judgment he acquiesced.

Beginning in the summer of 1656, when two Quakers were put ashore at Boston, another species of radical appeared in New England, one that claimed, among other novelties, that Christ *already* had come for the second time, ruling in the hearts of true believers.[43] Unlike other Protestants, who believed that God's revelation to mankind was closed, the Quakers claimed that divine revelation was not yet complete and that they themselves, who could know God's will through their acknowledgment of the Inner Light, were divinely ordained messengers who bore witness to the unfolding truth. Aflame with a desire to convert all people to their beliefs, the Quakers marched on New England as they had on old, unafraid to challenge those who questioned the testimony of their faith.[44] Willing, and often seemingly eager, to become martyrs for their cause, more than any other radicals of the 1650s they threatened to undo three decades of foundation work for the New English Sion.

Further, the Quakers' way was smoothed by members of radical groups we already have examined: in New England prior to 1660 the Quakers' success in winning converts often was directly proportional to the influence of other radical Puritans in those same areas. The Quakers' cardinal doctrine of the Inner Light that shined through all believers could be derived from the spiritists' emphasis on the free grace that liberated a Christian from all "legal" obligations; their concomitant rejection of a "hireling" ministry similarly was related to the anticlericalism of such groups as the General Baptists. Their vigorous attack on the special privileges accorded the ministry linked them to the Levellers and other radicals who stressed equality, religious and political, among all believers. The Quakers' further democratization of sainthood—through their belief that any believer, at any time, could become an instrument through which God revealed his eternal will—allied them to some of the antinomians banished to Rhode Island whose religious organization bore much resemblance to theirs. The very simplicity of Quaker ecclesiology, particularly their rejection of ordinances, indicated the extreme separatism of their position and so linked them to those among the Seekers who similarly had dispensed with the outward forms of the church.[45] By the mid-1650s, under the charismatic leadership of George Fox and, to a lesser degree, James Nayler, the Quakers had melded these and other ideas into a highly resilient faith that strongly appealed to those in England and America dissatisfied with the course of Puritan reform of church and society, and whose appeal was further strengthened by its adherents' fiercely maintained eschatology.

Although there were no self-proclaimed Quakers in New England until 1656, when Mary Fisher and Ann Austin arrived in Boston from the Barbados, once these Quakers and others who shortly thereafter joined them began to proselytize for their faith the Puritan magistrates had a frightening shock of recognition: many of the radicals who had already caused them so much difficulty had broached an ideology similar to that of these new immigrants and so might bolster their ranks. In his diary John Hull described this threat succinctly. Fisher, Austin, and the other Quakers, he wrote, came not only to upbraid the ministry and to "breed in the people contempt of Magistracy" but to "censure and condemn" all who disagreed with them because they thought themselves "the only knowing persons, and their spirit infallible." Thus when Nicholas Upshall of Boston openly sympathized with the plight of Fisher and Austin, who were imprisoned after their books and belongings had been seized and examined, the magistrates had good reason to worry.[46] If the Quakers were as persistent and well-organized as they were reputed to be, the government had to take immediate steps to eliminate any opportunities the recent arrivals might find to fan the smouldering radicalism among the colonists.

Reviewing the history of those who had disturbed the peace of the New England churches, Cotton Mather accurately located one of the first communities in which the ground had been turned for the receipt of the Quakers' vigorous "seed." "I can tell the world," he wrote in 1702, "that the first *Quakers* that ever were in the world, were certain *Fanaticks* here in the Town of *Salem*, who held forth almost all the Fancies and Whimsies which a few years after were broached by them that were so called in *England*, with whom yet none of ours," Mather added, "had the least Communication."[47] Although Mather did not mention whom he had in mind, he undoubtedly was alluding to those individuals who, after the departure of Roger Williams, persisted in their separatist ways, including radical spiritists and baptists. Elizabeth Truslar, brought to court in 1644 to answer for her open advocacy of Gorton's views, strenuously protested that "there was no love" in the Salem church and criticized the Puritans' scarcely veiled dependence on good works. Describing what she regarded as the Reverend Edward Norris's cynicism on this last point, she claimed that he said "that men would change their judgment for a dish of meat."[48] In the late 1650s, when the Quakers had visited Salem and made many converts, the group's meetings, not surprisingly, were held at the home of Truslar's son, Nicholas Phelps.

The persistence of other troublemakers in Salem through the 1640s and 1650s—Mary Oliver and Lady Deborah Moody the most prominent—kept the community's religious life unsettled, and the Quaker missionaries rapidly made converts among those dissatisfied with the Puritan oligarchy. Indeed, by the late fall of 1657 the group of converts had become large enough and well enough organized—it numbered about fifty individuals—to win for one of its number, Joseph Boyce, a position as selectman in the town; and Quakers as far away as the Barbados had heard that in Salem their emissaries would be graciously received. In 1657, for example, writing to his sister in England, Henry Fell related how he had heard that "Some there are . . . convinced who meet in silence at a place called Salem."[49] Though their meetings frequently were raided and their members harassed and punished under the colony's various laws against this "pernicious" sect, by the mid-1660s the Salem group had become the largest and most prominent in the Bay Colony.

The same letter from Fell to his sister Margaret tells of another area whose inhabitants were swayed by the Quakers' message; it too had a history of sectarian difficulties. "In Plymouth Patent," Fell noted, "there is a people not soe ridged as the others at Boston and there are great desires among them after the Truth," a report corroborated a year later by another Quaker, John Rous, who from his prison cell in Boston wrote

Margaret Fell that "Plymouth Patents" was "ripe" for Quaker mission-aries.[50] Salem's church, like Plymouth's, was based on separatist princi-ples and so attracted individuals who, like Williams at an earlier date, were predisposed to challenge the outward forms of church organization.

By the late 1630s Samuell Hickes had questioned the propriety of the instituted forms of worship as well as of the apostolic succession through which Puritan ministers claimed the prerogatives of their office. In 1642 George Willerd was arraigned on similar charges, for publicly announc-ing that any who contributed to the clergy's support were "fooles, and knaves and gulls."[51] By 1651, their population swelled by dissidents from Plymouth and the Bay Colony, the Cape Cod communities of Barn-stable, Sandwich, and Yarmouth showed signs of rejecting the principles of nonseparating congregationalism. William Leverich of Sandwich de-scribed his parishioners as so "transported with their . . . Fancies, to the rejecting of all Churches and Ordinances" that he despaired of ever hav-ing any evangelical success in his community. In 1653 he relinquished his post for a church on Long Island, and within three years of his departure the town was virtually given over to the Quakers.[52]

Sandwich was delivered to this sect by none other than Nicholas Up-shall, who spent the winter there after his attempt to purchase the books carried to New England by Fisher and Austin had brought upon him the displeasure of the Massachusetts General Court. Late in 1656 he was tried at Plymouth for holding private meetings on the sabbath and for slander-ing ordained ministers; with him appeared two women from Sandwich likewise accused of openly abusing the clergy.[53] A year later Ralph Allen, who in 1652 had been charged with "deriding God's word and ordi-nances," was arraigned for allowing the use of his home for religious meetings on the sabbath. When his fellow-townsmen Henry Saunders and Edward Dillingham refused to assist in his arrest and insulted the officer who finally apprehended him, they were brought before the court and admonished for abetting Quakers.[54]

In 1657, with the election of Thomas Prence to the colony's governor-ship, the campaign against this sect intensified. The new governor imme-diately initiated legislation to ensure public support of the ministry, to fine any who harbored Quakers within their domiciles, to jail and deport known members of this sect, and to require the colony's inhabitants to swear an oath of fidelity to the government, an act refused by Quakers, for whom oath-swearing was a sin. By early 1658 the group's stubborn-ness and penchant for martyrdom had become apparent; despite the sentences of banishment and the ensuing lashings, Quaker emissaries kept reappearing in the colony's towns. As James Cudworth, a Scituate militia man, put it in a letter to England, despite all the harshness of the colony's laws against the Quakers, in the Plymouth towns they still had "many meetings and many adherents."[55]

The third area in New England in which the Quakers found inhabitants predisposed to their faith was in the various Rhode Island settlements. As early as 1641, Governor Winthrop noted that at Aquidneck Nicholas Easton, a "very bold, though ignorant" tanner, maintained that "a Christian is united to the essence of God," and that "man hath no power or will in himself, but as he is acted by God," ideas that presaged the Quakers' emphasis on both the believer's ecstatic union with God and the doctrine of the Inner Light.[56] Similar views, probably derived from the same sources, soon were adopted by William Coddington and John Coggeshall, two prominent antinomians banished with Anne Hutchinson; when Upshall joined them in the spring of 1657, both these men (as well as Easton) converted to Quakerism. Anne Hutchinson's close friend Mary Dyer also eagerly embraced the Quakers' message; in 1660 she was hanged in Boston, a martyr for her cause.[57]

Too little is known of these Rhode Islanders' opinions to trace in detail their journey from John Cotton's church to Quaker meetings in Rhode Island; but such is not the case with Samuel Gorton, who in 1656 openly announced his support for the Quakers by offering asylum to several members of the sect then imprisoned in Boston.[58] For many years he had anticipated the Quakers' objections to the Puritan churches, even as he masked his doctrine of radical spiritism "under his Lambe-skin coate of *simplicity* and *peace*." In 1641 Plymouth's Edward Winslow wrote Winthrop about Gorton's obstreperous behavior in Providence, where in the sermons he preached "thrice a weake" he frequently condemned "all our churches and church ordinances, Sabbath, etc."; and in 1648 the author of *Good News from New-England* noted that for years Gorton had "rag[ed] and rail[ed] against all magistrates and general Courts, as murtherers, absolving from their obedience all such as would follow this opinion." Even more telling, when Gorton visited England between 1644 and 1648 and preached in Thomas Lamb's well-known conventicle, eyewitness Thomas Underhill, who later reported the fact in his *Hell Broke Loose* (1660), heard this New Englander affirm that "Baptisme, Lords, Chaplains, Ruling Elders, &c." were "carnal Ordinance[s], and from the Devil." Underhill wrote his pamphlet after a decade of trouble with

Nayler, Fox, and other Quakers and so was sensitive to ideas even re-
motely similar to theirs, but his conclusion about Gorton's opinions still
is revealing. Anyone could see, he told his readers, "what plain Quakerisme these things are."[59]

Underhill provided other evidence of Gorton's purported Quakerism,
from Samuel Rutherford's *Survey of the Spirituall Antichrist* (1647); from
Rutherford Underhill learned that the "Gortonians" believed "that whatever it is the Saints utter in point of Religion, must be the voice of the son
of God" and, concomitantly, "that Christ reveals his will in no voice, but
the voice of the Spirit in the Saints"—notions that directly foreshadowed
the Quakers' cardinal principles.[60] Gorton's four years spent at the center
of England's radical underground, then, may have had a significant impact on the subsequent religious history of New England, for his activities at Lamb's church and elsewhere had placed him in the same ideological crucible from which eventually was poured the spiritual amalgam of
Quakerism. The practice of lay exhorting, the strident anticlericalism
and anti-intellectualism, a belief in the indwelling of the Holy Spirit and
its supremacy over Scriptural law—all these "Quaker" ideas had been
broached in Lamb's church and other "Anabaptist" meetingplaces where
Gorton was known to have visited, and the books that he published after
his return to America offer plentiful evidence of his continuing interest in
the same ideas that had so moved the early Friends.[61]

Gorton never formally became a Quaker, but, having drunk deeply of
the spirit of toleration in England, upon his return to the New World he
did not neglect the sufferings of people persecuted for beliefs that flowed
from the same spiritual fountain as his own, hence his offer to aid the
Quakers imprisoned in Boston and his hospitality to members of the
group who later visited Rhode Island. Humphrey Norton, in his *New
Englands Ensigne* of 1659, reported that in Rhode Island he and other
Quakers had been "well received" by "such as were by the English accounted the basest of men," and who had been "barbarously banished" to
Rhode Island. While Coddington, Coggeshall, and Easton—all of whom
eventually became Quakers—obviously were instrumental in introduc-
ing the Quaker religion to this area and thus must have been among the
Quaker sympathizers Norton had in mind, none had undergone an in-
doctrination into religious radicalism comparable to Gorton's. By 1660
Rhode Island, of all the New England colonies, harbored the largest population of Friends. Gorton prepared the ground for such spiritual "seed."
Even though when George Fox visited Rhode Island in 1670 and spent

some time with Gorton, this prominent Quaker, by one report, displayed himself "a mere babe" in theology compared to his host, Gorton embraced a true spiritual brother.[62]

In the Massachusetts Bay Colony proper, Fisher and Austin quickly had been followed by other Quaker missionaries from England. Only days after these two women had been deported, eight other Quakers, led by Christopher Holder, were apprehended and imprisoned for eleven weeks. To these individuals Gorton had extended his invitation to Warwick, but soon they too were put aboard a ship bound for England. Anticipating a further influx of this sect, the General Court passed stringent laws to punish any who aided or abetted its members; any Quakers who still made their way into the colony were to be imprisoned and whipped; and then banished. But the next year Holder and another band of followers again came to New England. Finding succor in the Rhode Island colonies (particularly in Newport) and a good response to their gospel in some of the Plymouth Colony towns, they once more invaded the Bay Colony. Holder and John Copeland ventured to Salem, were apprehended for their disruption of a church meeting, and thereupon were brought to Boston, where they were flogged and then jailed for two weeks. Cassandra Southwick, who had invited the two to Salem, was fined and imprisoned for seven weeks for her hospitality to this outlawed sect.[63]

Seemingly unable to stem the Quaker invasion, the Bay Colony soon increased the penalties against them. In October 1657 the statute forbidding the entertainment of Quakers was made more severe, and any male member who returned to the colony after having been banished was to have his ear cropped. If he persisted in his stubbornness and returned yet again, the other ear was to be mutilated, and a third offense would call for boring his tongue with a hot iron. Female Quakers were to be whipped initially, with the third offense punishable in the same way as for the men. The following year Holder and Copeland each lost an ear, and the magistrates, astonished that all measures against the group had failed to prevent their proliferation, finally instituted the death penalty for those who returned after banishment. Thus, on 27 October 1659 William Robinson and Marmaduke Stephenson met their deaths by hanging. Within a year so too did William Leddra and Mary Dyer, Anne Hutchinson's close friend. The carnage was stopped only by the intercession of Charles II himself. Under pressure from English members of the Society of Friends, he issued an order for the colonists to revoke their severe laws against the group.[64]

For conservative Puritans the arrival of the Friends had confirmed their worst fears about the final tendency of radical spiritism. The Quakers' belief that "all men ought to attend to the Light within them to be the Rule of their Lives and Actions"; their claim that "the holy Scriptures were not for the inlightening of man, nor a settled and permanent Rule of Life"; their faith that "an absolute Perfection in Holiness or Grace is attainable in this life"—all undermined the Puritans' elaborately constructed Bible Commonwealth and threatened New England with the religious anarchy that in England eventually led to the reinstatement of Anglicanism as the nation's official faith.[65] The rapid success of the Quaker missionaries in many New England communities, as well as the psychological effect of their conversion of such prominent colonists as Isaac Robinson, John Robinson's son, and Samuel Winthrop, one of Governor Winthrop's sons, indicated to the Puritans that they could not be too diligent in their attempts to maintain the divine sanction accorded the New England Way, nor too harsh in their repression of error when it was openly voiced.[66]

Because the Quakers believed that God walked the earth with his true believers and asked of them the faith to bring the entire world under his reign, they, like the Fifth Monarchists, grew impatient with the slow progress hitherto made by Puritans toward the realization of God's kingdom on earth. And, for all their interest in millennial speculation, the New England Puritans simply refused to believe what the Quakers so confidently announced—that the new dispensation promised by God indeed had arrived, in the hearts of the faithful, who no longer needed scriptural rules to perfect their faith. There is a certain parabolic quality, then, in the story of Isaac Robinson, who was sent by the Plymouth General Court to a Quaker meeting to "reduce" the Quakers from "the error of their ways," for it was shortly thereafter that he embraced their faith and founded a Quaker meeting at Falmouth on Cape Cod.[67]

No doubt there were those among the Puritans who believed that the young Robinson only had brought his father's ideas to their logical conclusion, for the implications of separatist doctrine as taught by the elder Robinson at Leyden simply could not, to use one of the Puritans' favorite phrases, be hidden under a bushel. Its light shone with such brightness on some individuals that they accepted the justness of the Friends' separation from any and all dogma. The Quakers were the legitimate, if seemingly reprobate, offspring of the Pilgrim Fathers, as ready to risk danger for their faith as any of the *Mayflower*'s passengers. They too wanted "reformation without tarrying" and accused the New England Puritans of taking the wide road to hell. In various important ways they forced upon their sworn enemies behavior that by the 1660s made the Puritans accept, if not approve of, those among them who spoke and acted from an acknowledgment of God dwelling within them.

PART II

MEETING THE RADICAL CHALLENGE

PURITAN IDEOLOGY:

INHERENT

RADICALISM

The publication in 1644 of John Winthrop's *A Short Story of the Rise, reigne, and ruine of the Antinomians, Familists & Libertines* was meant to reassure English Puritans of the resiliency of the Congregational Way in the face of challenges from more extreme radical groups, but appearing as it did during the meetings of the Westminster Assembly, the governor's account of the Antinomian Controversy quickly was seized on by zealous presbyterians for use against the very Independents whose cause it was intended to serve. Robert Baillie's response was typical. In his 1645 *Dissuasive from the Errours of the Time* he made much of the Hutchinsonians' doctrinal aberrations and concluded his recitation of their opinions with the following rhetorical question. If "all this and more," Baillie asked, "we read of the Independents in *New-England*, in one short Narration of two or three yeers accidents among them," "what if we had their full History from any fruitful hand?" If some disgruntled colonist took it upon himself to portray accurately and completely New England's religious development, Baillie was convinced, "many more mysteries would be brought to light, which are now hid in darknesse."[1]

Baillie eagerly pounced on Roger Williams's reports of the Gortonists and other New England radicals, but he never had the full history he sought; his supposition concerning the widespread presence of such radicals was nonetheless, in general, correct. New England was so rank a breeding place for religious radicalism, as Baillie's friend Thomas Edwards put it, because "all Errors take Sanctuary in Independency, flie there and are safe, as the Chickens under the wing of the Hen." Within the very substance of nonseparating congregationalism there was an inherent radicalism that generated a diversity of beliefs. In New England this tendency was all the more dangerous because, in contrast to the situation in England, there was little organized opposition here to the Congregational Way. The New England Puritans had constructed and solidly reinforced a system that incorporated several elements which, interpreted with ever so slight a shift in emphasis, could combine with an individual's social and/or political unrest to form the religious radicalism of an Anne Hutchinson, a Samuel Gorton, or an Obadiah Holmes. Independency may well have been what its proponents argued, a fair copy of the order of the true apostolic churches, but it was formed of ideological components that had to be held in very delicate balance if they were not to initiate the kinds of radical speculation the magistrates so feared. Thus, while the New England Puritans did not openly encourage radical sectarians to settle among them, they did—to extend Edwards's metaphor—resemble a sitting hen whose chicks had more than a little in common with some radicals who easily could dash under her wing with the legitimate brood.[2]

The New England Puritans attempted to guard themselves against such radical religious and political ideas through constant adjustments to the ecclesiology and doctrine that defined the New England Way, increasingly inflexible responses to English Puritan demands that they become more tolerant of sincere Christian dissenters, and a gradual assumption of a corporate identity through which, by 1660, they had sharply distinguished themselves from their English brethren and essentially had defused the radicals' threats. In New England the thirty years prior to the Restoration were marked by the colonists' incessant attempts to absorb or neutralize the radicals' criticism of their church state, a criticism that was all the more difficult to answer because in part it was derived from the premises of the very congregationalism on which the colony's identity was based. New England Puritanism survived as a viable—indeed, a compelling—ideology because of, not in spite of, the nature of these responses to the radicals' challenges. New England did not become the veritable New Jerusalem for which its leaders prayed, but the radicals' willingness to read the implications of the New England Way more fully than many of its clerical architects and the New England Puritans' masterful co-optation of those readings brought the colonies, if not to the gates of an earthly paradise, then at least to a position enviable, in the seventeenth century, for its social and political stability.

The radicalism inherent in New England congregationalism was most evident in three areas—the colonists' conception of a gathered or covenanted church of "visible saints," their complex understanding of the relation of justification to sanctification, and the peculiar nature of their chiliasm, that is, their way of interpreting scriptural prophecy—each of which readily lent itself to varied interpretations that depended on an individual's understanding of the scriptural passages that announced and supported it. Because even in its most conservative—that is, presbyterian—manifestation Puritanism was a radical movement, the New Englanders' treatment of dissenters seems ironic. By their attempt to institutionalize what in 1630 was viewed by many English Puritans as itself a radical alternative to the socio-religious order, the colonists established what other Puritans regarded as a conservative church state. To form a theocracy was, in effect, to call a halt to an ongoing revolution that drew most of its support from a highly pietistic laity, some of whom were ready and eager to follow the logic of their own understanding of Scripture much farther than those who rested at the way-post of nonseparating congregationalism. A radically conservative society, New England was faced with the difficult task of maintaining its inhabitants' spiritual fervor even as it sought to channel that enthusiasm into socially acceptable streams.[3]

Since Perry Miller's study *Orthodoxy in Massachusetts*, published in 1933, scholars of American Puritanism, like the colonists themselves, have had to wrestle with the internal logic of the New Englanders' nonseparating congregationalism, which Miller isolated as the unique feature of their ecclesiology. Because the group of ministers who accompanied the Great Migration to Boston had been influenced more by Henry Jacob, William Ames, and William Bradshaw than by Robert Browne and Henry Barrow, upon their arrival in Massachusetts they organized their churches in what later was called a "congregational" manner, with people in each community covenanting to form their individual congregation, yet maintained that they still were members in good standing of the Church of England.[4] Men like Richard Mather, John Cotton, Thomas Hooker, and George Phillips believed that the Anglican church, with its hierarchy of regional and national officers, had to be replaced by a multitude of individual congregations, each overseeing its own affairs, even to the selection and ordination of its minister, and exercising church discipline on its delinquent members. But always, as Miller reminds us, the colonists sought to avoid the charge of separation by their insistence that their withdrawal, first to Holland and later to New England, was not an act of separation but of survival. They considered themselves a saving remnant of the English church who had been forced to move to safer locales to preserve intact the proper forms of church worship. To them, the English church was not the hopelessly corrupt body the separatists found it, for its purification depended only on the removal of the hierarchical structure that prevented its members from governing themselves as Scripture dictated. As John Cotton put it in one of his polemics against Roger Williams, nonseparating congregationalists believed that though the English churches obviously had fallen into the hands of the Antichrist's vice-regents, to make them "and their Ministers, and their Worship, and their Professors, either nullities, or Anti-christian, is a witnesse not onely beyond the truth, but against the Truth of the Lord Jesus."[5]

From the outset critics of the nonseparating congregationalists charged them with mere casuistry and argued that their ecclesiastical position was no less schismatic than that of the Brownists, who numbered among their offspring some of the Plymouth and Salem settlers. It was obvious to all, their various opponents claimed, that nonseparating congregationalists had adopted the separatists' church discipline, and, most important, their beliefs in the autonomy of individual congregations and the restriction of full church membership to those who had covenanted to form a new church. Their purported allegiance to the King and to the principle of national uniformity in religious affairs was specious. Nor did such assessments come only from Anglican bishops and presbyterian moderates. Even John Canne, one of the most influential separatists of the 1630s, used the works of Ames and Bradshaw to buttress his claim that Puritanism led logically to full separation.[6] The founders of Massachusetts, then, had to defend a system whose validity seemed framed on the gossamer threads of their clergy's rationalizations. Little wonder that the Bay Colony's first decade was given over to attempts to strengthen the logic on which the polity was based.

We already have seen how the Salem church was disturbed by Samuel Skelton's espousal of a near-separatist polity; for thirty years after his ministry the town was troubled by radical Puritans for whom the nonseparating congregationalism of Hugh Peter and Edward Norris proved inadequate to nurture their piety.[7] But often in the 1630s the advocates of this system were forced to rethink some of its premises, in England debated on the level of theory but in the New World tested by experience. Consider, for example, one ecclesiastical point, a New England minister's understanding of his former position in the Church of England. Good congregational theory (as it was practiced, for example, by the separatists in Holland) dictated that, though the minister's calling ultimately was derived from God, it was ratified only by a particular, covenanted congregation and was not transferable. If a minister moved to another church he no longer held an office until his election was ratified anew. Early in the colony's history, however, many ministers still were unsure about how strictly this rule was to be interpreted, particularly with regard to their original ordination in the Church of England.[8]

In 1630, George Phillips, a staunch congregationalist, consented to become Watertown's minister only if his congregation clearly understood that the "calling which he had received from the prelates in England" was null and void, a point on which he fully agreed with the separatists. But in the very same year in Charlestown John Wilson was ordained with the express understanding that the ceremony was only "a sign of election and confirmation" of his office and not an indication that he had renounced the "ministry he received in England."[9] The point may seem minor, but it was not that far, for example, from Phillips's position to Roger Williams's reason for refusing the offer to minister to Boston's church in Wilson's absence: that "he durst not officiate to an unseparated people." If a minister's ordination at the hands of a bishop were a nullity, what kept Phillips's congregation from rethinking other links to the Church of England, as Richard Browne later did?[10] The logic of nonseparating congregationalism may have been clear to ministers who lived in a world of ecclesiastical nuances, but to the laity, who expected general agreement on such matters, such discrepancies were the cause, if not for alarm, then for genuine confusion.

Even the estimable John Cotton was not immune to such problems, as is proved by his about-face regarding the discipline practiced in the Salem church. Cotton had known Skelton before Skelton's departure for New England and had tried to impress upon him the right guaranteed to any member of a true reformed church (even if by circumstance he still was nominally in the Church of England) to commune with covenanted churches, whether or not he was a member of a particular congregation. But Skelton was not persuaded by the logic of nonseparating congregationalism. He denied to William Coddington, who had arrived in the colony with Winthrop's fleet, the right of baptism for his newborn child because Coddington had neither become a member of the Salem church nor renounced his membership in the Church of England. When Cotton, still in England and communing with Puritans who expediently remained in the established church, received word of this, he sent Skelton a firm letter in which he sought to make clear to the Salem minister the dangerous tendency of such actions.[11]

Six years later, however, after his first skirmish with Skelton's friend Williams over *his* separatism, Cotton journeyed to Salem in an attempt to soothe the feelings of those who sought to install Williams in the Salem church but were prevented from so doing by the intervention of the General Court. In what must have come as a considerable surprise to his auditors, Cotton took that opportunity to "confess" that, after all, Skelton had been correct about the nature of the church covenant and asked the Salem church to regard what he earlier had written to their minister as an error in judgment. The reason for Cotton's confusion on this matter, and for his subsequent admission of error, no doubt was linked to the position of the Boston church, which upon his arrival in 1633 he found to concur with other churches in the colony regarding their refusal to commune with recent arrivals from England until such had joined a particular congregation, the very point of discipline about which he had communicated his displeasure to Skelton three years earlier. Cotton's subsequent ordination as Wilson's colleague rapidly indoctrinated him into a church order which in England he had not been willing to sanction but which, after viewing its operation in New England and searching the scriptures for more light on the question, he finally accepted.[12]

Cotton was a crafty pragmatist, and his willingness to offer the Salem church his confession of error regarding the nature of the covenant, which he came to understand as created by the faith of those who publicly confederated with other of the "seed" of Abraham, provides an early example in New England of what became the clergy's primary manner of meeting the challenge of more radical Puritans. For in his Salem sermon Cotton did more than admit his own error. By adding the weight of his reputation to Skelton's notion of congregationalism, which, after all, never had become out-and-out separatism and which, more important, had been adopted by other Massachusetts churches founded soon thereafter, Cotton sought to persuade the colonists to go no further than had Skelton in 1630.[13]

The fact of the matter was that by the mid-1630s the Salem church, under the influence if not the actual ministry of Williams, had indeed drifted toward a more radically separatist position. Among other things, Williams had objected to the ministerial meetings called to discuss ecclesiastical difficulties in Lynn and Weymouth because he believed that such gatherings constituted an abuse of congregational prerogative. He also had urged that the regenerate should separate as completely as possible from the unregenerate, to the extent that the latter should not administer civil oaths to the saints. In 1635, when several Salem residents, led by John Endecott, cut the cross from the English flag because it symbolized the Church of Rome, Cotton knew that he had to act. Thus his sermon in Salem, which was meant, as Larzer Ziff has written, "to check the zealous pace of reform at Salem so that Boston, if it did not become more independent, at least consolidated the position it now held rather than becoming even more closely separatist."[14]

By 1636, after only three years in Massachusetts, Cotton saw the necessity of permanently altering his own ecclesiastical position to prevent more radical elements of society from gaining power. He was willing to modify his understanding of church reformation in a more radical direction if through his action he persuaded others to follow him just so far *and no farther*; and the ploy, if we may so term it, worked. Soon after Williams's departure for the Rhode Island settlements in 1635, most of the Salemites consented to sit under the ministry of Hugh Peter, whose congregationalism was within the bounds outlined by Cotton. The structure of Cotton's argument—he granted the importance of an individual's covenant with a particular congregation while he still defended the existence of a more over-arching covenant of grace which some might hold even if they still were members of uncovenanted churches—was utilized in the formation of most of the subsequent churches in the colony.[15] Though the issue of separatism emerged again in slightly different form during the Antinomian Controversy and informed the dissent of such radical spiritists as the Gortonists, Cotton's *imprimatur* essentially set the rules for any future debate over the nature of the church covenant, particularly in the face of English Puritan criticism of it. That this was done at the expense of radical separatists displays Cotton's perspicacity regarding how the New England Way could best be institutionalized even as some members of the colony clamored for further reformation.

During the 1630s the very nature of membership in the covenanted congregation was an even thornier issue. Settling as they did three thousand miles from the bishops, the New England Puritans, for all their guilt and confusion over their relation to the Church of England, had de facto made separation an academic question. But once having used their freedom to organize their churches on the congregational order, they had to come to some agreement on *how* such churches were to be formed. It was here, both in their development of the notion of "visible sainthood" as a prerequisite for full church membership and in their use of the church covenant as a tool for social control, that the New England Puritans displayed a genius for confining revolutionary ideology within the boundaries of a conservative socio-political ethic.

As Edmund Morgan has shown, the decision to require prospective church members to describe the work of grace upon their souls—that is, to demonstrate that they were "visible saints"—was made sometime between 1633 and 1635; before that time an individual's consent to the church covenant was all that was necessary for his entry into church fellowship. By 1635, however, this new point of discipline appears to have met with general acceptance, and Morgan speculates that the narration of saving faith might have been an outgrowth of the lay prophesying that occurred in Cotton's church during an extensive religious revival in 1634. In any event, the requirement was firmly in place by the time Thomas Shepard and his co-settlers in Newtown (later Cambridge) asked the magistrates' and ministers' advice regarding the proper manner of organizing a new church in that community. They were told that "such as were to join should make confession of their faith, and declare what work of grace the Lord had wrought in them"; only after this would the church covenant be read and assented to.[16]

More important, by the following year this test of visible sainthood already was being used in a *conservative* way. At the attempted formation of a church in Dorchester, the assembled ministers, apparently led by Shepard, refused to approve the organization of Richard Mather's church because when the prospective members proceeded "to manifest the work of God's grace in themselves" they displayed tendencies toward both antinomianism and Arminianism. A few months later Mather made another attempt to organize his church, presumably after a more careful examination of his parishioners, and this time the candidates met with the colony's approval. But, as Morgan points out, it is very likely that the events in Dorchester (as well as the colony's earlier difficulties in Lynn with Stephen Batchelor and the Company of the *Plough*), had much to do with the General Court's enactment that same year of a law that required any people who sought to form a new church in the colony first "to acquaint the magistrates and the leders of the greater parte of the churches in this jurisdiction, with their intencions" and to gain their "approbacion." Moreover, the Court ordered that only those who were members of such approved churches could be "admitted to the freedome of this commonwealthe."[17]

However the requirement of visible sainthood had originated, by 1636 it was in place as one of the pillars of the ecclesiastical state then under construction in Massachusetts; even the recalcitrant Salem townsmen consented to a new covenant that essentially eliminated their separatism and instituted the new test for church membership.[18] Nothing like it ever had been demanded in such Independent congregations as Jacob's; in these churches personal assent to a confession of faith and to a church covenant constituted the sole requirement for full membership privileges. Further, while among the early radical spiritists a profoundly mystical experience often formed the basis for an individual's criticism of the established church, in no conventicle was the experience examined in the way it had been by Shepard and the other ministers at Dorchester. The New England Puritans had taken the radical step of demanding of their citizens proof that the mark of God's election was upon them, and only after an individual had convinced other saints of this fact could he be granted other religious and political privileges. As Stephen Foster has put it, "Not even the Levellers had so radical a conception of society, if the word *radical* is not taken as synonomous with *democratic*," for by defining citizenship by visible sainthood the New England Puritans took a large step toward the establishment of what they believed to be Christ's earthly kingdom.[19]

The institution of this requirement for church membership took place within the context of the colony's difficulties with an openly separatist element in their population. Perhaps more important, it also must be viewed against some of the ministers' and magistrates' fears that among the great numbers of emigrants arriving in the colony each year, some, as Thomas Weld later put it, came "*full fraught with unsound and loose opinions*" and "*after a time, began to open their packs, and freely vent their wares to any that would be their customers*"—fears that found expression in the 1637 law passed by the General Court regarding new arrivals in Massachusetts.[20] By imposing a test for church membership (and restricting the right of full citizenship to those who met it), the ministers were not only able to keep from their churches those whose religious experience seemed erroneous or extravagant—some of Mather's parishioners, for example, had based their faith upon "dreams and ravishes of spirit by fits," others on "duties and performances"—but also to encourage and preserve in their population the heightened piety that resulted from an acknowledgment that the spirit of God had worked upon their souls. The experience of grace, which had sustained so many Puritans during their difficult years in England but which could so easily be understood as the radical spiritists conceived it, was legitimized, but only within limits established by those with a vested interest in a definition of visible sainthood that did not run to radical extremes. In Massachusetts and Connecticut, then, religious ecstasy was allowed as long as it did not end in utter subjectivism; it was, after all, a *social* bond into which the member entered when he covenanted with a church.

Not that there was necessarily any insidious collusion on the part of Massachusetts clergy who began to demand a narration of grace from prospective members of their churches. But their institutionalization of this radical requirement and, subsequently, their conservative interpretation of it were attempts, akin to Cotton's sermon before the Salem church around the same time, to control Puritanism's revolutionary thrust for what they believed to be the good of their whole society. Even Winthrop himself, who was viewed by some ministers as inclined to too liberal an interpretation of the work of the Holy Spirit, agreed that the churches had to be "very carefull in admission of members," particularly because "there be some of these newe opinions that will simula[t]e and dissimula[t]e beyond expectation, to gett into our churches"; to his mind such care brought the highest possible reward. "He that in shooting aimeth at the top of a mountain," his minister Cotton wrote, "though he do not always reach it, yet he shall shoot higher, then he that aimeth at a molehill; so they that aime at receiving no church members into the Church, but such as in judgement of charity are Saints, . . . they shall keep their Churches more pure, then they that indifferently accept carnall persons, and grosse hipocrates. . . ."[21] Cotton and other ministers wanted just that: to make their churches more pure than any since the Apostles' times. They would try to achieve this goal through their demand that each church member report a heightened religious experience that conformed to their understanding, not to the individual's, of what saving faith really was.

The rapid spread of the notion of visible sainthood as a prerequisite for church membership was not accompanied by the unequivocal consent of all members of the colony, for both conservative and radical elements in Massachusetts frequently questioned the propriety of the requirement on both scriptural and practical grounds. Thomas Parker and James Noyes, for example, who had settled with their flock in Newbury, made no effort to disguise their support for a polity based on more inclusive church fellowship; they constantly reminded the other ministers that church membership should be open to all who resided in a certain geographical area and criticized the stringent rules applied to prospective church members. By 1643 their objections had become so disconcerting that a synod was called to discuss their and other ministers' support for wider church membership; this ministerial meeting was made all the more significant by the fact that the Westminster Assembly had just been called to discuss this same issue.[22]

Peter Hobart, Hingham's minister, also advocated presbyterian discipline and in 1646 lent support to the petition of Robert Childe, William Vassal, and others, who demanded an end to the restrictive membership requirements in the colony that infringed on their rights as freeborn Englishmen. From the Connecticut Valley at Springfield, William Pynchon wrote Winthrop to suggest that the petitioners' argument was not far off the mark. And in Dover, Scituate, Andover, and, later, Haverhill there was similar ecclesiastical discontent; presumably within these townships were many people like Salem's Mary Oliver, who, among other of her indiscretions, announced that "all that dwell in the same town, and will profess their faith in Christ Jesus, ought to be received to the sacraments there."[23]

More disturbing to the clergy, even some who called themselves congregationalists questioned the newly imposed test of sainthood. There is tantalizing contemporary evidence that Thomas Hooker's departure for the Connecticut Valley in 1635 was prompted in part by his disgust at the Bay Colony's institution of the requirement. In 1643 Robert Stansby broached this subject in a letter to Wilson when he reported that in England people had heard that in the colonies "there is great division in judgment in matter of religion amongst good ministers and people, which moved Mr. Hoker to remove." In England, Stansby continued, rumor had it that the colony was "so strict in admission of members" to their churches "that more than one halfe are out of your church in all your congregations"; more significantly, Stansby had a firsthand report "that Mr. Hoker before he went away preached against" this situation. Indeed, the Connecticut Valley seemed a veritable refuge for those who were disenchanted with the course of church reformation in Massachusetts. Upon his arrival in the colony, for example, Henry Vane seriously considered settling in the Valley. John Warham, who accompanied Hooker on his move, had been tutored in the moderate Puritanism of John White of Dorchester; William Pynchon later incurred the colony's wrath for the publication of his own latitudinarian ideas; and as early as 1639 Ephraim Huit, settled at Windsor, had been criticized by Ezekiel Rogers as among those who "have bene bold to vent Arminian and like foule errours, and then goe their way unquestioned, leaving an infectious savour behinde them." [24]

Not that these or other colonists actually wished to adopt the Scottish Presbyterian platform of discipline, a fact brought out in a letter written to John Wilson by William Vassal in 1643, at the height of the difficulties in Scituate between the pro- and anti-Chauncy factions. "I conceive the difference [between the groups]," Vassal wrote, "to be more in words than in substance, and not that we differ much in the main." "Those that know us," he continued, "fear not our inclining to the bishops, or to receiving profane persons to the sacraments." Rather, he and his party's wish was "that some care were taken to instruct all in religion by catechising, that we might win more to God and fit them for his ordinances." If one accepts a recent estimate that by around 1643 only 1,700 of 20,000 residents of Massachusetts had been admitted to freemanship, and this at a time when events in England promised more and more political power to the rank-and-file Puritans, the demands for wider church membership in Massachusetts assume more urgency. New England congregationalists may have extended the revolution of the saints in an unprecedented manner, but it was all too easy for individuals to feel that sainthood should be even less restrictively defined. [25]

New England Puritans managed to keep the presbyterians' retreat from splintering the colony in any significant way, though the highly visible disagreements among the clergy must have had an important psychological effect on the colonists. Still, with the publication of the Cambridge Platform in 1648, in which few concessions were made to the latitudinarians in their midst, the Puritans clearly announced their ongoing support for the strict membership requirement. [26] More difficult to control were objections of a very different kind, from those who maintained that, rather than forming the basis for a godly commonwealth, the test for visible sainthood was an unscriptural ordinance that encouraged "legalism" and hypocrisy. Such charges were particularly prevalent in the 1640s as ministers realized that membership in their churches was dwindling. Seeking to keep their membership roles filled without radically altering their notion of the covenant, they began to modify the membership requirement. At the synod called in 1643 to resolve the difficulties with Parker and Noyes in the Newbury church, the assembly recommended that more charity be used in deciding who became a church member and even conceded that some individuals, "though they are not always able to make large and particular relations of the work and doctrine of Faith," yet who did not "live in the commission of any known sin, or the neglect of any known duty," might be fit for membership. In the 1640s and 1650s, in response to such accommodations, the radical spiritists, against whom the membership requirement earlier had been imposed, attacked the Puritans for their undue reliance on "ordinances."[27]

Samuel Gorton's indictment in *Simplicities Defence against Seven-Headed Policy* (1646) indicates the substance of these objections. Describing his reason for so quickly leaving Massachusetts after his arrival in 1636, Gorton noted that he and others had "plainly" perceived "that the scope of their [the Bay Puritans'] doctrine was bent to maintain that outward form of worship which they had erected to themselves, tending only to the outward carriage of one man to another." Because he found "no ground or warrant for such an order in the Church," Gorton continued, "to bind men's consciences unto as they had established amongst them," he decided to set out for Plymouth, where the separatists were not such sticklers regarding church membership.[28] Gorton's criticism was repeated in the attacks by the Hutchinsonians, who objected to the "legalism" espoused by all the colony's ministers save Cotton; but even more telling was the clergy's own acknowledgment that the requirement of a narration of saving faith might be perverted to purposes quite different from those for which it had been intended. Some colonists essentially counterfeited their experiences to meet the ministers' expectations.

Concord's Peter Bulkeley, commenting on the shallowness of the colonists' faith, lamented that "Some rest in outward Reformation of grosse sins." "They make clean the outside of the cup," he wrote, "that they may seeme cleane before men; but they harbour many corrupt lusts within, which they doe not seek to cast forth. . . ." As long as things went their way, such people were "for Christ, for Religion, for Gospel, and for Ordinances," but "if the state of things and times should change," so, too, would they, "to be either enemies or Neuters." Bulkeley's friend Shepard, one of the major architects of the Congregational Way, sadly concurred. "This, if I may have leave to speak plainly, is the great sin, one of them, of New England," he wrote. "Men come over hither for ordinances, and when they have them, neglect them." "New England's peace and plenty of means breeds strange security," he continued, for "Here are no sour herbs to make the lamb sweet." John Josselyn, who made two separate trips to the colony and spoke with some degree of objectivity, was even more severe. Some of the colonists, he reported, "are of a *Linsiewoolsie* disposition . . . all like *Aethiopians* white in the teeth only."[29]

It was difficult for the clergy to acknowledge that what they had instituted to encourage vital piety instead brought deceit and formalism, but in the heightened atmosphere of the 1630s their actions had seemed necessary and proper to prevent their parishioners from, as Shepard put it in his election sermon of 1638, being led "like birds by glasses & larkes by lures" with the "golden pretences which Innovators ever have."[30] No matter what the subsequent history of the idea of visible sainthood, which by the 1650s had forced the colonists to redefine their understanding of the nature of baptism and, by extension, of the entire covenantal scheme, the notion had served the colony well through its earlier years. Even though by the 1640s, as Darrett Rutman has noted, there had been a significant shift in the New England churches from an emphasis on visible sainthood per se to the idea of the *church* of visible saints—that is, to the obligations of the covenanted group of believers toward the society at large—in the previous decade, when the whole notion of "sainthood" was hotly debated and easily misconstrued, New England Puritans had lit upon an ingenious way to permit their citizens the excitement that came in closing with Christ, while at the same time insuring that such fervor did not become anarchical.[31] Attacked by both latitudinarians and more radical Puritans, for three decades the concept of visible sainthood testified to the clergy's ability to use an individual's most private experiences for a larger social purpose.

If visible sainthood was the ecclesiastical point in which the inherent radicalism of New England Puritanism was most apparent, in the realm of doctrine it was most visible, and dangerous, in the Puritans' understanding of the relation of justification to sanctification; more specifically, in their belief that the imputation of Christ's righteousness to man (which depended on faith, not works) was a recognizable experience that preceded the progressive improvement of an individual's behavior in obedience to God and so was the efficient cause of it. Because, almost to a man, the New England clergy agreed on the primacy of the moment of justification and through their support of the concept of visible sainthood encouraged the belief that this instant was experientially ascertainable, it was all the more difficult for them to discipline those in the colony who, under the impression that they simply were further unravelling the logic of such mysteries, came perilously close to (and in some cases crossed the line into) radical spiritism.[32] The Puritans, particularly in the aftermath of the Antinomian Controversy, recognized that they had to refine what William K. B. Stoever has called the "theological dialectic of nature and grace" in conversion; still, they had to do so in a way that allowed for human initiative, even as they disclaimed the final efficacy of any such endeavor in the face of God's irresistible will.[33] This was no mean task and, as their defense of their church order had, it involved them in apparent casuistry; but the result again enabled them to anticipate the radicals' challenge by granting the precedence of faith over works while insisting that true Christians had to act as though justified, whether or not they had experiential proof of the momentous fact.

The root of the New England Puritans' difficulties with the radical spiritists lay in the Puritans' belief that a person could have some real knowledge of both the moment of his justification and the change of heart that flowed from it. For if an individual agreed that through a direct work of the Spirit, conveying God's irresistible grace, he could become radically transformed into a visible saint, he as easily could believe that upon the act of justification the Spirit literally dwelled within him and personally dictated his subsequent actions, thus abrogating any need on his part to adhere to outward or "legal" ordinances. The ministers, and particularly such masterful psychologists of the conversion experience as Shepard and Hooker, made it clear that once an individual was justified he still was restrained within the order God had established for the progress of salvation, but in the heightened emotion of one's conversion experience it was all too easy to feel as though such ministerial injunctions only crabbed and confined the work of grace.[34] By asking each prospective church member for a factual account of the working of grace within his soul, ministers implicitly encouraged a search for and reliance on the supposed promptings of the Spirit. Thus did the New England Way engender and, in a sense, institutionalize a fervent concern with the radical transformation wrought in an individual by the free grace of God. Once a person was "assured" of his salvation, however, he might very well reject the notion that the order of nonseparating congregationalism was the true Gospel order.

Put more simply, the New England Puritans' problems with the radical spiritists arose in part because of the often hard-to-discern distinction between trying to recognize a work of the Spirit on a human soul, a perfectly legitimate exercise, and believing that upon justification the Spirit literally dwells in the saint, a point of doctrine perilously close to antinomianism. The conservative English Puritan Stephen Geree, in his response to a book of sermons by the antinomian Tobias Crisp, clearly understood how difficult it was to maintain this distinction. "Now amongst all other Heresies and errours," he wrote in 1644, "those seem to me most dangerous, which are most plausible and pleasing to flesh and bloud, if

withall they have some alliance of semblance with saving truths." Antinomianism, he went on, was like this, "a sweet poyson" that was easily
swallowed because of the way it seemed "to magnifie the grace of God
and Christ." Not surprisingly, this is exactly what the New England Puritan ministers, in a more doctrinally orthodox way, stressed in their sermons. In his popular treatise *The Real Christian* (1670), Giles Firmin
made a similar point about the appeal of John Saltmarsh's works three
decades earlier. Saltmarsh had told his readers, Firmin explained, that,
like new light preachers, "legal" preachers also emphasized "Christ, Gospel, and Free-grace," but "they do by these, as some do by Wine, . . .
they offer it freely, and bid the people drink, but the Wine being burnt,
they give it so hot, that the people cannot, nor dare drink it, for scald-
ing their mouths." Too often, Saltmarsh continued, his contemporaries
among the Puritan ministry "so heat the Gospel with legal preaching"
that their parishioners "are afraid to meddle with it." Ironically, Firmin,
by that time ensconced in the presbyterian ranks, used this reminisence to
criticize the restrictive church membership requirements imposed in
New England by divines like Hooker and Shepard, but the similitude
still is revealing: part of antinomianism's appeal lay in the very manner in
which it magnified the act of justification, yet in a way that seemed to
accord with ministerial intentions.[35]

Peter Bulkeley, whose *Gospel-Covenant* (1646) in large part consists of
sermons delivered in the years immediately following the Antinomian
Controversy, also recognized how easily the ministers' doctrine could be
misinterpreted by the laity, particularly when they reflected on the mercy
of God in justifying sinners and thereupon seemed to "have the assurance
of revelation, seeing the very book of life unsealed and open unto them."
Such deluded individuals, he continued, "love to be wise above that
which is written" and so "despise" what they condemned as a "legall
course," claiming it was fit only "for novices, but not for such are perfect
as they are." These purported saints were not willing to allow others,
particularly "legall" preachers, to judge the fitness of their religious experience, nor were they about to subject themselves to church discipline
established and enforced by the will of the congregation, a situation that
hardly could be endured if civil order were to be maintained. Perhaps
weary of the insecurity demanded by a more orthodox understanding of
justification, such individuals, as Shepard put it, "say there is a sanctification in us" not in "any habitual holiness or graces in us," but in "the immediate actings of Christ," and so essentially argue that "the Lord makes
his music without any strings." Displaying a belief in the intimate and

progressive relationship between one's closing with Christ and the course of his life after this gracious event, Shepard reminded his listeners that "the same Spirit that seals the elect, the same Spirit commands the elect not to sit idle and dream of the Spirit, but to use all diligence to make it sure." Nature and grace thus were inextricably related; unless this was understood, people would be deluded by the "mere new-nothing, and dream of Master Saltmarsh and others" who erroneously distinguished between "Christ in the flesh, and Christ in the Spirit, as if one had a diverse ministry from the other." [36]

The persistence of this confusion or misinterpretation over how the Spirit worked in the soul is evident in the prevalence of such concerns in the sermons of the late 1630s and 1640s. And in the various crises of those years—particularly with the Hutchinsonians and Gortonists—doctrinal errors were all the more difficult to eradicate because of the spiritists' claims that they only emphasized what some of the ministers (particularly John Cotton) preached. [37] By looking more closely at parts of Cotton's theology, we can see how easily his words could have been misconstrued by the more fervent in his congregation, especially those of a spiritist bent who looked to Anne Hutchinson for further elucidation of Cotton's understanding of the indwelling of the Holy Spirit. Cotton's abandonment of the Hutchinsonians, an action finally dictated by the social implications of their radicalism, and his later articulation of the Congregational Way display in close focus his own attempts to come to terms with the radicalism inherent in the doctrine he preached.

Beginning with David Hall's assessment in *The Antinomian Controversy, 1636–1638*, recent historians of this episode in New England's history have stressed the centrality of Cotton's role in the whole affair. But as Stephen Foster recently has suggested, it probably is more accurate to view the protracted difficulties in Massachusetts as an inevitable consequence of the state of English Puritanism in the 1630s, which in those years was based on a volatile, ever-shifting ideology subject to endless variations by both its clerical and lay adherents. In this light, Cotton's role in the controversy is best understood not as pivotal, but, rather, as representative of the confusion into which Puritans could be thrown when they attempted to institutionalize the components of what at that time in England still was an underground, dissenting movement. [38]

In February 1637, as a ship was about to leave Boston for England, Cotton, already deeply mired in the controversy that had begun when members of his congregation criticized other clergymen in the colony for being under a covenant of works, "took occasion" to speak to the depart-

Rev. John Cotton, so-called. Portrait of Increase Mather su-
perimposed over portrait of man assumed to be Rev. John
Cotton.

ing passengers about the uproar the dissenters had caused. His words,
recorded by Governor Winthrop, are telling, for as usual Cotton tried to
make the best of a highly serious situation. He wished the passengers to
tell their countrymen, "that all the strife amongst us was about magnifying the grace of God; one party seeking to advance the grace of God
within us, and the other to advance the grace of God toward us," by
which he meant, as Winthrop indicated, that one group emphasized "justification," the other, "sanctification." And though Cotton was not, as his
most severe critics claimed, "in secret a Fomenter of the Spirit of Fam-
ilisme," in retrospect it is apparent that his spiritual relationship was

basically sympathetic to those who, "under a pretense of holding forth" what he had taught "touching union with Christ, and evidencing of that union,"[39] became radical spiritists. Cotton's magnification of the unconditional nature of grace and his concomitant emphasis on the overwhelming moment when man becomes aware of his justification all too easily could lead to the spiritist camp.

Early in the controversy Cotton, in a letter to Shepard, denied any connection to English spiritists, though he admitted that he knew the works of Robert Towne and others. Yet he clearly was disturbed by precisely the same thing that bothered so many of Hutchinson's party and, for that matter, the English antinomians of the 1620s and 1630s—an unwillingness on the part of many Puritans to acknowledge the powerful role of the Spirit in the act of justification. When, for example, in 1636 the colony passed a law requiring new immigrants to be examined before they were permitted to form a church, Cotton seriously considered leaving for New Haven, where his friend John Davenport had assumed the ministry. Twenty years later, when Cotton explained his reasoning at that time, he wrote that what had most upset him about the new law was how it seemed aimed at individuals who "held forth such a union with Christ by the Spirit giving faith, as did precede the acting of faith upon Christ: and such an evidence of that union, by the favor of God shed abroad in their hearts by the Holy Ghost, as did precede the seeing (though not the being) of sanctification," a fact that "made the deeper impression" upon him, he continued, because he saw that "by this meanes, we should receive no more members into our church, but such as must profess themselves of a contrary judgment to what I believed to be a truth."[40] Thus, although Cotton finally decided against removal and had to modify his emphasis on this point of doctrine, he bore the brunt of responsibility for having implanted in his parishioners' minds a belief in the unquestionable primacy of a saint's knowledge of his election.

William K. B. Stoever has thoroughly examined Cotton's doctrine of the indwelling of the Spirit in relation to reformed Protestant thought. It is our immediate purpose to understand how in Cotton's sermons and treatises his presentation of the work of the Spirit often was comparable to that found in the works of contemporary radical spiritists. In *The Way of Life* (1641), he dramatically insisted on the overwhelming power of the Spirit's presence in the saint. "A wind-mill moves not onely by the wind, but in the wind," he wrote; "so a water-mill hath its motion, not onely from the water, but in the water; so a Christian lives, as having his life from Christ, and in Christ." Or, as he put it more boldly in *The Covenant of Gods Free Grace* (1645), "A man is not a naturall man, but a spirituall man, when the Spirit of God dwelleth in him." Similarly, when he replied to Robert Baillie's attack on him in *A Dissuasive from the Errours of the Time*, in which the presbyterian argued that all the colony's ills could be laid at his door, Cotton refused to deny that there was "personal habitation of the Holy Ghost in the godly." Although, Cotton wrote, it was, as Baillie claimed, "Montanism" to believe that the Holy Ghost dwelled in the regenerate "so far forth as to make us one person with himself, or to communicate with us some personal propriety of his own," it was perfectly scriptural to maintain "the indwelling not only of the gifts of the Holy Ghost, but of his own person also in the regenerate." Such distinctions were easily lost on a laity eager for spiritual experience, and when such doctrine was linked to Cotton's belief that "once justified, for ever justified, for ever blessed . . . though after that time we should immediately fall frantick, not able to put forth an act of reason, much lesse an act of faith, yet we are blessed," the potential for the kind of spiritual self-assurance displayed by the antinomians greatly increased.[41]

Cotton was no antinomian and was quick to inveigh against those who "abrogate the Commandments, and in summe hold forth, Grace without Christ, Christ without Faith, Faith without the word of promise applyed particularly to me by the spirit, And the word of the Gospel without the word of the law." Indeed, as a letter of 27 March 1638 to Samuel Stone indicates, he himself never was possessed by the kind of spiritual self-assurance upon which the antinomians based their criticism of the colony's churches. He wrote to Stone, "God has so often exercised me with recurrent fears . . . about mine own spiritual estate, and the estates of some others depending on me, that I could not rest mine own spirit upon any sign thereof." Thus it is all the more remarkable that other of the clergy—particularly Shepard—went to such lengths to implicate him with the Hutchinsonians, a fact that finally may be explicable only if we consider the clergy's most paranoiac fear that a theology like his, while it may have offered saints the highest experience of rapture, implicitly threatened the very existence of a Christian commonwealth. Of course Cotton would have disagreed. He always maintained that the best church-state was one "where not the *will* of each man beareth the sway, but the *voyce of Christ* alone is heard," but the nagging belief that Cotton's emphasis on the preeminence of the Spirit denigrated the consequences of man's justification finally made his co-workers turn upon him, for all their deference to his reputation, with a terrible ferocity.[42] What the ministers did not count on, though, as they examined both Cotton and his parishioners, was the degree to which his purported recantation eventually provided him the freedom to remold portions of the New England Way in accordance with the very spiritism they so feared.

This is not to imply that Cotton did anything to mitigate the treatment received by the antinomians during and after their examinations in 1637 and 1638, for as their "teacher" he could not be blind to the error of their ways. To Anne Hutchinson's face, for example, he criticized her claim that "her faith was not begotten nor . . . scarce at any time strengthened, by the public ministry, but by private meditations, or revelations only," a fact that shows how far toward Quakerism she had travelled by 1638. Similarly, he was not loath to chastise her for discerning "little or nothing at all" of her sanctification, or for being "more sharply censorious of other men's spiritual estates and hearts, than the servants of God are wont to be."[43] It was he, too, in his position as teacher to the church of Boston, who had to pronounce the sentence of excommunication upon her, a task that must have pained him deeply, given her admiration for his preaching. But despite all his attempts to clarify his own doctrine and his final willingness to condemn the Hutchinsonians for the erroneous opinions they derived from a misunderstanding of his theology, Cotton still emerged from the Antinomian Controversy a marked man.

The measure of the synod's failure to bring Cotton into line—indeed, to forge any permanent consensus regarding the respective merits of nature and grace in conversion—was apparent even upon the immediate conclusion of the ministerial meetings. One colonist's letter that found its way into Thomas Hutchinson's paper is indicative. As the synod met, he wrote his correspondent in England, much time was spent "in ventilation and emptying of private passions"; and, though the assembly finally agreed upon such "divers truths" as "the nature of grace and faith, the necessity of repentance and good works, [and] the perfection of the scriptures," "when they came to the nature of the covenant, the qualifications preceding it, the use of it, the seal of the Spirit, the Helenaes for which they strive, they were as different as ever, resolved in nothing but this, that no one would be resolved by another. . . ." To this observer it was apparent that, as much as Cotton had tried to give satisfaction regarding his opinions, and as much as the others were willing to listen to, and finally to accept, his logic so that they might present a unified front against their English critics, "jarring and dissonant opinions" were only "covered."[44]

In the privacy of his journal, Shepard concurred, and was not afraid to name names. "Mr. Cotton repents not, but is hid only," he noted, for the Boston minister had not abandoned his belief in "the revelation of our good estate still, without any sight of word or work." The late seventeenth-century historian William Hubbard, who was old enough to have known some of the participants in the synod and whose account of it does not suffer from the ancestor-worship of men like the Mathers, also noted how Cotton had come to "an amicable compliance with the other ministers" only by "studiously abstaining . . . from all expressions that were like to be offensive." There was a "healing of the breach," Hubbard concluded; yet as Cotton brought out such treatises as *The Covenant of Gods Free Grace*, people recognized that "he did still retain his own sense and enjoy his own apprehension, in all or most of the things then controverted."[45]

To some colonists Cotton's purported duplicity had become the butt of jokes. Gorton reported that while he and his followers were imprisoned in Boston, Nathaniel Ward of Ipswich came to their cell window and urged them to repent, saying that it would be "no disparagement" to them, particularly since "here is our elder, Mr. Cotton, who ordinarily preacheth that publicly one year, that the next year he publicly repents of, and shews himself very sorrowful for it to the congregation." Predictably, the antinomians themselves, who had reason to feel betrayed by what they took to be Cotton's abandonment of their cause, were even more harsh, calling him a "timorous man, and a deceiver, and one that had lost his insight into the Gospel." One wit among the accused, it was reported, even sent him a pound of candles, "bidding his servant tell him that it was because he wanted light." Cotton himself, however, showed no open embarrassment about the resolution of either his own examination or the results of the synod. As he put it in 1648, "How far there arose any consent or dissent about these questions . . . is not material now to particularize." "It is enough," he continued, "that upon our clear understanding of one another's minds and judgments, and upon the due proceeding of our church against convinced notorious errors and scandals, we have ever since [had] . . . much amiable and confortable communion together."[46]

By 1648 Cotton obviously had become more objective about the events surrounding the Antinomian Controversy. But, more important, by that time he also felt confident about his subsequent role in the codification of the New England Way, an achievement in which he could justifiably take pride and that in part was made possible by the shift in emphasis in his works following his so-called "defeat" in the late 1630s. As noted earlier shortly after the conclusion of the synod he began a series of sermons on the Revelation; through the 1640s he continued to preach and publish on the subject of the millennium. During the 1640s, with the exception of *The Covenant of Gods Free Grace*, his treatises were almost exclusively concerned with ecclesiology, or, put another way, with discipline rather than doctrine.[47] Having learned a valuable lesson from his close contact with the radical spiritists, Cotton thereafter devoted his career to an elucidation of the order of New England's churches and of their role in the fulfillment of millennial prophecy. Thus, after he realized how easily his doctrine could be perverted into the kinds of errors that had surfaced in his own church, he made an expedient, if tenuous, peace with Shepard, Bulkeley, and other "preparationists" and channeled his energies into establishing further the means by which a saint could contribute to Christ's impending reign on earth.

His various defenses of the Congregational Way, particularly *The Keyes of the Kingdom of Heaven* (1644) and *The Way of the Congregational Churches Cleared* (1648), perfectly complemented the theology of Shepard and Bulkeley, who worked out elaborate descriptions of the morphology of conversion and sought to impress upon putative saints the never-ending task of testing the genuineness of their faith.[48] Shepard's position on justification and sanctification had been clarified at least as early as 1636, when he reviewed some of Winthrop's writings prepared by the governor to quiet the increasing difficulties in the Boston church. Responding to Winthrop's declaration that "Election is of gods free grace, without respect of any thing in the creature," Shepard reminded him that "Tis true nothing in the creature can be a motive cause or condition of election, antecedenter; but yet it may be," he continued, "and is the consequence of election, consequenter, for we are elected, not because we were holy, but that we might be holy." He told Winthrop that the "cheefe meaning" of the covenant of grace consists of "our conformity in our renewed Image to the morall law; which god promiseth to wright in our harts." By striking such emphases, which the Hutchinsonians had linked to a "Covenant of Works," Shepard clearly wished to use the covenant to hold people to the kinds of moral order on which Christian society, as he understood it, was based; the moment of one's justification had to be seen, from this perspective, as the starting point for a saintly pilgrimage in accordance with God's laws rather than an excuse for rank subjectivism. As he put it in his *Theses Sabbaticae*, written explicitly against those whose behavior fell into this latter category, "all these and such like quickening acts of the Spirit do not argue it [the Spirit] to be our rule, according to which we ought to walk, but only by which, only by means of which, we come to walk, and are inclined, directed, and enabled to walk according to the rule, which is the law of God without."[49]

It was to such doctrinal points that Cotton shaped his ecclesiology in the years after the Antinomian Controversy, never explicitly concurring with the doctrine, yet lending it his support by his general defense of New England's congregational church order. In the late 1640s, Cotton stressed that "there is a double state of grace, one adherent, (which some not unfitly call federall grace) sanctifying to the purifying of the flesh, . . . another inherent, sanctifying of the inner man." Thus far his formulation was unexceptional, but he went on to subdivide "inherent" grace into "two sorts, one wherein persons in Covenant are sanctified by common graces, which make them serviceable and useful in their callings, as *Saul, Jehu, Judas*, and *Damas*, and such like hypocrites," and another, "whereby persons in Covenant are sanctified unto union and communion with Christ . . . in way of regeneration and salvation." The point is clear: hypocrites had their uses in the covenantal scheme, for their outward attendance to convenantal obligations could not but help a society prosper. That personally they might be damned was, on one level, irrelevant, as long as they held to the rules by which all other members of the society walked in *their* covenants. In no sense had Cotton relinquished his concern for the truly sanctified among men, but in the aftermath of the Antinomian Controversy he saw fit to emphasize, as he had not before, the social obligations of all members of a Puritan commonwealth. To be sure, there could be ecstatic union with Christ, but now he added this caveat: "In all union, the things united are distinct from the bond by which they are united." "Christ is one thing," he continued; "the soul is another, the Spirit of God that uniteth them is distinct from both."[50]

Cotton now emphasized the joys of the covenant on which a community was built, and toward this end, as he had written to one of the exiled antinomians, mere promptings of the Spirit were not sufficient. "I know not how you can build up either church or commonwealth" just on the Spirit, he observed, for such would be "an house without a foundation."[51] Ordinances and discipline provided the true foundation, and once they were established properly, a society might expect outward prosperity as well as the eventual fulfillment of the millennial promises. With Cotton's support, the federal covenant as expressed in the Congregational Way became the colony's strongest defense against the radicals, for it allowed church members to harness their religious fervor for the good of the entire society rather than just for their own subjective satisfaction.

Yet here, again ironically, we must note the radicalism of the compro-

mise struck between Cotton and his erstwhile opponents; the kind of social experiment the Puritans were attempting was a veritable rule by the
saints, if by that term we understand, as Cotton himself eventually did,
those who outwardly conform to the ordinances of the church. The New
England Way did not in any way diminish the religious enthusiasm that
had carried the Puritans to the New World. Rather, as it developed in the
1640s and finally was codified in the Cambridge Platform of 1648, the
congregational system offered church members—the visible saints—an
opportunity to set the pace for the march toward the New Jerusalem.
Darrett Rutman has written with regard to the institutionalization of the
Puritan faith that the kind of identity crisis through which a Puritan had
to pass "is not resolved in the heat of the moment when the individual
takes hold of the ideology," that is, at his moment of conversion, but "in
the aftermath of that moment," when he "locates himself with relationship to the value system which the ideology affirms."[52] With Cotton's
concurrence, in the aftermath of the Antinomian Controversy that value
system more and more was identified with the federal covenant by which
New England asserted its corporate identity.

Cotton and his fellow ministers buttressed in yet another way the New
England Way against flank attacks by colonists who held more radical
notions of church reformation. Before 1637 there still was confusion over
the legitimacy of a ministerial candidate's former ordination in the Church
of England, but beginning in 1637, with Bulkeley's installation in the
Concord church, it became the rule for ministers to renounce their episcopal ordination and to assume the prerogatives of their new positions
only after their election by the visible saints in their new church. Any
charges by antinomians or other radicals that the colony's ministers were
unconverted or spiritually dead—a charge that surfaced quite often in
disputes with the baptists in the 1640s and 1650s—could be countered by
the fact that the colony's spiritual shepherds were saints elevated to their
position by other saints.[53]

Visible sainthood as it then was defined included among its privileges
the rights of saints to create a minister from among themselves, a prerogative that presumably would make them understand that within the congregational order privileges were based, as among more radical groups,
on the saint's uniqueness. To accept the doctrine and discipline of the
New England Way provided to a church member not only a sense of personal worth, as he declared the work of the Spirit upon his soul, but also
membership in a larger community dedicated to the cause of furthering
Christ's kingdom on earth through adherence to church ordinances. This

New England Way, which in the 1640s Cotton and others defended against both conservative and radical Puritans in England, was a clever, and compelling, mixture of institutionalism and subjectivity that enabled New England Puritanism, as Stephen Foster has written, to serve "the needs of those still seeking the comfort of salvation and at the same time work out means to give the self-professed saints the exclusive privileges and communion demanded as the token of sainthood."[54] By the 1640s a balance between justification and sanctification had been attained. Although it was not immutable, it enabled the New England Puritans successfully to resist any threats to the integrity of their church system.

William Haller has suggested adherence to radical Puritan ideology, especially the antinomians' notion of "free grace," liberated some English Puritans for revolutionary social action. In New England, where the Puritan theocracy insisted on a stricter commitment to ordinances, the saints' revolutionary potential was tapped in a different manner, by gradually modifying the colonists' belief in their community's millennial destiny. Millennial thought pervaded New England Puritanism, as it did its English counterpart, but because of the very different political situation in the colonies, no movement emerged comparable to that of the Fifth Monarchy in England. And yet, as many recent historians have pointed out, almost from its inception America was defined chiefly in terms of its sacred destiny. This interpretation of the meaning of New England, and by extension of America, may well have been the New England Puritans' most enduring accomplishment. It also proved one of their most effective counters to those colonists who, like their English counterparts, sought a major renovation of the social and political order.[55]

The New England Puritans' recasting of their sacred mission is closely linked to their rhetorical attempts to define and justify their corporate identity. Their understanding of millennial eschatology was modified so that it better fit the complex situation in which they found themselves as they struggled to maintain the allegiance, and spiritual fervor, of those who believed that the center of action in the Protestant world had shifted back to England. Christopher Hill and other historians of English Puritan radicalism have noted that the execution of King Charles and, later, the religious and political chaos of the Interregnum encouraged many Puritans to believe that the millennium was imminent. The months just before the Restoration, when proponents of radical reform saw all their dreams coming to a rapid end, only made more hysterical their anticipation of Christ's descent to earth to complete the renovation the Royalists had blocked.[56] How, in the two decades before the Restoration, did the New England Puritans stymie the radicals' attempts to enlist other colonists for their more drastic reformation of society and at the same time prevent the more evangelical among them from returning to England?

The answer lay in the way the ministers and magistrates subtly created what Sacvan Bercovitch has called the "myth of America," an overarching historical construct that allowed the colony's spiritual and political leaders to harness the insecurity and doubt that were a hallmark of their theology, for the purpose of maintaining an ideological consensus about America's divine destiny; or, as Bercovitch puts it, to foster the belief that "the future, though divinely assured, was never quite there." The colonists' religious and psychological anxiety was linked, constructively, to a belief in the colony's final direction and purpose. The personal dimension of their errand into the wilderness, which to antinomians and other spiritists had remained private and subjective, was subsumed into the social. Sainthood was linked to community; and the perfection of that community was progressively deferred into the future. The New England Puritans accepted the fact that, although because of their own errors and backsliding Christ had not yet come, his *eventual* appearance was assured because of the federal covenant into which they all had entered. The New England Way served as a complex and on-going act of rhetorical self-justification through which apparent failure was the best indication of eventual success.[57]

In exchange for the program of those radicals who wanted immediate reformation at the cost of severe social and political dislocation, the architects of the myth of America offered the colonists a belief in their destiny *through time* as a godly community, one maintained by strict adherence to ordinances that, like the concept of visible sainthood, eventually became integral components of the myth. Looked at in yet another way, in their refashioning of New England's millennial role, the ministers and magistrates combined the radical millenarians' demands for an immediate rule of the saints with the baptists' claims that any who so wished could come to Christ to help work his will. The proponents of the New England Way supported a church-state in which they maintained a distinction between visible saints and all others, and yet through their federal or social covenant they permitted all individuals a role in the construction of the New Jerusalem. Through their gradual redefinition of New England's destiny the Puritans also co-opted the Quakers' belief in a "realized" eschatology. It was Quakers, after all, who maintained that Christ's body is not in heaven, but in his true church members *at any given moment.* By claiming that Christ was identified with the very *act* of *building* a true Christian commonwealth, the New England Puritans stole the Quakers' thunder, maintaining the allegiance of those who might otherwise have been lured to the Friends' faith. Christ *is* his church, the myth declared; or, perhaps more accurately, the Puritan church embodies Christ. The Saviour had a special connection to the meaning of New England, and by enlisting as a visible saint, or a confederated Puritan, a person knew the satisfaction that came with such social commitment.[58]

Groups like the Seekers and baptists rejected this intimate connection between personal sainthood and social progress. To them, Christ's kingdom, as Williams so often argued, was of another world, never to be realized here, and they fought vigorously to carve themselves a place in the colonies where it was not demanded of them to give their consent to the ever-growing ideological consensus about New England's transformation into the millennial kingdom. But as history has shown, they too finally were subsumed into the myth as it later was expanded to include the concept of denominationalism. And if in the decades after 1660 the New England Puritans had to accept, grudgingly, that these dissenters were permanently among them, they still could maintain their exceptionalism. Their religious doctrine had enabled them to internalize the enemies they seemed so desperately to need to maintain their spiritual ardor. Instead of attacks upon religious or political rivals, or upon gentry and "university" men, New England Puritans waged psychological warfare on themselves, on their own insufficiencies, and thus created anxiety that in turn fueled their colony's dynamic sense of mission. Always they had to fight insecurity, carnality, and despair; by fighting the good fight against these states of mind their salvation became possible.[59] The myth, as it was spun out by generation after generation (and now has been synthesized for us by Bercovitch), was overpowering and belief in it inescapable. Against its irresistible force the program of a Ranter or Digger seemed an exercise in private fantasy.

By 1660, the millennial component of New England Puritanism was subtly transformed in a way that allowed for the partial harnessing of many of the radical ideas proposed by such groups as the spiritists, and the General and Particular Baptists. Rather than viewing their errand into America's wilderness as almost accomplished and the New Jerusalem virtually built, the colonists redefined it *geographically* and deferred it forward into *historical* time. As Robert Middlekauff has noted, the full assimilation of this ideological shift did not occur until the maturity of the second generation of settlers—in the framework of his study, in the days of Increase and not Richard Mather. It already was well under way by the 1640s and 1650s, as the colonies' major theologians closed ranks to promulgate a world-view that encouraged the same evangelical excitement that had heated the emigrants' imaginations in old England and yet kept fervor from exploitation in ways the colonies' leadership considered private and delusory. The New England Puritans' chiliasm, David Hall has written, "was directed toward the shaping of other institutions" and, when linked to "the concept of the reign of the pious," permitted New England's leaders to substitute for an anarchic individualism the promise of a future glory attainable by a community of saints. Unlike their English brethren, the New England Puritans obtained several generations of relative stability in their government because, for all the shortcomings of the New England Way, they were able to institutionalize a reign of the godly at the expense of those kinds of people whose extravagant demands had prevented any lasting Puritan settlement in England.[60]

During the late 1630s and the 1640s, especially, the New England Puritans were free from significant interference from an English government preoccupied with its own religious difficulties, and therefore able to develop congregationalism into a remarkably resilient and stable system. T. H. Breen and Stephen Foster have described that system as "flexible enough to accommodate moderate differences of opinion" yet able to detect and expel radical extremists who mobilized demands the colonies' leaders could not meet head-on. The colony was, in consequence, only infrequently required to wage extended battles over radical doctrine.[61]

The Congregational Way provided a common ideology to which such diverse individuals as John Cotton and Thomas Shepard could subscribe, allowing clergy and laity alike to believe that a radically religious vision was preserved. In the realm of Anglo-American politics, however, the issues proved much more divisive. New England Puritanism did allow for the absorption and redirection of more radical Puritan ideas, but one such idea, worked out in the free-for-all religious atmosphere of Interregnum England, proved unacceptable to most New England leaders. The notion of toleration of any and all sincere Christian dissenters, initially raised by New England's Roger Williams, provided to many English critics of New England's polity the largest target for attacking the transatlantic Puritan experiment. In meeting those attacks, which by the late 1650s and early 1660s threatened the integrity of the Massachusetts charter, colonists were forced to articulate the implicit assumption in their doctrinal and ecclesiastical statements, which was, Puritanism's revolutionary potential notwithstanding, commitment to a profoundly conservative social order. Their defense of their position on toleration clearly expressed their growing sense of exceptionalism, soon enough the hallmark of their identity as the redeemer nation. It was not enough that New England Puritans were able to direct into their own carefully reinforced channels many of the doctrinal and ecclesiastical streams that the radicals had raised above flood-stage. They also had to deal with the world of politics.

TOLERATION: THE GREAT CONTROVERSIAL BUSINESS OF THESE POLEMICK TIMES

When Nathaniel Ward, posing as "the Simple Cobler of Aggawam in America," sought to "help 'mend his Native Country,
lamentably tattered in the upper-Leather and sole," he was adamant about one fact: toleration of diverse religious opinions was deliver-
ing England into the hands of the Antichrist. "If the Devill might have
his free option," Ward declared, "he would risk nothing else, but liberty
to enfranchize all false Religions," for "Polypiety is the greatest impiety
in the world." The Simple Cobler heartily approved the New Englanders' willingness to brave criticism from their Independent brethren
in England by legislating against such dissenters as the "Anabaptists" and
so attempting to preserve purity of worship in their churches. "He that is
willing to tolerate any unsound Opinion, that his own may be tolerated,"
the Ipswich minister concluded, only hangs "Gods Bible at the Devills
Girdle." [1]

In 1647, though, when *The Simple Cobler of Aggawam* was published,
the notion that the state should allow toleration of all religions was supported to some degree by most radical English Puritans (including members of London's Independent congregations) and had become a rallying

point for many of New England's more radical settlers. As much as such groups differed in matters of doctrine or polity, they knew that their very survival depended on the magistracy's willingness to allow them to hold and promulgate their religious views in a culture in which they were viewed as extremists. But New England's magistrates and ministers were creatures of an age in which the notion of religious uniformity was sacrosanct; they were, in addition, insulated from the rapid flow of events that had convinced many English Puritans of the necessity for toleration, and heartily seconded Thomas Shepard's opinion that, no matter how easily the idea of toleration "dazzle[d] the eyes" of man, it was the "foundation of all other Errours and Abominations in the Churches of God."[2]

Thus, much more than their theology and ecclesiology, which had been decidedly influenced by the radicals' ideas, the New England Puritans' stand on this issue of freedom to practice any Christian religion gained them an almost unshakable reputation as ideological conservatives. Their response contributed to their increasing sense of isolation in the Protestant world. Their inflexibility on the issue of how far they would accommodate Christian dissenters before they took serious action against them reveals much about their conception of their role in the history of redemption. Their willingness to be pushed to a certain boundary, but no farther, indicates their inability fully to resist what, even in their splendid isolation, they knew to be the spirit of the age.[3]

Before the English civil wars, support for the principle of religious toleration was quite rare. Not until faced with the necessity of forming a unified front against the Royalist forces did dissenters of all stripes become odd bedfellows. In the second decade of the seventeenth century Thomas Helwys and several of the General Baptists gathered around him published tracts in which they cogently argued for separation of church and state. After one of John Eliot's parishioners had sent Roger Williams a portion of one of these pamphlets (*A Most Humble Supplication* [1620]) in manuscript, Williams drew from it many of the arguments he would use in his famous *Bloudy Tenent of Persecution* written two decades later.[4]

The writings of latitudinarians like William Chillingworth and John Hales espoused an enlightened rationalism in scriptural interpretation that in turn led to a belief that no one particular church could claim infallibility in matters of doctrine. Chillingworth's and Hales's ideas had a major impact on the debate over Socinianism in the 1650s, a controversy in which William Pynchon of Springfield was to become involved. But, for the most part, before 1620 extended defenses of religious toleration were restricted primarily to the Continental humanist tradition developed over a century and represented by the followers of Faustus Socinus, Michael Servetus, Jacobus Acontius, and Sebastian Castellio, who were to become known as Unitarians.[5]

Two arguments for toleration emerged from New England in the late 1630s, each in its way setting the grounds upon which the issue later would be debated in the colonies. One was made in 1637 by Henry Vane shortly after his defeat by Winthrop in his bid for reelection to the governorship of the Massachusetts Bay Colony and after the General Court passed a law excluding from Massachusetts any whose religious ideas were not consonant with the magistrates' own. Cotton had been sorely troubled by this legislation, and Vane, who like Cotton was closely associated with the antinomian faction, entered into a written debate with the reinstated governor over the legality of the law.

Well before Vane had arrived in New England in 1635 he had acquired a reputation as somewhat of a radical. For two years before his departure from England for the New World he had abstained from the Lord's Supper because no minister "would give him the sacrament standing." Consequently he decided to sail for New England "for conscience'[s] sake." In Boston he joined Cotton's church and, as difficulties with the antinomians escalated, emerged as one of their chief spokesmen, maintaining, as Winthrop noted in his journal, not only "the indwelling of the person of the Holy Ghost in a believer" but also, going "far beyond the rest," a "personal union" with this person of the Trinity. Following his return to England after he was discredited in the Antinomian Controversy, he drew around him a group of like-minded spiritists (termed "Vanists" by Richard Baxter, for lack of a better word), who included among their number the antinomian Joshua Sprigg, and who held radical ideas which, "though clowdily expressed," evidently included "Liberty of Conscience" and anticlericalism.[6]

Vane's objections to Winthrop's "Defence of an Order of Court" offered no abstract statement of the principle of toleration, but by objecting strenuously to the magistrates' power to make decisions about who was fit to be a member of the community he was openly asking by what authority the civil ruler claimed such a prerogative. "It is not," Vane wrote, "the refusing of some religious persons against which we except, but against the libertye which is given by this law of rejecting those, that are truly and particularly religious, if the magistrates doe not like them," a liberty that already had been taken against Mrs. Hutchinson's brother-in-law Samuel and other immigrants in the summer of 1637. Vane emphasized that the action taken by the magistrates was ill-founded not only because those whom they had excluded were professing Christians who as yet had done nothing to warrant such treatment, but also because the law was not consonant with the royal charter upon which the colony was based. Vane reminded the governor that as much as the "common wealth" was "christian," it was "dependent upon the grante also of our Souveraigne." Thus, "Members of a common wealth may not seeke out all meanes that may conduce to the welfare of the body, but all lawful and due meanes, according to the charter they hold, either from God or the King, or from both." By abridging the right of good Englishmen to settle within the Massachusetts patent, the magistrates quite literally took the law into their own hands.[7]

Vane's condemnation of the arbitrary nature of the Massachusetts government did not win any reprieve for the antinomians, but it did bring into the open the fact that, even though the New England Puritan settlers had risked the Atlantic crossing, like Vane, "for conscience's sake," they were not willing to extend any courtesy to those whose beliefs threatened their conception of proper church order. Another settler who strenuously objected to such presumptuous expediency, and on more philosophical grounds, was Roger Williams, who shortly after his settlement in Providence "did make an order," as Winthrop put it, "that no man should be molested for his conscience," a principle written into the colony's constitution along with the concomitant one that the civil magistrate's jurisdiction was restricted to civil affairs.[8]

During the years just before his first return to England in 1643 to try to secure a charter for the Rhode Island colonies, Williams systematically formulated his thoughts on religious liberty. He still was arguing with the Bay's ministers over his own banishment from the colony for his separatist views. Like Vane, who also had suffered at the hands of the intolerant Bay magistrates, Williams raised the issue of whether the state should control the spiritual lives of its charges. And more than Vane, whose criticism of the arbitrariness of the Puritan government was limited by his personal interest in their legislation—he was, after all, sympathetic to the antinomian faction—Williams in 1637 stood ready to defend the principle in the abstract, as all men's birthright.[9]

Though at the time they had little practical effect, the actions of Vane and Williams alerted the Massachusetts leaders that not all emigrants were ready to modify their behavior in accordance with the official orthodoxy and, more important, that some were beginning to defend their right to dissent on dangerous ideological grounds, the political challenge expressed by Vane's questioning of the authority of the magistrates in abridging English settlers' rights, and Williams's more fundamental challenge to the notion of religious uniformity.

The outward unanimity achieved at the synod of 1637–38 marked individuals like Vane and Williams as dangerous ideologues. But once events in England carried the issue of toleration into public debate, and when groups like the Gortonists and baptists brought their complaints against the Bay Colony in London and there aligned themselves with proponents of religious liberty, the statements of Vane and Williams returned to haunt the New England Puritans.[10] In 1647 one of Winthrop's correspondents warned him that "you have need to be carefull of your practice there, for whatever you doe that may have the least shaddow of severitie, is heightened here, and cast in your brethrens teeth," witness the magnified report of the presbyterian Ephraim Pagitt that "In New *England* they perswade the Magistrates to kill all idolaters and Heretickes, even whole Cities, men, women, and children. . . ."[11] Beginning, then, with Cotton's extended replies to Williams's eloquent defenses of religious liberty, the New Englanders were forced to face head-on what Lynn's minister, Thomas Cobbet, termed "That Great Antichrists masterpiece," the principle of toleration.

In the 1640s debates over religious liberty, the same two points were at issue that had been raised by Vane and Williams in the late 1630s: the power of the magistracy in spiritual affairs and the principle of religious uniformity in a Christian commonwealth. The principle of religious uniformity had been deeply ingrained in the Puritans at the time of their migration to New England and continued to be invoked by the colonies' ministers and magistrates well after it had come under serious attack in England. As late as 1651 the principle was defended by such laymen as Edward Johnson, who in his *Wonder-Working Providence* reminded his readers that "the Lord Christ hath said, *He that is not with us, is against us*: there is no room in his Army for tolerationists," as well as by such prominent ministers as Cotton and Norton.[12]

New England's leaders were not ashamed that their colonies had not become an asylum for persecuted Christians of all varieties. The settlements in Massachusetts and Connecticut were created by a group of English Puritans who wholeheartedly believed that the establishment of their commonwealth upon congregational church order fulfilled the will of the Almighty. In a letter in which he defended New England against charges of self-righteousness and persecution Cotton put it most clearly. There is, he noted, "a vast difference between men's inventions and God's institutions," and he and others had fled from the former to establish the latter. In New England "Wee compell none to men's inventions"; it was only to preserve what New England's leaders took to be God's institutions that the magistrates had been invested with those powers for whose use they were increasingly criticized. "To cut off the hand of the Magistrate from touching men for their consciences," Shepard wrote in 1645, "will certainly in time . . . be the utter overthrow, as it is the undermining, of the Reformation begun."[13]

In his major statements in support of toleration, *The Bloudy Tenent of Persecution* (1644) and *The Bloody Tenent Yet More Bloody* (1652), Williams directly challenged both these assumptions. By the 1640s in England the principle of religious uniformity had come under sustained attack for pragmatic reasons, as Puritan supporters of Parliament's case against King Charles mustered into their armies any who would fight for their cause, regardless of their religious opinions. But Williams, particularly as a Seeker who denied the validity of all outward church ordinances and so, by implication, the establishment of any church uniformity, did not rest his case on pragmatic arguments. For him, "soul liberty" was an inviolable right of each individual who wended his way through a world in which there would be no true religious guidance until Christ himself reestablished his true ministry and ordinances. Thus, Williams argued, just as "the forcing of a *Woman*, that is, the violent Acting of *uncleanlinesse* upon her *bodie* against her will, we count a Rape," so "that is *Spirituall* or *Soule-rape*, which is a forcing of the *Conscience* of any Person, to Acts of Worship." For the state to deny anyone the right to seek his own spiritual nurture, and thus to grow in knowledge and grace, blatantly obstructed the progressive unfolding of truth that God had promised his true believers. "I ask," Williams wrote rhetorically in 1652, "Whether in the present state and juncture of affaires in *England*, wherein . . . every *Sect*, every *Order* and *conscience* plead the integrity and purity of their way, and the People of God themselves are so divided and differently perswaded . . . I ask, Whether we may pray . . . that God would send us such *Magistrates*, who should authoritatively judge, whose *Conscience*, whose *Worship*, whose *Godlinesse* is true?" His answer, based in large measure upon his New England experiences with a "godly" magistracy, was an emphatic "No!"[14]

Curiously, Williams's belief, linked to his millennialism, in the Seeker's halting journey toward spiritual revelation was related to the latitudinarians' views of the progressive unveiling of truth to be realized through the proper use of reason in matters of religious doctrine. Thus, in the

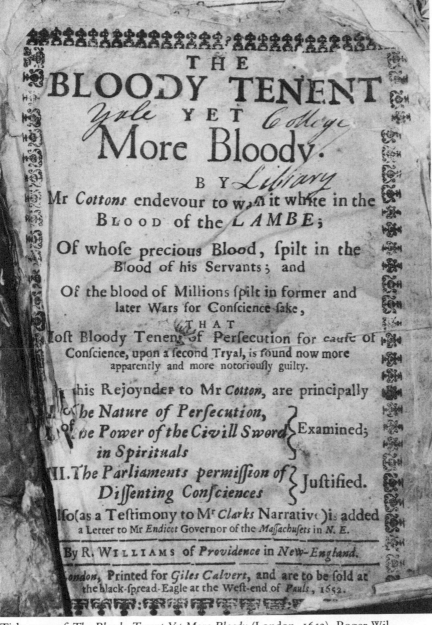

THE
BLOODY TENENT
Yale YET *College*
More Bloody.

BY *Library*

Mr *Cottons* endevour to wash it white in the
BLOOD of the *LAMBE*;

Of whose precious Blood, spilt in the
Blood of his Servants; and

Of the blood of Millions spilt in former and
later Wars for Conscience-sake,

THAT

Most Bloody Tenent of Persecution for cause of
Conscience, upon a second Tryal, is found now more
apparently and more notoriously guilty.

In this Rejoynder to Mr *Cotton*, are principally

I. *The Nature of Persecution,*
II. *The Power of the Civill Sword* } Examined;
in Spirituals

III. *The Parliaments permission of* } Justified.
Dissenting Consciences

Also(as a Testimony to Mr *Clarks* Narrative)is added
a Letter to Mr *Endicot* Governor of the *Massachusets* in *N. E.*

By R. WILLIAMS of *Providence* in *New-England.*

London, Printed for *Giles Calvert*, and are to be sold at
the black-spread-Eagle at the West-end of *Pauls*, 1652.

Title page of *The Bloody Tenent Yet More Bloody* (London, 1652), Roger Williams's answer to John Cotton's attack on his *Bloudy Tenent of Persecution*. Here Williams cited John Clarke's condemnation of the Massachusetts Bay Colony's treatment of baptists.

1640s and 1650s Williams's and other radical Puritans' defenses of religious liberty were championed by such purported "Socinians" as John Goodwin and John Biddle as well as by those who spun off from the Chillingworth-Hales circle, and all of whom joined in pressing Parliament for more liberty of the press and a blanket toleration of Christian dissenters. It was by this route, for example, that New England's William Pynchon came to warn Winthrop that the colony might have erred in so severely restricting religious freedom, and in 1650 to publish his *Meritorious Price of Our Redemption*, an overtly latitudinarian work.[15] Williams articulated what was on the minds of many spiritists and rationalists alike as they agitated for religious toleration. "In vaine," he wrote, "have *English Parliaments* permitted *English Bibles* in the poorest *English* houses, and the simplest man or woman to search the Scriptures, if yet against their soules perswasion from the Scripture, they should be forced . . . to beleeve as the Church beleeves."[16] The implications of such a statement, would only be, Cotton and other New Englanders were convinced, the death of true reformed religion.

Scholars like W. K. Jordan and William Haller have detailed the fortunes of those in England who, swayed by such arguments, rallied to the works of Williams, John Goodwin, William Walwyn, and others in the 1640s who used the opportunities presented by the liberalization (and eventual breakdown) of censorship to publish tolerationist tracts.

Cotton responded to the arguments for toleration "written long since by a witnesse of Jesus Christ close prisoner in *Newgate*" in *A Most Humble Supplication*, which one of Eliot's congregation had given Cotton for comment (Williams included it, along with Cotton's response, in the opening pages of *The Bloudy Tenent*). His arguments epitomize the New England clergy's party line on religious liberty in the decade of the 1640s, and serve as a benchmark against which to measure the evolution of the New Englanders' attitudes in the next decade as the demands for toleration, or at least for more open church membership, grew more strident.[17]

Cotton based his argument on a set of dichotomies that reflect his training in Ramist logic. Some points of doctrine, he began, "are fundamentall, without right belief whereof a man cannot be saved," while others are "circumstantiall or lesse principall, wherein men may differ in judgment without prejudice of salvation." The "points of Doctrine and Worship lesse principall" themselves could be subdivided into those that "are held forth in a meek and peaceable way" and those that "are held forth with such arrogance and impetuousnesse, as tendeth and reacheth . . . to the disturbance of civill peace." By this reasoning, in all good faith the New England clergy could tolerate the presbyterianism of Thomas Parker and James Noyes because, though their polity was not congregational, they agreed on other points of worship and doctrine with the majority of New England's ministers. So, too, the case of someone like Charles Chauncy, when he was elevated to the presidency of Harvard College: though he differed from the Puritans on the mode of baptism, his overall understanding of doctrine met with the Puritans' expectations. It was the doctrinal aberrations of an Anne Hutchinson or a Henry Vane, or the seditious carriage of a John Wheelwright or a Samuel Gorton, that brought down the wrath of the magistracy.[18]

Cotton made one more important distinction whose application assumed more significance in the 1650s as the New England Puritans scrambled to justify their intolerance of the baptists and Quakers. Because the Puritans believed that in fundamental points of doctrine and worship "the word of God" was "so clear" that an individual could not "but be convinced in conscience of the dangerous error of his way," Cotton and his fellow ministers felt no qualms about administering severe punishment to anyone who persisted in erroneous ways after firm and frequent admonition. "In things of lesser moment" the Puritans were quite willing to allow an individual his dissenting views (if they were held "in a spirit of Christian meeknesse and love" and not, say, like those of Gorton), "till God may be pleased to manifest his truth to him." But if the error was fundamental, no further toleration was possible.[19]

Before condemning the New Englanders as bigoted and extreme, Cotton concluded, his critics had to understand that in the colonies no one in fact was punished for his conscience, but rather "for sinning against his conscience." Ministers were to labor as diligently as possible to reclaim a man from error, but if against reason and revelation he maintained his erroneous opinions, he invited both temporal and eternal punishment. Finally, the Boston minister noted, the "question" was "whether an Heretique after once or twice admonition (and so after conviction) . . . may be tolerated either in the Church without excommunication, or in the Common-wealthe, without such punishment as may preserve others, from dangerous and damnable infection. . . ." Cotton was certain of the answer: the godly community simply could not be jeopardized for stubborn, aberrant individuals.[20]

Thus expressed, for its time the New England Puritans' stance toward toleration was moderate. The difficulty lay with those individuals who, as in the case of the Hutchinsonians or Gortonists, refused to accept the clergy's judgment about the fundamental error of their ways; for at a time when, as Cotton described it, "the Spirit of Error" was "let loose" and peoples' hearts had become "as Tinder, ready to catch and kindle at every sparke of false light," the extent of the Puritans' patience in way of "admonition" was limited. Their treatment of the Gortonists after they were captured in Shawomet and brought to Boston upon complaint of some of their Rhode Island neighbors is revealing. Though in 1643 the magistrates had compiled a lengthy list of "gross opinions" which they claimed the Gortonists held—among them, that they denied the humanity of Christ, as well as his churches and ordinances, and that they refused to acknowledge civil magistracy—the Gortonists were not allowed to answer the charges publicly. As Gorton later described the proceedings, they were "questioned and examined" in closed sessions of the court as the magistrates and invited visitors attempted "to get some matter against [them] from [their] own mouths." Nor was such badgering restricted to the courtroom; when the prisoners were returned to their cells the colony frequently sent as their agents "the elders and other members of the churches" to speak with and so "to get occasion" against them. By the clergy they were treated little better. Gorton claimed that for the three weeks before their formal examination John Wilson "ordinarily in his sermons, pressed the magistrates and the people to take away our lives," and for his part Cotton "encouraged the people in their lawfulness of dealing with us." The ministers' sermons also sought to show the Gortonists the error of their ways, but, as their leader later reported, such spiritual "meat" as was there offered was "not to be digested, but only by the heart or stomach of an ostrich." [21]

Gorton was summoned by the court and made to answer in writing, under penalty of death, a set of doctrinal and hermeneutical questions. Just as he had done earlier in his career when he had run into similar difficulties in the Rhode Island colonies, he claimed that, before any penalty could be carried out, he should have recourse to an appeal to England. But the Puritans' patience had worn thin: they told him "never [to] dream or think any such thing," for no appeal would be granted. Storing this threat for later use against them, Gorton complied without further resistance. After studying his responses, Winthrop announced that the court was "one with him in those answers" and asked only that he retract his earlier blasphemies and insults to the colony, tendered in several letters to the magistrates. This retraction was the acknowledgment the magistrates wanted of the Gortonists' errors in fundamental points of doctrine. Gorton stubbornly refused to comply, claiming that all he had previously written to them agreed with the present documents. Astounded by such insolence, an irate Thomas Dudley announced that he "never would consent to it whilst he lived, that they were one with him in those answers" and immediately called for the court to vote on whether the Gortonists should be executed for heresy.[22]

Their lives were spared by a few votes, but they were sentenced to wear irons and to do hard labor in towns surrounding Boston. The punishment was unpopular, however; the population was "much unsatisfied" and within a few months the General Court, without any further testimony, overturned the sentences, freeing the Gortonists to return to Shawomet and setting the stage for their leader's voyage to England to bring complaint against Massachusetts.[23]

As Gorton had charged in his examination by the court, the point upon which New England Puritans most easily could be challenged was the magistrates' abridgment of the sacred rights of Englishmen. Upon Gorton's arrival in London and the subsequent publication in 1646 of his *Simplicities Defence against Seven-Headed Policy* he aimed precisely at this vulnerable spot. In an England more and more receptive to the notion that freedom of worship should be granted to members of all Protestant groups, Gorton's historical narrative of his lengthy tribulations was cause for serious embarrassment, particularly among such hitherto stalwart supporters of the colony as Thomas Goodwin, Philip Nye, and other Independents who in 1644 had signed the ecumenical *Apologeticall Narration*. In June 1646, Edward Winslow of Plymouth, enlisted as Massachusetts' agent and dispatched to London with the particular charge to answer any of the complaints Gorton might bring before the Commission for Foreign Plantations, warned Winthrop of an "evill . . . long feared"—Gorton had been quick to find a "potent friend" among the radicals in that city. Winslow left the "friend" unnamed. It may have been Sir Henry Vane, the Independent Cornelius Holland, or perhaps the Earl of Warwick, head of the Commission. Two months later an anxious Theophilus Eaton, founder of New Haven, asked Winthrop for the latest news from London. "With your first conveniency," he wrote, "I desire to heare what issue Gortons complaints are brought to." "It wilbe an exercise to us all," he concluded, "if he returne with victory."[24]

Gorton eventually did just that, for the Commission for Foreign Plantations declared Shawomet beyond the formal jurisdiction of the Massachusetts Bay Colony's patent. Moreover, the Earl of Warwick guaranteed free passage through that colony for Gorton and his associate Randall Holden whenever they chose to return to New England. Gorton did not immediately avail himself of this privilege and soon enough found himself presented before another parliamentary committee to answer charges that some passages in his *Simplicities Defence* violated the so-called "Blasphemy Ordinance"; but his subsequent acquittal by that body only made his book the more serious a threat to the independence of the Bay Colony. Nor were matters for Massachusetts simplified by the fact that, as Winslow noted, in London many other "petitioners" were "very busie" attacking intolerance in old England and New. Gorton's complaints about the magistrates' repression of godly dissent, a topic to which he returned in his *Incorruptible Key* (1647), were part of a rising tide of concern over what kind of ecclesiastical polity would be imposed upon England should conservative Puritans have their way. To men like Goodwin and Nye, who had to answer increasing criticism of the actions of their Independent brethren across the Atlantic, Gorton's damning reports only cast more doubt on New England's claim to be the beacon for the course of Protestantism in the home country.[25]

Within a few months Winslow had to fulfill a second part of his charge as agent for Massachusetts, to counter the criticism of yet another group of colonists who, attempting to follow Gorton's lead, had brought their complaints directly to Parliament. In May 1646, encouraged by William Vassal of the Plymouth colony, Dr. Robert Childe, Samuel Maverick, and other disaffected New Englanders had petitioned the Bay government to extend the franchise, hitherto restricted to male church members, that is, to "visible" saints. Presbyterian in their orientation, these men had been disappointed by the failure of the ministerial assembly in Cambridge in September 1643 to endorse the liberal membership practices of Parker and Noyes, and they hoped to make their case in more explicitly political terms by appealing to the General Court to act where the ministers had been unwilling.[26]

Like Gorton in his *Simplicities Defence*, the petitioners stressed that in the Bay Colony their rights as freeborn Englishmen had been severely abridged; as they so bluntly put it, according to their judgment they could not "discerne a setled forme of government according to the lawes of England." As prime evidence they cited the recent law passed by the court that was aimed specifically at preventing "Anabaptists" from settling in the colony but which easily could be turned against members of other dissenting groups. They asked for a more liberal policy toward church membership, claiming that in the colony there were "divers, sober, righteous and godly men, eminent for knowledge and other gracious gifts of the holy spirit," in "noe weayes scandalous in their lives and conversations" and "members of the Church of England . . . not dissenting from the latest and best reformation of England, Scotland, &c.," who yet were kept from church membership.[27] A polity more akin to presbyterianism (in which all are members), the petitioners argued, was much more in line with Christ's expectations for the constant increase of his church.

One other of the petitioners' points, made more obliquely but still closely allied to this last, may well have been that to which the New Englanders were most sensitive. Not only did a congregational polity prevent many worthy Christians from enjoying full church privileges, the petitioners argued, but from it flowed "an ocean of inconveniences," among them "encrease of anabaptisme, and of those that totally condemn all ordinances as vaine," as well as a "decrease of brotherly love, heresies, [and] schismes." The presbyterian heresiographers frequently had made the same charge against the New England Puritans, and to hear it hurled at them also by their fellow-colonists not only gave more credibility to Baillie's and Pagitt's claims that an Independent polity was a breeding ground for error but also shocked New England's leaders into an awareness that some in their population were ready to train upon them the kind of ideological ammunition hitherto restricted to conservative English Puritans. Even so unlikely a figure as Williams repeated this same charge in one of his rebuttals to Cotton. "I am no more of Master *Gortons* Religion then of Master *Cottons*," he wrote, "and yet if Master *Cotton* complaine of their *obstinacy* in their way, I cannot but impute it to this *bloody tenent* and *practice*, which ordinarily doth give strength and *vigour*, *spirit* and *resolution* to the most erroneous. . . ."[28] Seen in this way, congregationalism and the intolerance which supported it only whetted peoples' appetites for dangerous, but spiritually fulfilling, alternatives. To return to the petitioners' line of reasoning: more open church membership, with the greater sacramental privileges such membership implied, was the best preventative against the heresies and schisms that wracked the New England Way.

Obviously Robert Childe and his associates were not radicals who sought immediate toleration of all different sects, but their petition had the effect of making more apparent the unusual strictness with which dissenters were treated in Massachusetts, Connecticut, and, to some degree, Plymouth. The petitioners' demands met with full rejection at the hands of the Massachusetts General Court and, subsequently, brought upon them considerable wrath from the magistrates. But much to the magistrates' chagrin, the petition gathered support from several quarters and severely rocked the colony. Early in 1647, Samuel Symonds of Ipswich wrote Winthrop that in his town "copies of the petition" had spread particularly among young men and women "apt to wonder why such men should be troubled that speake as they [the petitioners] doe; not being able to discerne the poyson in the sweet wine, nor the fire wrapped up in the straw." And from Springfield, where in the Connecticut River Valley the highly respected magistrate William Pynchon had heard of the commotion, Winthrop was given some surprising advice. Pynchon pointedly reminded the governor that, though he disapproved of the remonstrants' "manner of proceedinge," the colony would do well to acquiesce to some of their demands so as not to antagonize their sponsors in England. "We are not a Free state," he wrote, and "neather do I think it our wisdome to be." [29]

With the court's outright rejection of the petitioners' demands and the heavy fining of Childe and the other signees, the focus in this controversy shifted to London, where Vassal and Childe's brother John had brought their case before Parliament. Despite Gorton's success before the Commission for Foreign Plantations the year before, the Committee now, its composition having changed to a membership more Independent, and thus pro–New England, decided that in this case it had no reason to interfere in the affairs of Massachusetts. The other matter had involved a boundary dispute; here they perceived the issue as a strictly internal matter over which they had no jurisdiction. Two important results followed from Vassal's and Childe's agitation: a heightened criticism of the colony's policy toward dissenters, fueled by Childe's *New Englands Jonas Cast Up in London* (1647), Winslow's answers to it, and Gorton's writings; and the pressure exerted on Massachusetts by the colony's English supporters, hard-pressed to explain allegiance to the colony in light of their own courtship of English dissenters for help in countering the power of the presbyterians. In rejecting the petition of Robert Childe and his supporters, the New England Puritans were widely perceived in England as holding a position on toleration that ironically approached that of the English and Scottish presbyterians whose polity the petitioners championed. [30]

The virulent pamphlet war among the New Englanders began in earnest with Winslow's *Hypocrisie Unmasked* of 1647, a lengthy rebuttal to *Simplicities Defence*; in it the Plymouth colonist defended Massachusetts' action against Gorton by printing the colony's own set of documents relevant to the case, as well as a brief but revealing history of "*the ground or Cause*" of the Puritans' "*first planting* in New-England." Like Winthrop in his *Short Story of the Rise, reigne, & ruine of the Antinomians . . .* (1644), Winslow included a lengthy catalogue of errors culled from the Gortonists' writings. He also detailed their purported rejection of civil government, in general, and the office of the magistracy, in particular, arguing that it was for such civil insubordination that Massachusetts first had summoned them to Boston. The Gortonists expressly affirmed, Winslow reported, "that the Office to minister Justice belongs only to the Lord," and that therefore "men make themselves Gods . . . by ruling over the bodies and estates of men." But such a premise "strikes at all Magistracy," he continued; and their concomitant demand, which provides a strong hint of the group's ideological proximity to the Levellers and Diggers, that "a man may judge as a brother, but not as an Officer," if granted would result only in "the establishment of all confusion, and the setting up of Anarchy worse than the greatest Tyranny." Moreover, Winslow claimed, the Gortonists' doctrinal defense of this rejection of magistracy further indicated their connection to the most extreme radical sectarians: "They say men limit, and so destroy the holy one of *Israel*" if they "acknowledge that Christ rules on earth only by his Deputies, Lieutenants, and Viceregents." To acknowledge no law but that of Christ within one's heart opened "the sluce" to all the "violence, injustice, and wickednesse" that English Puritans witnessed in other members of this "peculiar fellowship."[31]

No doubt responding to the heresiographers' claims that, given a congregational polity, one had to expect such social aberrations, Winslow also strenuously denied that the New England churches "had been laid upon division or separation." The colonists were willing, even in separatist Plymouth, to accept into church fellowship members of other "Reformed Churches," particularly from Holland and France. Even more significant, he undertook to counter (as he would again in his reply to *New Englands Jonas*) the popular impression that the colonists would not "suffer" any that differed from them to "reside or cohabite" with them, not even presbyterians who differed "so little" from them in matters of doctrine. By way of proof he pointed to the Bay's lengthy toleration of Parker and Noyes, who were "in that way," and to "Mr. Hubbard" (Peter Hobart of Hingham), who similarly had been permitted to institute a more liberal membership policy without any molestation from the magistrates, and also to those who had signed the Remonstrance of 1646. When these last, Winslow insisted, had demanded the liberty to form presbyterian churches, the magistrates "freely and as openly tendred [it] to them," as long as they obtained their own ministers and did not seek to overturn the order of other churches in the colony. To those like Henry Jessey and John Tombes who condemned Massachusetts for its stringent laws against baptists, Winslow explained that, though the New Englanders indeed had instituted "severe" laws against them, they "never did nor will execute the rigour of it upon any . . . as long as they carry themselves peaceably" in their communities. There was a "broad difference," he concluded, "between evill doers" who had to be whipped for insubordination and others whose "tender consciences" made them "follow the light of Gods Word in their own perswasions" and walk according to "the rules of the Gospel." [32]

In *Hypocrisie Unmasked* Winslow sought to do more than defend the Bay Colony's treatment of the Gortonists, whose ideas, after all, still were anathema to presbyterians and Independents alike. Of equal importance was the agent's attempt to dispel the widespread belief that the colony was so intolerant that it would receive none but congregationalists and so had instituted a severe penal code to protect this system from any serious challenge, either conservative or radical.

When Major John Childe, who arrived in England ready to publish the relevant documents surrounding his brother's and the other remonstrants' attempts to challenge the political and religious restrictions of the New England Way, he discovered in Winslow's pamphlet open references to the very men he was charged with representing. He lost no time in sharply rebutting what he saw as Winslow's simplistic gloss of the colonists' response to presbyterians within their settlements. As much as the Remonstrance of 1646 and its subsequent rejection by the Massachusetts General Court spoke for themselves, Childe was not about to allow English Puritans to believe that the New England colonies, with the exception of Rhode Island, were anything but closed religious societies in which the power of the magistracy was used both for the persecution of sincere dissenters and the abridgement of the civil liberties guaranteed all Englishmen. [33] In *New Englands Jonas* Childe made clear that, as in the case of the Gortonists, the Massachusetts authorities' treatment of obstreperous dissenters often left little room for their much-vaunted "charity." Shortly after the presentation of the petition, for example, from their pulpits many of the ministers condemned it as seditious and "full of malignancie, subvertive both to Church and Commonwealthe in their foundations." The clergy took the lead in "publikely exhorting Authority to lay hold upon" the petitioners, advice that was expeditiously followed. The magistrates acted in a similarly high-handed manner. "One publikely, in open Court," Childe reported, "gave charge to the Jury" not in the least to consider dismissing the petitioners but to charge them with a capital crime, whose punishment was banishment or death. Childe reiterated what, after the Gortonists' success before the Commission for For-

eign Plantations, had become a most troublesome charge: that ever since
the Puritans had gone to New England they had worked to establish "an
Arbitrary government of their own" because they could not "endure" the
laws of England. By seeking "to stop all Appeals from all their unjust
Sentences," the New Englanders in effect had created an independent
state. "Mark his [Winslow's] great boasting that they are growing up into
a Nation," Childe concluded; "being begun at this Plantation, by the
same rule others might seek" to extend such freedom "to all other Plantations," even to Ireland, Wales, and Cornwall.[34]

Childe also condemned Winslow for the obvious smoke screen of connecting the petitioners to Gorton and his followers. Trying to excuse
their refusal to issue warrants in the King's name, Childe noted, the New
England Puritans cleverly began "to write against Gorton, a man whom
they know is notorious for heresie, that so behind him they may creep
and get a shot at a better game," namely the Commission for Foreign
Plantations, whom they wished to convince that the colony's seemingly
excessive laws were necessary to keep such troublemakers from destroy-
ing their commonwealth. It was all too obvious that Winslow had resorted to this ploy to "wash away the opinion that good men heretofore
have had of them" and to suggest "that they are Separatists and Schismatickes." Childe announced that the colonists' claims to "good agreement
& communion" between themselves and the presbyterians were a blatant
deception. Parker and Noyes were tolerated only because their church
had been founded in "the Independent manner" and they themselves still
held many Independent principles; and, contrary to Winslow's report,
Hobart, more outspoken in his views than the Newbury ministers, had
indeed been severely fined and harassed for advocating a presbyterian
polity. As to the magistrates' offer to allow the petitioners to establish
their own churches, "this is strange news to us," Childe wrote, "for we
hear not one word of that from those Petitioners," most of whom at that
time were still imprisoned. Childe could only conclude, in the light of
the distortion and exaggeration in Winslow's pamphlet, that "Independents are all of a peace, for subtiltie, designs, [and] fallacies, both in
New-England and in Old."[35]

With the publication of *New Englands Jonas* hard upon *Simplicities Defence*, the English public had before them complementary condemnations
of the colonists' abuse of their charter. With both conservatives and radicals attacking the colonies there seemed little reason to believe that New
England offered any suitable model for the reformation of the English
church. This fact was vividly brought home to New Englanders by the

rapidly escalating criticism of their enterprise by English Puritans. In a letter to Massachusetts in the mid-1640s, Hugh Peter, by that time one of the four or five most prominent Independents in the kingdom, exclaimed: "Ah sweet New England! & yet sweeter if divisions bee not among you, if you will give any encouragement to those that are godly & shall differ etc." "I pray you," he concluded, "doe what you can herein, & know that your example in all kinds swayse here." In another letter written at about the same time he was even more direct. "None will come to you because you persecute," he warned the colonists; "cannot you mend it?" In May 1646 Hannah Dugard wrote Mary Wyllys in Connecticut about the English Puritans' increasing disappointment in the colony. "For now here being Libberty of Conscience," she said, "many that heretofore sought to goe [to New England] will not heare of it now." "There is not any speech or inclination," she added, "in any that I heare towards new Ingland but Rather an expecttation of some from thence." The next year one of Winthrop's correspondents penned a sentiment that obviously had become all too common in the home country: "As for my good opinion of persons of New England, I do acknowledge some have lost it," he wrote, "and I thinke deservedly." [36]

New England Puritans did have reason to worry about the success of Winslow's rebuttal to Childe. The colonies' leaders realized that, as the sides then were being drawn in England, they were closer ideologically to the presbyterian faction than to some of the more radical Independents. They had to convince the conservative Puritans that their response to the Childe petition was not indicative of their policy toward all presbyterians but rather had been demanded by the seditious behavior of the petitioners themselves. As Winslow put it in *New Englands Salamander*, "there were none committed for petitioning, but for their Remonstrance and the many false charges and seditious insinuations tending to faction and insurrections sleighting the government, &c." By boasting that in New England there were "many thousands secretly discontented at the government," the petitioners opened the way for further unrest, encouraging those "so emboldened" to "discover themselves" and so to "kindle a flame in a peaceable Commonweale." [37] The New England Puritans were not at all concerned with the *act* of petitioning for changes in their ecclesiastical polity, but for the *manner* in which these particular individuals, led by Vassal, the "Salamander" who delighted in the fire of contention, had pressed their demands.

As Winslow was quick to point out, the petitioners themselves were hardly good presbyterians. Dr. Childe, though he had "found good acceptation" upon his first two voyages to New England, now had changed his "gentleman's carriage" and was willing "to close with such as are discontented" to further their seditious ends. Nor was Winslow willing to overlook the fact that Childe had traveled extensively in Italy and sometimes spoke "highly . . . in favour of the Jesuites." Some New Englanders, Winslow continued, even "suspect[ed] his agency for the great incendiaries of Europe"; after Hugh Peter had been "advised by letters from a forraign part that the Jesuites had an agent that sommer in New-England," attention logically was focused on Dr. Childe, who had taken a degree at Padua. The "presbyterianism" of some of his associates was just as specious. When, at a private conference with an "eminent person" the petitioners had been asked what sort of church government they wanted, one asked for the episcopal, another admitted that he was content with the present system in New England, and a third opted for "that particular government which Mr. John Goodwin in Colemanstreet was exercised in." By that time Goodwin, nicknamed "Socinian John," was known as one of the most advanced Independents, sympathetic to sectarians and latitudinarians alike; if the petitioners respected his views of church government, Winslow concluded, they hardly had any claim to sympathy from English presbyterians.[38]

There is little direct evidence of the influence of Winslow's second pamphlet on either the presbyterians or Independents, but by 1648 it was apparent that in their confrontations with those who challenged their repressive measures against dissenters the New England Puritans were forced closer and closer to the presbyterian camp. This had been clearly indicated in Ward's *Simple Cobler*, and even more so in Cotton's *Way of the Congregational Churches Cleared* (1648), a volume whose main purpose is partially obscured by its polemical title but which is clarified in Nathaniel Holmes's preface; there this English Puritan accurately described the book as "partly *apologetical*, partly *controversial*." In this lengthy response to Baillie's *Dissuasive*, Cotton, as much as he defended the propriety of congregationalism, took great pains to suggest to Baillie and other conservative Puritans that they were tilting their ideological lances at the wrong party. Rather than assuming that New England congregationalists spawned and then protected radical sectarians, presbyterians had to realize that success against the radicals would come only when they joined with congregationalists to combat the cancerous spread of fundamental error. Further, Baillie and others had to understand that "What offense soever in judgment of practice, hath been suspected or found among us, it hath not sprung from the government" but rather from "personal defects" in the individuals involved. The much-vaunted presbyterian discipline provided no better machinery to deal with the "opinionists." So close to each other in their attempts to eradicate error, it was high time, Cotton concluded, for congregationalists and presbyterians to make every attempt at reconciliation.[39]

For a while in the late 1640s it looked as though, at least with regard to the problem of toleration, New England congregationalists and Scottish and English presbyterians indeed might achieve some sort of rapprochement and convince English Independents of the final danger of defending the radical sectarians, but the events of 1649 and its aftermath made ineffectual any alliance between the two groups: during the Interregnum the presbyterians' star fell as quickly as it had risen a decade earlier. In 1650 plaintive cries like the one made to Giles Firmin (at that time still an Independent) by a New Englander—Firmin's correspondent was worried that the "godly Ministers" in England had been "too passive, and not so zealous against Errors and Heresies" as they might be, and thus deserving of the "inundations of hellish opinions" that God had released upon them—were drowned out by the myriad voices of those who saw the death of Charles as the signal event in their struggle for religious liberty. In England in the 1650s it was men like Williams, Goodwin, and John Milton, and not Cotton or Hooker, who captured the popular imagination.[40]

Increasingly in the 1650s New England was left alone to continue the campaign for religious uniformity, and the colonists' encounters with baptists and Quakers in that decade only led to more harsh measures. The Cambridge Platform of 1648, in which the Congregational Way was codified, guaranteed the civil magistrate's "duty" to "take care of matters of religion" and to punish "Idolatry, Blasphemy, Heresy, [and the] venting [of] corrupt & pernicious opinions" that destroyed the foundation of religion. When John Clarke, Obadiah Holmes, and John Crandall ventured to Lynn in 1651 to meet and comfort some baptist brethren, the full strength of these powers was marshalled against them.[41]

Within a few months of his release from prison, Clarke had his revenge, for the publication by the baptist printer Henry Hills of his *Ill Newes from New-England: or A Narrative of New-Englands Persecution. Wherein Is Declared That while old England is becoming new, New-England is become Old* brought to a new level the debate over the New England Puritans' treatment of dissenters. And, like Williams's *Bloudy Tenent*, which had elicited an official response by Cotton, Clarke's account of his and his

ILL
NEWES
FROM
NEW-ENGLAND:
OR
A Narative of *New-Englands*
PERSECUTION.
WHERIN IS DECLARED
That while old *England* is becoming new,
New-England is become Old.

Alſo four Propoſals to the Honoured Parliament and Councel of State,
touching the way to *Propagate the Goſpel of Chriſt* (with ſmall
charge and great ſafety) both in Old *England* and New.

Alſo four concluſions touching the faith and order of the Goſpel of
Chriſt out of his laſt Will and Teſtament, confirmed and juſtified

By J O H N C L A R K Phyſician of Rode Iſland in *America*.

Revel. 2, 25. *Hold faſt till I come.*
3, 11. *Behod I come quickly.*
22, 20. *Amen, even ſo come Lord Jeſus.*

L O N D O N,
Printed by *Henry Hills* living in *Fleet-Yard* next door to the *Roſe*
and *Crown,* in the year 1 6 5 2.

Title page of *Ill Newes From New-England,* by Particular Baptist John Clarke (London, 1652), praising England for its new tolerance of religious dissent and condemning New England for its persecution of the same.

THE
CIVIL MAGISTRATES
POVVER
In matters of Religion Modeſtly
Debated, Impartially Stated according to the
Bounds and Grounds of Scripture, And Anſwer
returned to thoſe Objections againſt the ſame
which ſeem to have any weight in them.

TOGETHER WITH
A Brief Anſwer to a certain Slanderous
Pamphlet called
Ill News from New-England ; *or, A Narrative*
of New-Englands *Perſecution.*
By J O H N C L A R K of *Road-Iland,* Phyſician.

By Thomas Cobbet *Teacher of the Church at* Lynne
in New-England.

Take us the foxes, the little foxes which ſpoil the vines, &c. Cant. 2. 15.
Rulers are not a terror to good works, but to the evill, &c. Rom. 13. 3.

This Treatiſe concerning the Chriſtian Magiſtrates Power, and the exerting thereof
in, and about matters of Religion, written with much zeal and judgement by Mr
Cobbet of *New-England,* I doe allow to be printed, as being very profitable for theſe
times.
Feb. 7ᵗʰ. 1652.   *Obadiah Sedgwick.*

L O N D O N,
Printed by *W. Wilſon* for *Philemon Stephens* at the Gilded Lion
in *Pauls* Churchyard. 1 6 5 3.

Title page of *The Civil Magistrates Power in Matters of Religion,* by Thomas Cobbet (London, 1653), affirming the government's right to legislate in matters of religious belief.

companions' sufferings at the hands of Massachusetts drew a lengthy rebuttal, this time by Lynn's Thomas Cobbet, whose *Civil Magistrates
Power in Matters of Religion* of 1653 further indicated the increasing inflexibility of the colonists' position on toleration. As Cromwell stripped the
presbyterians of their power to continue the campaign against religious
liberty, the New England Puritans only hardened themselves to their
brethren's criticism and proclaimed the righteousness of their course of
action against the baptists.

In addition to providing English readers with a graphic description of
his ordeal in Lynn and, later, in Boston, where the magistrates seemed
intent on making Clarke and his companions examples for other "Anabaptists" to consider before they dared broach such views, the author of
Ill Newes offered both a scriptural justification of his position on baptism
and a lengthy discussion of his belief that the magistracy had no right to
restrain a man's conscience, nor his "outward man for conscience sake."
To do so, Clarke argued, simply made men "outwardly and hypocriti-
cally to conform" to worship and thus usurped Christ's power over their
spiritual estates. Man's conscience, he wrote, "That which the Lord hath
reserved in his own hand, and hath intended to mannage as part of his
owne Kingdome by his own power or Spirit, and by another manner of
minnestry, and sword, than that which is put forth in the Kingdoms of
men," was not to be coerced, nor its power denied.[42]

"That which presupposeth one man to have dominion over another
mans conscience" was, Clarke wrote, but "a forcing of Servants, and
worshippers upon the Lord . . . which he seeks not for." Men had to be
free to follow the testimony of their consciences; to remove such freedom only destroyed the peace and well-being of a Christian commonwealth. In a catalogue of rhetorical questions that in retrospect seems
prophetic of the very problems the New England Puritans' intolerance
eventually brought upon them, Clarke displayed a profound insight into
religious psychology. If outward force or power was used to "maintain
and uphold the carnall interests and advantages of some upon religious
accounts" and so to persecute others who do not conform to that erroneous way, he wrote, "What hopes are hereby begotten and nourished
in some? what jealousies, suspitions and fears in others? what revengefull
desires in most? yea, what plottings and contrivings in all? and as a fruit
and effect hereof, what riding? running? troublesome, and tumultuous
assemblings together, and sidings?" Seen thus, Childe told his readers, a
forced conformity only bought the magistrates a little time against their
state's utter corruption.[43]

One example of the kinds of "assemblings" and "sidings" Clarke had in mind surfaced in Woburn a year after the appearance of his pamphlet when John Russell and nine others issued a "memorial for Christian liberty" in which they objected to a recent order of the General Court stipulating that "no person within this jurisdiction shall undertake any constant course of public preaching without the approbation of the elders of four of the next churches, or of the county court." By this time Russell was a Particular Baptist; and, though he had not yet signed off entirely from the Woburn church, he, like Clarke, was not averse to challenging what he regarded as an inordinate extension of both the civil magistrate's and the clergy's powers at the expense of the prerogatives of individual congregations.[44]

Russell, the acknowledged author of the petition, pointed out that by the institution of such a law the court greatly increased the powers of a "counsel of elders." Though he admitted that such counsel was desirable and, in "difficult" cases of discipline, often necessary, the law as worded allowed elders a voice in another congregation's affairs even before any rule of discipline had been broken. He nowhere openly said it, but Russell objected to "advice" remarkably similar to that tendered by a presbyterian classics. He made this point again when he warned that the law might work to "thrust" a minister upon a congregation, for if the full force of the ordinance was felt, "they must take such [ministers] as others approve or none." The General Court thus had empowered the elders of "approved" churches in a "superiorative" way because they had made the advice "binding from their authority." Clearly, then, although aimed at "Anabaptists" and other disturbers of New England's churches, the law ultimately threatened the very congregationalism it was meant to protect.[45]

To Russell's mind, the provision that allowed "approbation" to come as well from the county court was even more insidious, for this was a blatant extension of the civil magistrate's power into the religious sphere. The court's action, Russell claimed, took "the free course of church liberty into the hand of civil authority," for if the civil magistrate meddled in a church's affairs before he "discover[ed] any variation from a rule in her action by [her] . . . committing any practical or fundamental error of evil consequence," such action obviously "cross[ed] the lines" of the magistrate's designated authority. Russell added, "suppose elders and magistrates grow corrupt, where shall we be then?" Though at that time the court certainly intended no such inordinate extension of the law, who could predict how another body might choose to apply it? "If it may be

screwed up to such . . . a fair beginning," already to abridge the congregation's liberties, Russell argued, "posterity may rue when men of
worse conceits may be in place." In short, the ordinance seemed "to give
a supremacy where Christ gives none," and for a church to be asked to
perform an act "proportionable to a rule" would commit them to the
will, and whimsy, of fallible men. The civil throne was beneath Christ's,
the petitioners asked the court to remember, and "whilst churches keep
to the rule, they keep to their power and privilege." [46]

The Woburn "memorial" arraigned the Massachusetts General Court
for encouraging both presbyterianism and Erastianism, but, needless to
say, as in the case of the Remonstrance of 1646, redress was not granted.
The increase of such dissent within the colony, as well as the published
accusations of men like Childe and Clarke, forced New England Puritans
to defend the machinery by which they sought to maintain the New England Way even as more and more people were disaffected from it. When
Thomas Cobbet was asked by the colony to answer Clarke's *Ill Newes*—
he already had done doctrinal battle with the baptists in 1648 in his *Just
Vindication of the Covenant and Church Estate of Children of Members As Also
of their Right to Baptisme*—he prefaced it not with a tract attacking toleration per se, but with a lengthy discussion of the civil magistrate's coercive
power in matters of religion. As far as he and other Puritan clergy were
concerned, his debates with Williams Cotton already had settled the the-
oretical issue of religious liberty; Cobbet's job was the more practical one
of defining the civil magistrate's power to defend a Christian commonwealth from attack by those who would not keep erroneous opinions to
themselves. The extent to which the civil arm was to be used to discipline men in matters of belief, Cobbet announced, had become nothing
less than "the great controversal [sic] business of these polemick times." [47]

Cobbet was most troubled by the increasing contraction of the magistrate's power over "matters of the first Table," particularly his right to
punish those who drank "the Wine of Intoxicating and Infatuating doctrine." To the Lynn minister it seemed illogical (and unscriptural) that
magistrates should be left to attend only to political matters, "as if civill
maxims were more near and dear to Christ." If the civil arm of the commonwealth "be permitted to punish Witches, Sorcerers, and Inchanters,"
he wrote, those who play mischief with "Estates, Families, and Bodies,"
why could not magistrates arraign "white Witches, that out of pretence
of conscience, bewitch souls to death, by their inchanting doctrines"? To
prove once and for all that magistrates should resist being tied to so short
a "tether," Cobbet used as his main proof-text John 2:13–17, the descrip-

tion of Christ's purging of the temple, "one of his most glorious Acts," worthy of emulation by all those who had it within their assigned power to do likewise. If anyone objected that in cleansing the temple Christ had acted as Messiah, not as man, he had only to consider, Cobbet reminded his readers, that "Civil Rulers are Christs Vice-regents" on earth and as such were the "nursing Fathers and Mothers of his church."[48]

Cobbet was careful to point out that no one in civil authority could curb or punish ecclesiastical transgressions, for to do so infringed on the prerogatives of the congregation. Neither the magistrate nor the church could censure and punish corruptions in religion until they broke forth "into outward expression, and [were] brought into more open view," and even then only after sufficient means of conviction had been used with the offenders. But once such opinions had been broached and the individuals involved become "contemptuous" and "turbulent," the magistrate had every right to exercise his duty for the well-being of the state. Magistrates "may, yea must restrain," Cobbet concluded, "and seasonably and suitably punish all grosser corruptions in Religion, manifestly crosse to the Word," because such actions gave "just offence" to the saints and manifold "hurt" to others. Twenty years earlier such words would have been unexceptionable, but in 1653, in old England and New, many good Puritans seemed unsure just how the "Word" was to be taken, thus making irrelevant any one group's attempt to impose uniformity upon all others. To use another scriptural verse popular with Cobbet and other New Englanders in their sermons against toleration: though Christ had counseled his followers to take the little foxes that spoiled the vines, no one any longer was sure just who the foxes were or, if they were apprehended, for what crime they should be tried when so many others still ran free in the vineyard. But here again Cobbet was adamant. The civil authorities he defended would not impose "what form of Worship, or Church Discipline they please, as Erastus and some others since him affirm" but only upheld "the Laws of this their Supreme." As long as the civil magistrate was restrained by *that* tether, the commonwealth would prosper.[49]

Before he turned specifically to Clarke's charges, Cobbet answered the objection that the church had sufficient power to "attain her ends within her self." Here he fell back upon what in New England had become a familiar argument: "The State as well as the Church is injured by witchcraft, by perjury, by schism, and other sins, against the first Table," and so also must have "its defensive and vindictive power, Politically to attain its ends too, the good of safety and peace of the Subjects." The civil and religious "spears" both were to be drawn against anyone who seriously challenged church and state; both "polities" had to be "reciprocally help-ful to each other." Once the ecclesiastical powers had established the Way of God, when necessary they could request help in its maintenance; to reject the idea of such cooperation only opened the way for a serious dis-ruption of domestic peace. The church and state had to be in total agree-ment that "a set and fixed Toleration, is not to be given, by the Regulated Magistrate or higher Civill powers" when through such a toleration peo-ple "hold and profess" obvious and dangerous errors. All individuals, Cobbet concluded, were to obey the voice of conscience, as long as they remembered that by conscience they still were bound to the "very Word of God." "Neither Conscience it selfe simply considered, nor the direct-ing, instigating, and perswading of conscience" could be "in them selves nakedly considered."[50]

Cobbet had little sympathy for Clarke's difficulties in New England, and when he came specifically to answer the baptist's "scandalous pam-phlet" he wasted little time before claiming that *Ill Newes* was a patently "Anabaptist" tract in which the author argued that "no Christian may be a Magistrate, nor may use the Civil Sword." He attacked Clarke's objec-tions to the New Englanders' supposed intolerance with a barrage of scriptural texts and challenged him with a full range of practical consid-erations that demonstrated the magistrate's power in matters of the "first Table." To Clarke's charge that the suppression of dangerous dissent led to "Jealousies, Revengefull desires, Plottings Tumults and Sidings," Cob-bet pointed to England's recent experiences with "those opinionative Levellers" whose demands had come near irrevocably splintering the Pu-ritans' cause. Religious liberty obviously had done little to bring peace to England, and it was nonsense for Clarke to propose that a "generall Peace" would follow upon freedom to choose one's religion. The time of that sweet felicity promised in Micah 4:3–5 would occur only when all people and nations had become "resolute, and unanimous in the true paths and wayes of the true God."[51]

Cobbet disagreed with Clarke's recitation of the events that befell him in Lynn; and, as much as we must assume an equal amount of distortion on Cobbet's part, there is no reason to believe that, as in the cases of Childe and Gorton, the Bay government sentenced Clarke for his reli-gious belief—"you might have kept that to your self if you had pleased," Cobbet reminded him, "and so not merely conscience," for there was a degree of sedition in his action which tended "to draw away subjects from their obedience to the Laws of the Government" under which they lived. To the various charges made by Clarke (as well as by Childe, Gorton, and others) that the New Englanders disregarded English law in their persecution of dissenters, he pointed Clarke to the "established Law of the State of *England*, made May 2, 1648," a copy of which recently had been sent to a Salemite by a member of Parliament for the purpose of "tak[ing] off any apprehensions here of any, that they should tolerate corrupt opinions." This, the so-called Blasphemy Ordinance, still was in force, and to its original provisions had recently been added, Cobbet sharply noted, many aimed directly at baptists themselves. In England the civil magistrate still had the power, even if he only exercised it selectively, as against the Socinians in the 1650s, to prosecute individuals whose religious beliefs endangered the commonwealth. For Clarke to claim that the New Englanders' exercise of a similar power was illegal was, at best, specious.[52]

Cobbet's *Civil Magistrates Power* only made more apparent New England's increasing isolation from events in the rest of the Protestant world and did little to win the colonies any favor during the rule of Cromwell, to whom Cobbet had dedicated his work but who was discovering that to realize his dream of a godly commonwealth he had to permit a wide range of Protestant dissent. What made the New England Puritans' position even more difficult in the 1650s was the radically different attitude of the groups who then threatened them. Put most simply, the baptists and Quakers, unlike the earlier spiritists, made little effort to conceal their beliefs and seemed to thrive on the punishment their behavior brought upon them. John Norton's notion, offered in *The Orthodox Evangelist* of 1654, that "to add to the profession of error, suffering for it, is to add sin to sin," could not have been more alien to them. People like Clarke, Crandall, and Holmes, as well as the early Quaker emissaries to New England, were animated by the glory of personal witness for Christ's truth, regardless of what punishment ensued from such public testimony.[53]

One has to believe that the whippings, mutilation, and capital punishment administered to the Quakers finally were the result of the New England Puritans' increasing inability to comprehend what prevented such individuals from keeping their opinions to themselves in what Norton termed "Quiet Heresie." In reacting to them so harshly, the New Englanders, as Quakers were ever fond of pointing out, simply displayed how short and selective their memories were, and how dead to the spirit they had become. As the English Quaker Isaac Penington put it, though those who had emigrated to New England "no doubt thought and intended" to "lay a foundation" against the kind of persecution they had experienced in England, when their own condition changed, "in so much as it was now in their hand to determine the very worship, Church-Government, and order, there lay a great temptation before them to set up what they judged to be right, and to force all others to conformity with it." In retrospect, he observed, "it is plain, that which they sought was their own liberty" and "not the liberty of tender conscience towards God." The result of such a hard-fisted attitude, Penington concluded, was the ultimate corruption of their church way: "They have long had a form up, and it may have eaten out of the power [of their spirit], and they may not be so savoury now in their ease and authority in *New England*, as they were under their troubles and persecutions in Old England." [54]

On the whole such harsh judgments were convincing to English Puritans schooled in the civil wars and Interregnum. By the 1650s, even Governor Winthrop's son Stephen, a colonel in Cromwell's army, had become "a great man for soul liberty," and the ex-New Englander Hugh Peter, Williams reported in 1654, "crie[d] out against New English rigidities and persecutions" after word of them had reached his ears. A tract like Norton's *The Heart of New-England Rent*, written in 1659 after the imposition and final exercise of the harshest laws the New England Puritans yet had established against dissenters, announced New England's final admission of its ideological separation from the home country. Gone from this diatribe was all talk of due time for "conviction of one's errors," for the Quakers' "impunity" had to be "speedily and seasonably" punished to make others "more afraid of such evils." Gone, too, was any degree of charity toward these dissenters: Norton did not view them as erring brethren but rather as "*emissaries of Satan*" and "executioners of Gods coercive and vindicive displeasure" toward New England. "All experience proveth," Norton continued, "that the bitter root of Heresie, hath never prevailed where Doctrine, Catechism, and Discipline have been upheld in their purity and vigour." By the Quaker challenge New England was being called to its future glory; the punishment of such evil men was a necessary step toward the fulfillment of the colony's millennial role. "God forbid," Norton cried, "that after *New England* hath now shined twenty years and more, like a *light upon a hill*, it should at last go out in the *Snuff of Morellianism*," that is, be destroyed by too democratic a notion of church government. "Religion," he reminded his critics, "admits of no eccentric motions." [55]

New England's problem was that, to some degree, Puritanism always had been shaped by precisely the "eccentric motions" of those who found in this faith a release for their most profound spiritual longings, and for

New Englanders to attempt to cap so heady a mixture through its anti-tolerationist policies was at best a risky enterprise. Norton recognized as much when he admitted that already "too many" colonists were "perrilously disposed" to receive the Quakers' doctrines, and, "much disaffected" from congregationalism, they were eager "to live according to their own spirits." He could not discern as the basis for such social unrest the same power of faith that a few decades earlier had brought men like himself to America. One of the great apologists for the New England Way, Norton believed that "the Rule of Doctrine, Discipline, and Order is the *Center of Christianity*," but he made no mention of the spirit that shone so brightly in, say, the sermons of John Cotton.[56] By their very insistence on both the codification of New England congregationalism and the necessity to protect it in what they regarded its purest form, the New England Puritans had forgone an opportunity to perpetuate the kind of spiritual experience that in England, with the ascension of Charles II, had been outlawed again.

The politics of toleration, then, only confirmed the colonists in their belief that New England was a place apart, a bastion of consistency in a world that seemed to have expediently relinquished its claim to present Christianity as the Apostles had practiced it. The Puritans' carefully drawn distinctions between public and private offenses, their attempts to recall offenders from the error of their ways, their willingness to readopt excommunicated members who became penitent and accepted admonition, their trust in the lights of reason and revelation to awaken Christians to their waywardness: in all these ways the New England Puritans exercised charity toward brethren who had risked an Atlantic crossing to live according to God's rule. But the New Englanders set a line that could not be crossed. Once a dissenter disturbed the order of the New England churches and sowed the seeds of further discord, the arm of the magistrate was flexed against him. The last thing New England's leaders wanted was for the colonies to become the kind of spiritual bear-ring and circus they saw in the streets of London and elsewhere where religious liberty had been granted and abused.

Opposition to toleration for all sincere Christian dissenters had brought the Puritans to an implicit alliance with presbyterians, who in England similarly had refused to capitulate to the sectarians' demands for religious freedom. Implicit in the doctrinal and ecclesiastical treatises and in the ideological polemics of the 1640s and 1650s was the New England Puritans' recognition that they had more in common with the leaders of the Westminster Assembly than with those who preached in London's Independent churches. By linking themselves to those conservatives through an adamant insistence that they were neither schismatics nor separatists, they moved down a path that eventually led to Increase Mather's *Heads of Agreements* (1691), through which New England congregationalists made formal overture to union with presbyterians.[57]

Perhaps more significant, by the mid-1650s, particularly in Connecticut but in some Massachusetts churches as well, in debates over church membership, those inclined toward presbyterianism had gained much ground, a fact which the results of the Half-Way Synod of 1662 confirmed. Pushed by the radicals in the 1630s to incorporate into their discipline an acknowledgment of the work of the Spirit, thirty years later New England's leaders, seeking to head off a radical challenge in yet another way, acknowledged that their definition of church membership needed broadening in a way that, whether they wished it or not, aligned the colony with the kind of ecclesiastical settlement urged by Samuel Rutherford, Daniel Cawdrey, and other English and Scottish presbyterians.[58]

Admittedly, the battles over toleration did not lead directly to this modification of New England congregationalism. Rather, from the complex dynamic between New England congregationalists and those who sought freedom to worship as they pleased there was formed in the New England Puritans a willingness to acknowledge that some parts of their own discipline indeed might implicitly encourage dissent in the population. By opening their church doors to more individuals and so placing them under the elders' direct watch and care, the Puritans found yet another way to stem the tide of religious dissent as well as to combat the flagrant hypocrisy that men like Childe and Clarke had noted in the colony's churches. By 1662 in New England the church itself came to be defined in a more latitudinarian manner, not through the open toleration of dissenting opinions but by the liberal admission of those who, under the stringent membership requirements of the 1630s and 1640s, might have expressed their anxiety over their exclusion from the church by casting in their lot with the dissenters. Though men like Gorton and Clarke probably would not have recognized it, theirs and other challenges to the restrictions of the New England Way had borne healthy fruit. Convinced of its unique destiny as God's Promised Land, New England modified its ecclesiastical discipline in ways that ensured its survival long after the rule of the saints in England had ended with the reinstatement of the Episcopal clergy.

NEW ENGLAND'S IMAGE:

AT HOME AND ABROAD

By 1652, when Edward Johnson published his *Wonder-Working Providence of Sions Saviour in New England*, New England Puritans already had discovered and promulgated what Sacvan Bercovitch, following Perry Miller and other predecessors, has described as the myth of American exceptionalism. That is, they had willfully defined their community not so much through its political or territorial integrity as through a common ideology: specifically, their incessant rhetorical self-justification of what they regarded as their divinely ordained purpose. "When England began to decline in Religion, like lukewarm Laodicea," Johnson wrote, Christ erected "a New England to muster up the first of his Forces in," and as part of his commission to the settlers he had revealed that their new home would be "the place where the Lord will create a new Heaven, and a new Earth . . . , new Churches, and a new Commonwealth."[1] From that day forward, the Woburn militiaman believed, New England's destiny had been assured, and the many acts of God through which the emigrants and their churches were preserved only sealed the testament to the divine nature of their mission.

Robert Middlekauff has noted in his study of the Mather family that the New Englanders had not always thought of themselves in such terms, and though he dates this "invention of New England" much later, with the coming of age of Increase Mather's generation rather than Richard's, we do well to keep in mind his basic insight: in 1630 the Puritans were doing in New England what they would have gone *anywhere* to do—that is, preserving the true church polity—but by the 1650s they believed that *only* in *that* location could they accomplish this mission.[2] The process through which English Puritan emigrants became New England Puritans was inextricably linked to the colonists' various responses to the radical Puritan elements in their population. New England's self-image—that is, the colonists' way of understanding their identity and purpose in the New World, and thus their final difference from their brethren across the Atlantic—in large measure was determined by, or defined against, the ideology of more radical settlers who forced New England congregationalists to rethink their relationship both to the English Puritan movement, particularly as its leadership fell to Oliver Cromwell, and the Protestant Reformation as a whole. By 1650 ecclesiastically and politically separated from the majority of English Puritans, the New England Puritans had recourse to the world of myth, and the mythology about themselves that they presented to the rest of the Protestant world had within its texture many strands colored by exposure to ideas that had originated in the radical Puritan underground.

The single most important factor in the evolution of the New England Puritans' corporate identity lay in their typological reading of history, and, in particular, in their strong identification with the covenanted people of Israel. The doctrine of the national covenant, articulated most memorably in the "Modell of Christian Charity" which John Winthrop delivered on board the *Arbella* prior to his fleet's arrival in the New World, firmly established the colonists' strongest line of defense against any future challenges to the integrity of the Congregational Way. Unlike the early antinomians, the Gortonists, and the Quakers, all of whom promoted a mystical or allegorical reading of Scripture through which the drama of redemption was internalized and played out within the souls of individual believers, the majority of the New England Puritans assumed a biblical literalism that provided from the Old Testament's typological relation to the New a basis for belief in the progressive unfolding of the history of redemption *in this world*, a history that involved not only individual souls but an entire people in outward covenant with their God. And because to their minds the New Testament spoke of still-uncompleted things (particularly in the book of Revelation), when events in England radically altered the New England Puritans' relation to the home country, with relative ease they could come to believe that it was only they who remained to fulfill biblical prophecy.[3]

This linear conception of history formed one of the New England Puritans' basic points of contention with Roger Williams, whose millenarianism allowed for no successful reestablishment of the true Church until Christ himself reinstituted it at the end of time and thus left him and other faithful Christians to wander in the wilderness until the onset of the last days. In Williams's route his opponents perceived only the anarchic individualism they found among so many other dissenters, and in his case their judgment was borne out by Williams's subsequent career as a Seeker. So, too, did the majority of the New England Puritans reject the baptists' vision of the way God worked in human history, for by their denial of the efficacy of the rite of infant baptism, and so of the Abrahamic covenant of which it was the outward sign, they denied as well that God worked his will with special regard to a covenanted community. In place of the intricate genetics of salvation offered by the Puritans, baptists presented adults with the opportunity to decide for themselves to come to Christ and so willfully to join others who had made a similar decision. Their implicit premise was that no one could inherit membership in the Church; if asked to explain how God worked in human history, they pointed to those periods—spiritual pulsations we might term them—when through his grace God had revived the hearts of many dying sinners. Thus, as William McLoughlin has noted, revivalism, and not progressive reform, was at the heart of the baptists' understanding of Christian history.[4]

In contrast to such groups as the spiritists and baptists, who in different ways stressed the individuality of religious experience, the New England Puritans through their promotion of the ideal of the societal covenant sought to unite the entire population in what they took to be the furthering of God's divine will. All colonists, full church members or not, were given an important role in society, for even if their adherence to the covenant was only outward, their behavior still tended toward the good of the whole population. To ensure such visible allegiance to a corporate enterprise, New England's leaders, particularly its ministers, in the 1640s and 1650s came more and more to emphasize church discipline, the ecclesiastical forms that made visibly manifest the progress of the covenanted community toward the longed-for fulfillment of scriptural promise, over theological doctrine. But, as the colony's leaders asked from their charges a conscientious fulfillment of the terms of church discipline, they also opened themselves to criticism from those among them and in England who saw in such reliance on outward forms the death of true evangelical piety. "Discipline, or Church-Government is now the great businesse of the Christian World," one of Thomas Edwards's correspondents wrote after he had spent "almost eleven yeeres" in the "Wildernesse" of New England; and, he added, his experience there had only reinforced his belief that good Christians must "forget not the doctrine of Repentance from dead Works, and faith in the Lord Jesus."[5] At the price of true Gospel piety, some Puritans believed, had New England's grand covenantal scheme been purchased.

Like the Congregational Way itself, the New England Puritans' conception of their errand into America's wilderness and the public mythology they devised to strengthen it underwent considerable evolution in the first two decades of settlement. Even in the literature of the late 1640s some New Englanders reiterated the primary argument for emigration offered by the first colonists, but by that date such defenses had begun to sound more and more hollow. The argument stated that bands of courageous Puritan saints had come to the New World to nourish the seed of true religion after all indications pointed to its rapid extinction in England; if and when their home country was prepared to receive and nurture what the New Englanders by then would have raised into a vigorous plant, the emigrants' task would be successfully completed. Nowhere is the nature of this errand more eloquently expressed than in Cotton's words in *The Powring Out of the Seven Vialls* (1642) when he reminded New Englanders that it was their work "to wrastle with God, that they [their brethren in England] may not perish for lack of knowledge, nor mistake a false Church for a true," for "great pitty were it, that they should want any light which might possibly be afforded them."[6] In 1647 Samuel Symonds put it more pithily when he explained that New England had been created "to afford a hiding place for some of his people that stood for the truth while the nation was exercised into blood." In this view, New England was primarily expedient and the colonists' role intermediary. The New World had been planted by the Puritans for the good of the Church of England, and, by extension, of the entire home country.

The difficulty came when the New Englanders began to realize that, for all their countrymen's good will toward them, they still saw fit to criticize some of the decisions the emigrants had made as they began the practical business of establishing a colony. Even before the Antinomian Controversy had begun, some English Puritans were disturbed by reports that Winthrop and his cohorts "mainteine[d] opinions of the seperacion" and held other "opinions and tenents" that caused "a wonderfull disaffection of very many" toward the colony. "The whole kingdome begins, or rather proceeds to be full of preiudice against you," Winthrop's anonymous correspondent continued, "and you are spoken of disgrace-fully and with bitternes in the greatest meetings in the kingdome." Too many letters in which the colonists, finally free from the bishops' grasp, harshly criticized the English church had found their way to England, he went on to note, and he warned Winthrop to caution the settlers to be more discreet. For New Englanders to question the English Puritan min-istry and to call their brethren "doggs and swine" simply was not condu-cive to good relations between the two groups of reformers.[7]

The Antinomian Controversy provided a way to deflect such criticism of the colony's ecclesiastical path, for by so roundly condemning the Hutchinsonians and thus ensuring that any incipient dissidents would heed the lessons of the synod of 1637–1638, the New Englanders could claim that, contrary to reports of their purported separation and er-roneous doctrine, they were fully equal to the task of preserving the true faith in the face of so serious a challenge. This is the background to Zechariah Symmes's "fear," expressed at Anne Hutchinson's church trial, "that if by any meanes this should be carried over into England, that in New England and in such a Congregation thear was soe much spoken and soe many Questions made" about the plainest articles of the Puritans' faith, it would be "one of the greatest Dishonours to Jesus Christ and Reproch to thease Churches that hath bine done since we came heather." It had to be made clear to the colonists' English supporters that New En-gland was not a rat's nest of error and schism. By so forcefully destabiliz-ing the radical spiritists' position through the exile and excommunication of their leaders, they proved to their English brethren that they took their commission seriously. Let old England prepare the ground for the trans-planting of the true faith; the New Englanders were readying a hardy specimen to ship back for propagation.[8]

The first official account of the Antinomian Controversy was not pub-lished until 1644, and by then the New Englanders felt that the lessons learned during those trying years had become even more relevant to En-glish Puritanism. Throughout the 1640s, ministers like Bulkeley and Shepard, who had played such important roles in the synod, warned the home country to follow New England's lead and so to "Take heed of too much of that *new light* which the world is now gazing upon." "So much new light breaking forth," Bulkeley continued, "that the old zeale is al-most extinct by it." But the New Englanders' self-righteous boasting of how they had conquered the "antinomians," "familists," and "libertines" in their churches could be turned to serve their opponents' interests; viz., as proof that the kind of church polity established in New England *of ne-*

cessity produced such aberrant doctrines. After the calling of the Westminster Assembly, New Englanders were much abused for what men
like Baillie, Rutherford, Edwards, and Pagitt took to be the deleterious
effects of their "Independency." Baillie's attack, in particular, was so swift
and vituperative that Thomas Hooker suggested to Shepard that because
of the bitter struggle between presbyterians and Independents at the Assembly, Baillie, "a man of subtill and shrewd head," might have "had a
secret hand to provoke Mr. Weld to set forth his short story touching
occasions [in New England] in Mr. Vane his reigne" as a way of discredit-
ing both New England *and* the English Independents. Whether or not
this was the case, without doubt the *Short Story* caused New England
more harm than good.[9]

In 1645 the floodgates to toleration were not yet fully open, and the
colonists still could believe that, once the Independents had gained the
upper hand in England, the action Massachusetts had taken against
the radical spiritists would be viewed in its proper light. To the colonists'
increasing surprise and consternation, however, the Independents, realizing that they could not carry the Assembly, began to enlist the support of
more radical Puritans to counter their opponents' power. The *Apologeticall Narration* of 1644 gave the first indication of this reconciliation, and
within a few years hitherto-reliable Independents like Hugh Peter and
John Goodwin had heartily embraced some of their more radical brethren. At such moments the heresiographers again eagerly used the example of New England, if ironically. "We are made here to believe," Baillie
sarcastically noted in 1645, "that the Anabaptists and Antinomians are so
tame and harmless creatures." But "If it be so," he continued, "the Generall
Court at *New-Boston* hath been extreamly unjust, who professed their
well-grounded apprehension of a totall subversion not only of all their
Churches, but of their Civill State also," had the Hutchinsonians gone
unpunished.[10] Clearly, English Independents were causing a good deal of
trouble for the colonists, and the Bay Colony's official agents—particularly Weld and Winslow—gave much of their time to attempts to persuade the Independents to close ranks behind New England and reject
any compromise with more radical English Puritans.

Circumstances prevented any such agreement between the New Englanders and their erstwhile supporters in England, for the intensification
of the civil wars had put a different cast upon the colors the Independents
presented to their countrymen and had forced many New Englanders to
reconsider their commitment to their errand into America's wilderness.
What made the 1640s such a critical time for the colonies was the haunt-

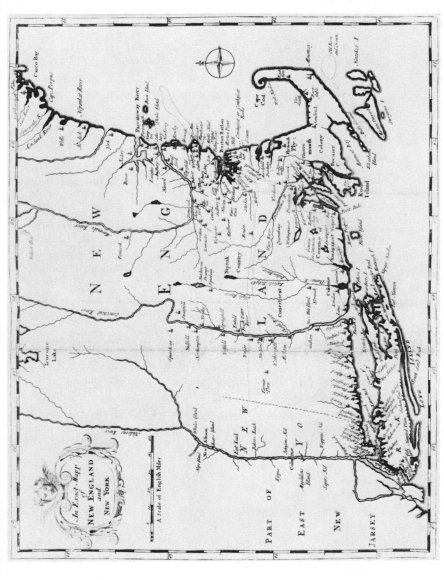

Map of New England at the end of the seventeenth century, from Cotton Mather's *Magnalia Christi Americana* (London, 1702), in which he defends the persecution of religious dissenters in seventeenth-century New England.

ing fear among many that the Great Migration had been an error in judgment, for with the onset of the civil wars and the ensuing victories by
parliamentary forces, New Englanders had good reason to wonder if the
center of action in the Protestant world had not shifted back to England,
if it ever had moved away in the first place. This doubt in the final purpose of their mission, and the equally painful burden of guilt they carried
for having deserted their fellow Puritans just before they were called on
to carry arms in defense of their faith, forced New Englanders to reassess
their purpose in coming to the New World and so to mark off permanently their differences from their English supporters. And toward that
end their confrontations with such radical groups as Gortonists, baptists,
and Quakers became the means by which they defined (and measured
their degree of commitment to) the task of being American Puritans.

    There is little doubt that the calling of the Long Parliament in 1640 and
the battles between royalist and parliamentary forces that followed within
two years seriously threatened the rationale behind the New England settlements, for many in the colonies did take these events as indications
that God once again intended great things for the home country and
decided to return across the Atlantic. Hugh Peter became Cromwell's
personal chaplain; Winthrop's son Stephen, as noted earlier, emerged as
major-general in the parliamentary forces; George Downing assumed the
post of chaplain to John Okey's regiment; Samuel Eaton, brother of
Theophilus, founder of New Haven, served the garrison at Chester; both
Thomas Larkin and Hanserd Knollys, discredited in the Antinomian
Controversy and its aftermath, preached to the Roundhead forces. Israel
Stoughton, Nehemiah Bourne, and John Leveritt all served as officers in
the famed regiment of Colonel Rainborough.[11] Some of the excitement
and anticipation these and other New Englanders felt as they enlisted in
the English Puritan cause is epitomized in a letter Thomas Weld sent to
New England in 1643 in which he explained to other New England ministers why he and Peter were remaining in England "six moneths longer."
"The present condition of the kingdom," he reported, "that is now upon
the verticall point, together with the incredible opportunities [for] very
many godly persons," kept them from immediately returning to New
England. "Things cannot stand at this passe here, as now," he continued,
"but will speedily be better or worse." "If better," he explained, "we shall
not repent as to have bene spectators and furthers of our deare countries
good, and to be happy messengers of the good newes thereupon you."
And "if worse, we are like to bring thousands with us to you."[12]

    The "thousands" were not to come until after the Restoration, and through the late 1640s and 1650s repatriation continued, reaching a high point during the Protectorate of Oliver Cromwell. During this heady period not the least among the incentives for return was what Weld had called the "incredible opportunities" for godly Puritans, in both the army and the ministry. As another New Englander, William Hooke of Taunton (who also served Cromwell's forces as a chaplain) proudly reported, in many circles New Englanders were in high regard. "When sometimes a New-England man returns thither," he wrote in 1641, "how is hee lookt upon, lookt after, received, entertained, the ground he walks upon beloved for his sake, and the house held the better where hee is? how are his words listened to, laid up, and related frequently when hee is gone?" Radical Puritans like Knollys and Gorton quickly took advantage of this situation, but even the most fervent Bay Puritans were wooed by their English friends with promises of the material and psychological rewards they could expect when they stepped again on English soil. In 1652 Hugh Peter invited John Winthrop the Younger to return with his family, "for certaynly," Peter informed him, "you will be capable of a comfortable living in this free Commonwealth." And earlier, in 1646, an attempt had been made to recruit Governor Winthrop himself "to assist in the parliament's cause." Neither of the Winthrops reemigrated, but the colony clearly was worried about losing such leadership. The Massachusetts General Court, for example, counseled against sending the elder Winthrop even as an agent to assist Weld in his representation of the colony's interest. They feared that so many already "were upon the wing" that the governor's departure would only "occasion more new thoughts and apprehensions."[13]

From reports in the heresiographies, particularly in Edwards's *Gangraena* (1646), it is clear that presbyterians did not welcome this influx of New Englanders, for in many cases they verified the suspicion that the religion practiced there would hinder the reformation sought by more conservative English Puritans, especially those who wished to fulfill the terms of the Solemn League and Covenant with Scotland and so bring all England under presbyterian rule. Charismatic leaders like Hugh Peter incensed the conservatives. The activities of this "Vicar Generall and Metropolitane of the Independents both in New and Old England" so rankled Edwards that he asked bitterly whether they in New England would "endure one or more Presbyterians to live among them, and to go up and downe their Countrey, and in chiefe Towns and places to preach against, cry downe their Churches and Church-government, and to extoll and cry up a contrarie way" as Peter himself did.[14] At times Peter's brashness knew no bounds. In the spring of 1643, he even had had the temerity to urge the House of Commons to send Archbishop Laud to New England as fitting punishment for his crimes.[15]

There were others like Knollys and Larkin who already were too radical for the colonies and who returned to the relative freedom of England to preach their doctrines more openly. "Poor England," Edwards complained, "must lick up such persons, who like the vomit had been cast out of the mouth of other Churches." Because of such unsavory types, he continued, England clearly had "become the common shore and sink to receive in the filth of Heresie and Errors from all places." And added to the problems posed by such characters were those raised by men whose very morality seemed to have disappeared during their years in the New World. One "Independent," for example, "who came some yeers ago out of *New-England*" and quickly rose to the position of captain in the army, had left behind "a wife and many children," Edwards reported, but now took no care for their subsistence. Further, "as it seems by Letters written to *New-England*, and from thence," Edwards noted disgustedly, without even a thought of divorce this man "hath been sometimes near the marrying of others" in England. Only rarely were good words spoken of New Englanders who had returned to their home country. Edwards did mention one individual who had lived for a time in Providence and become so tired of the "factions, fractions, and divisions" he encountered there that upon his return to England he renounced the Independents' polity for presbyterianism. But to conservative Puritans such rare exceptions only proved the rule. In the 1640s New England was thought of by many as a radical tinderbox which held countless errors ready to enflame any English Puritans disposed to champion an Independent course for the English Church.[16]

During these trying times the New England Puritan leaders watched anxiously as many of their friends and neighbors returned to aid the English Puritan cause and so to serve as well as more grist for the heresiographers' mills. Only in Rhode Island, where, as the baptist immigrant and prominent English printer Gregory Dexter noted, the people had not been "consumed with the overzealous fire of the Godly and Christian magistrates," did the colonists remain "quiet and drie from the streams of blood spilt by the warr in our native country." The implications of Dexter's observation—that, overall, people were more contented with their lot in the Rhode Island colonies—is difficult to prove but entirely plausible, given the undeniable strains between such groups as the deputies and magistrates in the Bay Colony in the 1640s and '50s. The Bay Colony's leadership was challenged during the imprisonment of the Gortonists and in the famous Hingham militia case and had to face the fact that the tumultuous political and religious situation in England quickly was bringing to nought all their initial rationalizations concerning their migration to the New World. They needed novel ways to justify their absence from what for many had assumed the proportions of the final battle between God's anointed and the forces of the Antichrist.[17]

This insecurity and guilt was not restricted to the magistrates and ministers. In 1647, Samuel Symonds of Ipswich told Winthrop that many of the populace were reexamining the wisdom of their move to New England. "The irregular departure of some" for England, he noted, "causeth a deeper search of heart wherefore God hath brought his elect hither." Peter Bulkeley's important treatise of 1646, *The Gospel-Covenant*, after reciting the usual litany about how God "hath dwelt with us as with his people Israel" and had brought the New Englanders "out of a fat land into a wildernesse" where their faith would be tested, lamented how "our hearts begin to faile us; yes, and our faith also." The reason for this apostasy was not hard to discern. "We begin to quarrel with Gods providence," Bulkeley explained, "and with our selves, and to question whether wee have done well to come hither or no." John Cotton, too, knew why a spiritual malaise had settled over the Massachusetts churches: "If men be weary of the Country and will back again to *England*," it was because "in heart they are weary." In such individuals he concluded, there was "no Spirit of Reformation."[18]

The opinions of English Puritans on this matter hardly mitigated the self-doubt experienced by New Englanders in the 1640s and 1650s. As early as 1640, Giles Firmin had "heard a conclusion gathered against [the New England] Plantations, that . . . it was not a way of God, to forsake" their country as long as they might have "enjoyed God in any comfortable measure" in England. Twenty years later the Quaker Isaac Penington was even more blunt. "That there was an honest intent" in many New Englanders "in transplanting into *New-England*," he wrote, "I do not doubt." But, he continued, "whether they had a sufficient warrant from God to transplant, was doubted and objected against them, by many of their conscientious fellow sufferers there in old *England*, who testified then they did believe it to be their duty not to fly." Those who migrated, Penington made clear, always had been at great pains to convince others, and themselves, of the final worth of their transatlantic venture.[19]

As long as their "fellow sufferers in old *England*" seemed to have need of them, the New Englanders marched confidently toward their goal of perfecting a church-state based on congregational polity. But in the world of English politics in the mid-1640s, to others, and, increasingly, to themselves, they seemed strangely disoriented, caught between a need to justify fifteen years of foundation work in the wilderness and their increasing knowledge that the path they had trodden might after all have led away from the New Jerusalem. But at this point, as they witnessed the disintegration of the English Puritan movement and themselves encountered such groups as the Gortonists and "Anabaptists," the New England Puritans began, half-consciously at first, to find light in this ideological tunnel. Reaching back to their treatment of Williams and the antinomians, they began to define themselves as those who had refused compromise with any of the kinds of sectarians then rending the fabric of English society. Ecclesiastically and politically separated from their English Puritan brethren, they emphasized this very separateness and, even in the face of more criticism of their measures against dissenters, to make of their ecclesiastical purity the touchstone of both their Christian virtue and corporate identity. The radicals in their midst—and through the 1640s and 1650s there seemed more and more of them—provided New Englanders with an opportunity to assert their godly difference from all other Puritans and to illustrate their willingness to defend their faith in battles every bit as trying as those in which the English Puritans then participated.

The Bay Colony's capture and imprisonment of the Gortonists in 1643 stands as a representative episode in the evolution of the New England Puritans' understanding of their mission in the New World. Brought to Boston under force of arms after two Indian sachems from whom they had purchased land around Shawomet complained that this land in fact had been seized unjustly, Gorton and his followers were not arraigned on this charge but for seditious and heretical statements uttered in previous exchanges with the General Court. Few people other than the magistrates and ministers seemed convinced of the Gortonists' threat to the colony, for "no other man or woman" appeared to testify against them. The populace finally, as noted earlier, was so dissatisfied with the sentences meted out to the group that the General Court shortly thereafter stepped in and overturned them. What are we to make of the colony's seeming overreaction to Gorton? Did the Bay Puritans, as Francis Jennings suggests, merely use the Gortonists as a ploy to extend economic and political control over the native American population on their southwestern border, or were they genuinely worried that this radical ideology

might spread to others in their settlements? Were they troubled only by
Gorton's seeming disregard for the laws of their Bible commonwealth
and his repeated threats to expose the colonists' own disregard for the
sovereign rights of Englishmen? Surely one could not compare the danger posed by the Gortonists to that of the antinomians several years earlier, when the entire colony was torn by the seriousness of the events in
Boston.[20]

New England would not become like old, even if, as one of their critics put it, their repressive and unenlightened posture made them "stinke
every where."[21] In New England the Gortonist episode epitomized a
time of communal identity crisis, of profound redefinition and redirection of an entire society's belief system; in Kai Erikson's terms, a new
"boundary" for acceptable behavior was being established at a point in
the society's history when its members sorely needed such a searching
reexamination of their communal goals. Under increasing pressure from
England to readjust their polity to square with the march of events there,
New England's magistrates began to pave the way for the synod of
1646–48, at which the New England Way, with all its strictures against
dissent, would be codified and published for all the Protestant world to
see. The Gortonists' very *difference* from the majority of New England's
colonists thus was put to ideological use, both to define and then, as such
dissidents were reprimanded, to reinforce the belief that New England's
destiny was different from England's.

After the Gortonists came Robert Childe and other of the Remonstrants; John Clarke, Obadiah Holmes, and John Crandall; William
Pynchon; Henry Dunster; the early Quaker emissaries; and numerous
other dissenters. None of these individuals nor the groups to which they
belonged had the means literally to overturn the New England Way.
Many never had any other intention but to live in harmony with other
Puritans in New England. But all eventually served a larger ideological
purpose: to direct the population to a renewed belief in the special nature
of their destiny and to impress upon English Puritans the progressive error of their ways, particularly through their espousal of religious toleration. If any of the colonists felt guilty about their separation from the
home country, here was good reason to accept that act as a necessary step
in God's plans for reformation. And if others were worried about not returning to England to fight the good fight against royalist troops, battles
for the Lord had to be fought in New England, too. With each subsequent "victory" over those who challenged the integrity of the New England Way, the magistrates buoyed the spirits of those in the colony's

population who had come to think that their presence in the New World had become irrelevant.

In the case of the Gortonists, as well as in the debate over whether to maintain the stringent immigration laws instituted during the Antinomian Controversy, the populace did not immediately endorse their leaders' actions nor recognize and affirm the "true" purpose for which they had peopled a wilderness. The redefinition of their mission—the shift from viewing New England as only one of many places where true church piety could be maintained to understanding it as the special preserve of ecclesiastical and doctrinal purity, God's chosen land—was gradual and, no doubt, at first only half-conscious. Through the late 1640s and 1650s the adjustment was indeed made and support for the colony's cause fervently recruited, primarily through the efforts of those clergy and magistrates who claimed that the direction in which the colony then was heading did not mark a sharp break with its past. Here, of course, the histories of Williams and Hutchinson had their uses; their early challenges to the New England Way, then only half-formed, were explained in terms of the now newly defined mission of New England. English Puritan criticism of the colony's intolerance and its supposed disregard for English law also served their purpose, for the profound doubts of English Independents and harsh condemnation by more conservative English Puritans, only proved to New Englanders that they had to suffer for their faith and struggle to maintain their righteousness as everywhere else in the Protestant world the true cause of Christ suffered.[22]

The radical Puritans in New England became a necessary scapegoat, helping the colonists redefine their errand and fueling its energy. By selecting various individuals whose behavior had crossed the boundaries of acceptable dissent and chastising them for their waywardness, the New England Puritans performed periodic rituals through which the population was brought to understand its communal purpose. And by allowing a modicum of dissent, as long as an individual kept his opinions to himself and was not openly seditious, the colony's leaders ensured that they would not have full-scale rebellion on their hands. The wisdom of this position was illustrated in the immediate aftermath of the Gortonists' trial when the magistrates chose not to protest the General Court's revocation of the Gortonists' sentences. Their imprisonment and trial had served the purpose of public spectacle; to press the issue further would only have been counterproductive. In the ensuing years there again would be sporadic disagreement with the colony's treatment of certain dissenters, but it never seriously threatened the authority of the magistrates and clergy. The fate of the Woburn "memorial for Christian liberty" in the early 1650s was typical: the court simply refused to consider it.[23]

New England's covenant with God (and the linear view of history upon which it was predicated) thus was indirectly served by those like the radical spiritists and baptists who refused to acknowledge its priority. Later in the century, when sectarianism had ceased to be a major issue in English Protestantism and New England finally was forced grudgingly to accept baptists, Quakers, and Anglicans, the colonists discovered yet other groups against whom they could assert their belief in themselves as a people under divine sanction. The native Americans in the aftermath of King Philip's War and, shortly thereafter, those in Salem accused of being in open league with Satan, provide the most memorable examples.[24] But through the 1650s the New England Puritans located *within* their society convenient enemies against whom they could prove their mettle, and convinced themselves of their own importance in the Protestant Reformation. If the radicals wished to be free from the psychological constraints such an understanding of history imposes, it is ironic that finally they were subsumed within it, not willingly to be sure, but through the New England Puritans' shrewd cooptation of the points of their revolutionary program for uses quite different from those which the radicals intended. Puritan radicalism was thus absorbed into the realm of the American Puritan imagination.

Nowhere is this more clearly seen than in Edward Johnson's *Wonder-Working Providence of Sions Saviour in New England*, the *locus classicus* for understanding the shift in the colonists' way of understanding their nature and destiny in the New World. The New England Puritans always had been interested in recording God's providences toward them; John Winthrop's journals and William Bradford's history of Plymouth are the most important but hardly the only examples of this. But Johnson's frenzied and chauvinistic history differs from theirs on several counts, not the least important of which is that it was the first large-scale published historical narrative of New England. Johnson's history, unlike, say, the narratives of Winslow that preceded it, was not at all apologetic or defensive in tone. Johnson took every opportunity to trumpet the fact that, because the ecclesiastical and civil polity of Massachusetts had been molded as closely as possible to the Word of God, the Lord had continuously blessed the colony and preserved it from all dangers. Gone now was the self-doubt and insecurity that in the 1640s had marked the colonists' polemics and treatises. In their place was the kind of bravado that came only with the author's belief that, despite all the abuse hurled at it, New England was assured of its true role in the history of redemption.[25]

More than any other kind of trial, the Indian wars included, the colonists' encounters with their radical brethren provided to Johnson his most important evidence of the extraordinary favor in which God held New England in general and Massachusetts in particular. Early in the narrative, as he described the divine commission the emigrants had accepted by leaving England, he reported that not the least among the many injunctions Christ had given to the Puritans was "never to make League with any . . . Sectaries," by which he meant antinomians, Seekers, familists, and the Gortonists, in addition to the "Papists" and other more conventional enemies.[26] Much later in his history, Johnson described at length the New Englanders' victories over these groups. From its commencement he obviously had an artful purpose—to impress upon English Puritans (and many New Englanders as well) the heroic nature of the colonists' resistance to the radicals' challenge. Toward this end he emphasized the kind of imagery that would have deeply moved anyone sensitive to the successive traumas of English Puritanism: he made frequent use of martial language, gave detailed descriptions of the foundation of each new outpost, and lavished praise on its minister, the ostensible leader of resistance to any outbreak of error. Equally important in his account were the foot-soldiers who formed the membership of the churches. Many of the most powerful passages concern the charge to each Puritan who had made the Atlantic crossing to stand firm in defense of the New England Way. "Can it possible [sic] be the mind of Christ," objected one English Puritan upon hearing of the call to attend God's word in New England, "that now so many Souldiers disciplined by Christ himselfe the Captaine of our salvation, should turne their backs to the disheartening of the Fellow-Souldiers?" Johnson's answer was an unequivocal "Yes," for, he argued, "although it may seeme a mean thing to be a New England Souldier," Christ had revealed that the New World would be the place "where the Lord will create a new Heaven and a new Earth." The colonists were to keep their "weapons" in "continuall readinesse" to fight the "Battails" of the Lord. "Not that he shall come personally to Reigne upon Earth," wrote Johnson in a moment that reveals his ardent post-millennialism, but because the "powerful Presence and Glorious brightnesse of his Gospell both to Jew and Gentile" soon would bring "the whole civill Government of people upon Earth" under his rule.[27]

Johnson insisted that "for England's sake" the emigrants had left England "to pray without ceasing for England." He also, however, made clear that the colonists had no good reason to return to their homeland; they were the "forerunners of Christs Army" whose destiny it was to "proclaim to all Nations, the neere approach of the most wonderfull workes that ever the Sonnes of men saw." In England armies could fight and crowned heads fall; those with open eyes would see America as a spiritual encampment of Christ's soldiers every bit as important as any in England. Its experience already had displayed God's special favor. As eminent a man of God as Rev. Cotton "hath declared some sudden blow to be given this blood-thirsty monster," Johnson confidently reported, and therefore "all men that expect [that] day" now had to "attend the means" of its arrival, and not "uphold some part of Antichrists kingdome." [28]

Throughout Johnson's narrative such pawns of the Antichrist as the antinomians, Gortonists, and baptists frequently test the resolution of Christ's soldiers. The author does not disguise the fact that, because of these troublemakers, the New England churches in the colony's earliest years had been very vulnerable. They were, he wrote, "like Sheepe let loose to feed on fresh pasture, being stopped and startled in their own course by a Kennell of devouring Wolves." But though the invective he hurled at these spiritual "Wolves" at times equalled the vitriol of the presbyterian heresiographers, Johnson had one polemical advantage over them. Because he wrote after some of the important battles already had been decided, he spoke convincingly of how completely the heretics had been crushed in campaigns like that waged at the synod of 1637–1638, when all good Puritans had gathered together "as one Man" to "undoe all the cunning twisted knots of Satans Malignity." Because Christ's New England army so diligently defended its communities against Satan's emissaries, certainly more than English Independents had protected theirs, the millennium seemed imminent. To those critics who recited the embarrassing fact of the continuing presence of radicals in the colonies, Johnson had prepared an equally assured response. "There's somewhat to be considered in it to be sure," he wrote, "that in these daies, when all look for the fall of Antichrist, such detestable doctrines should be upheld, and persons suffered, that exceed the Beast himself for Blasphemy." Johnson's was a rationalization that would be repeated many times in New England's subsequent history, most invidiously at the height of the witchcraft hysteria in the 1690s. He essentially argued that when the Devil's cohorts raged more angrily and mightily, it was the surest sign that Armageddon was near. With New England's soldiers leading Christ's forces, the outcome would not long remain in doubt. [29]

To a degree, Johnson's martial epic was wish-fulfillment pure and simple. What he articulated had not yet become popular opinion. *Wonder-Working Providence* is an important example—John Norton's *Orthodox Evangelist* and the Cambridge Platform itself are two others—of the attempts of New England Puritan leaders to salvage from the ideological wreckage of the English revolution an important role for New England in subsequent Christian history. Johnson's effort was especially significant because, much more than Winslow's or Norton's works, it was, for all its fidelity to the events surrounding the settlement of New England, primarily a work of the American Puritan imagination, a forerunner of Cotton Mather's monumental *Magnalia Christi Americana* of 1702, in which the myth of New England assumed its most eloquent formulation. Many of the components of the myth that Mather later so strikingly assembled already were present in Johnson's history—the hagiography of the first ministers and magistrates, the absorption of the individual colonist's destiny into that of the corporate enterprise, the use of typology to define the colony's historical role and thus the rhetorical conflation of New England with both New Canaan and New Jerusalem. While Mather's era most assuredly was not Johnson's, the impetus toward the creation of such historical monuments was the same: the insecurity the New England Puritans felt at not being sure of their mission, and hence their strong will to believe that through such books as *Wonder-Working Providence* and the *Magnalia* their leaders articulated that mission for them.[30]

The writing of history is itself a process of self-definition. As the New England Puritans began to realize more and more their difference from English Puritans, a fact brought home to them through their encounters with sectarians in England who were winning, if not outright acceptance, then grudging toleration, they self-consciously began through books like Johnson's to fashion a striking new identity. No longer was New England but a sanctuary where the light of God's truth would be kept burning until it could be brought back to illuminate the English church. It was the place from which Christ would take a more important fire, symbolized by the zeal with which the colonists maintained the integrity of their faith, and with which, as Johnson put it, he would then "burn up Babilon Root and Branch." Assured of their destiny by what they regarded as the favorable hand of God in all their affairs, in the 1650s New England's ministers and magistrates grew increasingly fierce in their treatment of those who, in straying from the Congregational Way, strived to sway other colonists to their side. Like English friends and relatives who wielded arms in the civil wars, they too could proclaim their bravery and resilience, and against enemies equally, if not more, threatening. The "Battails" of the Lord took many forms, Johnson reminded critics of New England, and no one could claim that New England's Christian soldiers had abandoned Christ's cause.

Nor, Johnson's literary descendents would claim, was it ever abandoned, no matter how severely New England's critics condemned the intolerance in the colonies. Williams, for example, asked the colonists to remember that "as your *Gifts* are rare, your *Professions* of Religion (in such way) rare, your . . . hidings from the storms abroad rare and wonderfull," so in proportion "your Transgressions" cannot but carry "a rare and extraordinary *Guilt*." As a theocratic experiment the New England Way survived an inordinately long time, much longer than any polity that emerged from the period of the English civil wars.[31] Its survival depended on the magistrates' and ministers' willingness constantly to adjust their ideology to the demands of each subsequent decade, but what remained inviolate at least through the seventeenth century—and historians like Bercovitch would say for two centuries more—was the colonists' sense of their specialness as guardians of the Christian faith against the attacks of any and all enemies, be they Indians, Papists, witches, or, eventually, opponents of "enthusiastic" religion, colonial agents, and deists. Even as they explicitly changed the principles of the Cambridge Platform through subsequent synods, and implicitly, in individual congregations as the clergy tried to maintain a heightened piety, the larger contours of the myth remained. New England was a special place made for a special reason, and its identity as such was assured as long as congregationalism and the complex ideology it supported held the allegiance of all the settlers. No matter that in 1680 the discipline of Boston's Second Church would have been scarcely recognizable, let alone palatable, to someone who had known Cotton's ministry in Boston's First Church. The larger myth of New England remained the cohesive factor.

In three different decades of New England's history the Puritans' responses to radicals in their midst contributed significantly to the development of the colonists' self-identity. The combination of the colonists' individual and group guilt at having "separated" from English Puritans just before their greatest trials and the increasing criticism of their ecclesiastical discipline by both conservative and radical English Puritans led to an oddly symbiotic relationship with those in their communities who sought more radical religious reform. As the New England Puritans sought to ensure the purity of their churches and, later, to disprove the presbyterians' criticism of the colony's schismatic tendency, they angered their Independent supporters in England. Yet by 1645 they also had begun to realize that these same radicals served the purpose of helping them to understand and justify their increasingly anomalous position in the Protestant world.

When they heard reports like that which came from John and Mary Trapp, that even though in England presbyterianism was carrying the day, "the Church swarme[d] with Antinomians, Anabaptists, & sects of all sorts," they could point with pride to their establishment of a commonwealth on the true primitive church model.[32] One might say, then, that there was no radical Puritan Revolution in New England because it already had occurred implicitly, in the magistrates' and ministers' incorporation of the notions of visible sainthood and corporate selfhood into the colony's public ideology, and thus in the creation of a state in which the individual, no matter who he was or what he did, possessed a dignity and purpose unavailable to him elsewhere in the Protestant world. Had the programs of the Levellers or Diggers been successful, of course, New England's achievements in comparison would seem minimal, but with Parliament's failure to implement any of the principles of *An Agreement of the People* and Cromwell's inability to forge a lasting coalition to carry out more radical religious and social reform, New England, where overt radicals were severely chastised, in fact encouraged a true revolution of the saints and maintained it throughout the seventeenth century.

PART III

NEW ENGLAND RADICALS: THREE CASE STUDIES

ANNE HUTCHINSON AND
THE "ANTINOMIANS"

In the 1630s, 1640s, and 1650s the range and diversity of New England Puritan radicalism was nowhere more clearly revealed than in the careers of Anne Hutchinson, Samuel Gorton, and William Pynchon, all of whom gathered around them disciples who promulgated their unorthodox ideas. All three were early immigrants to the colonies—Pynchon arrived in 1630, Hutchinson in 1634, and Gorton in 1636/7—and so provide more evidence that, though they and other New Englanders later contributed to the religious upheaval in England in the 1640s and 1650s, to a large degree such individuals developed their radical ideas independent of any extended contact with prominent English sectarians.[1]

Before their emigration each of these Puritans had drunk deeply at the same spiritual founts as had many of their countrymen and fellow emigrants, and in the freedom of the New World each drew upon his earlier experiences to develop a strain of Puritan thought decidedly at odds with the nonseparating congregationalism of Winthrop and other leaders of the Massachusetts Bay Colony. Gorton and Pynchon eventually returned to England, the former for a few years and the latter for the remainder of his life, and entered fully into the heated debates of the day, but their ideas had matured in New England and were simply refined in the crucible of religious dissent in the home country. Hutchinson, Gorton, and Pynchon, then, offer prime examples of the richness of Puritan thought as it had developed through the 1630s, and in particular of how it provided its lay adherents with significant ideological options, only one of which led to the theocracy of the Bay Colony.

One could quite justly argue that Roger Williams belongs with this group. No one would deny Williams's significance to radical Puritans in old England and New, particularly because of the range of his contacts in London's radical circles. But of all New England's dissenters he has received the most extended study, most recently by W. Clark Gilpin.[2] Hutchinson, Gorton, and Pynchon, each in his or her own way, allow us to study the development of many of the same radical ideas that Williams espoused; support even for his extreme stand on religious liberty, for example, was found in Gorton's and Pynchon's works, none of which has received serious scholarly attention in the last fifty years. Some may believe that Gorton and Pynchon were atypical because they gained access to the publishing outlets of London, or that Pynchon's prominence as one of the organizers of the Massachusetts Bay Colony was the sole reason for the magistrates' concern about his heresies and so disqualifies him as representative of any broad-based radical movement. Yet as lay Puritans all three of these people discovered in the doctrines of their faith support for a more radical renovation of the English church than that urged by New England's ministers and magistrates, and convinced a significant number of their contemporaries to consider seriously the logic of their criticisms. If Hutchinson, Gorton, and Pynchon were unusual or exceptional, it was because of their ability to articulate their ideas at length and with remarkable theological sophistication, a gift that three hundred and fifty years later provides a vivid evocation of the varied nature of Puritan radicalism in New England.

The careers of these New Englanders, each of whom came under attack in a different decade, illustrate the constellation of attitudes and events that dictated the nature of the magistrates' response. The course of reformation and revolution in England itself can be broken down by these same decades.[3] This is not to claim that within any given decade the Gortonists elicited the same reaction as, say, the Particular Baptists; but overall we can generalize with some intellectual profit about the official New England responses to such radical ideology. By the 1650s, with Pynchon's voice joined to a chorus of numerous baptists and Quakers, the New Englanders knew that they faced a revolution of sorts. Why and how they were able to prevent it from assuming the dimensions of England's is in good measure exemplified in these three case studies.

For many scholars the Antinomian Controversy that swept through the Massachusetts Bay Colony between 1636 and 1638 is the most memorable episode in New England's early history. It is usually pointed to, along with the colonists' difficulties with Roger Williams, as an indication of the Puritans' unwillingness to tolerate any deviation from congregational church order. During and immediately after the Antinomian Controversy, however, the colonists still were shaping the contours of their ecclesiastical system, an inevitable consequence of the fact that, as William Hubbard later noted, they had arrived in the New World without prior agreement about precisely how to establish the ecclesiastical reform they had contemplated.[4] The magistrates' and ministers' responses to Anne Hutchinson and her sympathizers must be seen not as a stubborn defense of long-held principles but as the consequence of the colony's process of self-definition. Those who held antinomian beliefs were no heretical invaders from outside the colony like, say, the Quaker vanguard in the 1650s, but a significant minority that, while as dedicated to the colonial experiment as Winthrop, Dudley, and Shepard, grounded their faith and piety in the moment of justification, not in its consequent effects.

Anne Hutchinson became the focal point of the authorities' frustration at their inability to resolve the colony's religious differences. Throughout the first year of the controversy, through the meeting of the synod of 1637 and its condemnation of eighty-two "erroneous opinions as were found to have been brought into *New-England*, and spread under-hand there," the authorities were concerned more with the increasing support for spiritist ideas than with Hutchinson herself. Hence, for example, their close examination of John Cotton until they were sure that he could be counted on to support the views of the majority of the colony's ministers; hence, the trial and banishment of John Wheelwright for his seditious behavior in support of the "opinionists," and the punishment of those who protested against the court's treatment of him. Although Winthrop and others argued to the contrary, Hutchinson herself clearly was not the source of all the erroneous doctrines in the Bay Colony but rather the articulate spokeswoman for a strain of radical spiritism; in Roxbury, Charlestown, and Newbury her cause found many sympathizers. With the final banishment and excommunication of Hutchinson and her closest adherents, the magistrates and ministers won an important psychological victory, but by the time the antinomians had left Boston for the Rhode Island colonies such radical ideas could no longer be eliminated. Stephen Foster recently argued that the lengthy roll call of "erroneous opinions" condemned by the synod may indeed have reflected the ministers' memories of English antinomians more than it provided a fully accurate list of errors voiced in Massachusetts; on the other hand, Hutchinson's departure from Massachusetts hardly coincided with the subsidence of radical spiritism in the colony's towns.[5]

In the middle and late 1630s, then, Hutchinson's activities in Boston's church were emblematic of a growing division in the Bay Colony between those who advocated the covenant theology elaborated by such English Puritans as William Perkins and John Preston, and in which good works—in particular the *act* of having faith in God—were thought to testify to one's state of grace; and those who, in Thomas Clap's words, were "for free Grace, and the Teachings of the Spirit" and attacked the legalism of ministers who through their notion of the covenant presumptuously bound God to their own limited perception of what was right and just.[6] Precisely how the latter came by their beliefs is now impossible to reconstruct, but we do know that, once in New England, this group drew much strength from the preaching of such Puritans as Cotton and, later, Wheelwright. Further, though the relationship of a person's justification to his sanctification undeniably was at the theological center of the colony's problems during the crisis, those who condemned the antinomian position were quick to indicate the corollaries to this doctrinal point which, as Winthrop put it, was so hotly debated that "it began to be as common here to distinguish between men, by being under a covenant of grace or a covenant of works, as in other countries between Protestants and Papists."[7] "By advancing free-grace," wrote Thomas Shepard, antinomians "deny, and destroy all being and evidence of inherent grace in us; by crying up Christ, they destroy the use of faith to apply him; by advancing the Spirit, and revelation of the Spirit, they destroy or weaken the revelation of the Scriptures; by depending on Christ's righteousnesse and justification, without the works of the Law, they destroy the use of the Law, and make it no rule of life unto a Christian. . . ."[8] The Hutchinsonian position undercut the entire covenantal scheme as Shepard and others understood it and challenged other colonists to reconsider both the means and end of the New England enterprise. As Woburn's Edward Johnson put it in words that rang true in many colonists' ears, "surely had this Sect gone awhile, they would have made a new Bible."[9]

It was the doctrine reviewed in Anne Hutchinson's conventicle in Boston beginning in the summer of 1635 that first brought her to the notice of the colony's ministers and magistrates. Born in 1591, the daughter of the nonconformist cleric Francis Marbury of Alford, Lincolnshire, in 1611 Anne married William Hutchinson, the son of a prosperous tradesman in the same shire. Sometime around 1620 she first heard John Cotton preach in St. Botolph's Church in Boston, the principal port of Lincolnshire, twenty-five miles south of Alford; from that time on, though she did not have the comfort of sitting under his ministry every week, she came more and more under the sway of his interpretation of Puritan doctrine. Pondering the substance of his distinctions between justification and sanctification, Anne worked out an understanding of her mentor's emphasis on salvation by the unconditional free grace of God. Then in the early 1630s, when Cotton became more and more involved with the Puritan migration to New England, her religious beliefs deepened and assumed the forms that within a few years not only carried her to America but also brought upon her both the condemnation of the New England authorities and, at least outwardly, the disapproval of her respected Cotton himself.[10]

From the records of her examination by the General Court in Newtown in the late fall of 1637 and her church trial in Boston in 1638 there emerge significant details of her religious experience just prior to her emigration. Much troubled by what she regarded as "the falseness of the constitution of the church of England," she recalled, she "had like to have turned separatist," a course of action later rejected but whose very possibility as a viable option suggests her incipient radicalism. Her decision to join the stream of emigrants to New England was accompanied by what she took to be "immediate revelations" from God, her description and defense of which later condemned her before the General Court. When Cotton had left for America, an event that she admitted to be "a great trouble" to her, the Lord revealed to her that, Cotton "being gone[,] there was none left that I was able to hear, and I could not be at rest but I must come hither." At these words William Bartholomew, a deputy to the General Court from Ipswich, who was on the voyage, recalled that when Hutchinson had come "within sight of Boston [in New England] and look[ed] upon the meanness of the place," she uttered the following: "if she had not a sure word that England should be destroyed her heart would shake." And another earlier time, when Bartholomew had walked with her through St. Paul's churchyard she had admitted that she was "very inquisitive after revelations and said that she had never had any great thing done about her but it was revealed to her beforehand." Nor were such beliefs unusual in her family. On board the *Griffin* as it made its way to New England, Anne's eldest daughter purportedly said that "she had a revelation that a young man in the ship should be saved, but he must walk in the ways of her mother."[11]

By the time of her emigration Hutchinson already had become a spiritual advisor of sorts and seemed particularly eager to offer others her judgment about the soundness of a minister's doctrine, a habit she was to continue after her admission to Boston's church. Zechariah Symmes, minister to Charlestown, told the General Court that the few times he had been in Hutchinson's company in England "she did slight the ministers of the word of God," and on the Atlantic crossing she aimed her criticism directly at him, disagreeing with his conception of "the evidencing of a good estate." He was surprised by "the corruptness and narrowness of her opinions" and was even more startled by her claim that "when she came to Boston there would be something more seen than I said," for she had "many things to say" that could not yet be uttered. Symmes's testimony, which supports Bartholomew's statements about her "inquisitiveness" after revelations, suggests that by this early date Hutchinson already had assumed the role of lay prophesier, perhaps taking as her model the "Woman of Elis [i.e., Ely]" whom, as Hugh Peter reported, Hutchinson "did magnifie . . . to be a Womane of 1000 hardly any like her." Whether this was the Elizabeth Bancroft who was reported preaching "in *Ely* in *Cambridgeshire*" in the late 1630s is unclear; but, whoever the "Woman" was, Hutchinson, though she "knew her not nor ever sawe her," clearly was aware of her activities and had been moved by her example to offer her own opinions on Christian doctrine to any who would listen.[12]

When Hutchinson arrived in New England she continued her spiritual development under Cotton's tutelage and offered guidance to any neighbors still unsure of the grounds of their faith, particularly if they labored in ignorance of the fact that they could be saved only by the free and unconditional grace of God. To her chagrin, she soon discovered that the source of so many of her fellow-colonists' doubts and errors was the ministers themselves, and in the private meetings for women—and later, at a second set of them, for mixed company—she unburdened herself of this disappointment by claiming that John Cotton was the only sound minister in the colony. In all accounts of the Antinomian Controversy, these two points—Hutchinson's open condemnation of a majority of the colony's ministers and her role as the leader of a well-known conventi-

An "Enthusiast," from Daniel
Featley's *The Dippers Dipt* (London, 1645). This group was often
associated with antinomian ideas.

cle—emerge as the pivotal circumstances for her arraignment by the
General Court.

Hutchinson's establishment of a private religious meeting itself was not
enough to warrant her condemnation, for the practice of organizing conventicles, as Patrick Collinson has shown, formed one of the most important components of Puritanism's extraparochial organization. Such meetings had continued when the emigrants reached New England, a fact
dramatically revealed at Hutchinson's examination before the court when
she testily reminded Winthrop that the establishment of conventicles
"was in practice before I came therefore I was not the first," and later corroborated by Cotton in *The Way of the Congregational Churches Cleared*.
Hutchinson's private exhortations, he explained in 1648, an outgrowth of
her physical ministrations to women in her capacity as midwife and herb-
alist, "suited with the public ministry," for the clergy had found that such
"private conferences did well tend to water the seeds publicly sown." But
when Hutchinson moved from "constraining" individuals "to all known
duties, as secret prayer, family exercises, conscience of Sabbaths" and the
like, to a sharp criticism of clergymen whom she believed to walk in the
way of "works," she began to lose the goodwill of those who had no
objection to her private meetings per se. Her critics most feared that her
example would contribute to a widespread anticlericalism that never lay
far beneath the surface of the Puritan movement.[13]

In her contemporaries' eyes, once Hutchinson crossed this line she revealed her ambition to become the equal of the ordained ministers. Edward Johnson complained that Hutchinson's and her followers' emphasis on "rare Revelations of things to come from the spirit" not only "weaken[ed] the Word of the Lord in the mouth of his Ministers" but was part of an attempt "to put both ignorant and unlettered Men and Women, in a position of Preaching to a multitude," a goal exemplary of their "proud desires to become Teachers of others." Thomas Clap similarly understood their motivations. Their endeavor "to bring up an evil Report upon our faithfull Preachers," was only "that they themselves might be in high Esteem," an attitude he linked directly to the machinations of Satan, who had "puffed up" the antinomians "with horrible Pride" so that they might better serve as his "Instruments." Clearly a premonition of the extreme anticlericalism of English radicals like William Dell and Gerrard Winstanley, the Hutchinsonians' condemnation of the New England clergy displayed a strong anti-institutional, if not anti-intellectual, bias. Johnson recalled that upon his arrival in New England at the height of the controversy he was approached by one of Hutchinson's party who promised to bring him "to a Woman that Preaches better Gospell then any of your black-coates that have been at the Ninneversity." "I had rather hear such a one," the opinionist told Johnson, "that speakes from the mere motion of the spirit, without any study at all, then any of your learned Schollers." [14]

By the late fall of 1635, what had begun as but another of the private religious meetings that characterized English Puritanism was increasingly perceived as the breeding ground for a large cadre of individuals whose religious fervor was channeled by Hutchinson into open criticism of all the colony's ministers. During these months the situation was complicated not only by the return of Cotton's colleague, John Wilson, who had been in England to tend to some family matters and who now, to his embarrassment, found himself compared unfavorably to Cotton, but by the arrival on the same vessel of Henry Vane, the son of a prominent member of the King's Privy Council. Despite his youth, Vane was from the outset treated with much deference, a fact borne out by Cotton's invitation to his new church member to board with him as long as Vane wished, a gesture that acquired more and more significance as the Antinomian Controversy escalated. By May of 1636 he had been elected governor of the colony, no doubt because of his close connections to inner circles of power in England. [15]

Vane displayed his theological colors by attending Hutchinson's conventicle and soon made it clear, as Winthrop was to note, that he not only "held, with Mr. Cotton and many others, the indwelling of the person of the Holy Ghost in a believer" but "went so far beyond the rest, as to maintain a personal union" with the third member of the Trinity. Clearly the group surrounding Hutchinson, which by now included such prominent settlers as William Coddington, John Coggeshall, and William Aspinwall, had become a force to be reckoned with in New England's affairs. With the arrival early in 1636 of Mrs. Hutchinson's brother-in-law John Wheelwright, the silenced vicar of Bilsby in Lincolnshire, those in Hutchinson's circle gained yet another powerful supporter, for this minister, who had known Cromwell in their student days at Cambridge and who later enjoyed his favor when he was Lord Protector, soon was singled out by the Hutchinsonians as the only other sound minister in the colony. Like Cotton, Wheelwright placed the joyful mystery of God's free grace in justification over and beyond any evidence of sanctification, a fact attested to by his friend Hanserd Knollys well before Wheelwright's emigration to New England, when the former still was vicar of Humberstone, near Bilsby. Once when Knollys had found himself spiritually discomfitted and turned to God for guidance, his prayer had been answered: "Go to Mr. Wheelwright," for he will "tell thee and show thee how to glorify God in his ministry." At Bilsby Wheelwright told him: "You cannot glorify God, either in the ministry or in anything else, for you are building on works, not on grace." The message might have been offered by Hutchinson herself.[16]

Wheelwright arrived in Boston in the same month when Vane was elected governor, a time that marked the height of Hutchinson's influence in the colony and the ministers' first recorded displeasure at the growing criticism of their work. The clergy's initial response was not to chastise Hutchinson herself but rather to go to him who by her own repeated admissions had fostered her theological opinions and who, before Wheelwright's arrival, had been the only minister to win her seal of approval— Cotton himself. Sometime between October 1635 and June 1636, Thomas Shepard wrote privately to Cotton to ask him to explain more fully some of his theological views, presumably those Hutchinson recently had been expounding to her own purpose. Through this initiative Shepard no doubt honestly intended, as he claimed, "to cut off all seeming differences and jarrs," but in questioning Cotton about the relationship between the Word and the Holy Spirit in salvation he sternly warned the Boston minister that, no matter how sound he was on this doctrinal point, his manner of expressing it was dangerous. "This I speake from the enforcement of my conscience," Shepard told him, "least under this color of advancing woord together with the spirit, you may meet in time with some members . . . as may doe your people and ministry hurt, before you know it," a warning he introduced by invoking the shibboleth of "Familists" who "doe not care for woord or ordinances but only the spirits motion." Shepard's parenthetical remark that at that time he "kn[e]w none nor judge[d] any" to have so misinterpreted Cotton seems disingenuous, particularly since in the very next sentence he noted that he had not "thus writ to breed a quarrell" but rather "to still and quiet those which are secretly begun and I feare will flame out unless they be quenched in time."[17]

Cotton thanked Shepard for his concern but did little to assuage his uneasiness, particularly when he stated that he "did not wish christians to build the signes of their Adoption upon [any] sanctification, but such as floweth from faith in christ jesus," and assured him that none of his church members "(brethren and sisters) doe hold forth christ in any other way." Whether Shepard immediately conveyed the substance of this exchange to any of his fellow-ministers is unknown, but it seems more than coincidental that at about this same time Peter Bulkeley of Concord also wrote Cotton for clarification of one of the doctrinal points upon which Shepard had queried him—the extent of man's role in the process of his salvation. Here, too, Cotton gave little satisfaction. He insisted, for example, that "In this union the soule Receyveth Christ, as an empty vessell receyveth oil"—that is, in a "passive" manner. By the fall of 1636, presumably after Shepard and Bulkeley had shared the unsatisfactory fruits of their interviews with Cotton with other of the colony's ministers, they decided to make public their concern about the final tendency of his preaching and to bring both Hutchinson and Wheelwright, as well as Cotton, under closer scrutiny.[18]

It is unclear what Shepard and Bulkeley had hoped to accomplish through their initial interrogation of Cotton, though presumably they hoped to encourage him to sway Hutchinson from the increasing errors of her ways. By this time they may have felt that ultimately Cotton's preaching would be dangerous even if Hutchinson herself were silenced, a speculation the more plausible in the light of the fact that shortly after his arrival the Boston church had undergone a spiritual revival, followed by a decline, that moved his parishioners to ponder the reasons for God's sudden withdrawal from them and so left them vulnerable to anyone who might try to rekindle their piety through an appeal to the docrine of "free grace." Edward Johnson explained the antinomians' appeal in light of "the bent of the peoples hearts" to "magnifie the rich Grace of God in

Christ"; when the colonists were in such a state, he went on to explain, they were eager and willing to condemn "all the Ministers among them [who] Preached a Covenant of workes."[19] By October, though, with Wheelwright and Vane now identified with Hutchinson's conventicle, it was clear that more stringent action had to be taken, if only to make Cotton declare publicly his differences with the "Opinionists." Now, for the first time, Hutchinson herself was brought before the General Court.

The Hutchinsonians in the Boston church, emboldened by the arrival of Wheelwright and the support of Vane, were attempting to install Wheelwright as the colleague of Cotton and Wilson, a signal insult to the man whose doctrine they had openly condemned. Late in the month, at a meeting of the court, the deputies and assembled clergymen questioned Cotton and Wheelwright about their understanding of the relationship of sanctification to justification, for supposedly their interpretation of this point of doctrine had led Hutchinson, as Winthrop had noted in his journal a short time before, to declare that "Our union with the Holy Ghost" was such that "a Christian remains dead to every spiritual action, and hath no gifts nor graces, . . . nor any other sanctification but the Holy Ghost himself." On this particular question Cotton "gave satisfaction" to the elders, as did Wheelwright: they "all did hold, that sanctification did help to evidence justification." But there remained some confusion over the matter of the indwelling of the Holy Spirit, for, though Cotton did not declare this to be a "personal union," as, say, Vane and Wheelwright had, he did nevertheless maintain that the spirit did indeed dwell in a saint. Five days later these and other questions again were raised in Boston's church as Hutchinson's party formally attempted to install Wheelwright as a "teacher"; but, with Cotton again hedging on the degree of his doctrinal agreement with the new arrival, the motion was defeated for final lack of unanimity. With the support of a number of Boston church members who had grants of land in the area, Wheelwright then settled at the outpost of Mount Wollaston.[20]

Following his removal matters did not improve, and Winthrop's journal entries for the months of November and December reveal an increasing disintegration of order in the Bay Colony. It evidently was then that Vane openly declared his belief in "a personal union with the Holy Ghost," a point he debated in writing with Winthrop, the deputy-governor, an activity which itself ended in such confusion that "they could not find the person of the Holy Ghost in scripture, nor in the primitive churches three hundred years after Christ." Wilson did little to improve matters by making "a very sad speech of the condition of our churches, and the inevitable danger of separation" if the "differences and alienations among brethren" were not remedied. Cotton took this speech "very ill" and moved to have his colleague censured for blaming all the trouble on the "new opinions" that Hutchinson and others were circulating, a motion subsequently denounced by Winthrop and the handful of Wilson's supporters in the Boston church. During this time, too, some ministers had "drawn into heads all the points, wherein they suspected Mr. Cotton did differ from them" and asked him for a direct yes-or-no answer to them all; at this request Governor Vane went into a fury because they had acted "without his privity." Neither was the activity in Hutchinson's meetings the least bit curtailed, for now even more serious "errors" became evident—"that the Holy Ghost dwelt in a believer as he is in heaven; that a man is justified before he believes; and that faith is no cause of justification"—the "ground" of them all, Winthrop concluded, was found to be "assurance by immediate revelation." The colony was experiencing an epidemic of radical spiritism, a situation summarized succinctly by Shepard in his "Autobiography." "No sooner were we thus set down and entered into church fellowship," he noted, "but the Lord exercised us and the whole country with the opinions of Familists, begun by Mistress Hutchinson, raised up to a great height by Mr. Vane too suddenly chosen governor, and maintained too obscurely by Mr. Cotton, and propagated too boldly by the members of Boston and some in other churches."[21]

Still the controversy focused on Cotton, for late in December, with many people still "taking offence at some doctrines" he had delivered, the rest of the colony's ministers drew up a list of sixteen points and "entreat[ed] him to deliver his judgment directly in them." He soon did. The ministers replied to these, in the hope that the Lord would make Cotton "the happy Instrument of calming the storms and cooling these hot contentions and paroxysms that [had] begun to swell and burn" in the colony, and Cotton offered a lengthy "Rejoynder," one that David Hall has termed "the most important exposition of Cotton's theology at the time of the Controversy." But with the Boston minister still maintaining, for example, that "the Seal of the Spirit is the Spirit himself," and its evidence "the stamping and engraving [of] a son-like disposition and Spirit in us," the ministers were not fully satisfied: Cotton's understanding of the way God worked in and on a man's soul obviously was significantly different from the opinions of other ministers in the colony on this matter.[22]

All this discussion—for the court evidently held public hearings in

Boston on these documents—only made the "differences of said points of religion [increase] more and more . . . so as all men's mouths were full of them." It was then that Cotton, addressing a shipload of passengers about to return to England, "willed them" to tell their countrymen "that all the strife amongst us was about magnifying the grace of God; one party seeking to advance the grace of God within us, and the other to advance the grace of God towards us . . . and so bade them tell them that, if there were any among them that would strive for grace, they should come hither." More ominously, it was at this time, too, that there was "great alienation of minds," a dramatic instance of which was provided by that Weymouth resident who "fell into sore trouble of mind, and in the night cried out, 'Art thou come, Lord Jesus?'" Leaping from his bed and then his window, he ran in the snow for seven miles and was found dead the next morning.[23]

Such confusion had spread even to Winthrop, who early in 1637, after having undertaken much soul-searching and having concluded that justification and sanctification never could be separated as distinctly as Wheelwright or Vane claimed, prepared two lengthy theological polemics through which he hoped to settle the controversy once and for all. Fortunately, he first took the step of showing these to Wilson, who in turn brought them to Shepard, and in a series of letters to their author the Newtown minister spelled out his doubts about the final soundness of Winthrop's positions. Some parts of his first paper, in which the deputy-governor sought to prove that "a man is justifyed by fayth, & not before he beleeveth," seemed to Shepard "doubtfull," others to "swerve from the truth," still others to bear "a colour of Arminianism." Shepard wondered whether it would be "most safe" for Winthrop to enter the fray and entreated him "not to send the papers as they are." Winthrop's second effort, a "Pacification" intended "to quiet & still" the colony's problems concerning justification by faith, also contained some "very doubtfull" doctrinal statements which Shepard undertook to correct. At this point in the controversy Winthrop, whether or not he would admit it, fell under the description that he offered of the colonists' growing confusion, "That no man could tell (except some few, who knew the bottom of the matter) where any difference was."[24]

In mid-January, however, the ministers and magistrates, unable to make Cotton change his doctrinal emphases, were serendipitously provided with the occasion to shift their attention from him to others among the spiritists and so eventually to discover the means by which they could initiate more formal charges against Hutchinson and her followers. This occasion was Wheelwright's "Fast-Day Sermon," which the magistrates considered seditious and which thus allowed them, for the moment at least, to shift the grounds of the debate from abstract theology to civil law. Wheelwright's inflammatory words, offered after Cotton had delivered an irenical sermon to the Boston congregation, set the stage for a prolonged political struggle in the colony, which reached its height that May in Vane's ouster from the governorship. After his defeat the authorities assiduously pursued a policy aimed to isolate and render powerless all the key members of the dissident faction. Put another way, early in 1637 the New England Puritans discovered that the kind of theological give-and-take that earlier marked the development of Puritanism in English churches and conventicles was too ineffective—and dangerous—a way to handle differences in doctrine once the Puritans themselves held the reins of power and sought to impose conformity of doctrine upon the population. From this point on they began to define, and, eventually, to refine, their notion of how, precisely, the civil and religious spheres intersected.[25]

All this was not accomplished without considerable struggle, for the arraignment of Wheelwright in March on charges of sedition and contempt prompted the sectarians to band together more tightly than they had had to when the conflict had been confined essentially to extended religious debate between Cotton and the other ministers. The novelty of the magistrates' attempt to step into a controversy hitherto almost exclusively under the purview of the ministry did not escape Wheelwright's supporters nor others in the colony who, while not necessarily sympathetic to his cause, were disturbed by such a turn of events. Hence, for example, the petition objecting to the court's treatment of Wheelwright was signed by no fewer than seventy-four of his supporters; in it the group beseeched the court to "consider the danger of meddling against the Prophets of God." Hence, too, "the brief Apologie in defence of the generall proceedings of the Court" against Wheelwright, in which the magistrates defended their reasons for not first referring the case to the elders. "The heat of contention and uncharitable censures which began to overspread the Country" as a result of the sermon, the court declared, "did require that the Civill power should speedily allay that heat, and beare witness against all seditious courses, tending to the overthrow of truth and peace amongst us." Once this justification was accepted—that is, once "truth" as well as "peace" became a legitimate concern of the court—the Hutchinsonians' fate was sealed.[26]

Suffice it to say that the magistrates' strategy prevailed. Examined

at length on the seditious nature of his sermon as well as on its doctrinal irregularities—like Hutchinson in her conventicle, he had openly
condemned the inordinate emphasis on a "covenant of works" in the
colony—Wheelwright was found guilty as charged, though his sentenc-
ing was deferred until October, at which time many of his prominent
supporters were called to answer for their own behavior and subsequently banished, as he was. In that interim even more important events
occurred. At the court of elections in Newtown in May, Vane, who one
of the New Englanders thought to be "altogether ignorant of the art of
government" and not content "to set the house on fire, but [he] must add
oil to the flame," was turned out from his position as the colony's leader,
depriving the sectarians of one of their most powerful supporters and in-
stalling in his place one of their most steadfast opponents, Winthrop himself. Further, no doubt due to the fact that the elections had been moved
from Boston, where the Hutchinsonians were solidly in the majority, the
electors present returned a slate of officers who firmly represented the
anti-Hutchinsonian position. For whatever reason, the tide was turning
inexorably against Mistress Hutchinson, and with the departure of Vane
for England a short time later, whatever power she held quickly began to
unravel.[27]

The summer of 1637 brought more theological debate, marked by
Cotton's growing realization that to maintain his power in the colony he
had to make peace with the other ministers, a task to be accomplished
only by separating himself from those like Hutchinson, Wheelwright,
and Vane, who under the pretense of expounding his doctrine in fact mis-
used it. After Wheelwright's first appearance before the court, Cotton
stated that he considered the "differences" between the parties "in a very
narrow scantling," and the next day Shepard "brought them yet nearer,
so as except men of good understanding, . . . few could see where the
difference was"; but because "men's affections" in these matters already
had become so "alienated," no reconciliation was forthcoming. Cotton
decided to argue his own case and not his brother Wheelwright's and
over the course of the summer met with other of the colony's ministers to
resolve their differences. By the end of August he and Wilson were reconciled, and finally only three questions, all having to do with justification, remained at issue between him and the rest of the colony's clergymen. His answers to these queries, later published in England, seemingly
satisfied the ministers as to his final orthodoxy, and Cotton's return—
even if only half-hearted, as Shepard thought—to the clerical fold set the

stage for the major offensive against the radical spiritists: the convocation of a synod to condemn "the erroneous opinions, which were spreading in the country."[28]

Clearly there was need for an undeniable display of ministerial unanimity, for in the months before the calling of the synod anticlerical feeling ran high. In the spring, Bulkeley had complained to Cotton that he had found "soe much neglect" toward his ministry that those who sometimes had made special efforts to visit him "passe by my dore, as if I were the man that they had not knowen." More ominously, the controversy undermined the morale of the troops mustered to combat the Pequot Indians. After Wheelwright's conviction, the town of Boston, angered because Wilson had been named chaplain to the expedition, contributed hardly a soul to the reorganized effort against the tribe. Even in such mundane affairs as the establishment of "Towne lots" and the setting of tax "rates," the question of "Free-grace" and "works" divided many communities. Magistrates like Winthrop were worried that the arrival of many more shiploads of immigrants that summer would swell the opinionists' ranks, a fear justified with the arrival of Samuel Gorton, who, as Edward Winslow later noted, helped "to blow the bellowes" upon the colonists' disagreements. At this time, the General Court instituted stiffer controls over who was allowed to enter and remain in the colony, with Anne Hutchinson's brother Samuel and other of Wheelwright's friends given permission to stay only for a few months; every day the governor expected "many of their [the Hutchinsonians'] opinion to come out of England from Mr. Brierly his church, etc."[29]

Winthrop's invocation of "Mr. Brierly"—that is, Roger Brearley of Grindleton in Yorkshire—is important because he was one of the few radical spiritists mentioned by name—Robert Towne was another—during the entire controversy, and the New England Puritans' memories of their experiences with such individuals or their works, as well as their imaginative reconstruction of the havoc wrought by John of Leyden in Münster, in large measure defined the manner in which they understood and responded to the Hutchinsonians. Brearley placed an inordinate emphasis on the workings of the Holy Spirit within the elect and believed that the promptings of the Spirit took precedence over scriptural law, which he regarded as primarily allegorical. Such notions earned him the epithet "Familist," though in fact he had little in common with the true continental familists.[30] Towne was in many minds linked with John Eaton, John Eachard, John Traske, and other English preachers of the 1620s and 1630s whose theology was based on the notion of "free grace" or "free justification" and who often were arraigned to account for the eccentricity of their teachings. Like the Hutchinsonians, these "Antinomians" commonly drew distinctions between themselves and mere "legal" ministers who labored under a covenant of "works"; their reliance on the apprehension of the Holy Spirit often led to the kinds of revelations to which Hutchinson herself had testified.[31]

But what is striking in contemporary accounts of the controversy is how rarely the clergy or magistrates mentioned the names of other "Antinomians" or "Familists," a fact that again suggests the indigenous nature of radical spiritist ideas in New England: as far as any of the records show, none of the New England antinomians claimed to have derived their ideas from any one source in England. Though later accounts of the difficulties stress how all the erroneous opinions in the colony came from Hutchinson herself, the exhaustive list composed by the elders at the Newton synod in August 1637 precludes the possibility that all of the errors had their origin in one conventicle, or even in one community. Cotton's statement in *The Way of the Congregational Churches Cleared* that "the thing attended to, for preparation to the synod, was the gathering up of all corrupt and offensive opinions that were scattered up and down the country" assumes great significance, as does Weld's, that the *"errors"* were conveyed *"not only into the Church of* Boston, . . . *but also into almost all the parts of the Country, round about."* With the widespread appearance of the spiritist ideas, the synod attempted to cast as large a net as possible in its attempt to list the erroneous doctrines that had surfaced in the colony, and the thrust of the ministers' efforts toward this end was two-fold: to set a framework within which the most troublesome members of Hutchinson's group could thereafter be arraigned and condemned, and to establish once and for all the boundaries of acceptable dissent within the colony. There is, of course, no way of knowing whether each of the eighty-two errors had in fact been voiced by some disgruntled colonist or another, but the ministry wished to make perfectly clear that members in good standing of the Massachusetts Bay Colony had to check any spiritist longings they might have.[32]

At a time of heightened emotions, the synod carried out its task expeditiously, working through its agenda in a mere three weeks. Weld's description of the sessions is worth noting, if only to see how thoroughly, and fairly, the elders fulfilled their charge. The synod's meetings in Newtown, he later reported, were open *"to any of the Countrey to come in and heare,"* and a particular invitation was extended to *"all the Opinionists . . . to take liberty of speech (onely due order observed) as much as any of our selves, and as freely."* The first week, he continued, *"we spent in confuting the loose opinions that we gathered up in the Country,"* and the remainder of the time was *"spent in a plain Syllogisticall debate,* (ad vulgas *as much as possible*) *gathering up nine of the chiefest points, (on which the rest depended) and disputed them all in order, pro and con."* Thomas Hooker, who at first had disapproved of the proposed synod because he thought it best first to "advise with the godly and learned of England about the uncommon errors of Mrs. Hutchinson," and Peter Bulkeley consented to act as moderators of the sessions, and the colony's magistrates also were present, *"as hearers, and speakers also when they saw fit."* With Cotton now sitting in judgment with other of the colony's ministers, the synod condemned any point that hinted of the radical spiritism advocated by the opinionists.[33]

It is not necessary to discuss each error in turn—to use Weld's words in which he explained his omission of the text of some of the debates, "the swelling of the booke" would be too great—but it is important briefly to suggest the range of errors the elders ferreted out. Many of the beliefs pertained specifically to the antinomian heresy; that is, to beliefs in the primacy of the Spirit over the injunctions of Scripture, hence their condemnation of the obvious, "that those that bee in Christ are not under the Law, and commands of the word, as the rule of life," or that "the whole letter of the Scripture holds forth a covenant of workes." Closely allied were errors that posited Christ's literal presence within the saint, a topic at the heart of the English Puritans' condemnation of men like John Saltmarsh and William Dell in the 1640s. The synod rejected all notions that "the new creature, or the new man mentioned in the Gospell, is not meant of grace, but of Christ," or that "there is no inherent righteousness in the Saints, or grace, and graces are not in the soules of believers, but in Christ only."[34]

Yet another class of errors centered on the kind of experiential knowledge that defined a saint and on his subsequent ability to judge whether others had undergone a comparable experience. "He that hath the seale of the Spirit," some opinionists claimed, "may certainely judge of any person, whether he be elected or no," for the saint's knowledge of his salvation comes by "a Testimony of the Spirit, and voyce unto the Soule, merely immediate, without any respect unto, or concurrence with the word." Or, as it was phrased in another error, "The Spirit giveth such full and cleare evidence of my good estate, that I have no need to be tried by the fruits of sanctification, this were to light a candle to the sun." The fear and trembling in which ministers like Shepard instructed their parishio-

ners to work out their salvation had been fully rejected by the antinomians. "There is no assurance true or right," another error read, "unlesse
it bee without feare and doubting." [35]

A final category of errors requires brief mention because of the manner
in which such ideas impinged on the New England Way as it then was
being formulated; that is, those ideas that challenged the authoritative role
of the ministry in determining the constituency of their own churches.
Some antinomians extended the notion that only saints could discern
each other and argued that to listen to unconverted or "legal" clergymen
was pointless: "No minister can teach one that is annoynted by the Spirit
of Christ, more then he knows already unlesse it be in some circumstances," nor can he "bee an instrument to convey more of Christ unto
another, then hee by his own experience hath come unto." Further, because "the Church in admitting members is not to looke to holinesse
of life, or Testimony of the same," but rather to a person's revelation of
the Spirit within, "All verbal Covenants," the opinionists claimed, "or
Covenants expressed in words, as Church Covenants, vowes, &c. are
Covenants of workes, and as such strike men off from Christ." Such
statements about the supremacy of personal experience with the divine
over any creeds or platforms did not make explicit the course a true saint
should follow if he found himself within such a restrictive ecclesiastical
structure, but other of the opinionists' ideas spelled it out: it simply was
his duty to separate. "If a member of a Church be unsatisfied with any
thing in the Church, if he expresse his offence, whether he hath used all
means to convince the Church or no, he may depart." [36]

The colony's ministers and magistrates reacted to such ideas that called
into question their notion of the New England errand not only by condemning them but also, more covertly, by incorporating some of their
premises into their own ecclesiology. "Although "the worke of the Assembly . . . gained much on the hearers, that were indifferent, to
strengthen them, and on many wavering, to settle them" both before and
after the synod the ministers subtly molded the New England Way to
conform to some of the radicals' demands. In particular, they adopted the
radicals' requirement of a narration of the work of grace upon one's soul
as evidence of sainthood, and their willingness to allow the individual
congregation to have a hand in the choice and creation of its minister and
to chart for itself a course that reflected the experiences and needs of its
parishioners, whether followers of a Thomas Hooker, a John Cotton, or
a Thomas Parker—as long as they paid lip-service to the congregational

order. By the time of the synod's conclusion, the colony had well under way a complex strategy to undermine many of the ecclesiastical and doctrinal positions the radicals had assumed.

In one regard the synod accomplished its purpose, for, as one New Englander put it, after its sessions "jarring and dissonant opinions, if not reconciled, yet [were] covered, and they who came together with minds exasperated, by this means depart[ed] in peace." But if the elders clearly had outlined what they considered the limits of acceptable doctrine, they only drove closer together those who believed the Bay Colony was doomed to tragedy if it persisted in an advocacy of salvation by works, a sentiment conveyed earlier in apocalyptical terms when in his "Fast-Day Sermon" Wheelwright had rhetorically asked: "Why should we not further this fire [that is, the contention between those who held salvation by faith as opposed to works], who knoweth not how soone those Jewes may be converted?" Thus, after the conclusion of the synod in late August, the "*Leaders*" of the opinionists, Weld claimed, "*put such life into the rest, that they all went on in their former course, not onely to disturbe the Churches, but miserably interrupt the civill Peace,*" actions which took the form of what often appeared to be outright "*sedition,*" to the "*indangering of the Common-wealth.*" By October, with the banishment and/or censure of Wheelwright and several of his most prominent supporters, the situation grew even more tense and the threat of physical violence more and more a possibility. As Weld put it, "*They said moreover what they would do against us (biting their words in) when such and such opportunities should be offered to them, as they daily expected.*" "*Insomuch that we had great cause to have feared,*" he continued, "*the extremity of danger from them in case power had beene in their hands.*"[37]

By the conclusion of Hutchinson's own examination before the General Court in early November, the ministers and magistrates had broken the back of the opposition by banishing several of the group's leaders, yet they openly displayed their fear of such violence by invoking the specter of the anarchy that had occurred a century earlier in Münster, Germany, where radical anabaptists finally had been defeated in bloody warfare with orthodox Protestant troops. Because part of Hutchinson's testimony had revealed her dependence on personal "revelations" from God, "the Court did clearly discerne," as Winthrop put it in *A Short Story*, "where the fountaine was of all our distempers, and the Tragedy of *Munster* . . . gave just occasion to feare the danger we were in. . . ." Whether or not one believes that there was any plot afoot to strike against the government and clergy, clearly the authorities took the threat seriously: "insomuch as there is just cause of suspition that they, as others in Germany, in former times, may, upon some revelation, make some sud-daine irruption upon those that differ from them in judgment," the court voted to disarm all known supporters of Hutchinson, a gesture unprece-dented in the colony's history and followed by the even more extreme measure of removing all the colony's arms and munitions from Boston, where the Hutchinsonians were strongest, to Roxbury and Newtown. It may have been paranoia pure and simple, but it announced to the dissent-ers that they had no future in the Massachusetts Bay Colony.[38]

By the time of Hutchinson's own appearance before the court in No-vember, the ministers and magistrates had gained considerable control over the flow of events, particularly in the ideological sphere: it was they and not the opinionists who were on the offensive. Such was the cha-risma of Anne Hutchinson, however, that they knew that even the banish-ment of Wheelwright and Aspinwall and the disenfranchisement of Cog-geshall and others would not fully settle the controversy. They had to dis-credit and humiliate her whom Bulkeley called "that wretched *Jezzabel*" whom "the Devill sent over hither to poyson these *American* Churches, with her depths of Sathan, which she had learned in the Schools of Famil-ists." In their minds she, as much as Wheelwright or the others, was guilty of sedition, and when in October the court began systematically to summon those involved in what it viewed as an organized threat to the colony, Mistress Hutchinson was among the number. Because the synod had dealt, as Winthrop put it, not with persons "but doctrines only," her examination before the court in Newtown provided her opponents with the most dramatic opportunity to display to the colony the ignorance and folly of her ways.[39]

The various "errors" discovered at Hutchinson's examination in No-vember and at her church trial the following spring reveal how easily or-thodox Puritan doctrine could be put to the use of radical spiritism. Al-though the court supposedly was concerned with behavior in the civil sphere—in this case, with sedition—the points on which it finally con-demned her were linked to the synod's recent pronouncements. In their decision to banish her the magistrates assumed that both her role as the leader of a private conventicle in which anticlerical statements commonly were uttered and her open reliance on personal "revelations" posed se-rious threats to social order. Hutchinson maintained that nothing she said or did differed very greatly from the actions or pronouncements of other Puritans, in old England or New. Objectively speaking, the difference was only a matter of degree, but it was precisely *that* that made Puritanism so volatile, and subversive, an ideology.

The practice of keeping conventicles at which doctrine was reviewed and further discussed had been a common feature of the Puritan movement since Elizabethan days and had been continued in New England. Thus Winthrop's charge, that "you have maintained a meeting and assembly in your house that hath been condemned by the general assembly as a thing of God not tolerable or comely in the sight of God" was quickly refuted by Hutchinson. "It is lawful for me to do so," she replied, "as it is all your practices and can you find a warrant for yourself and condemn me for the same thing?" More telling is her explanation in the same speech of the "ground" of her "taking it [the habit of presiding over a conventicle] up," for her explanation indicates how in New England such private meetings had constituted an expected part of worship. Hutchinson admitted that when she first arrived in America she did not go to "such meetings as those were," but because "it presently was reported" that she "did not allow of such meetings but held them unlawful" and thus "was proud and did despise all ordinances," she thereupon "took it up" to prevent such "aspersions." But "it was in practice before I came," she repeated, and "therefore I was not the first."[40] The irony, of course, was that her conventicle soon enough assumed precisely the function of those in Stuart England: it became a place in which disaffected individuals believed that they kept alive the true word while in all public meetings only error was preached.

Winthrop's second but related charge, that by keeping such a conventicle Hutchinson did something not "fitting" for her "sex," was equally problematic. Quoting Titus 2:3–5, Hutchinson claimed that she was within scriptural rule to instruct the women in her community, but Winthrop claimed that her rule "cross[ed] that in Corinthians [1 Cor. 14:34–35]." At this point, with Simon Bradstreet stating that he was "not against all women's meetings but [did] think them to be lawful," the examination quickly shifted to the substance of what Hutchinson preached; it was only at her church trial, which took place after more serious "errors" had been discovered in the colony, that the issue of female "prophecy" and the "Woman of Elis" became a serious issue. Instead, at this point deputy-governor Dudley, who throughout the trial had hounded her most persistently, sought to go "a little higher" and pressed the question of her condemnation of all the ministers but Cotton. Such behavior was "not to be suffered," he declared angrily, and since this charge was at the "foundation" of all the colony's difficulties—"Mrs. Hutchinson is she that hath depraved all the ministers and hath been the cause of what is fallen out"—this point had to be addressed by the Court.[41]

Once Dudley had introduced this topic, Hugh Peter followed his lead and reported that after he and other clergymen had spoken to Cotton about his troublesome parishioner, "who went under suspicion . . . from her landing, that she was a woman not only difficult in her opinions, but also of an intemperate spirit," they then had sent for Hutchinson to explain the reason for her derogatory comments. "Briefly," Peter reported, "she told me there was a wide and broad difference between our brother Mr. Cotton and our selves," one that turned on the question of who preached what kind of covenant. "Generally the frame of her course was this," Peter added, "that she did conceive that we were not able ministers of the gospel." After six different ministers, including Shepard, testified that she had indeed so spoken at their meeting, Hutchinson aggravated the assembly by asking the clergymen to swear oaths to their testimony, a request many of those present found insulting. Shepard told the assembly that he knew of no reason for the oath "but the importunity of the gentlewoman"; and when Coggeshall, one of her supporters, insisted on the matter, Endecott told him bluntly that his "carriage . . . tends to further casting dirt upon the face of the judges." Then, after Cotton, too, had corroborated the general drift of the others' testimony—he denied having heard her say specifically that they were under a covenant of works but admitted "that she looked at them as the apostles before the ascension"—Hutchinson provided the court with the crucial opening they needed.[42]

On her own initiative she turned the magistrates' attention to the manner in which she had become settled in her various beliefs, including the reason why she left England as well as how she could tell "which was the clear ministry and which was the wrong." God, Hutchinson related, quite simply had revealed these things to her as he had revealed to Abraham the necessity of Isaac's sacrifice—by immediate revelation. Speaking as though possessed by the Spirit, she reeled off example after example of God's so dealing with her, after which William Bartholomew recalled how in England she had evidenced similar behavior, even claiming that it had been revealed to her that England would be destroyed. Cotton thereupon was asked what he thought of such admissions, but before he had delivered his judgment Hutchinson complicated matters even more by declaring that "By a providence of God" she soon expected "to be delivered from some calamity" that would come to her. By then Winthrop had heard enough, for from Hutchinson's own words the assembly finally had been brought to the "ground" of all the disturbances: "this is the means," the governor declared, "by which she hath very much abused the country that they shall look for revelations and are not bound to the ministry of the word, but God will teach them by immediate revelations." Cotton tried one last time to persuade the court to reconsider the conclusions to which they were hastening, but his efforts only further angered those like Dudley who from the outset had wanted Hutchinson severely punished. When Winthrop thereupon asked "if it be the mind of the court that Mrs. Hutchinson for these things that appear before us is unfit for our society," all but three of those present consented. She then was banished from their jurisdiction "as being a woman not fit for [their] society" and was ordered imprisoned until the season permitted her to be sent away.[43]

To the dismay of the magistrates and elders, Hutchinson's confinement to the home of Joseph Weld of Roxbury did not quell the fires of contention in the surrounding towns, a fact that lends some degree of credence to Edward Johnson's suggestion that the errors associated with Hutchinson were "like those fained heads of Hidra, as fast as one is cut off two stand up in the roome." At this point the full bloom of radical spiritism appeared in the colony and in ways that at least partially justified later reports concerning the "familisticall" nature of the beliefs. Winthrop reported that soon after the censures of the court upon the most prominent Hutchinsonians, "divers other foul errors were discovered" among many of the colonists. Some of these "secret" opinions, he continued, were these:

That there is no inherent righteousness in a child of God.
That neither absolute nor conditional promises belong to a Christian.
That we are not bound to the law, but as a rule, etc.
That the Sabbath is but as other days.
That the soul is mortal, till it be united to Christ, and then it is annihilated, and the body also, and a new given by Christ.
That there is no resurrection of the body.

Clearly Cotton's fear, expressed at Hutchinson's examination before the court, had become justified: the "revelations" of the Hutchinsonians had bred "new matters of faith and doctrine" that unmistakably marked those who held them as genuinely radical ideologues.[44] No longer did the colony's theologians have to split hairs over doctrinal niceties; the opinionists had crossed the line into heresy.

The mystery is where such radical propositions came from, there being no hint in the earlier accounts or testimonies of such doctrinal vagaries; and for explanation one perhaps should rely on Hutchinson's own account, that she "did not hould any of thease Thinges before [her] Imprisonment" in the winter of 1637–38—that is, that she progressively generated the ideas from her initial Puritan tenets. To be sure, at her church trial that following spring she was not arraigned for all the "secret" opinions that Winthrop had enumerated. At that time the elders pursued her mainly for her "mortalist" heresy and did not mention the issue of the Sabbath nor the errors on Winthrop's list that preceded it, all of which easily could have been derived—as they had been in the case of the English antinomians of the 1620s and 1630s—from an insistence on the priority of the Holy Spirit in salvation. But as J. F. Maclear recently has demonstrated, Hutchinson's mortalism also could have been linked to "a developing spiritualization of eschatology" itself rooted in her antinomianism, for in the 1640s in England a very similar pattern emerged in such radicals as John Saltmarsh, Shepard's main target in *Theses Sabbaticae*, who argued for the spiritualization of the Bible, the ministry, and ordinances like the Sabbath; and Richard Overton, the radical spiritist and Leveller whose *Mans Mortallitie*, published in 1643, shocked the conservative Puritan community.[45] In this light, the evolution of the New England antinomians' doctrine directly anticipated the inevitable fragmentation of Puritan doctrine in England, where in the 1640s and 1650s radical ideas proliferated in a land in which no strong orthodoxy had emerged, as it had in Massachusetts, to check them.

When the elders discovered that such errors had begun to appear in other churches—testament, perhaps, to the colonists' general proclivity to such radical ideas—they took, as Winthrop later reported, "much paines (both in publike and private)" to suppress them. In Roxbury, Henry Bull, Philip Sherman, and Thomas Wilson were excommunicated for their erroneous opinions. But, again, the magistrates and ministers believed that the trail led back to Hutchinson herself, though how she could have spread such ideas when only ministers and members of her family were allowed to visit her is a question they did not address. Fixated now upon the undeniable dangers of "these new-sprung errors," the magistrates welcomed the church of Boston's "readinesse to deale with Mistris *Hutchinson* in a Church Way," and after a public lecture in mid-March she appeared in Reverend Cotton's meetinghouse to hear no fewer than twenty-nine erroneous doctrines attributed to her. If the list was accurate, and it may well have been, since a few days earlier she had been shown a copy of the statements, "All which she did acknowledge she had spoken," then there is undeniable evidence that during the months of

Hutchinson's imprisonment her radicalism had taken some decidedly dangerous turns.[46]

The first five errors were concerned explicitly with the "mortalist" heresy and in particular with the idea that through Christ the saint is provided with a wholly new body that supersedes the "fleshly" one. Thus, for example, the "resurrection" did not mean the literal resurrection of one's physical entity, but "our union [with Christ] here and after this life." In this view man was nothing—his soul merely "mortall like the beasts"—until Christ came to him in a moment of grace, at which time he underwent the resurrection to a new life, *in this life*. Such beliefs directly contradicted orthodox Puritan understanding of eschatology—that the Last Judgment would follow the establishment of Christ's earthly kingdom—and as such directly challenged the New England Puritans' notion of their role in Christian history. Further, as Maclear has noted, such beliefs made the Hutchinsonians "a connecting link between the 'radical Reformation' of the sixteenth century and the 'realized eschatology' [that is, the collapse of the historical time of Scripture into the life of each Christian] of Quakers in the next decade," a fact all the more important because the New England radicals' assumptions about the literal presence of Christ in one's soul seemingly developed independent of, and predated by several years, such ideas among their English Puritan brethren.[47]

Other errors charged to her were no less troubling and involved other such extensions of the doctrine of "free grace." Hutchinson evidently maintained that "The Law is no rule of life to a Christian" and that "There is no Kingdome of Heaven in Scripture but onely Christ." But although the elders began to examine her on some of these matters, they kept returning to the errors that comprised her denial of the orthodox understanding of man's immortality, particularly to the moral consequences of such beliefs, thus Wilson's outburst, that "if we deny the Resurrection of the Body than let us turn Epicures." "Let us eate and drinke and doe any Thinge," he continued, "to morrow we shall dye." And John Davenport's reminder to the church that "This Question of the Immortalitie of the soule is not new, but an Ayntient Heresie" that "gives way to Libertinisme." After such suggestions the congregation still did not comprehend the final tendency of such heretical notions. Hutchinson's erstwhile mentor Cotton, as teacher of the church charged with what for him must have been the uncomfortable task of admonishing his parishioner for her errors in doctrine, made it explicit. "Consider," he told her, "that by this Error of yours in denyinge the Resurrection of thease very Bodies you doe the uttermost to rase the very foundations of all Religion to the

Ground and to destroy our fayth." "Yea, consider," he continued, "*if the Resurrection be past than you cannot Evade the Argument* that was prest upon you by our *Brother Buckle* [that is, Peter Bulkeley, who had addressed her a few minutes earlier] and others, that filthie Sinne of the Communitie of Woeman and all promiscuous and filthie cominge togeather of men and Woeman without Distinction or Relation of Marriage, will necessarily follow." Such had been the course of anabaptists and familists who had questioned the Resurrection, and so would her own life become sordid if she continued to maintain that by "the *Resurrection* spoken of at [Christ's] appearance is ment of his *appearinge to us in Union*."[48]

At this juncture Hutchinson committed another grave error. She interrupted Cotton and maintained that she did not "*hould any of thease Thinges*" before her confinement at Weld's in Roxbury, although Shepard, to the contrary, had testified that when she had acknowledged such opinions to him "she added if I had but come to her before her Restraynt, she would have opened herselfe more fully to me and have declared many other Thinges about them, yea of thease very Opinions." Hutchinson had complicated her case—indeed, had sealed her fate—by apparent prevarication and shortly thereafter only seemed to add to it when she attempted to explain what she had meant by saying that there were no "graces" inherent in a saint, "but all is in Christ." "This day," Shepard concluded, "she hath shewed herselfe to be a Notorious Impostor," and since the issue now had shifted from "poynt of Doctrine" to "poynt of practice," Cotton left her to the mercy of Wilson, for it was "the Pastors Office to instruct and also to correct in Righteousnes when a lye is open and persisted in." Thereupon Wilson pronounced the words he had so long been waiting to utter: "*I command you* in the name of Christ Jesus and of this Church *as a Leper to withdraw your selfe out of the Congregation.*"[49]

Banished and excommunicated, Hutchinson soon thereafter left for the area in Rhode Island subsequently called Portsmouth, where Coddington and nineteen others who had been implicated in the Antinomian Controversy had, with the aid of Roger Williams, purchased land from the Indians. But Hutchinson found little peace here either. Four months after leaving Boston she suffered a miscarriage and expelled a hydatidiform mole. This "monstrous birth" (as Winthrop termed it) was minutely described by John Clarke, who had attended Hutchinson as a physician during her trauma, and when the Massachusetts Puritans heard of the event they pounced on it as further proof of God's judgment against the heretic.[50]

Politically, things went no better for her. Within a year of their arrival at Portsmouth, she and her husband, who had welcomed Samuel Gorton to the settlement, found themselves at odds with Coddington on both theological and political matters, and during the latter's absence in the spring of 1639, the Hutchinsonian and Gortonist factions pooled their votes to oust Coddington from his position as "Judge" of the community and installed Anne's husband, William, in his place. Coddington then moved to the southern tip of the island on which Portsmouth was located and founded Newport, and by March 1640, taking advantage of increasing friction between the Hutchinsons and Gorton over the latter's obstreperous behavior, he succeeded in uniting both settlements under a common administration with him at its head. Hutchinson remained in Portsmouth until 1642 and progressed in her radicalism to a position approximating that of the Seekers—Winthrop reported that she and her adherents "denied all magistracy" and "maintained that there were no churches since those founded by the apostles, nor could be any, nor any pastors ordained, nor seals administered" until the Church was redeemed from "the wilderness" by the second coming of Christ—but after her husband's death in that year, she and her six youngest children moved yet again, to a new settlement on Pelham Bay in New York. There, in the summer of 1643, she and her family were killed by a band of Indians. Again Winthrop saw the hand of God raised against her for her errors.[51]

Hutchinson's death, however, hardly put a stop to her influence, and we need to explore how her radicalism directly affected other prominent radical spiritists in some way associated with her, for, as Cotton himself put it in his admonition to Hutchinson, her opinions were wont to "frett like a Gangrene and spread like a Leprosie, and infect farr and neare."[52]

In addition to the members of Hutchinson's immediate family, a number of individuals, including many of those in Boston who regularly attended her conventicle, were directly nurtured by her, William Balston, John Compton, and Jane Hawkins, among them. We know little about such individuals except that they were disarmed in the aftermath of the controversy or were otherwise singled out for chastisement because of their close association with her. The notable lack of mention in contemporary documents of any of their specific doctrinal errors suggests that their notions of "free grace" were akin to hers and probably were acquired through her preaching.[53]

Another group about which there similarly is very little documentation consists of those in other of the infected communities, particularly in Salem, Newbury, and Roxbury—for example, John Porter and Richard

Morris of Roxbury, and William Alford, Robert Moulton, and William
King of Salem—who went on record in support of Wheelwright by signing the various petitions on his behalf or who were disciplined by their
own congregations or the General Court for errors similar to those of
Hutchinson's conventicle, but whom we cannot trace directly to Hutchinson's meetings. It is impossible to ascertain whether their radicalism
developed specifically through exposure to her doctrines or whether
these colonists came to support her because of their general sympathy
with the criticisms she and Wheelwright leveled at the Puritan clergy.[54]

A far more interesting group consists of those who had little in common except having passed through an antinomian phase on their way to
very different and, in many cases, much more radical positions. Among
these colonists were not only such prominent individuals as Aspinwall,
Coddington, and Coggeshall; also some who became Quakers, like William and Mary Dyer, William Freeborn of Boston, Richard Burden of
Newbury, and Henry Bull of Roxbury; others who eventually adopted
Samuel Gorton's spiritist and General Baptist views, like Richard Carder,
Robert Potter, William Wardall, Christopher Helme, and Francis Weston; and John and Thomas Clarke, John Peckham, and John Thornton,
who became Particular Baptists.[55] Many of these had been closely tied to
the Hutchinsonian faction. The adoption of the doctrine of "free grace"
provided to them the momentary comfort of a half-way house as they
expanded their understanding of Puritanism. Like so many of their
counterparts in England, once they rethought the doctrine of salvation
by faith they became powerless before its logic and unable to resist its
overwhelming conclusion—that Christ literally dwelled in and directed
the life of the true saint. Nicholas Easton of Newbury provides the most
striking example of this dynamic. One of Hutchinson's early supporters,
Easton was part of the group who left with her for Rhode Island, and by
1638 maintained that "every [one] of the elect had the Holy Ghost and
also the devil indwelling." Three years later he had adopted the Ranter-
like positions that "man hath no power or will in himself, but as he is
acted by God," and that because "God filled all things, nothing could be
or move but by him." By the late 1650s he had become a prominent
Quaker in Newport.[56]

Aspinwall, whose behavior at his examination by the court had been
"so contemptuous, and his speeches so peremptory" that its members
voted to banish him rather than to rest with a verdict of disenfranchisement, early in 1638, with eighteen others who had been punished for their
association with Anne Hutchinson or had sympathized with her cause,

signed a civil compact by which they promised to live when they reached Rhode Island. Not finding the new settlement to his liking, Aspinwall eventually confessed to his "errors" and was readmitted both to the Bay Colony and the Boston church. By the 1650s, his spiritual wanderlust had brought him back to England, where he became a prominent Fifth Monarchy pamphleteer. It is tempting to suggest that his fervent millennialism was influenced by Wheelwright's obsession with the last days—it was Wheelwright who counseled, for example, that "All the valiant men of David . . . all must out and fight for Christ, curse the Meroz, because they came not out to helpe the Lord against the mighty"—but more likely it was nurtured by Cotton himself, who emerged from the Antinomian Controversy to preach at length on the Revelation and other prophetic texts. Aspinwall, unlike, say, the Gortonists or Quakers, refused to internalize his eschatology. For him the discovery of salvation by God's free grace only whetted a desire to witness in his own lifetime the onset of the millennium.[57]

The subsequent history of the colony of Aquidneck suggests how varied were the religious beliefs of those who settled it; those who chose not to follow Aspinwall's example in asking the Bay Colony for forgiveness soon found that constant bickering led to outright schism. Randall Holden, one of the original settlers, no doubt had a hand in welcoming Samuel Gorton to the area after he had been banished from Plymouth; and by the end of 1639, after Gorton disrupted the civil order of the infant community, calling the town's leaders "great asses" and its judges "corrupt," Holden followed him to Providence and then Shawomet, where "Gortonism" as a movement acquired its greatest influence.[58] By 1641 other, more novel opinions surfaced at an alarming rate in the Rhode Island colonies. Several of the settlers at Aquidneck, evidently prompted by the Hutchinsons, "turned professed Anabaptists, and would not wear any arms, and denied all magistracy." Others adopted the Seeker belief that "there were no churches since those founded by the apostles and evangelists, nor could any be, nor any pastors ordained, nor seals administered but by such, and that the church was to want these all the time she continued in the wilderness, as yet she was." Then Coggeshall and Coddington, then in Newport, continued their rapid development toward Quakerism by joining Easton in his advanced spiritist beliefs, an event that caused John Clarke, Robert Lenthall, and others in that settlement to break from them and openly declare their sympathy for the Particular Baptists.[59] By the mid-1640s, Rhode Island was composed of several small colonies, almost all formed by the centrifugal force generated by the Antinomian Controversy in Massachusetts.

The continuing influence of Sir Henry Vane among these Rhode Island settlers, particularly in the Hutchinson family itself, should not be underestimated, for though his departure for England in 1637 had delivered a severe blow to the antinomians' cause, he continued to take an interest in the exiles' fortunes. They looked to him for both moral and political support. In April 1638, shortly after the Hutchinsonians had stopped in Providence on their way to their new home at Aquidneck, Williams wrote Winthrop that he found the group's "longings great after Mr. Vane, although they think he cannot return this year." "The eyes of some," Williams continued, "are so earnestly fixed upon him that Mrs. Hutchinson professeth if he comes not to New, she must to old England," Vane evidently having assumed in her mind the place once occupied by Cotton.[60] In 1639 the town of Newport instructed Easton and Clarke "to informe Mr Vane by writing of the state of things" in the colony "and desire him to Treate about the obtaining of a patent of the Island" from the King. Vane, however, soon enough was caught up in the turmoil of English politics and did not make good his efforts for Rhode Island until 1652, when Clarke and Williams finally acquired just such a patent.[61]

Vane's radicalism was never in doubt—Richard Baxter even claimed that the ex-New Englander had given rise to a sect of "Vanists"—but the case of John Wheelwright, who with Hutchinson and Vane was singled out for the most abuse both during and immediately after the controversy, is more difficult to assess. Clearly he was a strong partisan of the embattled members of Boston's church, but before delivery of his "Fast-Day Sermon" he, like Cotton, seemed drawn into the affair primarily through Hutchinson's approval of his preaching. After that performance —and particularly after his appearance before the General Court in March 1637—the authorities believed his role among the antinomian faction more and more significant. In late August, after the synod had completed its work, Wheelwright and Cotton were summoned to a private meeting with other of the clergy to try to resolve some remaining questions about points of doctrine; the result was that "Mr. Cotton and they agreed, but Mr. Wheelwright did not." Neither these "points," all of which were linked to the debate over sanctification and justification, nor any others ever were formally marshaled against Wheelwright. As Winthrop later put it, the General Court "had not censured his doctrine, but left it as it was." He was punished rather for his "Application," by which he "laid the Magistrates, and the Ministers, and most of the people of God in these Churches, under a Covenant of works, and thereupon declared them to be enemies of Christ." The court did not so much argue with his distinction between the covenants of grace and works but with his reckless invocation of the distinction, a fact that, when linked to Hutchinson's dependence on "revelations," had brought the colony to its crisis.[62]

In most accounts of the controversy Wheelwright was painted with the same brush applied to Vane, Hutchinson, and other *bona fide* radical spiritists, but there is a strong likelihood that, doctrinally, he indeed was closer to someone like Cotton, if only because as a well-trained and highly regarded minister he was sensitive to the dangerous implications of some of Hutchinson's pronouncements. Cotton himself proposed this view in 1648 when he noted that "though [Wheelwright] gave some offense in some passages at the assembly [i.e., the synod] . . . yet neither the church, nor myself . . . did ever look at him, either as an Antinomian or Familist." The proof that "he had taken good pains against both" was provided by a parishioner who later became a Gortonist. This man had "openly contested," Cotton observed, "against his doctrine as false and unchristian."[63]

Wheelwright's later relationship to the Bay Colony also suggests that in good measure the disagreements between them were caused by passions inflamed during the controversy. Immediately upon his sentence of banishment, he moved to the area surrounding Exeter in present-day New Hampshire but by the spring of 1643/4 sought permission to return to the Bay for a short time. His request granted, he was allowed to speak with the colony's clergymen in an attempt to repair the damage to his reputation. The results of this visit evidently were constructive, for a few months later he sent Winthrop and the General Court a letter in which he admitted that "Upon the long and mature consideration of things," he perceived that the main difference between the court and "some of the reverend elders" and him "in point of justification and the evidencing thereof" in fact had not been "of that nature and consequence as was then presented to [him] in the false glass of Satan's temptations and [his] own distempered passions." He now was "unfeignedly sorry" that he had "had such an hand in those sharp and vehement contentions" surrounding Hutchinson. After apologizing for the inflammatory effect of his "Fast-Day Sermon," he "repent[ed]" that he "did so much adhere to persons of corrupt judgment, to the countenancing of them in any of their errors or evil practices," for he truly had intended no such thing. He also regretted his "unsafe and obscure expressions" at the meeting of the

synod, words which had fallen from him "as a man dazzled with the buf-
fetings of Satan."[64]

Winthrop wrote back that the Court was indeed willing to consider a
reversal of its actions against him, but from Wheelwright's subsequent
reply it is apparent that some questions about the nature of his recantation
remained. He had made it clear to Winthrop that in front of the court he
was willing to say what he had said in his letter, but only that and no
more: "I cannot with a good conscience," he wrote, "condemn myself
for such capital crimes, dangerous revelations and gross errors, as have
been charged upon me." At its next meeting the court, without further
debate, voted to overturn his sentence. The principal clue to their uneasiness about his initial recantation is found in Winthrop's *Short Story*, the
one piece of hard evidence that Wheelwright was a radical spiritist. One
of his supporters evidently had reported that Wheelwright, in his fare-
well sermon to his Mount Wollaston parishioners, had preached open
"Antichristianisme" and "set up a Christ against a Christ." This same
"Scholar" himself subsequently "maintained immediate revelations" and
claimed that "every new creature is a dead lumpe, not acting at all, but as
Christ acts in him," declarations that led Winthrop and others to assume
that, because this "poore man" was "newly come on to the profession of
Religion," Wheelwright's preaching must have been at the root of these
and other of his errors. Even though at that time Wheelwright "could not
but contradict him" because the man's testimony was so "grosse," yet
"hee did it so tenderly," Winthrop reported, "as might well discover his
neere agreement in the points."[65]

Even with his sentence of banishment overturned, Wheelwright still
rankled at the memory of the General Court's accusations. The publication of Winthrop's *Short Story* in 1644 prompted him to write and publish
in London his *Mercurius Americanus, Mr. Welds his Antitype, or Massachusetts great Apologie examined* (1645), a pamphlet that offered a sharp rejoinder to Winthrop's characterization of many of the individuals implicated in the controversy and a lengthy vindication of Wheelwright's own
theological positions during it; needless to say, he concluded that the
Short Story was "mythologie" plain and simple. Like Gorton a year later,
Wheelwright accused the New England Puritans of being "*prelaticall*" because they "did not admit these men [the Hutchinsonians], who left
Bishops" as they had, "to a freedome of spirit, and conscience." He criticized the colony's leaders for their lack of patience with those who had
come to New England with "a good opinion" of the other colonists but
whose inevitable "dispositions to errours at first" were "forced into a

habit" by the "*Anti-peristasis*" of the Puritans' "vehement persecution."
Wheelwright claimed that when some of the immigrants—"spirituall
Chymists," he called them, who had "extract[ed] the sweetnesse of all
into freedom of conscience"—became frustrated by their inability to find
this "*Elixar*," their "melancholy" disposed them "to strange fancies in
Divinity." [66]

Wheelwright clearly intended people to know that he was not among
the "*Chymists*" and to prove his point focused on Winthrop's anecdote
about the "Scholar" at Mount Wollaston who presumably had descended
into his errors by way of his minister's teachings. Wheelwright noted,
quite logically, that this "illiterate man" could hardly have derived his
doctrines from his own preaching if the man had considered Wheelwright's doctrine "Antichristian," and then proceeded to outline his own
beliefs, which flatly contradicted Winthrop's account of them. The Exeter minister saw no reason to rebut all eighty-two errors listed by the
synod, for he did not wish to draw himself into "the same height of bab-
ling" as Winthrop. He attacked what he considered the most representative charges and through a rigorous application of logic and divinity
stiffly maintained his orthodoxy. The purportedly contemptuous and seditious behavior exemplified in his "Fast-Day Sermon" was reduced to
nought. He simply refused to admit that his explication of the covenant
of grace contributed to "disobedience to civill discipline" or to "neglect
of Authority." All he had done in that sermon, he reminded his readers,
was to have "set up Christ, whose absence was the cause of fasting."
Then, touching on what in the colony still were tender nerves, he added
that "Mr. *Cotton* and *He* agreed in the main," for "both their labours
[were] directed at the same scope," to bring men to Christ, the difference
between them being one "of *precision*" in doctrine. He slyly suggested
that Winthrop's malice toward him was fed in good measure by the governor's own "melancholy" over not having received the respect the colonists had accorded to "that worthy gentleman then *Governour*, Sir *Hen:
Vain*." [67]

Given his disenchantment with New England, it should come as no
surprise that between 1656 and 1662 Wheelwright was in England, where
he enjoyed the favor of both Vane and Oliver Cromwell before their
deaths. Before and after this interlude, he lived in settlements in present-
day Maine and New Hampshire—in Wells, Hampton, and finally Salis-
bury—an area populated by a number of exiled antinomians and their
fellow-travelers.

One of these exiles was Hanserd Knollys, prevented from settling in the Bay Colony because he was said to hold "some of Mrs. Hutchinson's opinions." He moved to the Piscataqua territory, in what later became Dover, New Hampshire, where he was settled over a church of "very raw" men. One of his parishioners was Captain John Underhill, banished from Massachusetts for complicity in the Antinomian Controversy. To the Bay's magistrates and ministers these two individuals offered vivid proof of the final tendency of "Antinomian" and "Familist" beliefs. The escapades of these two radicals contributed to the popular impression of what befell those who voiced aberrant doctrines.[68]

Underhill's difficulties began in the summer of 1638 when he petitioned the General Court to grant him a tract of land previously promised for his duties in the Pequot War. Because he had been directly implicated in the controversy over Wheelwright's "Fast-Day Sermon" (and indeed soon joined that minister in the Piscataqua region), the court took that opportunity to question him about derogatory "speeches" about the colony, particularly his claim that the New England Puritans were zealous "as the Scribes and Pharisees were, and as Paul was before his conversion." He denied these charges, whereupon the court produced as its witness "a sober, godly woman," whom, as Winthrop reported, Underhill "had seduced . . . and drawn to his opinions." From her testimony, the magistrates learned of the remarkable way that the militia captain had come to his "assurance" of salvation: "He had lain under a spirit of bondage and a legal way five years," he had told her, "till at length, as he was taking a pipe of tobacco, the Spirit set home such an absolute promise of free grace with such assurance and joy, as he never since doubted of his good estate, neither shall he, though he should fall into sin." Neither confirming nor denying this, Underhill dug his pit even deeper when he admitted that in a recent "retractation" of his earlier actions in behalf of Wheelwright, he had intended to repent "only of the manner" of his behavior, not of the "matter." He was ordered banished for attempting to deceive the court.[69]

The next Sabbath he was questioned for another sexual impropriety, "suspicion of incontinency with a neighbor's wife." Witnesses reported that the woman was "young, and beautiful, and withal of a jovial spirit and behavior," and that Underhill "did daily frequent her house, and was divers times found there alone with her, the door being locked on the inside." Captain Underhill "confessed" it looked "ill, because it had an appearance of evil in it," but he explained that the woman was "in great trouble of mind, and sore temptations, and that he resorted to her to comfort her." Behind the locked door, "they were in private prayer together." The elders rejected this as a lame excuse and condemned such licentious behavior, all the more vigorously because only a few months earlier they had warned the populace that just such sin would be the final effect of Hutchinson's "mortalist" heresy. As noted earlier, Cotton had warned Hutchinson at her church trial, "*if the Resurrection be past than you cannot Evade the Argument* . . . that [the] filthie Sinne of the communitie of Woeman and all promiscuous and filthie comminge togeather of men and Woeman without Distinction or Relation of Marriage, will necessarily follow." Hutchinson had not yet fallen into such immorality, but Underhill's behavior seemed to bear out the magistrates' opinion and Cotton's admonition.[70]

Wheelwright later tried to defend his supporter by asking whether "every little error touching *Divinity* in militarie men, whose stirred humors may easily attenuate the spirits, . . . [should] be heighten'd into heresie," but by that time Underhill had sullied his reputation even more. A year following the events mentioned above, he made the mistake of sending a letter full of reproaches against the Bay Colony to a young man who subsequently showed the document to Winthrop. From that point on all Underhill's requests for pardon fell upon deaf ears, particularly after the Boston church learned that he had attempted adultery with other women. In 1639 he withdrew from Wheelwright's settlement to Dover, where Knollys had been installed.

Knollys, too, had recently been taken to task for bitterly inveighing against the Bay government and clergy. He retracted and the colony accepted his retraction, but his sincerity was questioned the following year by obstreperous behavior in the northern settlements.[71] Knollys's difficulties began when his ministry was challenged by a recent arrival from England, Thomas Larkham, who got himself elected in Knollys's stead. Knollys formed a second church in the tiny settlement. The resulting uproar within days turned violent, with Larkham, whom Thomas Edwards later described as "a feirce [sic] Independent," a man of "ill behavior," laying "violent hands" upon his opponent. One day Underhill and Knollys led a farcical assault on Larkham's home, one of their supporters carrying "a Bible upon a staff for an ensigne" and Knollys a loaded pistol. Larkham sent for aid, and the attacking party was surrounded and contained while Larkham tried them for riot. A commission from the Bay, requested by Underhill, cooled the tensions, but not before Knollys was found an "unclean person" who had "solicited the chastity of two maids" and "used filthy dalliance with them." Winthrop recorded the delightful irony that this "sin of his was the more notorious" because the improprieties were discovered "the same night after he [Knollys] had been exhorting the people . . . to proceed against Captain Underhill for his adultery." A more comical state of affairs could hardly be imagined, but, predictably, Winthrop made a more serious generalization. "It is very observable," he wrote, "how God gave up those two, and some others who had held with Mrs. Hutchinson, in crying down all evidence from sanctification, etc., to fall into these unclean courses, whereby themselves and their erroneous opinions were laid open to the world." With such evidence, he believed, none could doubt the justness of the colony's actions against the antinomians during 1637 and 1638.[72]

Within a few months of this embarrassment Knollys returned to England, where among the baptists in the sectarian underground his fortunes took a turn for the better. Underhill, by 1644, had wandered to a new settlement on the shores of Long Island Sound, scattering his antinomian seed as he went. In 1644 Wheelwright apologized to the Massachusetts government and clergy. Aspinwall had offered his recantation in 1642. A year later Hutchinson and several members of her family were slaughtered by Indians on Long Island near Pelham Bay. Thus by the mid-1640s the first major episode in the history of New England radicalism essentially had come to a close, most of its main actors silenced, some reconciled to the ecclesiastical polity in Massachusetts or content to leave well enough alone and to pursue their radical visions in other colonies, free from persecution by those whom they had considered their closest brethren. But the 1640s hardly brought peace to New England, for at the same time that Aspinwall and Wheelwright were asking forgiveness of their enemies, others like John Clarke, Gorton, and Coddington, who had remained on the periphery of the Antinomian Controversy, were beginning to offer their own vigorous, if less direct, challenges to New England congregationalism, challenges that proved every bit as threatening as Hutchinson's.

During the next phase of Puritan radicalism in New England, the views of chief radical ideologues frequently were reinforced by the larger world of English sectarianism. This is not to suggest that someone like Gorton was the appointed disciple or representative of any prominent English radical, but rather, that if such a man had come to his own understanding of the marrow of Puritan doctrine and thereupon rejected the main tenets of the New England Way, he was very likely to establish connections with Puritans in England who had arrived at similar conclusions about the nature of their faith. This was particularly so after the triumph of the Long Parliament and the successes of the New Model Army had liberated English Puritans to explore the implications of proscribed doctrine. As often as not, too, in the 1640s these spokesmen for New England radicalism traveled to England—perhaps to bring complaints against the intolerance of Massachusetts, or to attempt to secure patents for their own settlements—and found themselves at the center of a veritable revolution of thought and values in a land of increasing toleration of sincere Christian dissent. Other colonists encountered the excitement of English radicalism secondhand, through the reports of new arrivals to New England, or in the books and pamphlets such immigrants carried with them. Some New Englanders—Hugh Peter, Samuel Gorton, and Roger Williams are the most notable examples—made a significant contribution to the development of English Puritan radicalism. If, like Williams and Gorton, they later returned to America, they often brought with them a much richer and more militant conception of Puritan reform.

Measured against developments in the English Puritan movement in the 1640s, the Antinomian Controversy shrinks to an undeniably provincial event, important to the larger Protestant world primarily in how its irrepressible dynamic provided an object lesson about the dangers inherent in an emphasis on justification by faith alone. Its importance to the evolution of New England thought itself cannot be overstated; for the magistrates and ministers it sharply revealed the tension between Puritan faith and a viable social order. As one historian has put it, the strange-sounding doctrines debated in Massachusetts between 1636 and 1638 really involved "an assertion of self-esteem, of one's inner feeling as more trustworthy than logic or convention, of the individual's right to decide religious questions for himself (and in his interests), of a need for relief from the strain of rectitude and other-worldliness."[73] And, as Leonard W. Levy recently has written, the antinomians' emphasis on the overwhelming power of grace implied that "salvation begins here and not beyond the grave, and that the righteous or moral man does not or cannot sin," for sin is only a "temporary aberration pardonable through spiritual regeneration." By rejecting the model of a "fallen and depraved Adam" for the saint redeemed through Christ, Hutchinson and her supporters announced that they no longer would support an ideology whose adherents refused to recognize God's true mercy or His son's true purpose. Aware of the implications of antinomian doctrine, the established order in New England knew as well that such notions were incompatible with their own goal of a theocratic, hierarchical society.[74]

Hutchinson's cause drew so many supporters because there already existed in New England—as in the Puritan movement as a whole—a predisposition to her doctrine: Hutchinson did not so much start the Antinomian Controversy as become its most intense focus. What the Antinomian Controversy "meant," then, was not so much that the New England theocrats had encountered an individual who had intentionally started a new sect, but rather that she, and others like Vane and Wheelwright, had harnessed what the author of *Good News from New-England* (1648) described as a "new Engine" to influence popular opinion that was "somewhat like the Trojan horse for rarity." Hutchinson's fame was raised to such heights because of the colonists' willingness—one almost could say *desire*—to have clarified for them the true nature and meaning of their spiritual longings, a task for which she was admirably suited.[75]

One other important consequence of the Hutchinsonian episode was that, as soon as the Antinomian Controversy officially ended, it served in both New England and old as a benchmark by which to evaluate all subsequent encounters with radical sectarians. The publication in 1644 of Winthrop's *Short Story* provided the measure; within a few years such prominent presbyterians as Ephraim Pagitt, Robert Baillie, and Samuel Rutherford fleshed out their attacks on congregationalism with facts about New England gleaned from its pages, and predicted from events in the Boston church their own country's inevitable decline into heresy and immorality.

Any subsequent outbreak of radicalism in New England—most notably the challenge of the Gortonists, and, later, of the Quakers—immediately was put into perspective by a ritual invocation of the Hutchinsonians. Edward Johnson's *Wonder-Working Providence* is representative: his obsession with the antinomians and the countless children they begat runs through its pages like a sharply pulled thread. The influence of Anne Hutchinson and the Antinomian Controversy on the development of the American Puritan imagination is undeniable, for throughout the seventeenth century and into the period of the Great Awakening, when Charles Chauncy recalled the events that had occurred in his own Boston church a century earlier to condemn the "enthusiasm" of the New Lights, the "defeat" of the antinomians never outlived its usefulness as an emblem of the purity of the New England churches. In this light, the title of Cotton Mather's own description of the difficulties in which his esteemed grandfather had been so deeply implicated is highly ironic. "*Hydra Decapita*," he called the chapter; but, contrary to what he wished his readers to believe, the many-headed monster first discerned in Anne Hutchinson's conventicle was anything but destroyed in the spring of 1638.[76]

SAMUEL GORTON

Until recently, Samuel Gorton had remained one of the most enigmatic characters in early New England history, primarily because his doctrinal link to prominent English radicals was insufficiently understood. Most historians' accounts of him fall into the historical typecasting that echoes Nathaniel Morton's vituperative description of him as "a proud and pestilent seducer . . . deeply leavened with blasphemous and familistical opinions," or insists he was an early American advocate of religious freedom second only to Roger Williams in vehemence for the cause. Even so profound a scholar as Perry Miller described Gorton's beliefs as "part and parcel" of a "lunatic fringe" of Puritanism in Stuart England, but he never took the time to investigate the precise nature of Gorton's relationship to the radicals whose thought his so closely mirrored.[1] Yet perhaps more than those of any other New Englander, Gorton's ideas illuminate the complexity of the relationship of English and American Puritanism. The development of his radical spiritism, first in Rhode Island and then for four years at the center of London's sectarian underground, permits close examination of the links between the "antinomianism" of the 1630s and the doctrines of the Levellers, the Ranters, and, finally, the Quakers.

Gorton's prose style was relatively inaccessible; one nineteenth-century historian remarked that his religious discourse "employ[ed] a dialect utterly incoherent to the uninitiated." Most students have therefore glossed over his religious opinions and have accepted the simplistic exaggerations of earlier historians. They overlook the fact that while in England in the mid-1640s Gorton enjoyed great success as a preacher in the General Baptist conventicles, particularly in that of the infamous Thomas Lamb; and that his political ideology was similar to that of such English Puritan radicals as John Saltmarsh and William Dell, chaplains in the New Model Army and men prominent in the Seeker and Ranter movements of their day; and that after he returned to New England in 1648 he was one of the first men to defend the Quakers when they attempted to land in Boston in the 1650s. Instead, Gorton has been tossed haphazardly into the murky and seldom-stirred cauldron that contains Anne Hutchinson, John Wheelwright, William Aspinwall, and other "Antinomians" who obstructed the Bay Colony's march to the New Jerusalem but whose radical ideas differed significantly from Gorton's.[2]

An examination of Gorton's profoundly held mysticism reveals much about Massachusetts' prolonged attempts to slander him for his deviance. While their deepest fears about him stemmed from the ideological implications of his radical spiritism, they also were profoundly troubled by his threat to broadcast to the Protestant world that New England's "pure" congregational polity offered a fertile spawning ground for the chaos threatening England during the civil wars. Such presbyterian divines as Thomas Edwards, Robert Baillie, and Samuel Rutherford were quick to point out that he brought into dangerously close focus not only the questions of the political and ecclesiastical jurisdiction of magistrates and the proper use of ordinances, but also the more basic issue of how Puritans committed to a congregational or "Independent" polity could control individual and social behavior that stemmed from a fervent mystical faith. Claiming victory over Gorton, the New England Puritans could more confidently march to the synod at Cambridge in 1648 and proclaim with Nathaniel Ward that "all Familists, Antinomians, Anabaptists, and other Enthusiasts shall have free Liberty to keepe away" from the American strand.[3] The colonists dramatically announced that, despite the military successes of the New Model Army and the increasing toleration for Christian sects in England, New England would not become the mirror image of old.

A sketch of Gorton's New England career demonstrates how violently the Massachusetts Puritans reacted to anyone whose behavior reminded them of their recent difficulties with the antinomians. Born about 1592 in Gorton, England, an area near Manchester known from the 1580s on as a Puritan stronghold, Samuel Gorton eventually found his way to London, where he engaged in the respectable middle-class trade of a clothier.[4] The motive for his removal to the Puritan colony is unknown, but in 1636/7 he arrived in Boston at the height of the troubles with Anne Hutchinson and her followers. Remaining apart from the immediate controversy, although Winslow claimed that he helped "to blow the bellowes" upon the colonists' contentions, Gorton, by 1638, was within the boundaries of the Plymouth patent. He had left Boston—at least so William Hubbard and Cotton Mather would have us believe—because he was dunned for one hundred pounds by the agent of a Londoner, the Reverend George Walker, from whom he had solicited such an advance before coming to New England.[5]

A more plausible explanation for the brevity of his stay in Boston is that he recognized the direction in which the ministerial winds were blowing. If Gorton sensed that his religious beliefs were similar to those held by the beleagured Hutchinsonians and did not want to risk bringing the wrath of the synod on himself as well, he was wise to move to more peaceful Plymouth. But as much as he tried to stay clear of those not likely to tolerate his peculiar religious opinions, once he began acting on the Word as it was revealed to him he was bound for trouble. Nathaniel Morton's account sets the tone for later reports. Though harboring little affection for Gorton, Morton admitted that upon Gorton's first coming to Plymouth there was hope that he would be "a useful instrument," but that all too quickly Gorton showed himself "a subtle deceiver, courteous in carriage to all, at some times (for his own ends) but soon moved to passion." Gorton's passions were aroused by difficulties over his wife's serving woman, whom the Plymouth authorities threatened to banish when "nothing was laid to her charge, only it was whispered privately that she had smiled" in the Sabbath meeting. He soon condemned Plymouth's government.[6]

The animosity displayed toward Gorton was caused by more than his uncivil behavior in his defense of the serving woman, for the Plymouth records charge him not only with "misdemeanours in the open Court, towards the elders, the Bench, and [with] stirring up the people to mutynie in the face of the Court," but with heresy as well. It was rumored that Gorton had already begun "to sow such seeds . . . whereby some were seduced," and among those he influenced was none other than the wife of Ralph Smith, the colony's minister, whom Gorton had known in Lancashire; she frequented Gorton's home for daily prayer and told her neighbors "how glad she was that she could come into a family where her spirit was refreshed in the ordinances of god as in former dayes." The scenario was all too familiar, especially since Gorton, like Anne Hutchin-

SIMPLICITIES DEFENCE

againſt
SEVEN-HEADED POLICY.

OR

Innocency Vindicated, being unjuſtly Accuſed,
and ſorely Cenſured, by that

Seven - headed Church - Government

United in

NEW-ENGLAND:

OR

That Servant ſo Imperious in his Maſters Abſence
Revived, and now thus re-acting in Nɛvv-Enɡland.

OR

The combate of the United Colonies, not onely againſt
ſome of the Natives and Subjects, but againſt the Authority alſo
of the Kingdme of *England,* with their execution of Laws, in the name and
Authority of the ſervant, (or of themſelves) and not in the Name and
Authority of the Lord, or fountain of the Government.

Wherein is declared an Act of a great people and Country
of the *Indians* in thoſe parts, both Princes and People (unanimouſly)
in their voluntary Submiſſion and Subjection unto the Protection
and Government of Old England (from the Fame they hear thereof) together with the true manner and forme of it, as it appears under their own
hands and ſeals, being ſtirred up, and provoked thereto, by
the Combate and courſes above-ſaid.

Throughout which Treatiſe is ſecretly intermingled, that
great Oppoſition, which is in the goings forth of thoſe two grand
Spirits, that are, and ever have been, extant in the World
(through the ſons of men) from the beginning and
foundation thereof.

Imprimatur, *Aug.* 3ᵈ. 1646. Diligently peruſed, approved, and
Licenſed to the Preſſe, according to Order by publike Autho ity.

LONDON,
Printed by *John Macock,* and are to be ſold by Lukɛ Favvnɛ,
at his ſhop in *Pauls Church-yard,* at the ſign of the *Parrot.* 1 6 4 6.

Title page of *Simplicities Defence against Seven-Headed Policy,* by Samuel Gorton
(London, 1646), wherein he attacked his persecution at the hands of the Massachusetts Bay Colony's government.

son, was engaged in lay preaching that alienated the community from the settled ministry. Not about to risk more dissension—or the further embarrassment of Smith—the elders tried Gorton for religious and civil insubordination. Charging him with preaching (among other things) "no more happiness than this world affords," they banished him from the patent.[7]

By 1639 Gorton reached the newly established settlement of Aquidneck (later Portsmouth) where William Coddington, John Clarke, and others forced out of Massachusetts in the Antinomian Controversy had joined the Hutchinsonians.[8] But Gorton soon upset the political alignment of that infant colony, and Coddington, from the outset suspicious of Gorton's religious eccentricities, moved swiftly against him. Thomas Lechford, who had his own bones to pick with New England, described the proceedings with precious understatement. "They began about a small trespasse of swine," he noted, but "it is thought some other matter was ingredient." Indeed it was, for after Gorton refused to acknowledge the authority of the local government in a trespassing complaint, he behaved as he had at Plymouth, calling the town's magistrates "great asses" and its judges "corrupt," and taunting Coddington with the words, "all you that are for the King, lay hold on Coddington!" Mather sarcastically pointed out that Gorton had affronted "what little government they had." For his seditious behavior he was whipped and banished.[9]

Matters went no better in Roger Williams's settlement of Providence. Gorton again became embroiled in disputes. Within a few months of Gorton's arrival, the usually mild-mannered Williams wrote an exasperated letter to John Winthrop, complaining that Gorton, "having foully abused high and low at aquedneck [was] now bewitching and bemadding poor Providence." Besides censuring "all the Ministers of this Countrey," he was "denying all visible and externall ordinances," and his opinions seemed to be spreading, for "all most all suck in his poyson as at first they did at aquedneck."[10] Then, on 17 November 1641, Gorton's name was brought officially to Governor John Winthrop's attention in a petition from thirteen inhabitants of Providence, who requested aid in settling the disputes Gorton had complicated. They "counted it meet and necessary to give . . . true intelligence of the insolent and riotous carriages of Samuel Gorton and his company," who had "no manner of honest order of government, either over them or amongst them" and who taunted, threatened, and assaulted those who sought to resist their "lewd, licentious courses." Faced with this unusual complaint (the settlement was not within his jurisdiction), Winthrop cautiously replied that the Bay "could

not levy war, etc. without a General Court," and "except they [the peti-
tioners] did submit themselves to some jurisdiction, either Plymouth or
ours, we had no calling or warrant to interpose in their contentions."
Then in September 1642 the petitioners formally subjected themselves to
the authority of Massachusetts Bay and solicited its protection.[11]

Massachusetts now had the opportunity not only to drive a wedge into
the plantation refuges for those seeking "soul-liberty" but also to secure a
strategic window on Narragansett Bay, facing the Dutch plantations to
the south. Winthrop soon issued a warning for the Gortonists to halt further agitation among the inhabitants of Providence.[12]

Gorton's patience—never his prominent virtue—became strained, and
he sent the Bay Colony an immoderate reply unequivocally refusing
compliance with their directive. He objected to the Bay Colony's attempt
to enlarge its jurisdiction without the consent of a majority of the inhabitants, for by English law "neither the one nor the other [that is, neither
William Arnold and the other petitioners nor the Bay Puritans] . . . have
power to enlarge the bounds, by King Charles limited" to them. He
claimed that Massachusetts betrayed the true intent of its actions by its
willingness to honor the request for aid from men like William Arnold
whom it once had banished from its society because they had been associated with Anne Hutchinson. "We know very well," he argued, "that it
is the name of Christ, called upon us which you strive against, whence it
is that you stand on tiptoe to stretch yourselves beyond your bounds, to
seek occasion against us. . . . We know, before hand, how our cause will
be ended, and see the scale of your equal justice turned already, before we
have laid our cause therein."[13] His band would not capitulate to the Bay's
jurisdiction, for they had "wronged no man" and "will not be dealt with
as before; we speak in the name of our God, we will not; for, if any shall
disturb us . . . secret hypocrites shall become open tyrants, and their
laws appear to be nothing else but mere lusts, in the eyes of all the
world." Hurling a final insult, Gorton maintained that if any people
thought his words "unchristian" it was because their magistrates had
kept them "ignorant of the cross of our Lord Jesus." Gorton accused the
Puritan leaders of setting up their own cross, "Seighnirim," signifying
"horror and fear," and he dared tell Winthrop that this was the cross the
governor held and taught and by which he thought to be saved.[14]

Gorton was openly challenging the Puritans to persecute him as they
had the antinomians, but his only defense was the location of his settlement beyond the boundaries set in the Massachusetts charter. To ensure
his safety—and because of bitter feelings in Providence—Gorton moved

even farther south, finally purchasing a piece of land called Shawomet (later Warwick), where he felt secure from any intrusion by Massachusetts. But to his immense surprise and consternation the Massachusetts magistrates summoned him and his followers to Boston on the complaint of two Indian sachems who claimed that he had seized their land unjustly. Urged on by Gorton's enemies (one of the Providence petitioners acted as the Indians' interpreter in Boston), both sachems had appeared before the authorities, submitted to the jurisdiction of Massachusetts, and asked aid in recovering the property they claimed was swindled from them. The Massachusetts magistrates had lost their quasi-legal hold on Gorton when he moved from Providence; they were outraged at the numerous heresies and blasphemies in his letters to them, and now took the new opportunity to strike.[15] An expeditionary force led by Edward Johnson captured the Gortonists after a duplicitous attempt at negotiations and brought them to Boston for trial as heretics and enemies to civil government.[16]

The magistrates were unable to reach a verdict from the available evidence and directed Gorton to answer in writing, under penalty of death, a set of doctrinal and hermeneutic questions.[17] Gorton complied, but refused to retract his earlier insults to the Massachusetts magistrates. The court sentenced them to hard labor in towns surrounding Boston.[18] Within a few months, though, bowing to public pressure and without soliciting any further testimony, the General Court overturned the Gortonists' sentences. Gorton was free to voyage to England to bring complaint against Massachusetts.[19] There he found frequent opportunity to preach his theological doctrines to people sympathetic to the ideology he represented, and to publish treatises that clearly reflect the nature of his radicalism.

At first Gorton's presence in London drew little attention, but by the late fall of 1645 none other than Roger Williams had given to Robert Baillie, a Scottish presbyterian minister and member of the Westminster Assembly of Divines, a manuscript "Paper" in which he described some of Gorton's opinions. While the precise nature of Williams's "Paper" and his reasons for bringing it to Baillie's attention remain unknown, the document contained enough information to convince Baillie that the Gortonists' behavior was a further indication of the degeneracy to which an Independent or "Separatist" ecclesiastical polity tended.[20]

Soon after Baillie read Williams's manuscript he brought Gorton to public attention in his *Dissuasive from the Errours of the Time* of 1645–46, one of the earliest of what soon proved a spate of heresiographies. Among the many "errours" he assiduously documented, Baillie included the ideas about divorce propounded by John Milton in his *Doctrine and Discipline of Divorce* (1643), and to a discussion of Milton's treatment of this subject he appended what he knew of others who supported similarly radical views. "What ever therefore may be said of M. *Milton*," Baillie noted, "M. *Gorting* and his Company," who were "men of renown among the *New-English Independents*, before Mistresse *Hutchinsons* disgrace," also had to be numbered among those who maintained that it was "lawfull for every woman to desert her husband when he is not willing to follow her in her Church-Way." Gorton and his followers openly avowed, Williams had written (and Baillie dutifully reported), that a woman who saw "into the mystery of Christ" and thereupon entered "the Lords House" had every right to abandon a spouse who had not been granted similar insight. "The Church of God is a Christian home" where the saints dwell, Gorton had proclaimed. In leaving a husband who would not inhabit the same spiritual domicile a woman did no wrong; it was her husband who had forsaken her.[21]

Whatever Baillie's disagreements with Williams over church polity, he felt no hesitancy about using the colonist's own words to condemn others who purportedly espoused so unholy a doctrine concerning matrimony. Considering his prominence in the Westminster Assembly, he frequently had the opportunity to share such information with other presbyterians. It probably was Baillie himself who apprised Thomas Edwards, the most renowned of the English heresiographers, of Gorton's activities in New England. In *The Second Part of Gangraena* (1646) Edwards reported that among the religious radicals then proliferating in England was "one *Gorton*," "a great Sectarie" from New England who had been severely chastised by the Massachusetts Puritans for his many "desperate opinions," and about whom he had learned from "a Reverend Minister at London" whose own knowledge had come from a document given him "by Mr. *Williams* of New-England." When Edwards decided to compile more accounts of sectarian activity, Baillie presumably gave him direct access to the Williams material, which, as Edwards put it, he had "seen and perused." Eager to add another heretic to his already lengthy list, Edwards solicited information about Gorton's whereabouts, and by the late spring of 1646 he had located the New Englander in one of London's most famous conventicles. "This I am assured of from divers hands," Edwards reported; "*Gorton* is here in London, and hath been for the space of some months." "I am told also," he continued, "that hee vents his opinions, and exercises in some of the meetings of the Sectaries," particularly at "*Lams* Church," in Bell Alley, off Coleman Street.[22]

In Bell Alley Gorton found a kindred spirit who like himself had been harshly persecuted for his religious beliefs. In 1640, Lamb had been arraigned before the Star Chamber for preaching to a separatist group in his home town of Colchester. Found guilty of this and later of other similar charges, he was in and out of prison over the next year until the Long Parliament removed Archbishop William Laud and granted to Lamb and countless other nonconformists a degree of freedom they hitherto had not known. In 1641 Lamb joined the congregation of John Goodwin, famed Independent minister at St. Stephen's, Coleman Street, where he was ordained as an elder; and a few months later, moved by the same spiritual hunger that possessed so many other Puritan preachers of that decade, he formed his own conventicle, first in Bell Alley and then in other parts of London. By 1644 "Lams Church" had become a byword for the most extreme forms of religious radicalism; and, while Lamb himself usually was considered a member of the group loosely termed the "General Baptists," from the extant descriptions of the meetings at his church in the 1640s, it is clear that the practice of adult baptism was only one of many radical principles espoused by him and his associates, and hardly the most extreme.[23] Bell Alley assuredly was not Puritan Boston, and in Lamb's church Gorton found an audience who would not chastise him for his ideology as the Massachusetts settlers had. By his frequent presence at this particular meeting, Gorton showed that he was a very different creature from any of Anne Hutchinson's immediate supporters.

When Edwards complained of the "very Erroneous, strange Doctrines" that were "vented there continually," he had foremost in mind Lamb's predilection to preach "universal Grace" and "Arminian tenets," two points of doctrine usually attributed to the General Baptists but shared at one time or another by many members of England's sectarian underground. At Lamb's church, such ideas were staple fare for the people who filled the "house and yards" for the meetings. "Especially young youths and wenches flock thither," Edwards continued, to hear "all of them preach *universal Redemption*." It was widely known that Lamb openly welcomed others who preached a similar version of the good news. Henry Denne, who as early as 1643 had rejected infant baptism and had been rebaptized by Lamb himself, made a point of visiting the Bell Alley meeting whenever he was in London. "The usual Theam that he is upon," noted one of his critics, "is Christs dying for all men." The

Baptist Samuel Oates, another regular visitor at Lamb's church and father of the infamous Titus Oates, frequently preached "*That the Doctrine of Gods eternal Election and Predestination was a damnable Doctrine and Error.*" By late 1646 Baillie, writing in his *Anabaptism, the True Fountaine of Independency* (1647), declared what all London already knew: "Mr. *Lambs* Congregation, the greatest, as they say, and the most fruitfull of all their [the General Baptists'] Societies," was thoroughly "pestered" with the "gangren" of universal redemption.[24]

Lamb's church was as infamous for the nature of the preaching found there as for the doctrines preached, for the crowds that gathered in Bell Alley "in the latter end of the Lords day" were assured of hearing not only from Lamb and a variety of popular preachers like Denne and Oates, but from members of the congregation itself who were encouraged to speak out in the meeting. Such open participation in the church service by "illiterate mechanicks" and other representatives of London's lower classes understandably shocked conservative clergymen, who felt threatened by the political implications of such behavior. In Bell Alley "they have many 'Exercisers,'" Edwards reported, "in one meeting two or three." After someone like Lamb, Denne, or, for that matter, Gorton, had preached and prayed, one critic observed, the exhorter often called out to the audience "to know if any be not satisfied." If there indeed was any disagreement, "then they stand up that will, and object, and he answers." Even more disconcerting to London's established clergy than this breach of clerical prerogative, these raucous discussions were not limited to regular members of the meeting nor to individuals unaffiliated with established churches. Edwards complained that not only did "some of other separate Churches" find their way to Bell Alley, but "some of our Churches," too, went "to this *Lams* Church for novelty, because of the disputes and wranglings that will be there upon Questions."[25]

Those who attended Lamb's church for doctrinal and ecclesiastical "novelty" were seldom disappointed. At one point in his *Gangraena*, for example, Edwards related the story of a young man who went to "*Lams* meetingplace" and encountered "one Sectarie who maintained and affirmed that he was Jesus Christ." When the youth challenged him, the sectary "still maintained it stiffly" and told him that "hee would poure out his judgements on him for opposing and speaking thus against him." We are given no indication of this man's identity, though it is tantalizing to recall that when Gorton was whipped in New England his disciples cried out, "Now Christ Jesus has suffered." The astonished youth assured his parents that the fellow was indeed "in his wits" when he made such statements and had been given a sympathetic hearing by those at the meeting. "He spoke sensibly," the youth reported, "and to the things that were spoken of, though in a blasphemous and abominable way." Well-known preachers like Denne and Oates uttered similarly shocking beliefs. They not only maintained that "the common doctrine of election and pre-destination" was "false" but also broached the heretical notion, later the hallmark of such Ranters as Abiezer Coppe, "that the Sun, Moon, and other creatures do sufficiently preach Christ to all the world," thus obviating the saint's need to search endlessly through Scripture for proof of the glorious work of redemption.[26]

Contemporary accounts report that in the mid-1640s the "novelty" of Lamb's church extended to preaching by women, and although the identity of the "Sister *Stag*" at whose meetings Edwards also located Gorton is unknown, the New Englander could hardly have escaped notice of Mrs. Attaway, "the mistresse of all the she-preachers in Coleman Street," who in the presbyterians' eyes stood as one of the most unholy incarnations of the "mechanick" preachers who taught the doctrine of universal redemption. Early in January 1646, in Bell Alley, this woman reiterated the message of Lamb, Denne, and Oates and told the assemblage that "it would not stand with the goodnesse of God to damn his own creatures Eternally," for her reading of the Bible revealed an impending "general restauration" wherein "all men shall be reconciled and saved."[27]

Like many others whose association with radical Puritanism began in the Baptist conventicles, she expressed some of the views most often linked to the "Expecters" or "Seekers," of whom Roger Williams was the most famous representative. Like Williams, she believed that through the Church's corruption the true apostolic succession had been lost, thus preventing any individual from claiming a divine commission to dispense church ordinances or even to preach. Like Williams, too, she viewed herself as an individual witness to Christ's glory, alone "in the Wildernesse, waiting for the pouring out of the Spirit" that would initiate the new dispensation. The true ministers of God's word would only appear when the Holy Ghost was "poured out upon all flesh," Attaway claimed, and she was content to await this "restauration" in the corners of Bell Alley, making it "the subject of divers of her Sermons, that the Kingdom of the Holy Ghost, and of love more excellent than that of Christs was now at the doors."[28]

As her own behavior indicates, however, Mrs. Attaway was not totally idle as she awaited this outpouring of the Spirit, for she fueled her critics' charges that doctrines like those daily broached in Bell Alley ended in libertinism. When two representatives of the Inns of Court interrogated her about her beliefs, one question they posed concerned her approval of "Master *Miltons* Doctrine of Divorce," which she had found "a point to be considered of" because she herself had an "unsanctified" husband. Not one to be accused of hypocrisy, Mrs. Attaway shortly thereafter ran off with one William Jenney, who like her, was still married to someone else! So well known was this case of alienated affections in the radical underground that by late 1646 Baillie admitted that though he had no proof that the "Anabaptists" doctrines were "yet so extremely obscene" as those of David George and other "familists," "yet here [on the matter of divorce] they are come pretty near him." "Two of their Teachers," Baillie continued, "M. *Gorting* and Mistresse *Attaway* with their Disciples have declared themselves for the dissolution of all unequal Marriages," which they defined as "all those with persons of a different mind from themselves." [29]

Baillie's decision to associate Gorton and Attaway was based on more than rhetoric, for the reports of Edwards and others make it clear that upon his arrival in England Gorton had lost little time in establishing his reputation among London's radicals, for whom Bell Alley was one center. How he found his way *there* is anybody's guess, though it may have been through the mediation of Giles Calvert, the radical printer and bookseller whose shop on Ludgate Hill was a well-known clearinghouse for sectaries and who in 1655 would publish Gorton's *Saltmarsh Returned from the Dead*. More simply, Gorton's participation in the New England experiment made him a sought-after visitor in the radical conventicles, for, as one disgruntled clergyman observed, in the 1640s there was "hardly a noted Sectary, lately come out of *New-England, Holland*, &c, who is in any way capable of an office, place, gift, or respect, but he is in some one or other, and hath beene the better for these times." The experience of "Master Nicholas Davison," who had returned to London after a brief stay in America, supports this contention. He noted that upon his re-arrival in England he met "with one who came from *New-England*, and held himself there an Apostle, for which he was whipped." In England, however, this man was considered "a great Preacher, and in great account." [30]

Davison no doubt was describing Gorton himself, who had been flogged for his obstreperous behavior in Aquidneck in Rhode Island but who then was drawing crowds of admirers in Bell Alley. It was there in

1647 that Thomas Underhill, who later reported the fact in his scathing *Hell Broke Loose: Or An History of the Quakers Both Old and New* (1660), heard "this Gorton affirm . . . that what ever shall have *an end*, was a *carnal Ordinance*, and from the Devil," for to Gorton's mind such institutions as "Baptisme, Lords, Chaplains, Ruling Elders, &c" were the inventions of men, not of God. In 1660 Underhill directly linked this and other of Gorton's ideas, which he had gleaned from Samuel Rutherford's *Survey of the Spirituall Antichrist* (1647), to those propounded by the Quakers. Considering England's recent experience with the followers of James Naylor and George Fox, any of his readers, Underhill claimed, could see "what plain Quakerisme these things are."[31]

Underhill spoke with hindsight, but his judgment about the radicalism of Gorton's sermons only corroborated the suspicions many had harbored about Gorton almost from the moment of his rearrival in London. In March 1646, Sir Nathaniel Barnardston reported to his friend John Winthrop that "Gorton is under examination for his opiniones & blasfemies," news that must have pleased the Massachusetts governor because such a formal inquiry could have influenced the resolution of Gorton's case against the Bay Colony. When Gorton recalled this event years later, he claimed that he had been "examined" by a "Committie of Parliament" on the complaint of "three or four malignant persons" who accused him of preaching without being "a university man"; but it is clear that Gorton, who had been summoned along with Hanserd Knollys, William Kiffin, and Thomas Patience, was arraigned specifically for preaching unorthodox doctrine. Gorton's accusers—one of whom was "a Schoolmaster in Christs hospitall" and two others, "Elders of independent or seperatist Churches"—claimed that the doctrines expressed in his sermons were so erroneous that they only served to make "the people of God sad." Gorton's critics strengthened their case against him by producing a copy of his recently published *Simplicities Defence Against Seven-Headed Policy*, "which they said contained divers blasphemies" against the Christian religion.[32]

After the committee had examined the book, and had interrogated its author about his right to preach—Gorton answered their questions, he later recalled, according to his "knowledge and conscience"—he was cleared of all charges and "Dismissed as a preacher of the Gospel," a decision that greatly pleased the "multitude of people" assembled to hear his case. Gorton's difficulties with London's established clergy, though, were not yet over, for Rutherford and other presbyterians had seized on *Sim-*

plicities Defence as proof of this New Englander's—indeed of all New England's—complicity with the program of England's sectaries. A Parliamentary committee might have been willing to ignore the book's radical ideology, but not so those members of the Westminster Assembly who still were struggling to wrest control of the nation's churches from the Independents and radicals, who had their own plans for the reorganization of England's ecclesiastical polity.[33]

In his *Survey of the Spirituall Antichrist* Rutherford offers one final piece of evidence of Gorton's links to the General Baptist conventicles, for in his account of the New Englander, drawn primarily from the documents in *Simplicities Defence*, he clearly intended his readers to believe that Gorton was personally acquainted with another radical who was in London at the same time, one "*R. Beacon*," a "grosse *Familist*" whom he claimed was the author of the prefatory poem to *Simplicities Defence* and from whose "Catechisme" (unfortunately not extant) he quoted to justify his condemnation of Gorton's ideas. The identity of this individual is not certain, but the most likely candidate is Robert Bacon, a Gloucester nonconformist who in the mid-1640s was cast out of that city for preaching "several Erroneous Doctrines" and who then found his way to London, where, Edwards noted, he was "entertained in the house of a great man, one *Barber* [,] an Anabaptist about *Thredneedlestreet*." This Edward Barber, who, as a merchant-tailor, followed the same occupation as Gorton before he departed for New England, had organized what became a well-known General Baptist conventicle, at "his great house in Bishopsgate-street." If Bacon indeed was the "*Beacon*" to whom Rutherford attributed the prefatory poem, Gorton could easily have met him either at Edward Barber's conventicle or at the bookstore and print-shop of Calvert, who published several of Bacon's works.[34]

Bacon enjoyed a bit of notoriety for the "close Antinomianism" displayed in his *Spirit of Prelacie* (1646) and later was attacked by Richard Baxter for spreading this same error among Cromwell's soldiers. Like Gorton, Rutherford noted, "*M. Beacon* in his Cathechisme" unashamedly turned "all Christ in[to] a Metaphoricall Imaginary Christ." Those two "Antinomians" both taught "*that Christ reveales his will by no voyce but the voyce of the Spirit in the Saints*," and thus it was "no marvel" that they also were "*Antiscripturians*" who affirmed that the Bible was but "*a humane thing of Inke*."[35] Because his theology was so similar to Gorton's, Bacon could only have delighted, so Rutherford would have us believe, to supply an introductory testament to *Simplicities Defence*, particularly consid-

ering how rapidly Gorton's star had risen in London's sectarian underground. And, presumably, Gorton was pleased to cultivate Bacon's (and
so Barber's) acquaintance and thus to extend his influence into another of
those conventicles whose members formed another in the seemingly infinite series of intersecting circles that in the mid-1640s defined the left
wing of English Puritanism.

Although Gorton might have safely returned to Rhode Island as early
as 1646, after his favorable hearing before the parliamentary commission
on plantations, through the spring of 1648 he remained in England and
continued his association with the city's radical preachers.[36] In 1647 he
further established his radical credentials by publishing *An Incorruptible
Key to the CX. Psalme*, a tract that, despite its condemnation of the power
of civil magistrates to interfere in matters of conscience, did not cause a
stir comparable to that of *Simplicities Defence*. No doubt this was because
the presbyterians had increasingly shifted their attention from the doctrines of the city's spiritist preachers to the more pressing political demands of the Levellers. It also is likely that during this same year Gorton,
following the example of Lamb, Denne, Oates, and other "mechanic"
preachers in London's baptist conventicles, traveled to other parts of England to proselytize for his radical ideas. From the "Epistle Dedicatory"
to *Saltmarsh Returned from the Dead*, for example, we learn that once back
in New England Gorton felt obligated to thank not only his "honoured
and beloved friends in *London*, who in a solitary season . . . were so great
refreshment" to him, but also some "respected and honoured friends in
and about *Lynne* in *Norfolke*," in whom he "perceived grave and joyfull
Acclamations at the publication of the Gospel." Evidently he was as well
received on these trips to the provinces as in Bell Alley, for his hosts'
"carriage" toward him, Gorton remembered, when he was "for a short
time" among them, was "sufficient encouragement" forever to bind him
to them.[37]

Despite his continuing successes as a radical preacher in London and
elsewhere, early in 1648 Gorton finally turned his thoughts to New England. It is unclear why he chose to return to his settlement at Shawomet
at that time, though the Levellers' failure to implement their political
program in the aftermath of the Putney debates may have convinced him
that his vision of the kingdom of God on earth might more easily be realized in the "rude, incumbring, and way-less wilderness" of the Narragansett country. With the territorial integrity of Rhode Island and Providence guaranteed by the royal patent granted to Roger Williams in
1644, and Gorton's own safe passage through Massachusetts assured by

the protection of the Earl of Warwick, in the summer of 1648 Gorton resumed his role as the spiritual leader of the "Gortoneans," a position he held until his death in 1677.[38]

Although none of Gorton's treatises was published until he returned to England in the mid-1640s, the implications of the theology later outlined in such works as *An Incorruptible Key, composed of the CX. Psalme* (1647), *Saltmarsh returned from the Dead* (1655), and *An Antidote against the Common Plague of the World* (1657) already were evident in the late 1630s in his dealings with the Bay Colony, Plymouth, and Rhode Island authorities, suggesting that prior to his initial removal to New England he may have ingested the germs of his "heresies" from some of the same sources as his English counterparts and only refined his doctrines at such places as Lamb's church. Like many seventeenth-century mystics, he argued for an essential divinity in all human beings, a divinity that was defined for him by the miracle of Christ's presence and that precluded any arbitrary distinctions (be they religious or political) between saints and sinners. For Gorton, conversion consisted in the true and full apprehension of this indwelling divinity and a willingness to follow its dictates against human authority. Like others in the General Baptist conventicles, as well as some Seekers and Ranters, he strongly maintained the all-sufficiency of Christ's image in the true Christian, a concept that exempted the believer from obedience to mankind's perverse and troublesome laws, whether they stemmed from the English Parliament or the Massachusetts General Court.[39]

The tap-root of Gorton's theology was vividly exposed during the time of his trial in Boston. At that time the question of his guilt had revolved around not only his civil insubordination but also his doctrinal understanding of the process of regeneration and Christ's historical role in freeing man to receive salvation, a subject that had been broached during the earlier months of the Antinomian Controversy. Winthrop noted that after one of John Cotton's sermons Gorton desired "leave to speak" and openly pronounced that "if Christ lived eternally, then he died eternally." He further remarked that Christ had been "incarnate in Adam" and had been the "image of God wherein Adam was created." Christ's "being born after of the Virgin Mary and suffering" was, then, but "a manifestation of his suffering, etc., in Adam." To these heretical suggestions that the image of Christ had been present in Adam and so was present in all his descendants, points of doctrine that informed the General Baptists' universalism, Cotton, who had been using "all due pains to

charm these *adders*, with convincing disputations," replied that a true
Christian had to believe that the death of Christ was the cause of "our
redemption, whereas the fall of Adam was . . . but the cause of our condemnation." Intent on showing how through Christ's death God was rec-
onciling *all men* to Himself (and not just "imputing their sins"), Gorton
countered that, when Christ died, the image of God died just as His
image had died in Adam's fall.[40]

Gorton stubbornly maintained that "Christ was incarnate when Adam
was made after God's image" because God could have but one image. In
human terms "that image was Christ," and "this making of Adam in that
image was the exinanition [humiliation, abasement] of Christ." Further,
Gorton understood that God Himself was unknowable, making Christ
the only rational object of worship; or, as he later put it, "the Father was
never knowne nor is he knowable but in Christ." Man's spiritual contact
with God was made through His son, and since man's literal ancestor,
Adam, had been formed in the image of God (that is, Christ was "present" in him), so could the Holy Spirit, through Christ's sacrifice, be
present in and available to all believers, enabling them to be justified not
through works, but through faith: "That doctrine which ties the death of
Christ to one particular man in one time and age of the world, as being
the scope and intent of God's will concerning the death of his son in the
salvation of the world, that doctrine falsifies the death of Jesus Christ, and
sets men upon the law of workes in the ground and matter of their salvation, by which law no man is justified." Gorton expressed the same sentiment later in his life in a letter to John Winthrop the Younger in which he
maintained that "to hold that Christ Jesus was not exhibited in the Church
from the beginning, is a point of [the] soules disease and sicknesse . . .
[for if He] was in purpose and promise in the begining, but not actually
[in existence] till some thousands of years after [, this belief] idolizeth the
Lord to be like a corruptible man." If men understood the true meaning
of God in Christ, they would discover the inherent divinity of all mankind—what Gorton termed "the equal nearness of the divine spirit to
[both] the sinner and the saint." Through this spiritual union, all believers in Christ partook of the perfection of God Himself. In the very same
act of the Son of God descending into the world and becoming a finite
man, man himself was raised to a state of dignity equal to that of the Son
of God.[41]

Such doctrine argues Gorton's spiritual connection to a number of
prominent English radicals whose conceptions of free grace and its implications were quite similar, a point made at length by Rutherford in his

Survey of the Spirituall Antichrist. Analyzing Gorton's *Simplicities Defence*, Rutherford first combed its pages for passages that connected the author to previous "*Familists and Antinomians.*" It was his predilection to find attributes of the Antichrist in any but the most zealous presbyterians, and he discerned that *Simplicities Defence* was "stuffed with wicked principles" and smelled "ranckly of the abominable Doctrines of *Swenckefield, Muncer, Becold, David Georgius,* and of *H. Nicholas* the first elder of the Family of Love, of the piece called *Theologia Germanica,* and the *Bright Starre.*" It was, in short, an unmistakably "*Familist*" tract.[42]

In the 1640s the epithet "Familist" was indeed part of the stock-in-trade of any conservative minister who attacked spiritist preaching; thus by far the more revealing part of Rutherford's recitation of Gorton's theological pedigree consists of the names of those English radicals whom he considered Gorton's contemporary first-cousins. He compared Gorton's ideas to those of Robert Towne, John Eaton, and Tobias Crisp, the most well-known English "Antinomians" and those whom Winthrop and other New Englanders had in mind when they condemned Anne Hutchinson's errors; and to those of John Saltmarsh, William Dell, and other prominent chaplains in the New Model Army who throughout the civil wars were the targets of presbyterian abuse for the radicalism of their preaching. When Rutherford complained of Gorton's annoying tendency to "change all histories of the word in allegories" and so "to put us to a stand in all the Articles of our Faith," he first likened such allegorizing to that practiced by "*H. Nich.* and unclean *Familists,*" and then to the preaching of one "*Del,*" particularly in his recent "Sermon before the House of Commons." Both Dell and Saltmarsh, Rutherford continued, also shared Gorton's blatant antinomianism, for like the Rhode Island radical they openly denied that Scripture was "an obliging rule to the Saints." These spiritists contended, Rutherford argued, that those who truly knew Christ owed their allegiance only to "the inward word written in the heart."[43]

Later in his *Survey,* when Rutherford devoted a considerable number of pages explicitly to Saltmarsh, whose recent *Sparkles of Glory* (1647) had so alarmed the conservative clergy, he again noted the similarity between this army chaplain's message and Gorton's in *Simplicities Defence.* "The *Familists* of *New England,*" Rutherford complained, "take on them to judge who are elect and who are reprobate" in just the same way that "*Saltmarsh* will have one Saint to know another . . . as we know one another by voyce, features, [and the] statures of the outward man." Saltmarsh's unorthodox view of the Atonement recalled the troublesome

New Englander and his tendency to allegorize. "Hee hath a good head," Rutherford sarcastically wrote, "that can take these giddy fleshly notions of *Saltmarsh*, and can render the sense either of *Gortyn's* book or of this." To those credulous enough to believe such gibberish, Rutherford concluded, every saint must be seen as Christ, for spiritists like Saltmarsh and Gorton argued that "Christ hath no body of his owne, but every beleever, Goded, deified, and annoynted with the Spirit, is Christ."[44]

There is no reliable evidence that Gorton knew Saltmarsh or Dell, though he did invoke Saltmarsh's name on the title pages of two of his later works. And Rutherford never claimed any overt collusion between them, nor with the two other members of the army, Lamb's sometime associate, Henry Denne, and another prominent General Baptist, Paul Hobson, to whose ideas he compared Gorton's. It was enough for him to trace all their heresies to a common source—the sink-hole of "Familism" to which "Separatist" doctrines led—and so to damn them all by ideological association.[45]

Gorton's extreme christocentrism had its counterpart in the theology of Saltmarsh and Dell. Gorton argued that Christ offered us "a fulness of freedome and liberty" that obviated the necessity of adherence to the moral law, for "to affirme that we are able to give Christ a true forme and being, out of our selves doctrinally, and yet that he is not in our selves, operating and working effectually, is as much to affirme, that we can give Christ a true forme and being without mans nature." "I acknowledge no bond," Gorton concluded, "but what is only found in him." Similarly, Saltmarsh, in his *Free Grace; Or The Flowings of Christs Blood Freely to Sinners*, published in 1646, proclaimed that one should not "serve the *oldnesse* of the Letter . . . but the *newnesse* of the Spirit," and that because of Christ's sacrifice all Christians were no longer "under the Law, but under Grace." His comrade-in-arms Dell spelled out the political implications of such doctrines. Once a man understood the meaning of salvation through Christ he became a new being: "it is not I that live, but *Christ* that lives in me." Dell convinced his soldiers that if they were true saints nothing could stand in the way of their uprooting England's carnal government. Gorton directly echoed such sentiments. "God is *all in all* in every one of the Saints," he claimed, "and they onely passive in them selves or in their owne nature, but powerfull and operative in their Lord." Radical Puritans like Gorton, Saltmarsh, and Dell believed that Christians who placed too strong an emphasis on outward ordinances at the expense of an experience of Christ's saving presence (for example, magistrates like those at Aquidneck and Boston, as well as King Charles) were forcing people to live by the wisdom of men rather than by faith and had no true sense of the freedom the saint possessed.[46]

Gorton's contempt for the New England Puritans' magistracy and its efforts to prescribe matters of faith and belief stemmed from similar doctrinal premises. Believing in the liberty Christ offered mankind, he was dismayed that even the inhabitants of the City on the Hill were willing to subject themselves "to the hand or skill of the devised ministrations of men," as though God "made man to be a vassal to his own species." Rather than ushering in the millennium by listening to the voice of God, New England Puritans were establishing another worthless set of "idols," best evidenced by their ridiculous concern with turning "the juice of a poor silly grape . . . into the blood of our Lord Jesus" through the "cunning skill of their magicians," an act that effected no lasting change in the character of its participants. New England's polity was becoming just another arm of Antichrist. The New England saints always had "some fast to keep, some Sabbath to sanctify, some sermon to heare, some Battel to fight, some church to constitute, some officers to raise up"; and they erroneously believed that such issues had to be settled before they took "God upon his word, *that we are complete in Christ.*" Winthrop and his fellow-colonists, as well as many persons in England, depended on the contrived ordinances of man and not on the Lord; and when their idolatry was threatened by the likes of Hutchinson, Williams, or Gorton, they could "never rest or be quiet" until they had put the witness "under a bushel," that is, "bounded and measured the infinite word of God" according to their own "shallow, human, and carnal capacities."[47]

Such disregard for the magistrate's power in matters of conscience linked Gorton to Williams, for, like his erstwhile neighbor in New England, Gorton knew that the churches in Massachusetts were "*labouring in the fields of their home-made* covenants and performances." From what Williams told Baillie, promptly publicized in Baillie's *Dissuasive*, it is clear that Gorton went even further, to claim the saint's freedom from *any* laws enforced against them. In Gorton's colony of Shawomet, Williams reported, the settlers believed that "the Saints are not to submit to the powers of the world or worldly powers, and that the powers and governments of the world have nothing to doe with them for civill misdemeanours." "These Governours," the Gortonists argued, must keep in their own sphere, "as Whales, not to governe Whales, but other fishes; Lions, not to governe Lions, but the beasts of the forrest; Eagles, not to governe Eagles, but the other foules of the ayre." It was not that "we hold government useless and unlawful," Gorton explained elsewhere;

rather, he wished "that all things were considered according to their nature, and exercised and kept within their proper confines and cercuits."
The man who had Christ within him simply could not be treated as just
another man.[48]

But while New England Puritans "contended" and made "great stirre"
about such outward displays of piety, and while "the life and spirit of the
Gospel" lay "buried under humane ordinances and carnall traditions," the
voice of God in Christ was every day revealed to Gorton and his followers. It offered a higher calling than the Puritans' legalisms, which
"tend[ed] only to the carriage of one man toward another" and neglected
those "principles of divinity . . . tending to faith toward God in Christ."
If Christ were a "sufficient King and Ruler in his Church," Gorton maintained, "all other Authority and Government erected therein is superfluous, and as a branch to be cut off." Sounding a note as militant as any
uttered by Saltmarsh or Dell, he warned Massachusetts that "if you put
forth your hands to us as a countryman, ours are in readinesse for you
. . . [but] if you present a gun, make haste to give the first fire, for we are
come to put fire on the earth . . . and it is our desire to have it speedily
kindled."[49]

This intense belief in Christ's animating presence fostered more than a
suspicion of religious forms and ordinances, for Gorton's ideology supported an antiauthoritarianism that threatened the social hierarchy most
New England Puritans accepted. To Gorton, as to Saltmarsh, Dell, and
other spiritists who eventually moved to the Leveller camp, the equality
of all men was so literal a fact that deference to a hierarchical system, civil
or religious, denied the true priesthood of all believers. Gorton criticized
the Massachusetts Puritans for insisting that only men who were "honorable, learned, wise, experienced and of good report" could rule; they did
not realize that, to be judged honestly, a man had to be brought before his
spiritual peers. Edward Winslow insisted that to preach free grace as Gorton did was to offer an inconceivable political liberty. He feared that if
"the administration of Justice and judgement belongs to no officer, but to
man as a Brother, then to every Brother, and if to every Brother, whether
rich or poore, ignorant or learned, then every Christian in a Commonwealth must be King, and Judge, and Sheriffe, and Captaine."[50]

This was precisely the Gortonists' point and the reason for much of
their uncivil behavior—for example, their addressing Winthrop as the
"great and honored Idol General . . . whose pretended equity in distri-
bution of justice unto the souls and bodies of men, is nothing else but a
mere device of man." After studying such brash statements, Winslow cor-

Hypocrisie Unmasked

BY

A true Relation of the Proceedings of the
Governour and Company of the *Massachusets* against
SAMVEL GORTON (and his Accomplices) a notorious
disturber of the Peace and quiet of the severall Governments
wherein he lived: With the grounds and reasons thereof, examined and allowed by their Generall Court holden at *Boston* in
New-England in *November* last, 1646.

Together with a particular Answer to the manifold slan-
ders, and abominable falshoods which are contained in a Book
written by the said GORTON, and entituled, *Simplicities defence
against Seven-headed Policy, &c.*

DISCOVERING

To the view of all whose eyes are open, his manifold
Blasphemies; As also the dangerous agreement which he and his
Accomplices made with ambitious and treacherous *Indians*, who
at the same time were deeply engaged in a desperate Conspiracy
to cut off all the rest of the *English* in the other Plantations.

VVhereunto is added a briefe Narration (occasioned by
certain aspersions) of the true grounds or cause of the first Planting of *New-England*; the President of their Churches in the
way and Worship of God; their Communion with the *Reformed
Churches*; and their practise towards those that dissent from
them in matters of Religion and Church-Government.

By Edw. Winslow.

Psal. 120. 3. *What shall be given unto thee, or what shall be done unto
thee thou false tongue?*
Vers. 4. *Sharpe arrows of the Mighty, with coales of Juniper.*

Published by Authority.

London, Printed by *Rich. Cotes* for *John Bellamy* at the three Golden
Lions in *Cornhill,* neare the Royall Exchange, 1646.

Title page of *Hypocrisie Unmasked* (London, 1646), Edward Winslow's defense of the Massachusetts Bay Colony's treatment of Samuel Gorton.

THE
Danger of Tolerating
LEVELLERS
In a Civill State:

OR,

An Historicall Narration of the dangerous pernicious practices and opinions, where-
with *SAMVEL GORTON* and his
Levelling Accomplices so much disturbed and molested the severall Plantations in *NEW-ENGLAND*;
(Parallel to the positions and proceedings of the present
Levellers in *OLD-ENGLAND*:)

Wherein their severall Errors dangerous and
very destructive to the peace both of Church and State,
their cariage and reviling language against Magistracy
and all Civill power, and their blasphemous speeches
against the holy things of God:

TOGETHER,

With the Course that was there taken for suppressing them,
are fully set forth;
With a Satisfactory Answer to their Complaints made
to the PARLIAMENT:

By Edw. Winslow of Plymouth in New-England.

London, Printed by *Rich. Cotes* for *John Bellamy* at the three Golden
Lions in *Corn-hill,* neare the Royall Exchange, 1649.

Title page of *The Danger of Tolerating Levellers in a Civill State* (London, 1649). Edward Winslow reissued *Hypocrisie Unmasked* under this new title at the height of the Levellers' agitation in England.

rectly reported that to Gorton "to be a Brother, and consequently a coheire in Christ, is a higher sphere than to be a civill Officer." Winslow well understood where such doctrines led. When in 1649 he republished his *Hypocrisie Unmasked* (1646), New England's defense of its actions against Gorton, he had it printed with a new title page aimed directly at Englishmen already suspicious of such radical ideas: it could be purchased under the title of *The Danger of Tolerating Levellers in a Civil State*. Later, in *Saltmarsh returned from the Dead*, Gorton further clarified his democratic beliefs. "The ground of these particular and nominal religions, (as Independent, Presbyterian, Anabaptist, Papist, Generallist, for they all stand on one root) is [that] they limit and infringe the grace of the Gospel" and so disregard the universality of the Holy Spirit. Dell, too, in his *The Way of True Peace and Unity in the True Church of Christ*, proclaimed that, while "according to our first Nativity" men are born into different stations and religions, "yet according to our new or second birth, whereby we are born of God, there is exact equality . . . [and] all have the same faith, hope, love." The Kingdom of God on earth was based on spiritual and political equality.[51]

Gorton's anticlericalism was equally pronounced. As one recent critic correctly asserts, Gorton recognized the allegiance between the "Puritan reliance on learning and Puritan social control" and held that any community built on a formal church covenant and supported by an educated, paid ministry was a form of Antichrist. Many left-wing Puritans during the English civil wars agreed, among them Dell and William Erbury, the Welsh Puritan radical who linked clergymen and lawyers as the "chiefest oppressors" of the age. Gorton's persistent anticlericalism was most evident in *An Antidote*, which attacked the "ignorance and vanity of such men that go about to bring men unto the knowledge of God, by telling them stories out of scripture not analyzing them with something written in their own hearts." Gorton sharply disapproved of the ministry's status as a privileged class and its perpetuation through claims to the power of learning. "The Spirit of prophesie is out of date in these own daies," he continued, because "all must be hewed out by study . . . and so kept in schools of humane learning, Libraries, and in men who have most means and time to exercise themselves in such things." He saw such a system for what it was, an exercise of blatant power, for the established ministry always "set up men in temporary authority, to praise the able and wealthy, and to press the poorer sort with burdens of sins, and such abundance of servile obedience, as to make them slaves to themselves and others." Like those Ranters who shocked society by flouting all of its most cherished

values, Gorton knew that what most men called "sin" was but another
link in the chain by which unenlightened men bound themselves to the
prison walls of this world.[52]

The true saints had to reject any ministry whose authority came from
book learning. Answering Nathaniel Morton's attack on him in *New Englands Memoriall*, Gorton maintained that, although Morton had termed
him nothing but "a Belcher out of Errours, . . . I would have you know
that I hold my call to preach . . . not inferiour to the call of any minister
in the country. . . . [I have not] bin drowned in pride and ignorance
through Aristotle's principles and other heathen philosophers, as millions
are and have bin, who ground the preaching of the Gospell upon humane
principles to the falsifying of the word of God." His call to preach the
Word was "as good as the Degrees in Schooles" or any authorized by
bishops, elders, or the "call of a people"; and though never formally ordained, he "doubted not *but there hath bin as much true use made of languages
. . . for the opening of Scripture in the place where I live, as hath bin in any
church in New England.*" To require a more formal "call" than that of the
Holy Ghost was to institute another crass idol. Speaking to some "praying Indians" who had wandered to Shawomet, Gorton argued that,
while New England Puritans "teach that you must have Ministers," these
church officers "cannot change men's hearts, God must do that, and
therefore there is no need of Ministers." Because true religion depended
on a unique personal experience of Christ, formal training in language,
arts and sciences, and divinity was superfluous; any man could address
others from his own experiences, and under the true dispensation no external education could reform one's life as Christ could.[53]

Such beliefs perfectly complemented his approval of the kind of preaching he saw in Bell Alley and other General Baptist conventicles and
informed the organization of his own meetings in Rhode Island. "The
spirit," he claimed in 1647, "uttereth it selfe freely without respect of Persons in all the Congregations and Assemblies of Saints, giving words for
edification and comfort of the Church sometimes in one, and sometimes
in another." Thus, "yee may all prophecy one by one for the edification
of the Church, but if any thing bee revealed to another that sits by, let the
first hold his peace." Nor was this anticipation of a Friends meeting restricted to men. Learning well his lessons from Mrs. Attaway and "Sister
Stag," Gorton allowed either sex to prophesy or speak, for "The Man is
not without the Woman nor the Woman without the man in the Lord."
To have "hewen out unto themselves a Ministry . . . *by the art, wisdome,
and will of man, prostrating themselves thereunto*," he concluded, vividly

showed how a people's "vision" had "failed." God's word was available
to all, and thus the true saints had to "listen unto the Oracle of God by
whom hee is pleased to utter it." [54]

The moral implications of such beliefs were not lost upon the Massachusetts magistrates when they examined the Gortonists in 1643, but
they are made more clear in a heated exchange between Gorton and Nathaniel Morton in 1669, after Morton's condemnation of Gorton in his
recently published *New Englands Memoriall*. Gorton resented the charge
that he denied life after death and that his preaching of the doctrine of
universal salvation encouraged hedonism. Morton had claimed that Gorton had told a disciple "That all the felicity we are like to have, we must
expect in this life, and no more," and so urged what at Hutchinson's
church trial had been called "Epicureanism." But Gorton stoutly maintained that there was "not a man[,] woman[,] or childe upon the face of
the earth that will come forth and say that ever they heard any such
word[s] come out of my mouth." He was "farre from understanding"
John's message that Christ died for the sins of the whole world in the
"sense of the generallists," because they "exterpate[d] and roote[d] out"
Christ's role in the work of redemption. They denied any more "Divine
or eternall nature th[a]n is in the elements or beginnings of all earthly and
transitory things" and, because of this incipient pantheism, were prevented from being witness to an "eternall power manifest in that which
in it selfe is temporary," that is, the power of Christ himself. [55]

The subtlety by which Gorton maintained his innocence involved his
belief that a soul touched by the spirit of God *already* was in eternity, a
point of doctrine which had been spread in England by such men as the
spirit-mystic John Everard. To Gorton as to Everard, who had translated
works of such Continental mystics as Nicholas of Cusa and Sebastian
Franck, righteousness was in itself eternal life, and sin eternal death and
punishment. A penalty was not assessed arbitrarily at some future time
but was the natural and inevitable result of evil action. Such doctrine,
Gorton declared, "as sets forth a time to come, of more worth and glory
than either is, or hath been, keeps the manna till tomorrow, to the breeding of worms in it." "We see it," he continued, "to be . . . deceipt also of
the world, not to give Christ a present being, but [instead to] hold men in
expectation" of him. "By *new heavens* and *new earth* . . . we understand
the state of Christ, or of that *holy unction* or *Christianity* . . . that make
one durable and fruitfull *condition, wherein righteousness dwells*." [56]

Heaven was a condition of the soul on earth, and the divine spark of
regeneration implied the immediate and eternal destruction of evil as well

as the salvation of good, opening the way for man's final perfection in this life. "The righteousness of God is of eternal worth and duration," he maintained, "but the one and the other [course of life] being wrought into a change at one and the same time, thence comes the capacity of an eternall life and eternall destruction." Or, as Everard suggested, men who are estranged from Christ crucify Him anew in their own hearts and so "live in Hell . . . in the very condition of Devils and Reprobates," while a "good man hath God in him, and he seeth, knoweth, and believeth it." Heaven and hell were psychological conditions, and morality was to be upheld because it made one feel spiritually healthy. "Whose oxe or whose asse have I taken[?]" Gorton asked when Morton accused him of leading a "sordid" life. "Or when and where have I lived upon other men's labours and not wrought with mine owne hands for things honest in the sight of men[?]" Possession by Christ ruled out such immoral activities.[57]

Viewed against the background of English Puritan radicalism, then, Gorton's theological doctrines and "political" activities appear less eccentric than most historians have suggested; indeed, perhaps even more than Williams he emerges as the New Englander whose religious experience best serves to guide us through the netherworld of Puritan radicalism in the 1640s and 1650s. Before his death in 1677 he made one last political gesture, again directed at the Massachusetts Puritans, and perfectly consistent with the behavior of others whose faith had been nurtured in the General Baptist meetings. When in 1656 four Quakers arrived at Boston and were imprisoned by the authorities, Gorton dispatched a sympathetic letter offering asylum if they "had a mind to stay in these parts." Several missives were exchanged, but before any further plans could be made the captives were returned to England. Gorton never formally became a Quaker; indeed, oral tradition has it that when George Fox "came over [to Rhode Island] he went to Warwick to see Gorton" but found himself "a mere babe" in theology compared to his host. In the spirit of toleration absorbed in England and taken up in *An Incorruptable Key*, Gorton allowed no points of doctrine to prevent his hand from reaching out to those persecuted for beliefs that stemmed from the same spiritual fountain as his own. The Quaker Humphrey Norton acknowledged in 1659 that he and other Friends were "well received" by "such as were by the English accounted the basest of men, whom many of them they had barbarously banished . . . [to] Rhode Island."[58]

The most important effect of Gorton's radicalism may well have been in his sympathy for the early Quaker movement in America. Others in the colony—most notably William Coddington and Nicholas Easton—were instrumental in introducing Quakerism to Rhode Island, but none had undergone an indoctrination into religious radicalism comparable to Gorton's. By the end of the seventeenth century Rhode Island, of all the New England colonies, harbored the largest population of Friends. Gorton's role in preparing the soil for such spiritual "seed" must not be underestimated: when he returned to America in 1648 he carried with him those ideas that had made the General Baptist conventicles popular with people who distrusted the inflexible rule of both "visible" saints and Scottish presbyters. Gorton knew firsthand the exciting possibilities of a more tolerant, and democratic, ecclesiastical polity. At least in part, it was through him that the "wranglings and disputes" that informed the debates of Bell Alley, and the radical ideology of Saltmarsh, Dell, and Bacon, entered the religious and political discourse of Rhode Island, and, eventually, of all New England.

The immediate lesson to be gleaned from a careful study of Gorton's ideology is that he is best comprehended in the context of English radical spiritualism. Historians should be aware that New England Puritans regarded his presence as proof of the presbyterians' charge that an Independent or "Separatist" polity gave rise inevitably to aberrant doctrines like his own. The true significance of Samuel Gorton becomes apparent when one understands him not just as a belligerent Rhode Island mystic but as a threat to the New England Puritans' self-image and to the representation of that image in England.

The magistrates' treatment of Gorton did not sit well with English Independents, under pressure in 1644 to take a more liberal stand toward toleration. In 1645, Winthrop's son Stephen could write his father that in Cromwell's army there was "great complainte ag[ains]t us for our severetye ag[ains]t Anabaptists," and a short while later the governor heard from Giles Firmin that even Hugh Peter, who had so staunchly fought the antinomian element in Salem, now did "too much countenance the Opinionists, whom we did so cast out of N. England." Gorton's petition to the Commission for Foreign Plantations had suggested that the New Englanders paid little attention to English law and sharply criticized the magistrates' repression of religious opinions not consonant with their own. This stance found many sympathetic ears and cast further doubt on New England's claim to be the beacon for the course of Protestantism in the home country. The gist of Theophilus Eaton's warning to Winthrop was in many people's minds. "It will be a great exercise to us all," he wrote, "if Gorton returneth with victory."[59]

By the early 1640s it was clear that conservative English and Scottish Puritans, disgusted and frightened by the explosion of radicalism among their contemporaries, had settled upon New England as a scapegoat, particularly after word of the controversy over Hutchinson had reached them. Even one of Winthrop's friendly correspondents wrote him that "this seede of pride and contention" among the English radicals "had [its] first beginning in your partes."[60] Conservative English Puritans viewed New England and its "Independent" or "Separatist" polity not as the guiding light for English reformers but as another training ground for radicals who threatened to split England's social fabric at its seams. Gorton's rapid rise through the sectarian ranks only provided further proof of the errors found in a land where congregationalism had been established.

Massachusetts Puritans believed that the risk Gorton posed to their communities demanded his prosecution, despite the implications the English would draw. Soon after Gorton's arrival his complaints had been reinforced by those of John Childe who, from the opposite end of the political spectrum, criticized the lack of rights granted English citizens in Massachusetts. But as the Massachusetts Puritans reevaluated their communal purpose they decided that the danger of open accommodation of dissent was too great to allow it. All they asked was to be left alone with their God, and their ordinances. Gorton introduced to New England the leaven that filled the General Baptist conventicles in England and thus served to refine the New Englanders' conception of their City on a Hill. In moving against Gorton they moved one step farther toward the summoning of the second synod, which would codify their understanding of Puritanism. He could not be tolerated, but he certainly could be used.

WILLIAM PYNCHON

In the 1650s New England Puritanism experienced ideological fragmentation like that of its English counterpart, though on a smaller scale. Historians have noted that in the 1640s and 1650s colonial Puritans felt threatened by radical spiritists and baptists with links to the English sectarian underground, but they have paid little attention to the fear of infection by corrupt opinions of those associated with English latitudinarian or, as it often was called, "Socinian" thought. Such ideas played no small role in the theological upheavals during the civil wars in England.[1] Although hardly widespread in New England, liberal opinions of this sort were held by William Pynchon of Agawam (later Springfield) in the Connecticut River Valley, who, despite his prominence as a leader of the colonial enterprise, was severely chastised by the Massachusetts General Court.

The Puritans' harsh treatment of Pynchon stemmed from their alarm at finding that the demand for wider toleration of religious opinions could come from respected adherents of the New England Way and not only from such Seekers as Roger Williams and Samuel Gorton. While basing their theological opinions in a biblicism as scrupulous as that of the orthodox divines, those individuals allotted significantly greater importance to the place of individual conscience in matters of fundamental doctrine. Unlike Rhode Island radicalism, which was derived from the mystical strain of Puritanism, Pynchon's thought was linked to a rational tradition of English dissent. His thoughts on the atonement and his intellectual justification for them allied him to apologists for religious toleration like Jacobus Acontius, Anthony Wotton, and John Goodwin, men commonly slandered as "Socinians," after the liberal religious movement in Poland, but who in fact represented a significant rationalist strain within English Puritanism itself.[2]

The publication of Pynchon's *The Meritorious Price of Our Redemption* in 1650, at a time when New Englanders were especially sensitive to both internal and external criticism of their intolerance, announced the presence of a new kind of theological maverick within their borders. This and other of Pynchon's published works illustrate the startling heterogeneity of theological opinion within seventeenth-century New England Puritanism and demonstrate how difficult it was to control the centrifugal dynamic at the core of Puritan ideology, even in the relative isolation of the New World.[3]

William Pynchon was associated with the Massachusetts Bay Colony from its inception. A flourishing merchant, he was one of the men who obtained a royal charter for the colonial undertaking in 1629 and took a large part in the preparations for the departure of John Winthrop's fleet. Arriving in Boston aboard the *Ambrose*, he settled in Roxbury, became one of the original members of the church John Eliot founded there in 1631, and quickly assumed such important political positions as assistant, magistrate, and finally treasurer of the colony. He rapidly established himself as one of the Bay Colony's most powerful merchants. Based in large measure on a fur-trading empire, his mercantile success was acknowledged by the General Court in 1632 when it granted him a fur-trading monopoly. Despite all such preferments, however, by 1635 Pynchon turned his attention to the fertile valley where he would spend the remainder of his New England years.[4]

In moving west Pynchon joined what soon proved a sizable emigration. Whatever his motives—whether primarily religious, like Thomas Hooker's, or perhaps economic—he laid out the town of Agawam at the junction of the Westfield and Connecticut rivers, expanded his fur-trading activities with the Indians, and built an important trading post just below Enfield Falls.[5] He was among the men to whom the General Court gave a special one-year commission to rule the Connecticut River settlements, and when this charge expired and the towns established a de facto independent government, with each community electing magistrates and deputies to attend the Connecticut General Court, Pynchon continued to exercise a significant role in the area's government by serving as magistrate in Agawam.[6]

Portrait of William Pynchon, first settler of Springfield, in the Connecticut River Valley of Massachusetts, who was arraigned for purportedly Socinian beliefs.

Within a few years, relations between Agawam and the other river towns began to deteriorate, in large part because of Hooker's animosity toward Pynchon. In March 1637/8, for example, after a poor harvest due to the disruptions of the Pequot War, the Connecticut General Court asked Pynchon to buy corn from the Indians at a set price in order to supply towns downriver. He reported that the tribes would not sell at the requested price, whereupon the court sent Capt. John Mason—as the soldier who had led the assault on the Pequots, not the best man to drive a bargain with the Indians—to secure the supplies. Frustrated in his turn, Mason returned to Hartford convinced that Pynchon was attempting to manipulate the natives for his own profit. Pynchon was summoned to Hartford to answer the charges, and, after Hooker offered his judgment that Pynchon had indeed obstructed Mason's mission, intending to "have all the trade to himself . . . and so rack the country at his pleasure," the court fined him forty bushels of corn.[7]

This severe treatment soon had political consequences that further strained Pynchon's relations with Connecticut. In the summer of 1638, when Connecticut and Massachusetts commissioners met to discuss a confederation, they disagreed about the boundary between the colonies, particularly around Agawam, and Pynchon startled his cocommissioners by expressing his willingness to have his settlement brought under the jurisdiction of the Bay. Massachusetts refused to continue the discussions unless Agawam were ceded. Although the Connecticut government was openly displeased by Pynchon's betrayal—his settlement, after all, had more in common with the Connecticut towns—it had no choice but to agree to the change in status, and by the late winter of 1638–39 Agawam's inhabitants formalized their separation by selecting Pynchon as the magistrate of the plantation. A year later they changed the name of their town to Springfield, Pynchon's birthplace in England.[8]

Through the 1640s Pynchon enjoyed the freedom provided by Springfield's distance from Boston, but in 1646 he began to assert his independence in a way that spelled trouble for him and his settlement. The occasion of his indiscretion was the Remonstrance of 1646, drawn up as a petition to the Massachusetts government by Robert Childe, Thomas Fowle, and five others under the instigation of William Vassal of Plymouth Colony. The remonstrants argued for relaxed standards for church admission and for freemen's privileges and accused the General Court of "not owning the fundamental laws of England as the basis for their government." Pynchon took the liberty of offering Governor Winthrop some advice; though he disapproved of the remonstrants' "manner of proceedinge," he urged the governor to remember that "the Courte both of magistrates and deputies, should not turne of[f] all the particulars wherein they [the petitioners] desyre a Reformation, without making a right use of so much of their petition as doth justly cale for reformation." He acknowledged that the petitioners' endeavors could not "but have an ill construction," particularly in England, but he maintained that acquiescence to some of their demands would greatly benefit the colony.[9]

In this same letter Pynchon returned to an argument concerning the relationship of church and state that he had made in his reply to Connecticut in the corn-dealing controversy. Since "we had the happinesse to be

bredd and borne under such lawes for civill government as I conceive no
nation hath better," he declared, "so it should be our care . . . to preserve
and adhere to what ever lawes or customes they have except those that be
contrary to god." Pynchon knew that in some regards the remonstrants
threatened the religious and political fabric of the colony; nevertheless, he
concurred in their belief that in important respects, particularly by restricting freemanship to church members, the colony's laws did indeed
deny the inhabitants certain of their legal privileges as English citizens,
and not in such matters where the magistrates could claim authorization
by the laws of God. As Samuel Gorton's successful appeal before the
Commission for Foreign Plantations had made clear, the colony's presumptuous disregard of the prerogatives of the crown could only lead to
greater strain in relations with England.[10]

Pynchon's pointed reminder that "we are not a Free [that is, indepen-
dent] state . . . [and] neather do I think it our wisdome to be" made
Winthrop aware that support for the Remonstrance (as it had been for
Gorton) was more widespread than he had believed. A more telling hint
of future difficulties came in Pynchon's discussion of the petitioners' demand for a more liberal system of church government that would make
the seals of the covenant available to any in "no wayes scandalous in their
lives and conversations." Noting the bifurcation of English Puritanism
into presbyterians and Independents, Pynchon observed that the best
frame was not necessarily presbyterian or congregational but rather one
"where zeale of gods glory and godly wisdome are joyned together." He
went on to maintain that a "world of good hath bin don by godly ministers even in England, that have held no certaine fourme of discipline."
On the other hand, "where a could [that is, cold] spirit doth rule in ministers," the people may "yet be but dead christians." What mattered was
less the form of the polity than the zeal of the clergy.[11]

It would be a few more years before the Springfield magistrate publicly defended such statements, but his letter of 1646 revealed his concern
for the legal rights of English subjects and his belief that no magistrates,
not even in Massachusetts, had a monopoly on wisdom concerning the
true form of church government. These two propositions, when linked
to his intellectual justification for so believing, would bring the colony's
wrath upon him. It would be provoked by the publication of his controversial treatise on the atonement, a subject that, in one way or another,
had been at issue in Massachusetts since the antinomians had been accused of misunderstanding the meaning and purpose of Christ's role in
history.[12]

The Meritorious Price was printed in London in 1650 and arrived in Boston that same year. Although the book nowhere overtly displayed that inflammatory mixture of politics and theology that marked the tracts of such groups as the Levellers and Diggers, since Pynchon restricted himself to a logical and exegetical defense of his interpretation of the atonement, it was promptly seized and condemned by the General Court, which by coincidence had recently been hearing testimony in the witchcraft cases of Hugh and Mary Parsons of Springfield.[13] To its credit, the court did not openly declare that the witchcraft episode was linked to Pynchon's doctrinal aberrations, but the speed and severity of its condemnation of the book suggests that it may indeed have perceived such a connection. On October 16 the court declared that because *The Meritorious Price* contained "many errors & heresies generally condemned by al[l] orthodox writers that we have met with," they ordered "the said book to be burned in the Market Place, at Boston by the Common Executioner, on the morrow immediately after lecture." The court protested its "innocency, as being neither partyes nor privy to the writing, composing, printing, nor divulging thereof" and commanded Pynchon to appear before it "with all convenient speed" to find out whether he would "owne the said book as his or not."[14]

The magistrates' sensitivity to criticism from conservative English Puritans who contended that New England's church system encouraged such doctrinal aberrations partially explains their anger at the book's publication, and the rapidity with which they condemned it. They "perceiv[ed] by the Title Page that the Contents of Book were unsound, and Derogatory" and considered its ideas intrinsically dangerous. Accordingly, they threatened to proceed with the book's author "according to his demerits, unless he retract the same, & give full satisfaction both here & by some second writing, to be printed and dispensed in England." They voted to appoint "some fitt person to make particular answer to all materiall and controversyall passages in said book," a task that fell to the redoubtable John Norton of Ipswich, whose effort was published as *A Discussion of That Great Point in Divinity, the Sufferings of Christ*.[15] Important as Pynchon was to the colony, the General Court felt required to make apparent their extreme disapproval of his doctrines, and, if possible, force him to a retraction so that their presbyterian critics would not pounce on his book as more evidence of the deleterious effects of a congregational or Independent polity.

Pynchon appeared as requested at the May 1651 session of the court to answer charges against the book as well as to testify in the Springfield witchcraft case. After meeting privately with John Cotton, Edward Norris, and Norton and being apprised of his "errors," he admitted to the court that he had "not spoken in [his] booke so fully of the price and merit of Christ's sufferings" as he should have done, and he promised to take Norton's manuscript rebuttal home with him to enlighten his understanding. "Under the penalty of one hundred pounds" the court required him to appear again at its October session, but, as one report had it, "in the interim . . . he received letters from England which encouraged him in his error," and he did not comply with the court's demands for a further retraction.[16] No doubt stung by his humiliation before the magistrates and at the hands of the ministers—an experience reminiscent of his earlier difficulties in Connecticut—Pynchon had already made plans to return to England, perhaps at the behest of those who recently had written him.

When news of Pynchon's case crossed the Atlantic it elicited sympathetic letters not only from "some Brethren" who sought to "incline" New England "to a favorable construction of the Tenants held forth" in the book, but from none other than Sir Henry Vane, ex-governor of the colony and an important figure in Puritan revolutionary circles. Though no proponent of Socinian thought, Vane was as much disturbed by the court's repression of the theological inquiry of a respected citizen as by its objection to Pynchon's doctrinal propositions, and he openly criticized its course of action.[17]

The New England officials responded that they had indeed considered Pynchon's high public standing when they called him to account for his ideas. It had been more important to them, however, that he had "take[n] upon him[self] to condemn the judgment of most, if not all, both ancient and modern divines . . . in a point of so great weight and concernment"—that is, the atonement. They intimated that had he "kept his judgment to himself, as it seems he did above thirty years," all would have been well. Once he published his thoughts, thus "spreading . . . his erroneous books here amongst us, to the endangering of the faith of such as might come to read them (as the like effects have followed the reading of other erroneous books brought over into these parts)," the court had been compelled to move against him.[18] Pynchon had no illusions about the difficulty of remaining in a land where he had suffered such embarrassment for his opinions, and preferred to return to a country in which, especially during the heady days of the Interregnum, he might find a more sympathetic hearing. By the late spring of 1652 he was back in England seeing through press another book, *The Jewes Synagogue*, which broadened his attack on the New England Way by challenging its narrowly defined restriction of church membership to the "visible saints." During the next three years he busied himself with two more argumentative volumes, one on the Sabbath in 1654, the other a reply to Norton, under the title *The Meritorious Price of Mans Redemption* (1655), which reaffirmed and refined his views on the atonement.[19]

Pynchon's *The Meritorious Price of Our Redemption* met severe condemnation from New England Puritans because it promulgated an intolerable heresy concerning the personality of Christ and a line of argument that linked its author to the acrimonious debates over the limits of free inquiry within English Puritanism at a time when what Thomas Shepard called the "contagion of corrupt opinions" threatened to spread across the Atlantic. Although in their chastisement of Pynchon the New Englanders nowhere used the specific term "Socinian," English Puritans, who were combating an outbreak of anti-Trinitarian thought, quickly placed Pynchon's work within this tradition and blamed him for encouraging the growth of theological skepticism in Puritan circles.[20] In 1650, however, the epithet "Socinian" was linked by Massachusetts Puritans not only to a specific anti-Trinitarian doctrine of the atonement but also to the latitudinarian principle that all men—including ministers and magistrates—are fallible and thus have no right to impose ecclesiastical or doctrinal norms on an individual otherwise directed by his conscience.[21]

Pynchon's view of the atonement differed in many particulars from the position held by the New England Puritans; it suggested his allegiance to anti-Trinitarian thought as it had been developed by Faustus Socinus and his followers in sixteenth century Poland. *The Meritorious Price of Our Redemption* (which took the form of a dialogue between a "Trades-man" and a "Divine") located the price of man's redemption "in the merit of [Christ's] Mediatorial Obedience, whereof his Mediatorial Sacrifice of Atonement was the Masterpiece" rather than in Christ's "suffering of Gods wrath for us in full weight and measure," a distinction which Socinus maintained in his attack on the divinity of Christ and which orthodox Puritans strenuously denied.[22] Since sin had come into the world through Adam's archetypal transgression, Christ's perfect obedience to the Father's will—evidenced by his passion and death—and not the Father's transference of the burden of men's sins to him, redeemed the elect from Adam's curse. Thus Christ's actions provided a perfect moral example, but, as Socinus claimed, nothing that he had done necessitated a belief in his divinity.

Extending this "moral" argument of the atonement further, Pynchon argued against the orthodox belief that Christ suffered and died on the cross and briefly descended into hell, all by order of God the Father to atone for men's sins, claiming instead that Christ "did not satisfie Gods wrath for our sins by suffering the extremity of his Wrath, [and] neither did he suffer the torments of hell neither in his body, nor his soul, nor any degree of Gods wrath at all." Rather, the sufferings and death of Jesus were the experience of mankind writ large, "inflicted upon him from the age and enmity of the old Serpent and his wicked instruments," Christ's persecutors, who were testing the strength of his mediatorial obedience, just as they daily tested all true Christians. It is unclear whether Pynchon was a certifiable Socinian who maintained the immutable unity of God— in his treatise he defended both the human *and* divine natures of Christ. Still, his book contained enough anti-Trinitarian "Novelismes" to make it objectionable to New England and old.[23] To orthodox Puritans the de- nial of the imputation of men's sins to Christ called into question the whole doctrine of the atonement, and thus of Christianity itself.

Pynchon's critics, like the critics of the early Socinians, attacked the reasoning on which they perceived such theological opinions to be based and warned of the danger such arguments posed to civil and ecclesiastical peace. Socinus and his followers claimed that Trinitarians abused the gift of reason in their arguments for a triune God; they insisted that a mind unshackled by ecclesiastical authority would find in the Bible a Christ who, rather than being a part of the godhead, was a mere man, albeit one whom God had greatly exalted so that his moral example would inspire emulation. Thus Socinians called for a general toleration of religious opin- ions so that such truth could be discovered, and, not surprisingly, their pleas met with bitter resistance from those in ecclesiastical authority.[24]

Pynchon's book was similarly attacked. In the preface to his answer to *The Meritorious Price*, Norton focused sharply on the issue of religious toleration and on the role of the magistrates in setting and patrolling its limits and only then moved on to rebut Pynchon's doctrinal arguments. Speaking as much to the colony's critics abroad as to his New England audience, Norton assured his readers that in condemning Pynchon's work the General Court had done only what God required, for it was "a Stratagem of the Old Serpent and Father of lies" to deny to magistrates control of ecclesiastical affairs that in their judgment the common welfare required. The sword of the clergy and the sword of the civil rulers make up "a compleat Medium of all our good and remedy of all evil," and both "are of speciall use to each other mutually." Thus in any truly holy commonwealth the magistrates always "need the Ministery to fix them in the Conscience of Men, and the Ministers need the Magistracy to preserve them from men that have no conscience, or worse."[25]

Norton acknowledged that although in the past the General Court had successfully demonstrated that "the care of Religion is the duty of the Magistrates," there remained "a great Quaery" over "when and how far to bear, in case of errour concerning matters of Religion," particularly in doctrinal matters such as the atonement. No doubt recalling the famous exchange between John Cotton and Roger Williams on this same topic, Norton claimed that "unity in judgement" on points of doctrine always "is to be endeavoured as much as possible, because truth is one and indivisible." Therefore, although some differences touching the truth "must be endured because of the weaknesse of men," in a true Christian commonwealth the magistrates had power from God to determine and enforce the limits not to be transgressed.[26]

It followed that Pynchon had been arraigned in Boston only because the magistrates in their wisdom decided that his doctrinal error was indeed "Fundamental" on points that had been "clearly" and "orderly decided with due time for conviction," as distinct from things that still were "disputable and of depending disquisition." The General Court held that even though "toleration is not an approbation," Pynchon's views were liable to stimulate dissension. His doctrine was plain "heresie," unequivocally defined by Norton as "Fundamental Error, . . . such as he that knowingly liveth and dieth therein cannot be saved"; but equally dangerous was the intellectual license Pynchon had assumed in publishing his treatise. Norton and the court had found in his arguments a threat to civil peace that necessitated quick and sharp action.[27]

The magistrates and their clerical watchdogs were not wholly mistaken. Pynchon's intellectual allegiance to Puritan rationalists amply supported Norton's contention that, his theory of the atonement aside, Pynchon's line of reasoning posed a threat to New England's city on a hill, just as English latitudinarians endangered the polity the presbyterians tried to construct at the Westminster Assembly. In *The Meritorious Price* Pynchon attempted, unsuccessfully, to mask the intellectual origins of his thought—he was careful to cite only those divines who would least offend the New England Puritans—but his later theological works openly revealed, as his critics had charged, that his theory of the atonement owed its origin to writers, particularly Anthony Wotton, who argued for latitudinarian principles in religion and whose works formed the immediate background to the outbreak of overtly Socinian thought in England in the 1640s and 1650s.[28]

When Nicholas Chewney, a presbyterian divine and erstwhile minister of St. Nicholas at Wade, issued his book *Anti-Socinianism* (1656) as an attack on *The Meritorious Price of Mans Redemption* (1655), he spent many pages challenging the scriptural arguments Pynchon used to support his view of redemption. He inveighed against him as "a dangerous Socinian Sophister" who abused God's gift of reason by "ignorantly, if not willfully, corrupt[ing] some texts of Scripture." Although he himself had "not wrote any thing to the prejudice of the person of the *Author* of the *Dialogue* [*The Meritorious Price of Mans Redemption*], whose Christian moderation in many things is known to many [and] whose holy conversation may be a pattern to most," Chewney was unwilling "that Truth should suffer by the hand of any whatsoever, much less wounded by those that pretend to be her best friends, and make an escape in a croud, without any notice taken of it." Orthodox Puritans could not stand by idly as Pynchon, who "baited his tract" with a "glorious title," "hooked in many, and some no smal fools in the eye and judgement of the World."[29]

We do not know exactly whom Pynchon "hooked in," but Chewney made clear by whom he thought Pynchon himself was ensnared. To the scriptural arguments in *Anti-Socinianism* he appended a lengthy description of *A Cage of Unclean Birds*, "containing the Authors, Promoters, Propagators, and chief Disseminators of this damnable *Socinian* Heresie," the pedigree of which he detailed, not altogether accurately, from the first days of the church through the early seventeenth century. Chewney concluded this genealogy with a discussion of "Antonius Wottonus," whose writings expressed "in plain words his desent [dissent] from all our *Orthodox Divines*, which had before written any thing concerning the necessary *Doctrine* of a sinners justification before God." Fortunately for Christ's cause, Chewney reported, Wotton's books had been virtually "extirpate[d]" shortly after their publication, but, he lamented, recently "our *Dialogue* by the New-English Gentleman revived some, *John Biddle* others, of these *diabolical doctrines*: The one having the very words, the other the *opinions* of *Socinus* and his followers."[30]

In his *True Doctrine of Justification Asserted and Vindicated* (1654), Anthony Burgess, vicar of Sutton Coldfield and a member of the Westminster Assembly, had the good will not to damn Pynchon as irretrievably as Chewney. He accurately described him as a problematic fellow traveler of the Socinians, one of "the eminent and Learned men" among the Protestants who maintained "the *Non*-Imputation of Christs Active Obedience, as the matter of our Justification," but who did not deserve "such a severe Condemnation" as true Socinians did. Although Burgess admitted that he was "grieved publickly to manifest a difference from such who are eminently usefull in the Church of God," his arguments proved every bit as sharp as Chewney's.[31]

In the late 1640s and early 1650s English Puritans were encountering increasing difficulties with such representatives of anti-Trinitarian thought as Paul Best and John Biddle, England's first avowedly Socinian writers who not only questioned the divinity of Christ but also agitated for general toleration.[32] When Chewney linked Pynchon to Wotton, he threw fuel on the fire in nonconformist circles. Wotton had been suspended in 1604 by Archbishop Richard Bancroft from a lectureship at All Hallows, Barking, and seven years later was accused of the Socinian heresy by one George Walker, a charge that brought him under examination by a conference of divines. He was acquitted; but in 1641, fifteen years after Wotton's death, Walker resurrected the charges, at which point Wotton's son Samuel rose to defend his father's name. So, too, did John Goodwin, the leading Independent minister, whom Walker termed "Socinian John" and who perhaps was his real target in the renewed attack on Wotton. It was in this controversy with Walker that Goodwin penned his famous *Imputatio Fidei, or a Treatise of Justification* (1641), which one historian of Puritanism has called "the most impressive statement that had yet come from a Puritan preacher of a theological formula for toleration, for intellectual freedom in the widest sense."[33]

Since the late 1630s, conservative churchmen like Thomas Edwards and Robert Baillie had placed Goodwin in the "Socinian" camp because of his open espousal of the thought of Jacobus Acontius, an Italian divine who settled in England in the mid-sixteenth century and through whom the ideas of Socinus were introduced to that country.[34] In his *Satanae Stratagemata* (Basel, 1565), Acontius had maintained that in religious matters no earthly authority took precedence over a man's own conscience and, further, that no human judgment was infallible. Even before this work was translated into English in 1648 (under the sponsorship of Goodwin), it had become the intellectual progenitor of both Wotton's and Goodwin's writings on toleration and had influenced such liberal theologians as William Chillingworth and John Hales as well.[35] Because Acontius and his English followers so passionately defended the claims of reason and individual conscience and de-emphasized the importance of a belief in the divinity of Christ in the work of redemption, their enemies impugned them as "Socinians," but they were not so much anti-trinitarian heretics as Puritan latitudinarians who argued that the few truths essential to salvation and recorded in the Scriptures were revealed directly to the heart of man and corroborated by his reason. Thus they carried to its logical conclusion the Protestant tenet of the supremacy of private judgment in matters of religion and urged toleration of various theological positions.

Basic to the arguments of Wotton, Goodwin, and other English latitudinarians was their belief that the truths of the Christian religion could be known by any person, regardless of intellectual achievements or official position in church or state, and, as much as their call for a general toleration of opinions, this implicit antiauthoritarianism was one of the main reasons for the sharp condemnation from conservative churchmen. When Chewney warned that there was no more "dangerous and desperate" a sect than the Socinians because their "Spseudo-Divinity ariseth from no other fountain than the abuse of the principles of *reason*," he rehearsed the argument that the exercise of reason in matters of religion was reserved for those who were best educated in theology. By maintaining that the divine truth in the Bible could be ascertained by such "unfit" people as "Taylors," "Physicians," "Sailers," and others untrained in theology, Chewney concluded, the Socinians threatened to "raze . . . the very foundation of *Religion*." [36]

As Puritan rationalists like Wotton and Goodwin saw it, then, for too long the church had restrained healthy inquiry, by laymen as well as clergy, into scriptural questions that could be addressed by the reasoning faculty without detriment to the essential truths of Christianity. By the 1650s such repression had greatly contributed to the divisive sectarianism that so weakened English Puritanism, and neither Parliament nor the Westminster Assembly had helped matters by arraigning latitudinarians whose books smacked of Socinianism. In 1645, Biddle (whom Chewney had mentioned in the same breath with Pynchon) had been jailed for spreading the unorthodox doctrine of the trinity that he later published as *Twelve Arguments against the Deity of the Holy Ghost* (1647), and through the late 1640s and early 1650s he frequently was called before Parliament for examination of his theological opinions. [37] In 1652 he was implicated in the publication of both Latin and English editions of the *Racovian Catechism*, the seminal codification of Socinian principles first issued in Rakow, Poland, in 1609, and two years later he again was summoned by Parliament, this time for organizing Unitarian conventicles in London.

Although the dissolution of Parliament in early 1655 prevented any immediate action against Biddle, he was removed in 1656 from Newgate and banished to the Isle of Scilly, but not before his case had drawn the attention of dissident groups like the baptists and Fifth Monarchy Men, who feared the repercussions of the "Blasphemy Ordinance" under which Biddle and Best, another man often harassed for his Socinian opinions, had been arraigned. Though the marriage of convenience was short-lived between such rationalists as Goodwin and Biddle and the more radical sectarians—for a time, Goodwin became an ally of the Levellers in pressing their political demands—it gave more basis to the belief that latitudinarian thought encouraged the same kinds of antiauthoritarianism displayed by the Seekers, Ranters, and other spiritist groups.[38] To no small degree it was just such reasoning that had instigated the Bay Colony's condemnation of Pynchon's *Meritorious Price*.

However well disguised in *The Meritorious Price*, Pynchon's affinities to this rationalist strain in Puritan thought were distinctly revealed once he attained the relative safety of England. There is no overt proof of his association with any of the participants in the controversies over Socinianism—though Chewney claimed that Pynchon was "acquainted with Socinian John" (either Goodwin or, perhaps, Biddle)—but the works he published from 1652 on display no hesitance on his part to admit his support of the latitudinarians' program.[39]

His advocacy of a more open ecclesiastical polity than that instituted in the Bay Colony was publicly announced in *The Jewes Synagogue*, a treatise probably composed in Springfield, published in London shortly after his arrival. In this volume, which everywhere displays the strict biblicism that characterized the treatises of Wotton and Goodwin, Pynchon entered a debate over church polity that had long preoccupied English Puritans. The passages he explicated supported a less dogmatic and less restrictive ecclesiastical system than that established in New England and corroborated the English latitudinarians' belief that matters of fundamental doctrine should be decided not by the invocation of clerical authority, but rather by each individual's reasoned study of scripture.[40]

Pynchon maintained "that the word *Church* is of so large a capacity that it may well comprehend" all visible professors: "I do fully accord with those Divines that describe the *Church of Christ* to be outwardly visible farre and wide over the face of the earth," though it was not explicitly a "national" church like Scotland's. When the "Scholar" in this book's dialogue remarked that "very learned men do think that none ought to be admitted to a particular visible Church as a member thereof, until the

same Church shall judge them to have a true grace in their souls by trying and examining the marks of their effectual conversion," a cardinal
tenet of the New England Way, Pynchon, responding as the "Teacher,"
squarely opposed all membership restrictions that forced an individual to
adhere to requirements verified neither by his conscience nor his reason.
"If none ought to be admitted into a particular visible Church," he answered, "until they manifest the Truth of Grace in their souls, then
doubtless Christ hath given infallible rules, whereby the Church may
discover aright the Truth of their Grace," a position New England congregationalists still staunchly maintained. But, Pynchon added, in a voice
that recalled Wotton (and anticipated Solomon Stoddard),

I must confess that I am to seek where to find those rules. For though the Scriptures have perfect rules in general, yet when these rules come to be adopted to
particular persons, then am I to seek for certainty of judgement. I conceive it is
one of the royal Prerogatives of the Lord Jesus, to know what particular persons
have the Truth of Grace in their Souls. Questionless, all such are the most fit persons that are to be joyned as Members of particular Churches. . . . But yet, if
there be any others that do call upon the name of the Lord, and depart from iniquity, our Lord Jesus Christ would have us to esteem them also as fit matter for a
particular visible Church[,] until by their scandalous walking they deserve to be
excommunicated.[41]

By the mid-1650s many churches in Massachusetts and Connecticut,
where strict membership qualifications had resulted in declining numbers
of communicants, were splintering themselves against just this point of
doctrine, and Pynchon, like some English Puritans, felt that a large number of Christians were left abandoned because of such restrictive rules.[42]
He urged more liberality on the clergy so that parishioners would not be
forced to enter the gates of the church as hypocrites. "I would say," he
concluded, in words that might have served Goodwin or even Baillie,
"let Churches, both Teachers and Members, be careful that they be not
too censorious and pragmatical, lest they turn men upon the stumbling
blocks of Anabaptistry, etc."[43]

Pynchon's generosity in matters of church membership was shared by
others in New England, notably among the churches of Connecticut, but
the justification for his theological liberalism derived more from the
spirit of the English Puritan rationalists, especially Wotton and Goodwin,
both of whom similarly resisted the establishment of stringent tests of
faith within English Puritanism, than from that of the Connecticut presbyterialists.[44] Never in all his theological treatises did Pynchon approvingly quote any New England divines; this strategy is explained by

his observation, offered in *The Time When the First Sabbath Was Ordained*, that dogmatic ecclesiastical practices like those codified in New England had only proved stumbling blocks to true Christians. "Whole Churches," he noted, "do many times erre, both in their judgement and practice," in such matters as ascertaining the precise time of the Sabbath or setting the qualifications for membership, two questions the Massachusetts clergy believed they had answered for all time. How, then, Pynchon asked (with the full support of Wotton and Acontius behind him), "could so much Corruption, Superstition, Idolatry, and Prophaneness creep in to several reformed Churches[?]"[45] The obvious answer to this rhetorical question was that too many restrictions on the individual conscience would palsy the spiritual life of any Puritan.

Like the Puritan rationalists, too, Pynchon did not wish to halt or reverse reform of the English church but to make it intellectually consistent. In his later writings he often turned to illustrations of human fallibility to point out the error of establishing too formal an ecclesiastical system. Answering Norton, he urged readers to consider "*Lev.* 4.13, 14, where a Church, a Synod, and a Court of Elders and Magistrates, may see that they are sometimes subject to Error in the things of God," adding that "therefore they, as well as persons of a lower capacity, had need to watch and pray, and to study daily and earnestly, that God would guide their judgement unto the sound understanding, and righteous preserving of the truth of his blessed Scriptures."[46] Implicitly combining an attack on New England's Cambridge Platform with a criticism of his own treatment at the hands of the Hartford church and the Massachusetts General Court, Pynchon answered Norton blow for blow, always reminding him that he, like his Massachusetts sponsors, was, after all, a mere mortal and subject to error in matters of both doctrine and polity.

In this same reply to Norton, Pynchon admitted his intellectual affinity with the English Puritan latitudinarians. Like Wotton and Goodwin, he urged his readers, if they wished "to escape the *odium* of a Persecutor," to search the Scriptures "not only superficially, and by some common received Expositors," but by the lights of reason and conscience, "look-[ing] well to the Context, and . . . to the force and use of the original word." He thereafter peppered his arguments with quotations from Reformed theologians: William Ames, John Preston, Henry Ainsworth, Richard Baxter, and, most prominent, Wotton himself, who at one point received at Pynchon's hands as glowing a commendation as he would a rude slander at Chewney's. Pynchon hailed Wotton as "a man of approved integrity, one that suffered much for Christ, through the iniquity of the times." He was "a man of great reading in all kinds of writers, both Ancient and Modern, and a man of deep judgement" whose "book of Reconciliation" (*De Reconciliatione Peccatoris*) only "was printed in his old age, after much debate, and study, and revising." Pynchon concluded, "what he saith in this point [the imputation of man's sins to Christ], ought not, and will not be slighted by the Judicious."[47]

Once in England, Pynchon was not timid in making known his intellectual indebtedness to men such as Wotton. Indeed, he claimed that through all its pages, his *The Meritorious Price of Mans Redemption* "doth approve and follow Mr. Wottons sense," and even in the earlier version of this work, in which Wotton went unnamed, his influence is very evident.[48] It is important to note, however, that Pynchon's inclusion of quotations from more orthodox writers like Preston and Ames, even in his later treatises, was consistent with his position as a latitudinarian *within* the English Puritan tradition. Like Wotton and others, he believed in the final truth of scriptural revelation, but he also championed the place of individual reason in man's perception of that truth. On the one hand, Pynchon warned in his response to Norton, men had to take heed "of framing a model of [their] own, as to think, that because such a thing is just, therefore the Lord wills it." But he also stressed that clergymen had no ex officio monopoly on the interpretation of divine truth and gravely injured the cause of Puritanism by believing that "god must go by [their] rule." The fundamental doctrines of the Christian religion were not the property of a choice few but were available to all men, including laymen, who examined the Bible with a pious heart and an open mind. The betrayal of one's conscience resulted in the illiberality that characterized contemporary religious debate.[49]

Further light is thrown on Pynchon's link to the Puritan rationalists by considering briefly his friend and neighbor in the Connecticut Valley, Edward Holyoke, another of the original settlers of Agawam. Like Pynchon, Holyoke was deeply interested in theology; in 1658, after his friend returned to England, he published *The Doctrine of Life, or of Mans Redemption*, a lengthy work in which, among many other topics, he discussed the atonement and praised Pynchon's words on the subject. Holyoke displayed the same latitudinarian emphases as Pynchon, particularly on the subject of toleration, and he, too, made use of Wotton's arguments.[50]

Emboldened by the increasing criticism of Massachusetts for its repressive measures against dissenters, though fully aware of the danger of tolerating "wicked opinions in pretence of conscience," Holyoke believed it appropriate to reexamine the question of the atonement. He urged readers to obtain Pynchon's reply to Norton; there they would "have plentifull satisfaction" for the ideas that he would "enlarge" in his own book. Like Pynchon, Holyoke asked every man to search the Scriptures to ascertain true doctrine for himself and strongly indicted ecclesiastical polities like New England's that officially discouraged theological inquiry among its members. Though he strongly disagreed with the orthodox view of the atonement defended by Norton, Holyoke recognized that such arguments raised even larger questions about the search for truth. He implored "Reverend Teachers of salvation" not to think that he and Pynchon wrote "out of any sinister end and purpose," but rather "out of conscience." Because Holyoke believed that the cause of Christianity never could be served by harsh repression of dissent, he strongly defended the individual's right to inquire into the scriptural foundations of his or her faith. "We ought not to maintain errour, much less foul heresie[;] neither ought we to be silent at other mens errours, but to contest for the truth." Only when Christian soldiers displayed such courage, taking the "paines of the mind to dive into the true sence and scope" of biblical texts and seeing them "with their owne and not with other mens eyes," would a true Christian commonwealth be established.[51]

The remarkable similarity between Holyoke's position on toleration and Pynchon's leaves little doubt that the Connecticut Valley harbored a small but active group of Puritan rationalists who by the 1650s were beginning to broadcast their opinions and whose presence suggests that historians have underestimated the great variety of Puritan thought in New England. To be sure, in the colony's history the condemnation of Pynchon's *Meritorious Price* was not as significant an event as the protracted battles against the Antinomians, the Gortonists, or Roger Williams. Yet coming as it did at a critical moment, as the New England authorities were drawing a hard line against toleration, their action against Pynchon revealed their fear that church and state could be undermined as insidiously by latitudinarians like Pynchon as by radical spiritists like those in the Rhode Island settlements. The intellectual basis for Pynchon's arguments could too easily be adopted by those who found license for spiritual (and therefore civil) anarchy in its defense of an individualistic, egalitarian definition of religious experience.

Massachusetts Bay's esteemed minister John Cotton had sparred with Roger Williams, one of the best known of the radical spiritists, and in turning loose Cotton's soon-to-be successor, John Norton, on a different but similarly dangerous representative of free thought the General Court clearly announced its view of the apostolic succession in Boston. As though oblivious to the fact that the world of English Puritanism was turning, and turning decidedly, toward an accommodation with sincere dissenters, Norton, like the magistrates he represented, refused to admit that a man like Pynchon had his uses in a Puritan commonwealth. In 1650 enlightened rationalism was not the rock upon which Boston's First Church, or the New England Way, was to be built.

Try as they might, the New England theocrats finally were powerless to control the antiauthoritarian, democratic impulse at the heart of the Puritan revolution, for after Pynchon they soon had to contend with baptists, Quakers, and other critics of their ecclesiastical regime. And though they would not view the broad spectrum of sectarian thought with any comfort until later in the seventeenth century, Pynchon's voice reminded them that the revolution of the saints could not be restricted to nonseparating congregationalists, even if they were convinced that they had both reason and revelation on their side.

EPILOGUE

TOWARD THE GREAT

AWAKENING

AND BEYOND

In New England, Hutchinson, Gorton, and Pynchon were exceptional Puritans only because their radicalism was publicly voiced and promoted. Throughout the several colonies, other individuals, families, and small groups of settlers, some influenced by the example of those whom they had known in England or America, others simply unraveling what they considered the inner logic of their faith, adhered to an ideology decidedly at odds with that codified in the Cambridge Platform of 1648. In the great majority of cases such individuals, in good conscience, chose to remain within the Puritan churches in which they had been nurtured, for by 1660 the nonseparating congregationalism that marked New England's ecclesiology had been adapted to co-opt the radicals' appeals to the disgruntled. To be sure, the New England churches could not satisfy all the demands made by the region's varied population—among the settlers there were, after all, the John Crandalls, the Thomas Venners, and the Nicholas Eastons—but for many who demanded a greater lay participation in church affairs, an acknowledgment of the overpowering presence of the Holy Spirit in the work of conversion, or an increased effort to identify New England with the veritable New Jerusalem, the New England Way had been elaborated to provide convincing reinforcement for their beliefs. Ministers like Cotton, Hooker, Shepard, and Bulkeley had created, if nothing else, a remarkably resilient polity.

Beginning in 1661, when Charles II ordered New England to suspend its recently imposed (and implemented) death penalty for Quakers and to return to England any of this sect whom they still held in prison, the history of New England Puritan radicalism entered a new phase, one further marked by the founding, four years later, of a baptist church in Charlestown. Whether or not the ministers and magistrates approved—and some most vociferously did not—by the late seventeenth century "that cursed Brat Toleration" had gained the run of all the New England colonies.[1]

But the grudging toleration accorded such dissenters after the Restoration was only part of the story of the further development of New England Puritan radicalism, for, as in the years prior to 1660, in addition to flowering openly in the meetings of such groups as the baptists and Quakers, the ecclesiastical and doctrinal emphases that always had identified Puritan radicalism continued to appear within nonseparating congregationalism itself. This was the case during the protracted debates that followed the institution of the Half-Way Covenant in 1662, which granted some of the privileges of church membership to the children of those who had been baptized because of *their* parents' status as visible saints but who never had experienced the work of Christ in their own souls. Ministers like Jonathan Mitchel and Richard Mather who argued for this "half-way" membership knew that such new measures represented a departure from the ecclesiastical purity of the 1630s, but they believed that the declining membership in their churches was linked directly to the strict polity established by the first colonists, one that too closely resembled radical separatism.[2]

Opponents of the half-way measures, particularly John Davenport and Charles Chauncy, defended their position in terms that indeed made them sound like baptists. Like the Particular Baptists of the 1650s, they rejected the argument that the Hebraic rite of circumcision was typologically linked to the Christian ordinance of baptism and thus implicitly challenged the intricate genetics of salvation through which New Englanders had justified their place in the work of redemption. Then, too, though consenting to the baptism of children of visible saints, opponents of the Half-Way Covenant clearly viewed that ordinance more as a reminder of a young Puritan's covenantal obligations than as a seal of divine promise to him, and constantly reminded children so baptized that they would not be considered true members of the church until years later when they gave convincing evidence of true repentance and conversion. Outwardly, of course, most opponents of the Half-Way Covenant were not the "anabaptists" some termed them; still, the nature of their opposition to the ecclesiastical innovations of the 1660s brought them dangerously close to those the colony earlier had disciplined for strikingly similar beliefs.[3]

Also at issue in these and other arguments, of course, was the same problem that had divided New England Puritans since the Antinomian Controversy, and Protestants generally at least since the mid-sixteenth century—that of the relative value of human initiative in Christian salvation, or, put another way, the relation of outward ecclesiastical forms to inner spiritual assurance. Thus, opponents of the Half-Way Covenant argued that the liberal measures sanctioned at the synod of 1662 could only breed a lifeless formalism in the religious life; and later in the century, as the traumas of Indians wars, pestilence, drought, and the horror of witchcraft stunned the colonies, this charge was repeated and extended, seemingly with some legitimacy. Covenant renewals, the rhetoric of the jeremiad, less restrictive church membership policies and the ensuing liberalization of sacramental privileges—all were construed as contributing to what some colonists viewed as unforgivable apostasy. Such increased emphasis on outward forms was like a cancer on the life of the spirit, these individuals argued, and God's judgments upon New England the logical consequence of an extensive communal retreat from the dreams of the first generation.[4]

But as many historians recently have demonstrated, in the late seventeenth century such conservative views more often than not were held by the populace rather than by the ministry, for once again, as in the aftermath of the Antinomian Controversy, the clergy took it upon themselves subtly to mold their ecclesiology either to rob such arguments of their appeal or to harness them to forward their own understanding of New England's destiny. Thus by 1700 sacramental piety had replaced evangelism as the chief method of filling the churches; and New England's ministers, as they had in the late 1630s and 1640s when they gathered behind Shepard and Bulkeley to insist on the necessity of preparation for salvation, argued that salvation most often flowed through the discipline of outward piety. In these years what one historian recently has termed the "iconoclastic, anti-sacramentalist tendency in Puritanism," manifested in the antinomians, Gortonists, baptists, and Quakers, was successfully re-

pressed as congregations were vigorously instructed in forms of sacramental devotion. Though dissenters like the Quaker George Keith continued to attack such sacramentalism as a return to mere popery, through
the early eighteenth century New Englanders came to believe that the life
of the spirit could indeed be attained through discipline and devotion.
Gradually led to accept the innovation of the Half-Way Covenant, many
colonists found it increasingly easy to define their Puritanism more
through a belief in sacramental efficacy than through spiritual ecstasy.[5]

American Puritans, nevertheless, finally were powerless fully to eliminate the spiritist and millennial tendencies within their culture. Between
1660 and 1735 those who spoke for the traditions of Puritan radicalism were driven underground, but, as Edward Johnson had reported
of the Hutchinsonians after their banishment, they "sometimes like Wiz-
ards" emerged "to peepe and mutter" their "blasphemies." In the 1670s,
Thomas Shepard the Younger, who had inherited his father's distrust of
spiritist ideas, still could inveigh against "Anabaptists" as "an Engine
framed to cut the throat of the Infantry of the Church" and "Rigid Separatists" as those who buried the churches in "Confusion," and through
the remainder of the century such shibboleths as "anabaptist," "antinomian," and "familist," continued to inform ministerial diatribes against
those for whom the presence of the Spirit assumed greater meaning than
any moralism the ministry preached.[6]

Cotton Mather might have been exaggerating when in the late seventeenth century he concluded his historical account of Quakerism in New
England with anecdotes worthy of the most prurient English heresiographers of the previous century—he spoke, for example, of one Mary
Ross, who had been "possessed with as Frantick a *Daemon* as ever was
heard of," and had called herself Christ and danced naked with her two
male "Apostles." Nevertheless, as had been the case throughout the seventeenth century, the mere perception and articulation of such behavior
was as persuasive to critics as its verifiable existence. What such individuals as Mary Ross, Anne Hutchinson, Obadiah Holmes and other radicals
kept alive within Puritanism was, as Christopher Hill has put it, a belief
"in the evolution of truth, continuous revelation," and "a reliance on the
holy spirit within one, of one's own experiential truth as against the traditional truth handed down by others."[7]

Knowing this, and appreciating its importance to the development of
other, more liberal and, finally, democratic ideas, we should consider
whether America's true radical revolution finally arrived in the late 1720s
and 1730s with the excitement of the first religious revivals in the Con-

necticut River Valley of New England. During the turmoil of the Great Awakening, the "Old Light" opponents of the revivals assumed doctrinal and ecclesiastical positions in many ways comparable to those maintained by the English and Scottish presbyterians a century earlier, and, not surprisingly, they often attacked the threats to civil order posed by the "New Lights" in rhetoric derived from the pamphlet literature of the English civil wars. The most striking instance of this occurs in Charles Chauncy's *Seasonable Thoughts on the State of Religion* (1743), which owes much to the heresiographical literature of Thomas Edwards, Robert Baillie, and Samuel Rutherford, and in which Chauncy makes extensive use of Winthrop's attack on the antinomians in his *Short Story*, but fears of "Antinomianism" and "Anabaptism" permeate the literature of the Awakening. Nor were the lessons of the Interregnum and Protectorate lost on some of the more moderate pro-revival ministers. In 1746 in his *Treatise Concerning Religious Affections*, for example, Jonathan Edwards approvingly cited Samuel Rutherford's condemnation of such "enthusiasts" as David Jorus, Henry Niclaes, and Caspar Schwenckfeld, as well as "the followers of Mrs. Hutchinson," as Edwards tried to direct the course of the New Lights between the Scylla of Arminianism and the Charybdis of antinomianism. The religious and social programs of such New Lights as James Davenport and Benjamin Pomeroy were indeed comparable to those of the radical sectarians of the 1640s and 1650s, and by their challenge to the established social and ecclesiastical norms they, too, threatened to turn the world upside down, and at a time more suited to the reception of such liberating ideas.[8]

In one form or another Puritan radicalism was unquestionably an important influence in American theology until at least the time of the Great Awakening; whether it contributed significantly to the political ideology of the American Revolution is still very much open to consideration. Historians like Alan Heimert and Nathan O. Hatch have examined the immediate effects of the religious rhetoric of the Awakening on the revolutionary cause, but no one has yet detailed the connections between this radicalism—particularly the American patriots' powerful antiauthoritarianism and their millennial aspirations—and the tradition of seventeenth-century American radicalism.[9] What the Americans of 1776 rejected from this radical heritage, however, is as significant as what they may have integrated into the public ideology of the new nation. As important as it is to inquire why in the seventeenth century New England's radicals failed to turn the New World upside down, we also should ask, in all candor, why some of the most revolutionary and democratic components of the radical sectarians' plans for bringing the kingdom of God to America—those, for example, of the Levellers and Diggers—were enshrined only in the rhetoric of the founding fathers, if even there.

There is no denying that in one important fact the history of Puritan radicalism in seventeenth-century New England mirrored that of its English counterpart, for in both lands the radicals' attempts to create a commonwealth in accord with what they took to be God's explicit intentions were failures. But in New England more than anywhere else in that century, the inhabitants moved closer to this goal, and in good measure through the promptings of those among them who refused to dismiss the visions of individuals like Hutchinson, Gorton, Pynchon, and a host of others. If, as Joseph Haroutunian has said of another group of American reformers, knowing what they did of human nature, they were indeed "great optimists," in their own hearts and minds, and occasionally in the words and deeds of some of their more conservative fellow colonists, New England's radical Puritans at least had glimpsed Sion's glory.[10] This was no meager accomplishment.

For my self, God hath been here with me, and done me much good, learning me something of himself, and of my selfe, and of men. N[ew] E[ngland] is not Heaven, and here we are men still.

ANONYMOUS NEW ENGLAND MINISTER
quoted in Thomas Edwards,
The Second Part of Gangraena (1646)

They, who of late were called fifth Monarchy-men did err . . . especially two ways. First by anticipating the time, which will not be till the pouring out of the sixth and seventh Vials [and] Secondly, By putting themselves upon a work which shall not be done by man, but by Christ himself.

JOHN DAVENPORT,
"An Epistle to the Reader," in
Increase Mather, *The Mystery
of Israel's Salvation* (1669)

BIBLIOGRAPHY

This bibliography lists primary and secondary sources cited throughout the text. Full bibliographical references to other works are found in the notes to the chapters in which those sources are used.

PRIMARY SOURCES

Anderson, Philip J. "Letters of Henry Jessey and John Tombes to the Churches of New England, 1645." *Baptist Quarterly* 28 (1979): 30–40.

Baillie, Robert. *Anabaptism, The True Fountaine of Independency*. London, 1647.

———. *A Dissuasive from the Errours of the Time*. London, 1647.

———. *The Letters and Journals of Robert Baillie*. Edited by David Laing. 3 vols. Edinburgh: Bannatyne Club, 1841–42.

Bartlett, John Russell, ed. *Records of the Colony of Rhode Island and Providence Plantations in New England*. 7 vols. Providence, 1856–62.

[Baxter, Richard.] *Reliquiae Baxterianae*. London, 1696.

Bradford, William. *Of Plymouth Plantation, 1620–1647*. Edited by Samuel Eliot Morison. New York: Alfred A. Knopf, 1953.

Bulkeley, Peter. *The Gospel-Covenant; or The Covenant of Grace Opened*. London, 1646.

Callender, John. *Historical Discourse on the Civil and Religious affairs of the Colony of Rhode Island*. 1739. Reprinted in Rhode Island Historical Society, *Collections*, vol. 4. Providence, 1838.

Chapin, Howard M. *Documentary History of Rhode Island*. 2 vols. Providence: Preston and Rounds, 1916–19.

Chauncy, Charles. *Gods Mercy, shewed to his people*. . . . Cambridge, Massachusetts Bay Colony, 1655.

Childe, John. *New Englands Jonas Cast Up at London*. 1647. Reprinted in Massachusetts Historical Society, *Collections*, 2d Ser., vol. 4, 107–20. Boston, 1846.

[Clap, Roger.] *Memoirs of Roger Clap.* 1731. Reprint. Boston: David Clapp, 1854.

Clarke, John. *Ill Newes from New-England.* 1652. Reprinted in Massachusetts Historical Society, Collections, 4th Ser., vol. 2, 1–113. Boston, 1854.

Cobbet, Thomas. *The Civil Magistrates Power in Matters of Religion.* London, 1653.

Cotton, John. *A Brief Exposition of the Whole Book of Canticles.* London, 1642.

———. *A Briefe Exposition with Practicall Observations upon the Whole Book of Ecclesiastes.* London, 1654.

———. *The Churches Resurrection.* London, 1645.

———. *The Covenant of Gods Free Grace.* London, 1645.

———. *The Grounds and Ends of Baptisme of the Children of the Faithful.* London, 1647.

———. *The Powring Out of the Seven Vialls.* London, 1642.

———. *The Way of the Congregational Churches Cleared.* 1648. Reprinted in *John Cotton on the Churches of New England.* Edited by Larzer Ziff. Cambridge: Harvard University Press, 1968.

———. *The Way of Life.* London, 1642.

Crosby, Thomas. *The History of the English Baptists.* 4 vols. London, 1738.

Cushman, Robert. "Reasons and Considerations touching the lawfulness of removing out of England into the parts of America." Reprinted in *A Journal of the Pilgrims at Plymouth: Mourt's Relation.* Edited by Dwight B. Heath. New York: Corinth Books, 1963.

Denison, Stephen. *The White Wolfe.* London, 1627.

Edwards, Thomas. *Antapologia.* London, 1646.

———. *Gangraena: or A Catalogue and Discovery of many of the Errours . . . of this Time.* London, 1646.

———. *The Second Part of Gangraena.* London, 1646.

———. *The Third Part of Gangraena.* London, 1646.

Felt, Joseph B. *The Ecclesiastical History of New England.* 2 vols. Boston: Congregational Library Association, 1855–62.

Firmin, Giles. *A Brief Review of Mr. Davis's Vindication.* London, 1693.

———. *The Real Christian.* 1670. Reprint. Boston, 1742.

———. *Separation Examined.* London, 1652.

———. *Stablishing against Shaking.* London, 1655.

Forbes, Allyn B., et al., eds. *Winthrop Papers, 1498–1649.* 5 vols. Boston: Massachusetts Historical Society, 1929–47.

Gaustad, Edwin S. *Baptist Piety: The Last Will & Testament of Obadiah Holmes.* Grand Rapids, Mich.: Christian University Press, 1978.

Geree, Stephen. *The Doctrine of the Antinomians . . . Confuted.* London, 1644.

Gorton, Samuel. *An Antidote against the Common Plague of the World.* London, 1657.

———. *An Incorruptible Key, composed of the CX. Psalme.* London, 1647.

———. "Letter to Nathaniel Morton, 30 June 1669." Reprinted in *Tracts and Other Papers.* Edited by Peter Force. 4 vols. Washington: Force, 1836–46. Vol. 4, no. 7.

———. *Simplicities Defence against Seven-Headed Policy.* 1646. Reprint. Rhode Island Historical Society. *Collections,* vol. 2. Providence, 1835.

———. *Saltmarsh Returned from the Dead.* London, 1655.

Hall, David D. *The Antinomian Controversy, 1636–1638: A Documentary History*. Middletown, Conn.: Wesleyan University Press, 1968.

———. "John Cotton's Letter to Samuel Skelton." *William and Mary Quarterly*, 3d Ser., vol. 22 (1965): 478–85.

Haller, William, ed. *Tracts on Liberty in the Puritan Revolution, 1638–1647*. 2 vols. New York: Columbia University Press, 1934.

——— and Godfrey Davies, eds. *The Leveller Tracts, 1647–1653*. New York: Columbia University Press, 1944.

Hooker, Thomas. *The Covenant of Grace Opened*. London, 1649.

———. *Survey of the Summe of Church Discipline*. London, 1648.

Hubbard, William. *A General History of New England from the Discovery to MDCLXXX*. Cambridge: Massachusetts Historical Society, 1815.

[Hutchinson, Thomas.] *The Hutchinson Papers*. Publications of the Prince Society. 2 vols. Albany, N.Y.: For the Society, 1865.

[Johnson, Edward.] *Johnson's Wonder-Working Providence, 1628–1651*. Edited by J. Franklin Jameson. Original Narratives of Early American History. New York: Charles Scribner's Sons, 1910.

Lechford, Thomas. *Plain Dealing; or, News from New-England*. 1642. Reprint. Boston: Wiggin and Lunt, 1863.

Mather, Cotton. *Magnalia Christi Americana*. London, 1702.

Mather, Richard. *A Heart-Melting Exhortation*. Cambridge, Massachusetts Bay Colony, 1650.

———. *The Summe of Certain Sermons*. Cambridge, Massachusetts Bay Colony, 1652.

Morton, Nathaniel. *New Englands Memoriall*. Cambridge, Massachusetts Bay Colony, 1669.

Norton, John. *The Orthodox Evangelist*. London, 1654.

Pagitt, Ephraim. *Heresiography*. 1645. 5th edition. London, 1654.

Penington, Isaac. *An Examination of the Grounds or Causes . . . .* London, 1660.

Plymouth Church Records. 2 vols. New York: The New England Society, 1920.

Rutherford, Samuel. *A Survey of the Spirituall Antichrist*. London, 1648.

[Shepard, Thomas.] *God's Plot: The Paradoxes of Puritan Piety: Being the Autobiography and Journal of Thomas Shepard*. Edited by Michael McGiffert. Amherst: University of Massachusetts Press, 1972.

———. *New-Englands Lamentations for Old Englands Present Errours and Divisions*. London, 1645.

———. *Works*. Edited by John Albro. 3 vols. 1853. Reprint. New York: AMS Press, 1967.

Shurtleff, Nathaniel B., and David Pulsifer, eds. *Records of the Colony of New Plymouth, in New England*. 12 vols. Boston: W. White, 1855–61.

———. ed. *Records of the Governor and Company of the Massachusetts Bay in New England*. 5 vols. Boston: W. White, 1853–54.

Trumbull, James H., and C. J. Hoadly, eds. *The Public Records of the Colony of Connecticut, 1636–1776*. 15 vols. Hartford, 1850–90.

Underhill, Thomas. *Hell Broke Loose: Or An History of the Quakers Both Old and New*. London, 1660.

Walker, Williston. *The Creeds and Platforms of Congregationalism*. 1893. Reprint. Boston: The Pilgrim Press, 1960.

Ward, Nathaniel. *The Simple Cobler of Aggawam in America.* 1647. Reprint. Edited by P. M. Zall. Lincoln: University of Nebraska Press, 1969.

Wheelwright, John. *Mercurius Americanus.* 1645. Reprinted in *John Wheelwright.* Publications of the Prince Society, vol. 9. Boston: Prince Society, 1876.

White, John. *The Planters Plea.* 1630. Reprint. Rockport, Mass.: The Sandy Bay Historical Society and Museum, 1930.

Whitefield, Henry. *The Light Appearing more and more . . . Or, A Farther Discovery of the . . . Indians in New England.* 1651. Reprinted in Massachusetts Historical Society, *Collections,* 3d Ser., vol. 4, 100–148. Boston, 1834.

———. *Strength Out of Weakness.* 1652. Reprinted in Massachusetts Historical Society, *Collections,* 3d Ser., vol. 4, 149–96. Boston, 1834.

Williams, Roger. *Complete Writings.* Edited by Perry Miller. 7 vols. New York: Russell and Russell, 1963.

Winslow, Edward. *Hypocrisie Unmasked.* 1646. Reprint. Providence: Club for Colonial Reprints, 1916.

———. *New Englands Salamander Discovered.* 1647. Reprinted in Massachusetts Historical Society, *Collections,* 3d Ser., vol. 2, 110–45. Cambridge, 1830.

Winthrop, John. *Winthrop's Journal, "History of New England, 1630–1649."* Edited by James Kendall Hosmer. 2 vols. Original Narratives of Early American History. New York: Charles Scribner's Sons, 1908.

Young, Alexander. *Chronicles of the First Planters of the Colony of Massachusetts Bay.* Boston: Little and Brown, 1846.

SECONDARY SOURCES

Arnold, Samuel Greene. *History of the State of Rhode Island and Providence Plantations.* 2 vols. New York: Appleton and Company, 1859.

Barclay, Robert. *The Inner Life of the Religious Societies of the Commonwealth.* London: Hodder and Stoughton, 1876.

Battis, Emery. *Saints and Sectaries: Anne Hutchinson and the Antinomian Controversy in the Massachusetts Bay Colony.* Chapel Hill: University of North Carolina Press, 1962.

Bercovitch, Sacvan. *The American Jeremiad.* Madison: University of Wisconsin Press, 1978.

———. *The Puritan Origins of the American Self.* New Haven: Yale University Press, 1975.

Brailsford, H. N. *The Levellers and the English Revolution.* Stanford, Calif.: Stanford University Press, 1961.

Breen, T. H. *Puritans and Adventurers: Change and Persistence in Early America.* New York: Oxford University Press, 1980.

Bridenbaugh, Carl. *Fat Mutton and Liberty of Conscience: Society in Rhode Island, 1636–1690.* Providence: Brown University Press, 1974.

Burns, Norman T. *Christian Mortalism from Tyndale to Milton.* Cambridge: Harvard University Press, 1972.

Burrage, Champlain. *The Early English Dissenters in the Light of Recent Research.* 2 vols. Cambridge, Eng.: Cambridge University Press, 1912.

Bush, Jr., Sargent. *The Writings of Thomas Hooker: Spiritual Adventure in Two Worlds.* Madison: University of Wisconsin Press, 1980.

Capp, Bernard S. *The Fifth Monarchy Men: A Study in Seventeenth-Century English Millenarianism*. London: Faber and Faber, 1972.

Cohn, Norman. *The Pursuit of the Millennium: Revolutionary Messianism in Medieval and Reformation Europe and Its Bearings on Modern Totalitarian Movements*. 1957. 2d ed. New York: Harper and Row, 1961.

Collinson, Patrick. *The Elizabethan Puritan Movement*. Berkeley and Los Angeles: University of California Press, 1967.

Corey, Deloraine Pendre. *The History of Malden, Massachusetts, 1633–1785*. Malden: The Author, 1899.

Cragg, Gerald R., *Freedom and Authority: A Study of English Thought in the Early Seventeenth Century*. Philadelphia: Westminster Press, 1975.

Deane, Samuel. *History of Scituate, Massachusetts, From Its First Settlement to 1831*. Boston: James Loring, 1831.

Dexter, Henry Martyn. *The Congregationalism of the Last Three Hundred Years as Seen in Its Literature*. New York: Harper, 1880.

Dow, Joseph. *History of the Town of Hampton, New Hampshire*. 2 vols. Salem, Mass.: Salem Press and Publishing Company, 1893.

Erikson, Kai T. *Wayward Puritans: A Study of the Sociology of Deviance*. New York: John Wiley and Sons, 1966.

Foote, Henry Wilder. "George Phillips, First Minister of Watertown." Massachusetts Historical Society, *Proceedings*, vol. 63, 193–227. Boston, 1931.

Foster, Stephen. "New England and the Challenge of Heresy, 1630–1660: The Puritan Crisis in Transatlantic Perspective." *William and Mary Quarterly*. 3d Ser., vol. 38 (1981), 624–60.

———. *Their Solitary Way: The Puritan Social Ethic in the First Century of Settlement in New England*. New Haven: Yale University Press, 1971.

Gildrie, Richard P. *Salem, Massachusetts, 1623–1683: A Covenant Community*. Charlottesville: University of Virginia Press, 1975.

Gilpin, W. Clark. *The Millenarian Piety of Roger Williams*. Chicago: University of Chicago Press, 1979.

Hall, David D. *The Faithful Shepherd: A History of the New England Ministry in the Seventeenth Century*. 1972. Reprint. New York: W. W. Norton, 1974.

Haller, William. *Liberty and Reformation in the Puritan Revolution*. 1955. Reprint. New York: Columbia University Press, 1967.

———. *The Rise of Puritanism*. New York: Columbia University Press, 1938.

Hill, Christopher. *Antichrist in Seventeenth-Century England*. London: Oxford University Press, 1971.

———. *Milton and the English Revolution*. 1977. Reprint. New York: Penguin, 1979.

———. *The World Turned Upside Down: Radical Ideas During the English Revolution*. 1972. Reprint. New York: The Viking Press, 1978.

Holifield, E. Brooks. *The Covenant Sealed: The Development of Puritan Sacramental Theology in Old England and New, 1570–1720*. New Haven: Yale University Press, 1974.

Jennings, Francis. *The Invasion of America: Indians, Colonialism, and the Cant of Conquest*. Chapel Hill: University of North Carolina Press, 1975.

Johnson, George Arthur. "From Seeker to Finder: A Study in Seventeenth-

Century English Spiritualism Before the Quakers." *Church History* 17 (1948), 299–315.

Jones, Rufus M. *Mysticism and Democracy in the English Commonwealth.* Cambridge: Harvard University Press, 1932.

———. *The Quakers in the American Colonies.* 1911. Reprint. New York: W. W. Norton, 1966.

———. *Studies in Mystical Religion.* London: Macmillan, 1923.

Jordan, William K. *The Development of Religious Toleration in England.* 4 vols. Cambridge: Harvard University Press, 1932–40.

Kittredge, George L. "Dr. Robert Child the Remonstrant." Colonial Society of Massachusetts, *Publications*, vol. 21 (1920): 1–146. Boston, 1920.

Koehler, Lyle. *A Search for Power: The "Weaker Sex" in Seventeenth-Century New England.* Urbana: University of Illinois Press, 1980.

Lamont, William M. *Godly Rule: Politics and Religion, 1603–1660.* London: Macmillan, 1969.

Langdon, George D. *Pilgrim Colony: A History of New Plymouth, 1620–1691.* New Haven: Yale University Press, 1966.

Levy, Leonard W. *Treason against God: A History of the Offense of Blasphemy.* New York: Schocken Books, 1981.

Lewis, Alonzo. *The History of Lynn.* Boston: J. H. Eastburn, 1829.

Lucas, Paul R., *Valley of Discord: Church and Society along the Connecticut River, 1636–1725.* Hanover, N.H.: University Press of New England, 1976.

Lyon, Thomas. *The Theory of Religious Liberty in England, 1603–39.* Cambridge, Eng.: The University Press, 1937.

Mackie, John M. "Life of Samuel Gorton, One of the First Settlers of Warwick, in Rhode Island." *Library of American Biography.* Edited by Jared Sparks. 2d Ser., vol. 5. Boston, 1864.

McLachlan, H. John. *Socinianism in Seventeenth-Century England.* London: Oxford University Press, 1951.

Maclear, James Fulton. "Anne Hutchinson and the Mortalist Heresy." *New England Quarterly* 54 (1981), 74–103.

———. "'The Heart of New England Rent': The Mystical Element in Early Puritan History." *Mississippi Valley Historical Review* 42 (1956), 621–52.

———. "New England and the Fifth Monarchy: The Quest for the Millennium in Early American Puritanism." *William and Mary Quarterly*, 3d Ser., vol. 32 (1975), 223–60.

McLoughlin, William. *New England Dissent: The Baptists and the Separation of Church and State.* 2 vols. Cambridge: Harvard University Press, 1971.

Middlekauff, Robert. *The Mathers: Three Generations of Puritan Intellectuals, 1598–1728.* New York: Oxford University Press, 1971.

Miller, Perry. *Errand into the Wilderness.* Cambridge: Harvard University Press, 1956.

———. *Nature's Nation.* Cambridge: Harvard University Press, 1967.

———. *The New England Mind: From Colony to Province.* Cambridge: Harvard University Press, 1953.

———. *Orthodoxy in Massachusetts, 1630–1650.* 1933. Reprint. New York: Harper and Row, 1970.

————. *Roger Williams: His Contribution to the American Tradition*. Indianapolis, Ind.: Bobbs-Merrill Co., 1953.

Morgan, Edmund. *Roger Williams: The Church and the State*. New York: Harcourt, Brace, and World, 1967.

————. *Visible Saints: The History of a Puritan Idea*. Ithaca, NY: Cornell University Press, 1965.

Morton, A. L. *The World of the Ranters: Religious Radicalism in the English Revolution*. London: Lawrence and Wishart, 1970.

Nuttall, Geoffrey. *The Holy Spirit in Puritan Faith and Experience*. Oxford: Basil Blackwell, 1946.

————. *Visible Saints: The Congregational Way, 1640–1660*. Oxford: Basil Blackwell, 1957.

Oliver, Peter. *The Puritan Commonwealth*. Boston: Little and Brown, 1856.

Petit, Norman. *The Heart Prepared: Grace and Conversion in Puritan Spiritual Life*. New Haven: Yale University Press, 1966.

Pope, Robert G. *The Half-Way Covenant: Church Membership in Puritan New England*. Princeton: Princeton University Press, 1969.

Rogers, P. G. *The Fifth Monarchy Men*. London: Oxford University Press, 1966.

Rosenmeier, Jesper. "New England's Perfection: The Image of Adam and the Image of Christ in the Antinomian Crisis, 1634–1638." *William and Mary Quarterly*, 3d Ser., vol. 27 (1970), 435–459.

Russell, John H. "A Cobbler at His Bench: John Russell of Woburn, Massachusetts." *New England Historical and Genealogical Register* 133 (1979), 125–33.

Rutman, Darrett. *Winthrop's Boston: A Portrait of a Puritan Town, 1630–1649*. 1965. Reprint. New York: W. W. Norton, 1972.

————. *American Puritanism: Faith and Practice*. Philadelphia: Lippincott, 1970.

Sanborn, V. C. "Stephen Bachiler and the Plough Company." Maine Historical Society, *Collections*, 3d Ser., vol. 2, 342–66. Portland, Maine, 1906.

Solt, Leo F. *Saints in Arms: Puritanism and Democracy in Cromwell's Army*. Stanford, Calif.: Stanford University Press, 1959.

Stearns, Raymond Phineas. *Hugh Peter: The Strenuous Puritan, 1598–1660*. Urbana: University of Illinois Press, 1954.

Stoever, William K. B. *"A Faire and Easie Way to Heaven": Covenant Theology and Antinomianism in Early Massachusetts*. Middletown, Conn.: Wesleyan University Press, 1978.

Thomas, Keith. *Religion and the Decline of Magic*. New York: Charles Scribner's Sons, 1971.

Tolmie, Murray. *The Triumph of the Saints: The Separate Churches of London, 1616–1649*. Cambridge, Eng.: Cambridge University Press, 1977.

Toon, Peter, ed. *Puritans, The Millennium and the Future of Israel: Puritan Eschatology 1600 to 1660*. Cambridge and London: Clarke and Company, 1970.

Wall, Jr., Robert Emmet. *Massachusetts Bay: The Crucial Decade, 1640–1650*. New Haven: Yale University Press, 1972.

White, B. R. *The English Separatist Tradition: From the Marian Martyrs to the Pilgrim Fathers*. London: Oxford University Press, 1971.

Whitley, W. T. *A History of the British Baptists*. London: Griffin, 1923.

Williams, George H. *The Radical Reformation*. London: Weidenfeld and Nicolson, 1962.

Ziff, Larzer. *Puritanism in America: New Culture in a New World*. New York: The Viking Press, 1973.

———. *The Career of John Cotton: Puritanism and the American Experience*. Princeton: Princeton University Press, 1962.

NOTES

Full bibliographic citations are provided at the first reference.

PROLOGUE   NEW ENGLAND PURITAN RADICALISM: AN OVERVIEW

1. James Kendall Hosmer, ed., *Winthrop's Journal, "History of New England, 1630–1649*," in the series Original Narratives of Early American History, 2 vols. (New York: Charles Scribner's Sons, 1908), 1:65, 67, hereafter cited as *Winthrop's Journal*. Also see V. C. Sanborn, "Stephen Bachiler and the Plough Company," Maine Historical Society, *Collections*, 3d. Ser., 2 (Portland, 1906), 342–369.

2. *Winthrop's Journal*, 1:65, 81, 169, 266; 2:45–46, 179, 221.

3. Most scholars have approached Puritan radicalism in New England through studies devoted wholly to one figure or movement and thus have not provided any systematic overview of the subject. See, for example, W. Clark Gilpin, *The Millenarian Piety of Roger Williams* (Chicago: University of Chicago Press, 1979); William K. B. Stoever, *"A Faire and Easie Way to Heaven": Covenant Theology and Antinomianism in Early Massachusetts* (Middletown, Conn.: Wesleyan University Press, 1978); and Emery Battis, *Saints and Sectaries: Anne Hutchinson and the Antinomian Controversy in the Massachusetts Bay Colony* (Chapel Hill: N.C.: University of North Carolina Press, 1962).

4. See especially Christopher Hill, *The World Turned Upside Down: Radical Ideas During the English Revolution* (1972; rpt., New York: The Viking Press, 1973) and *Milton and the English Revolution* (1977; rpt., New York: Penguin, 1979); and Keith Thomas, *Religion and the Decline of Magic* (New York: Charles Scribner's Sons, 1971). Important studies of individual groups or movements will be noted in future chapters.

5. Perry Miller, *The New England Mind: The Seventeenth Century* (New York: Macmillan, 1939), pp. 391, vii.

6. Miller, *The New England Mind: From Colony to Province* (Cambridge: Harvard University Press, 1953), p. ix.

7. Larzer Ziff, *Puritanism in America: New Culture in a New World* (New York: The Viking Press, 1973), pp. 70, 90; and Kai T. Erikson, *Wayward Puritans: A Study in the Sociology of Deviance* (New York: John Wiley, 1966), passim.

8. Darrett Rutman, *American Puritanism: Faith and Practice* (Philadelphia: Lippincott, 1970), p. 112.

9. Ibid., and Rutman, *Winthrop's Boston: A Portrait of a Puritan Town, 1630–1649* (1965; rpt., New York: W. W. Norton Company, 1972), p. 274.

10. Stoever, "*Faire and Easie Way*," p. 23.

11. Charles M. Andrews, *The Colonial Period of American History*, 4 vols. (New Haven, Conn.: Yale University Press, 1934–1938), 2:2; William Haller, *Liberty and Reformation in the Puritan Revolution* (1955; rpt., New York: Columbia University Press, 1967), p. 192.

12. See, for example, Stephen Foster, "New England and the Challenge of Heresy, 1630–1660: The Puritan Crisis in Transatlantic Perspective," *William and Mary Quarterly*, 3d Ser., 38 (1981), 626–628; and Patrick Collinson, *The Elizabethan Puritan Movement* (Berkeley and Los Angeles: University of California Press, 1967), pp. 372–381.

13. David Grayson Allen, *In English Ways: The Movement of Societies and the Transferal of English Local Law and Custom to Massachusetts Bay in the Seventeenth Century* (Chapel Hill, N.C.: University of North Carolina Press, 1981), passim; and T. H. Breen, "Persistent Localism: English Social Change and the Shaping of New England Institutions," in *Puritans and Adventurers: Change and Persistence in Early America* (New York: Oxford University Press, 1980), pp. 3–23.

14. See below, chap. 10, and pp. 118–120.

15. See below, chap. 11, and pp. 138–143.

16. See especially Stoever, "*Faire and Easie Way*," passim, but especially pp. 34–57, 161–183; Geoffrey Nuttall, *The Holy Spirit in Puritan Faith and Experience* (Oxford: Basil Blackwell, 1946), passim; James Fulton Maclear, "'The Heart of New England Rent': The Mystical Element in Early Puritan History," *Mississippi Valley Historical Review*, 42 (1956), 621–652, and "New England and the Fifth Monarchy: The Quest for the Millennium in Early American Puritanism," *William and Mary Quarterly*, 3d. Ser., 32 (1975), 223–260; and below, chap. 6.

17. Ziff, *Puritanism in America*, pp. 53–54, 75–79, 94–99, briefly discusses the social and political dimensions of New England Puritan radicalism. Battis, *Saints and Sectaries*, analyzes the psycho-social dimensions of the Antinomian Controversy. Robert Emmet Wall, Jr., *Massachusetts Bay: The Crucial Decade, 1640–1650* (New Haven, Conn.: Yale University Press, 1972), pp. 121–156, relates Gorton to the political pressures upon the colony.

18. Sacvan Bercovitch, *The American Jeremiad* (Madison, Wis.: University of Wisconsin Press, 1978), passim, but especially pp. xi–xv, 16–30.

19. Perry Miller, *Orthodoxy in Massachusetts, 1630–1650* (1933; rpt., New York: Harper and Row, 1970), passim; "The Marrow of Puritan Divinity," in *Errand into the Wilderness* (1956; rpt., New York: Harper and Row, 1964), pp. 48–98; and "Preparation for Salvation in Seventeenth-Century New England," in *Nature's Nation* (Cambridge: Harvard University Press, 1967), pp. 50–77; Edmund Morgan, *Visible Saints: The History of a Puritan Idea* (1963; rpt., Ithaca, N.Y.: Cornell

University Press, 1965), pp. 1−112; and Sacvan Bercovitch, *The Puritan Origins of the American Self* (New Haven, Conn.: Yale University Press, 1975), esp. pp. 35−108.

20. Bercovitch, *American Jeremiad*, pp. 3−30.

21. William Haller, ed., *Tracts on Liberty in the Puritan Revolution, 1638−1647*, 3 vols. (New York: Columbia University Press, 1934), 1:1.

22. J. Franklin Jameson, ed., [Edward] *Johnson's Wonder-Working Providence, 1628−1651*, Original Narratives of Early American History (New York: Charles Scribner's Sons, 1910), p. 25, hereafter cited as Johnson, *Wonder-Working Providence*.

23. [Thomas Goodwin], *A Glimpse of Syons Glory: or, The Churches Beautie . . .* (London, 1641), p. 17.

24. Johnson, *Wonder-Working Providence*, p. 49.

25. Harrison T. Meserole, ed., *Seventeenth-Century American Poetry* (Garden City, N.Y.: Doubleday, 1968), pp. 397−398; Allyn B. Forbes, et al., eds., *Winthrop Papers, 1498−1649*, 5 vols. (Boston: Massachusetts Historical Society, 1929−1947), 4:159−160; Joseph B. Felt, *The Ecclesiastical History of New England*, 2 vols. (Boston: Congregational Library Association, 1855−1862), 1:593; Massachusetts Historical Society, *Collections*, 4th Ser., 1 (Boston, 1852), 247−248; and Wilbur Cortez Abbott, ed., *The Writings and Speeches of Oliver Cromwell*, 4 vols. (Cambridge: Harvard University Press, 1934−1947), 2:482−483.

26. Edward T. Corwin, *Ecclesiastical Records of the State of New York*, 7 vols. (Albany, N.Y.: J. B. Lyon, 1901−1916), 1:399−400.

27. Quoted in Cotton Mather, *Magnalia Christi Americana* (London, 1702), Book III, p. 118.

28. Bercovitch, *American Jeremiad*, passim, and Robert Middlekauff, *The Mathers: Three Generations of Puritan Intellectuals, 1596−1728* (New York: Oxford University Press, 1971), esp. pp. 96−112.

29. Thomas Goodwin, *Works*, 12 vols. (Edinburgh: J. Nichol, 1861−1866), 4:237.

30. Roger Williams, *Complete Writings*, 7 vols. (New York: Russell and Russell, 1963), 1:35, marginal notation; Isaac Penington, *An Examination of the Grounds or Causes . . .* (London, 1660), p. 47; Peter Bulkeley, *The Gospel-Covenant; or The Covenant of Grace Opened* (London, 1646), p. 15; and Mather, *Magnalia*, Book III, p. 53.

31. See Murray Tolmie, *The Triumph of the Saints: The Separate Churches of London, 1616−1649* (Cambridge, Eng.: Cambridge University Press, 1977), esp. chap. 5.

32. Stephen Foster, *Their Solitary Way: The Puritan Social Ethic in the First Century of Settlement in New England* (New Haven, Conn.: Yale University Press, 1971), p. 161.

CHAPTER I   A NURSERY OF *SCHISMATICKES*

1. Thomas Shepard, *New Englands Lamentations for Old Englands Present Errours and Divisions* (London, 1645), pp. 1−2, 5.

2. Nathaniel Ward, *The Simple Cobler of Aggawam in America*, ed. P. M. Zall (Lincoln, Neb.: University of Nebraska Press, 1969), pp. 5−6.

3. See below, pp. 195–196.

4. Chapter 4 below, passim.

5. Wall, _Massachusetts Bay_, pp. 157–224; Ward, _Simple Cobler_, p. 6.

6. Stoever, "_Faire and Easie Way_," p. 22.

7. Henry Ainsworth, _The Communion of Saints_ ([Amsterdam], 1607), p. 319.

8. William Bradford, _Of Plymouth Plantation, 1620–1647_, ed. Samuel Eliot Morison (New York: Alfred A. Knopf, 1953), pp. 146–169, 222–223, 292–293.

9. _Winthrop Papers_, 3:111.

10. John Clarke, _Ill Newes from New-England_ (1652), rpt. in Massachusetts Historical Society, _Collections_, 4th Ser., 2 (Boston, 1854), 23.

11. _Winthrop Papers_, 4:159; Bulkeley, _Gospel-Covenant_, p. 104.

12. See pp. 278–282 below.

13. _Winthrop Papers_, 4:456; Samuel Gorton, _Simplicities Defence against Seven-Headed Policy_ . . . (1646), in Rhode Island Historical Society, _Collections_, 2 (Providence, 1835), 147.

14. Nathaniel B. Shurtleff and David Pulsifer, eds., _Records of the Colony of New Plymouth, in New England_, 12 vols. (Boston: W. White, 1855–61), 1:92; hereafter cited as _Plymouth Colony Records._

15. Charles Chauncy, _Gods Mercy_ . . . (Cambridge, Massachusetts Bay Colony, 1655), p. 19.

16. Jeannine Hensley, ed., _The Works of Anne Bradstreet_ (Cambridge: Harvard University Press, 1967), p. 244.

17. Thomas Shepard, _Works_, ed. John Albro, 3 vols. (1853; rpt., New York: AMS Press, 1967), 2:513.

18. Robert Cushman, "Reasons and Considerations touching the lawfulness of removing out of England into the parts of America," in Dwight B. Heath, ed., _A Journal of the Pilgrims at Plymouth: Mourt's Relation_ (New York: Corinth Books, 1963), p. 94. Also see John White, _The Planters Plea_ (1630; rpt., Rockport, Mass.: The Sandy Bay Historical Society and Museum, 1930), pp. 17–20.

19. Cushman, "Reasons and Considerations," pp. 94–95; Hill, _World Turned Upside Down_, pp. 16–17, and chap. 3; and _Society and Puritanism in Pre-Revolutionary England_ (1964; 2d ed., New York: Schocken Books, 1967), chap. 7; Carl Bridenbaugh, _Vexed and Troubled Englishmen, 1590–1642_ (New York: Oxford University Press, 1968), passim; and M. M. Knappen, _Tudor Puritanism: A Chapter in the History of Idealism_ (1939; rpt., Chicago: University of Chicago Press, 1970), chap. 22.

20. Cushman, "Reasons and Considerations," p. 96.

21. White, _Planters Plea_, pp. 49, 65–66; Thomas Edwards, _Antapologia_ (London, 1646), p. 34.

22. Thomas Dudley, "Letter to the Countess of Lincoln," in Alexander Young, ed. _Chronicles of the First Planters of the Colony of Massachusetts Bay_ (Boston: Little and Brown, 1846), pp. 315, 324–25, 331.

23. Ibid., pp. 324–25.

24. _Winthrop Papers_, 2:303; 3:216, 112; _The Hutchinson Papers_, 2 vols., Publications of the Prince Society (Albany, N.Y.: For the Society, 1865), 1:62. John White, quoted in Miller, _Orthodoxy in Massachusetts_, p. 220.

25. William Hubbard, _A General History of New England, from the Discovery to MDCLXXX_ (Cambridge: Massachusetts Historical Society, 1815), pp. 181–82.

26. John Cotton, *Answer to Williams*, in Williams, *Complete Writings*, 2:14–15.

27. The best introduction to Puritan radicalism in this period remains Hill, *World Turned Upside Down*, but also see A. L. Morton, *The World of the Ranters: Religious Radicalism in the English Revolution* (London: Lawrence and Wishart, 1970); Leo F. Solt, *Saints in Arms: Puritanism and Democracy in Cromwell's Army* (Stanford, Calif.: Stanford University Press, 1959); William M. Lamont, *Godly Rule: Politics and Religion, 1603–60* (London: Macmillan, 1969), esp. pp. 106–62; and Nuttall, *Holy Spirit*.

28. Battis, *Saints and Sectaries*, pp. 254–55.

29. Lyle Koehler, *A Search for Power: The "Weaker Sex" in Seventeenth-Century New England* (Urbana, Ill.: University of Illinois Press, 1980), p. 216.

30. Morton, *World of the Ranters*, p. 16.

31. William Haller and Godfrey Davies, eds., *The Leveller Tracts, 1647–1653* (New York: Columbia University Press, 1944), p. 38.

32. Background material to each of these categories of Puritan radicalism will be found below, in the chapters on each.

CHAPTER 2   SEPARATISM: THE DEVIL'S *ALPHA* AND *OMEGA*

1. [Anonymous], *A Blow at the Root, Or some Observations towards a Discovery of the Subtilties and Devices of Satan* (London, 1650), pp. 151–52.

2. See Morgan, *Visible Saints*, pp. 1–33, for a good discussion of Browne and other early separatists. Also B. R. White, *The English Separatist Tradition: From the Marian Martyrs to the Pilgrim Fathers* (London: Oxford University Press, 1971), pp. 44–66; Champlin Burrage, *The Early English Dissenters in the Light of Recent Research*, 2 vols. (Cambridge: Cambridge University Press, 1912), 1:94–116; and Henry Martyn Dexter, *The Congregationalism of the Last Three Hundred Years as Seen in its Literature* (New York: Harper: 1880), pp. 61–128.

3. William Haller, *The Rise of Puritanism* (New York: Columbia University Press, 1938), pp. 183–90; White, *English Separatist Tradition*, pp. 91–115; and Burrage, *Early English Dissenters*, 1:136–82.

4. Morgan, *Visible Saints*, p. 25.

5. Dexter, *Congregationalism*, pp. 225–412 passim; White, *English Separatist Tradition*, pp. 142–59; Morgan, *Visible Saints*, pp. 1–63; and Miller, *Orthodoxy in Massachusetts*, pp. 53–101.

6. George D. Langdon, *Pilgrim Colony: A History of New Plymouth, 1620–1691* (New Haven, Conn.: Yale University Press, 1966), pp. 100–105; and Miller, *Orthodoxy in Massachusetts*, pp. 73–101 passim.

7. Ibid., pp. 81–82, 86.

8. Langdon, *Pilgrim Colony*, p. 105.

9. *Plymouth Church Records*, 2 vols. (New York: The New England Society, 1920), 1:115–16, 140; Langdon, *Pilgrim Colony*, pp. 105–06.

10. Tolmie, *Triumph of the Saints*, pp. 7–11; Miller, *Orthodoxy in Massachusetts*, pp. 75–82; and Morgan, *Visible Saints*, pp. 78–79.

11. Tolmie, *Triumph of the Saints*, p. 11.

12. Gilpin, *Roger Williams*, pp. 30–38.

13. Richard P. Gildrie, *Salem, Massachusetts, 1623–1683: A Covenant Community* (Charlottesville: University Press of Virginia, 1975), pp. 8–9; Morgan, *Visible*

Saints, pp. 85–86; David D. Hall, "John Cotton's Letter to Samuel Skelton," *William and Mary Quarterly*, 3d Ser., 22 (1965), 482–85.

14. Hall, "John Cotton's Letter," pp. 481–82. The controversy over Cotton's remarks can be traced in the following: Burrage, *Early English Dissenters*, pp. 133–34; Miller, *Orthodoxy in Massachusetts*, pp. 127–43; Larzer Ziff, "The Salem Puritans in the 'Free Aire of a New World,'" *Huntington Library Quarterly*, 20 (1956–57), 373–84, and *The Career of John Cotton: Puritanism and the American Experience* (Princeton, N.J.: Princeton University Press, 1962), pp. 78–79; David D. Hall, *The Faithful Shepherd: A History of the New England Ministry in the Seventeenth Century* (1972; rpt. New York: W. W. Norton, 1974), pp. 78–86; Langdon, *Pilgrim Colony*, pp. 107–114; Lewis J. Robinson, "The Formative Influence of Plymouth Church on American Congregationalism, *Bibliotheca Sacra*, 127 (1970), 232–40; and Sladen Yarborough, "The Influence of Plymouth Colony Separatism on Salem: An Interpretation of John Cotton's Letter of 1630 to Samuel Skelton," *Church History*, 51 (1982), 290–303. Also see Hall, "John Cotton's Letter," passim.

15. Tolmie, *Triumph of the Saints*, pp. 16–18.

16. Ibid., p. 13; Winthrop, *Journal*, 1:66, 71; Hubbard, *General History*, p. 187; Henry Wilder Foote, "George Phillips, First Minister of Watertown," Massachusetts Historical Society, *Proceedings*, 63 (1931), 211–13.

17. *Plymouth Church Records*, 1:64; Tolmie, *Triumph of the Saints*, p. 13. Lynell may have been the member of Lathrop's congregation whom Skelton allowed to take the Lord's Supper in Salem in 1630.

18. Tolmie, *Triumph of the Saints*, pp. 16–18; Winthrop, *Journal*, 1:134, 136; Felt, *Ecclesiastical History*, 1:99; Samuel Deane, *History of Scituate, Massachusetts, From Its First Settlement to 1831* (Boston: James Loring, 1831), pp. 59–60.

19. Deane, *History of Scituate*, pp. 59–70.

20. Tolmie, *Triumph of the Saints*, pp. 15–34.

21. Gildrie, *Salem*, pp. 24–32, 35–37.

22. Gilpin, *Roger Williams*, pp. 34–35; Winthrop, *Journal*, 1:61–62; Williams, *Complete Writings*, 6:356.

23. Nathaniel Morton, *New Englands Memoriall* (Cambridge, Massachusetts Bay Colony, 1669), p. 78; Bradford, *Of Plymouth Plantation*, p. 257.

24. Winthrop, *Journal*, 1:112–113, 120; Hubbard, *General History*, pp. 204–205; Miller, *Orthodoxy in Massachusetts*, p. 58.

25. Winthrop, *Journal*, 1:116–117, 137.

26. Ibid., 1:154; Cotton, *Answer to Williams*, in Williams, *Complete Writings*, 2:13–14.

27. Gilpin, *Roger Williams*, pp. 50–62 passim.

28. Winthrop, *Journal*, 1:168, 175; Gildrey, *Salem*, pp. 51–54; Felt, *Ecclesiastical History*, 1:243; Koehler, *Search for Power*, p. 217.

29. Gorton, *Simplicities Defence*, p. 113, note 1; Edwin S. Gaustad, *Baptist Piety: The Last Will & Testament of Obadiah Holmes* (Grand Rapids, Mich.: Christian University Press, 1978), pp. 51–52; Felt, *Ecclesiastical History*, 1:360–361.

30. Felt, *Ecclesiastical History*, 1:159, 161, 209, 238; Winthrop, *Journal*, 1:148; 2:45ff., 179ff.; Sanborn, "Stephen Bachiler," pp. 363–366; Alonzo Lewis, *The History of Lynn* (Boston: J. H. Eastburn, 1829), pp. 51–57; Joseph Dow, *History*

of the Town of Hampton, New Hampshire, 2 vols. (Salem, Mass.: Salem Press Publishing and Printing Company, 1893), pp. 343–348; *Winthrop Papers*, 4:447–449.

31. Winthrop, *Journal*, 1:83, 160.

32. Tolmie, *Triumph of the Saints*, p. 43.

33. See, for example, Thomas Lechford, *Plain Dealing: or, News from New-England* (1642; rpt., Boston: J. K. Wiggin & Wm. Parsons Lunt, 1863), pp. 12–58; White, *Planters Plea*, pp. 59–69.

34. Giles Firmin, *Separation Examined* (London, 1652), sig. B4ᵛ.

35. See below, p. 219ff.

36. Dudley, "Letter to the Countess of Lincoln," in Young, *First Planters*, p. 331; *Winthrop Papers*, 3:54–55, 397–402; Williams, *Cotton's Letter . . . Examined* (1644), in *Complete Writings*, 1:109–110.

37. See, for example, Tolmie, *Triumph of the Saints*, p. 42ff.

38. Williams, *Cotton's Letter . . . Examined*, in *Complete Writings*, 1:112.

39. *Winthrop Papers*, 3:54–55.

40. Robert Baillie, *Anabaptism, The True Fountaine of Independency* (London, 1647), pp. 51, 65.

CHAPTER 3   RADICAL SPIRITISM: SWEET SUGAR–CANDY RELIGION

1. Foster, "New England and the Challenge of Heresy," p. 642.

2. Stoever, *"Faire and Easie Way,"* pp. 10, 18; Peter Sterry, *The Spirits Conviction of Sinne* (London, 1645), p. 26.

3. Ward, *Simple Cobler*, p. 20.

4. *Winthrop Papers*, 3:335.

5. *Memoirs of Roger Clap* (1731; rpt. Boston: David Clapp, 1854), p. 33; Johnson, *Wonder-Working Providence*, pp. 134–135; Thomas Weld, preface to John Winthrop, *A Short Story of the Rise, reign, and ruine of the Antinomians, Familists, & Libertines* (1644), in David D. Hall, ed., *The Antinomian Controversy, 1636–1638: A Documentary History* (Middletown, Conn.: Wesleyan University Press, 1968), pp. 201–202, 208.

6. Giles Firmin, *A Brief Review of Mr. Davis's Vindication . . .* (London, 1693), sig. A2ʳ. The phrase "faire and easie way to Heaven" is found in Weld's preface to Winthrop, *Short Story*, in Hall, ed. *Antinomian Controversy*, p. 203.

7. Stoever, *"Faire and Easie Way,"* p. 181.

8. Shepard, *Works*, 2:377; Weld, preface to Winthrop, *Short Story*, in Hall, ed., *Antinomian Controversy*, p. 204; Richard Mather, *The Summe of Certain Sermons* (Cambridge, Massachusetts Bay Colony, 1652), sig. A5ʳ; Stephen Geree, *The Doctrine of the Antinomians . . . Confuted* (London, 1644), p. 136; at p. 35 Geree calls spiritism a "sweete sugar–candy Religion."

9. Hall, *Faithful Shepherd*, p. 118.

10. See, for example, Hill, *World Turned Upside Down*, pp. 21–23; and Foster, "New England and the Challenge of Heresy," pp. 631–637.

11. J. W. Martin, "Elizabethan Familists and English Separatism," *Journal of British Studies*, 20 (1980–1981), 53–73; Felicity Heal, "The Family of Love and the Diocese of Ely," in Derek Baker, ed., *Schism, Heresy, and Religious Protest*, in the series Studies in Church History (Cambridge, Eng.: Cambridge University

Press, 1972), pp. 213–222; Jean Dietz Moss, "Variations on a Theme: The Family of Love in Renaissance England," *Renaissance Quarterly*, 36 (1978), 186–195; Hill, *World Turned Upside Down*, pp. 22–24; and Alastair Hamilton, *The Family of Love* (Cambridge, Eng.: J. Clarke, 1981).

12. Stephen Denison, *The White Wolfe . . .* (London, 1627), p. 39; Ephraim Pagitt, *Heresiography* (1645; 5th ed., London, 1654), pp. 87–88. Also see Rufus M. Jones, *Mysticism and Democracy in the English Commonwealth* (Cambridge, Mass.: Harvard University Press, 1932), chaps. 3–4; Ronald A. Marchant, *The Puritans and the Church Courts in the Diocese of York, 1560–1642* (London: Longmans, 1960), pp. 40–41; and Hill, *World Turned Upside Down*, pp. 65–68.

13. Geree, *Antinomians*, p. 46; also see p. 48.

14. Winthrop, *Journal*, 1:219; Felt, *Ecclesiastical History*, 1:288; Thomas Shepard, "Autobiography," in Michael McGiffert, ed., *God's Plot: The Paradoxes of Puritan Piety, Being the Autobiography and Journal of Thomas Shepard* (Amherst, Mass.: University of Massachusetts Press, 1972), pp. 42–43. Also see Hubbard, *General History*, p. 346. Both titles mentioned by Shepard are by Richard Rogers, preacher at Wethersfield, Essex. *Seven Treatises* was published in 1603; *The Practice of Christianity* (1618) is a shorter version of the same work.

15. Foster, "New England and the Challenge of Heresy," pp. 632–636; Stoever, "*Faire* and *Easie Way*," pp. 138–160; Gertrude Huehns, *Antinomianism in English History, With Special Reference to the Period 1640–1660* (London: The Cresset Press, 1951), chaps. 3–4 passim.

16. Geree, *Antinomians*, pp. 46, 48.

17. Foster, "New England and the Challenge of Heresy," p. 634.

18. See below, pp. 171–179; and letter of Cotton to Shepard, c. 1636, in Hall, ed., *Antinomian Controversy*, p. 32. Also, George Selement, "John Cotton's Hidden Antinomianism: His Sermon on Rev. 4:1–2," *New England Historical and Genealogical Register*, 129 (1975), 278–283.

19. Edward Norris, *The New Gospel, not the True Gospel* (London, 1638), pp. 1–2, 5–6, 12. Also see *Winthrop Papers*, 4:456; and Gildrie, *Salem*, pp. 79–80.

20. "The Examination of Mrs. Anne Hutchinson at the Court at Newtown," in Hall, ed., *Antinomian Controversy*, p. 314. Also see above, "Introduction," note 12; and Winthrop, *Short Story*, in Hall, ed., *Antinomian Controversy*, p. 207.

21. *Plymouth Records*, 1:105; Samuel Gorton to Nathaniel Morton, 30 June 1669, in Peter Force, ed., *Tracts and Other Papers . . .* , 4 vols. (Washington, D.C.: Force, 1836–1846), 4, no. 7; Morton, *New Englands Memoriall*, p. 108.

22. Richard Vines, *The Impostures of Seducing Teachers Discovered* (London, 1644), p. 11.

23. John Woodbridge, Jr., to Richard Baxter, 31 March 1671, in Raymond Phineas Stearns, "Correspondence of John Woodbridge, Jr., and Richard Baxter," *New England Quarterly*, 10 (1937), 572–573.

24. Mather, *Magnalia*, Book VII, p. 14, quoting Weld; Giles Firmin, *Stablishing against Shaking* (London, 1655), p. 35; Samuel Gorton, *An Antidote against the Common Plague of the World* (London, 1657), sig. F2ʳ; and *An Incorruptible Key, composed of the CX. Psalme* (London, 1657), part 2, p. 25. Hubbard (*General History*, p. 303) reported that one of the Hutchinsonians so stubbornly maintained that "Christ and the new creature were all one" that it called to mind a Catholic

who was "heard to say, he not only believed Christ was really present in the sacrament, but that he was there booted and spurred, as he rode to Jerusalem."

25. For good discussions of this complex issue see Stoever, *"Faire and Easie Way,"* passim, but especially chaps. 3–6; Norman Pettit, *The Heart Prepared: Grace and Conversion in Puritan Spiritual Life* (New Haven, Conn.: Yale University Press, 1966), pp. 1–21, 125–157; and Miller, *The New England Mind*, pp. 25–28.

26. Winthrop, *Short Story*, in Hall, ed., *Antinomian Controversy*, p. 259; Battis, *Saints and Sectaries*, p. 68; and Felt, *Ecclesiastical History*, 1:320. John Wheelwright, "A Fast-Day Sermon," in Hall, ed., *Antinomian Controversy*, p. 161.

27. Winthrop, *Journal*, 1:209–210, 230; other such incidents are reported elsewhere in the *Journal*, 1:282–283, 2:60–61, and in *Winthrop Papers*, 5:14.

28. "Examination of Hutchinson at Newtown," in Hall, ed., *Antinomian Controversy*, pp. 337–342; Winthrop, *Journal*, 1:297.

29. Shepard to Cotton, c. 1636, in Hall, ed., *Antinomian Controversy*, p. 28; Holden to Massachusetts General Court, 15 September 1643, in Gorton, *Simplicities Defence*, p. 269; Johnson, *Wonder-Working Providence*, p. 129; Gorton, *Saltmarsh Returned from the Dead . . .* (London, 1655), sig. a1ʳ.

30. See Morton, *World of the Ranters*, chap. 4 passim; Hill, *World Turned Upside Down*, chaps. 9–10 passim, but especially pp. 163–168; and Norman Cohn, "The 'Free Spirit' in Cromwell's England: The Ranters and Their Literature," in *The Pursuit of the Millennium: Revolutionary Messianism in Medieval and Reformation Europe and Its Bearing on Modern Totalitarian Movements* (1957; 2d ed., New York: Harper and Row, 1961), pp. 321, 380. [John Reading], *The Ranters Ranting* (London, 1650), pp. 1–2.

31. Winthrop, *Journal*, 1:284; Hubbard, *General History*, p. 337; Felt, *Ecclesiastical History* 1:341; Gaustad, *Baptist Piety*, p. 60.

32. Gorton, *Incorruptible Key*, part 2, pp. 111, 119; Joseph Salmon, *A Rout, A Rout* (London, 1649), quoted in Nuttall, *Holy Spirit*, p. 105. Compare to John Saltmarsh, *Sparkles of Glory* (London, 1647), pp. 49–53.

33. John Josselyn, quoted in Carl Bridenbaugh, *Fat Mutton and Liberty of Conscience: Society in Rhode Island, 1636–1690* (Providence, R.I.: Brown University Press, 1974), p. 3. Winthrop, *Journal*, 1:177; Shepard to Mather, c. 1636, in Shepard, *Works*, 1:cxxviii.

34. Winthrop, *Journal*, 1:187, 2:22–23.

35. Ibid., 1:292; Hubbard, *General History*, pp. 275–276; Felt, *Ecclesiastical History*, 1:373; John Callender, *Historical Discourse on the Civil and Religious Affairs of the Colony of Rhode-Island* (1739), in Rhode Island Historical Society, *Collections*, 4 (Providence, 1838), 116. Also see J. Hammond Trumbull, ed., "Conference of the Elders of Massachusetts With the Reverend Robert Lenthall, of Weymouth, Held at Dorchester, Feb. 10, 1639," *Congregational Quarterly*, 19 (1877), 239.

36. Felt, *Ecclesiastical History*, 1:342; Raymond Phineas Stearns, *Hugh Peter: The Strenuous Puritan, 1598–1660* (Urbana, Ill.: University of Illinois Press, 1954), pp. 146–147; Winthrop, *Journal* 1:294, 309.

37. *Winthrop Papers*, 4:317–319; Tolmie, *Triumph of the Saints*, pp. 49, 55–57; Thomas Edwards, *Gangraena: or A Catalogue and Discovery of many of the Errours . . . of this Time* (London, 1646), pp. 97–98, reported on Knollys's activities in Suffolk. Hubbard, *General History*, p. 357, claimed that John Bastwick "once not

untruly styled" Knollys, "with a little varietie of the letters of his name, Absurdo Knowless."

38. Deloraine Pendre Corey, *The History of Malden, Massachusetts, 1633–1785* (Malden: The Author, 1899), pp. 132–150; Felt, *Ecclesiastical History*, 2:42–43; Massachusetts Historical Society, *Collections*, 3d Ser., 1 (1825; rpt., Boston, 1846), 29–32.

39. Johnson, *Wonder-Working Providence*, p. 192; John Wheelwright, *Mercurius Americanus* (1645) in *John Wheelwright*, Publications of the Prince Society, IX (Boston: Prince Society, 1876), 194–195; *Records of the Governor and Company of the Massachusetts Bay in New England*, ed. Nathaniel Shurtleff, 5 vols. (Boston: W. White, 1853–1854), 1:189, hereafter cited as *Massachusetts Records*; Felt, *Ecclesiastical History*, 1:361, 465–466; Winthrop, *Journal*, 2:7–8.

40. Shepard, *Works*, 3:339; Hill, *World Turned Upside Down*, chap. 2.

41. Winthrop, *Short Story*, in Hall, ed., *Antinomian Controversy*, p. 233.

42. *Massachusetts Records*, 1:252, 336; Weld, preface to Winthrop, *Short Story*, in Hall, ed., *Antinomian Controversy*, p. 209.

43. Gildrie, *Salem*, p. 77; Felt, *Ecclesiastical History*, 1:531, 2:16, 62; Sumner Chilton Powell, *Puritan Village: The Formation of a Puritan Town* (Middletown, Conn.: Wesleyan University Press, 1963), p. 127; Langdon, *Pilgrim Colony*, p. 61; Henry Whitefield, "The Light appearing more and more towards the perfect Day, Or, A farther Discovery of the present state of the Indians in New England (1651)," in Massachusetts Historical Society, *Collections*, 3d Ser., 4 (Boston, 1834), 135–137.

44. Gorton, *An Antidote*, sig. G4ᵛ and p. 27; and "Letter to Morton," in Force, *Tracts*, 4, No. 7, p. 14.

45. Firmin, *Separation Examined*, pp. 6–7; Edward Winslow, *Hypocrisie Unmasked . . .* (1646; rpt., Providence, R.I.: Club for Colonial Reprints, 1916), p. 7.

46. Firmin, *A Brief Review*, pp. 31–32; Edwards, *Gangraena*, 2d pagination, pp. 16–17.

47. Johnson, *Wonder-Working Providence*, p. 173. On Dell see, for example, George Arthur Johnson, "From Seeker to Finder: A Study in Seventeenth-Century English Spiritualism Before the Quakers," *Church History* 17 (1948), pp. 299–315; and Nuttall, *The Holy Spirit in Puritan Faith and Experience*, passim.

48. Williams, *Complete Writings*, 6:286; Chauncy, *Gods Mercy*, pp. 16–17, 41.

49. Gorton, *An Antidote*, sig. E3ᵛ; *Incorruptible Key*, pp.3–4.

50. Winthrop, *Journal*, 2:39; Felt, *Ecclesiastical History*, 1:460–461, 2:46, 149; Winslow, *Hypocrisie Unmasked*, p. 5; Koehler, *Search for Power*, p. 242; Henry Whitefield, "Strength Out of Weakness (1652)," in Massachusetts Historical Society, *Collections*, 3d Ser., 4 (Boston, 1834), pp. 180–183; *Plymouth Records*, 3:74.

51. David Laing, ed., *The Letters and Journals of Robert Baillie*, 3 vols. (Edinburgh: Bannatyne Club, 1841–1842), 2:211–212.

52. Thomas Edwards, *The Second Part of Gangraena* (London, 1646), pp. 13–14; *Letters and Journals of Baillie*, 2:191; *Answer to Williams*, in Williams, *Complete Writings*, 2:11; Gilpin, *Roger Williams*, chap. 3; Morton, *New Englands Memoriall*, pp. 80–81.

53. Cotton, *Answer to Williams*, in Williams, *Complete Writings*, 2:19; Hill, *World Turned Upside Down*, pp. 148–163.

54. Winslow, *Hypocrisie Unmasked*, p. 7; Winthrop, *Journal*, 1:309.

55. Ward, *Simple Cobler*, p. 20.

56. Edwards, *Second Part of Gangraena*, p. 14; Johnson, "Seeker to Finder," passim.

57. Baillie, *Anabaptism*, p. 79; and *A Dissuasive from the Errours of the Time* (London, 1647), p. 150.

58. Whitefield, "A Farther Discovery," p. 137; Gorton, *An Antidote*, p. 17; and *Incorruptible Key*, sig. C1$^{r + v}$.

59. White, *Planters Plea*, pp. 19, 35.

60. Winthrop, *Short Story*, in Hall, ed., *Antinomian Controversy*, p. 239.

61. Ibid., p. 262; Battis, *Saints and Sectaries*, pp. 249–285, especially p. 262; and Rutman, *Winthrop's Boston*, pp. 125–126.

62. *Winthrop Papers*, 4:267; Robert C. Winthrop, *Life and Letters of John Winthrop*, 2 vols. (Boston: Ticknor and Fields, 1864–1867), 2:430.

63. Shepard, *Works*, 3:332, 341, 350. Shepard implored his readers to "maintain in the heart a holy fear of abusing liberty, every one in his place." "Know it assuredly," he wrote at the same time, "It is service and subjection which the Lord aims at, and which the Lord looks for" (Ibid., 3:351, 353). Also see 2:441.

64. Howard M. Chapin, *Documentary History of Rhode Island*, 2 vols. (Providence, R.I.: Preston and Rounds, 1916), 2:142; Winslow, *Hypocrisie Unmasked*, pp. 38–46; Gorton, *Simplicities Defence*, p. 239.

65. Winslow, *Hypocrisie Unmasked*, pp. 43–45.

66. Ibid., pp. 32, 44. See p. 298 below for Winslow's republication of *Hypocrisie Unmasked* under a different title, aimed against the Levellers.

67. Ibid., p. 47; Shepard, *Works*, 2:441; 3:347; Baillie, *Dissuasive*, pp. 116, 145.

68. On the Levellers see H. N. Brailsford, *The Levellers and the English Revolution* (Stanford, Calif.: Stanford University Press, 1961); Joseph Frank, *The Levellers; A History of the Writings of Three Seventeenth-Century Social Democrats: John Lilburne, Richard Overton, and William Walwyn* (1955; rpt., New York: Russell and Russell, 1969); and G. E. Aylmer, ed., *The Levellers in the English Revolution* (Ithaca, N.Y.: Cornell University Press, 1975). On the Diggers see George H. Sabine, "Introduction," *The Works of Gerrard Winstanley* (Ithaca, N.Y.: Cornell University Press, 1941), and Hill, *World Turned Upside Down*, pp. 86–106; *Winthrop Papers*, 5:212–213; Williams to John Winthrop the Younger, 10 December 1649, in Williams, *Complete Writings*, 6:189.

69. Bulkeley to Cotton, 4 April 1650, in Lemuel Shattuck, *A History of the Town of Concord; Middlesex County, Massachusetts, from its earliest settlement to 1832* (Boston: Russell, Ordione and Company; Concord: J. Stacy, 1835), pp. 155–156.

70. Hill, *World Turned Upside Down*, pp. 130–136; Morton, *World of the Ranters*, pp. 77–82 and passim; Cohn, *Pursuit of the Millennium*, pp. 321–378 passim.

71. Stoever, *"Faire and Easie Way,"* p. 158, and chap. 8 passim; also Hill, *World Turned Upside Down*, chap. 8. On Lamb and Denne see W. T. Whitley, *A History of the British Baptists* (London: Griffin, 1923), pp. 36, 38, 68–70; Robert Barclay, *The Inner Life of the Religious Societies of the Commonwealth* (London: Hodder and Stoughton, 1876), pp. 157, 160–164, 289; Rufus M. Jones, *Studies in Mystical Religion* (London: Macmillan, 1923), pp. 421–423; and Thomas Crosby, *The History of the English Baptists*, 4 vols. (London, 1738), 1:305.

72. Shepard, *Works*, 3:111; Massachusetts Historical Society, *Collections*, 3d

Ser., 1 (1825; rpt., Boston, 1846), p. 31; Bulkeley, *Gospel-Covenant*, pp. 378–379.

73. Shepard, *Works*, 3:90–91; Winthrop, *Journal*, 2:17; Hubbard, *General History*, p. 277; *Massachusetts Records*, 1:312.

74. Gorton, *An Antidote*, sig. C4ᵛ; on Winstanley see Hill, *World Turned Upside Down*, chap. 7 passim; Sabine, *Works of Winstanley*, "Introduction" and p. 530; and Brailsford, *Levellers*, pp. 658–670. Also see Leonard W. Levy, *Treason against God: A History of the Offense of Blasphemy* (New York: Schocken Books, 1981), p. 231ff.

75. Winslow, *Hypocrisie Unmasked*, p. 58; Hill, *World Turned Upside Down*, chap. 7 passim; Sabine, *Works of Winstanley*, "Introduction."

76. Koehler, *Search for Power*, p. 333, note 65, quoting from Dexter's letter to Vane, 27 August 1654; Winslow, *Hypocrisie Unmasked*, p. 61.

77. Mather, *Magnalia*, Book VII, p. 20; Koehler, *Search for Power*, pp. 322–323, note 65, quoting from Essex Court Records, 1:210–212. "Gingoes" refers to the gingko or maidenhair tree; hence, in the colloquial, its sexual connotation.

78. Morton, *New Englands Memoriall*, pp. 108, 110; Gorton, *Simplicities Defence*, pp. 86–87, note 1.

79. On Winstanley, see note 74 above; on Walwyn, see Morton, *World of the Ranters*, pp. 143–196; Hill, *World Turned Upside Down*, pp. 136–145.

80. Whitefield, "A Farther Discovery," p. 136; cf. Walwyn, quoted in Haller and Davies, *Leveller Tracts*, pp. 296–297.

81. Gorton, *Saltmarsh*, sig. 23ᵛ.

82. Morton, *New Englands Memoriall*, p. 110.

83. Winthrop, *Journal*, 1:275, 277, 281; 2:12. Also Thomas Edwards, *The Third Part of Gangraena* (London, 1646), pp. 187–188, where the author claims that he can tell "of rapes and forcing young maidens too young for the company of men, of which I could tell some sad stories of Independents in *New-England* in this kind, and upon whose daughters; but I forbeare out of my respect to the Parents."

84. See Norman T. Burns, *Christian Mortalism from Tyndale to Milton* (Cambridge: Harvard University Press, 1972), passim; and J. F. Maclear, "Anne Hutchinson and the Mortalist Heresy," *New England Quarterly*, 54 (1981), 74–103, especially 98–100.

85. Winthrop, *Journal*, 1:259.

86. "A Report of the Trial of Mrs. Anne Hutchinson before the Church in Boston," in Hall, ed., *Antinomian Controversy*, pp. 351–352, 355, 357, 358.

87. Maclear, "Mortalist Heresy," p. 99. It should be noted that the mortality of the soul was a frequently debated topic at Thomas Lamb's church in London, where Gorton preached in the mid-1640s. See Edwards, *The Second Part of Gangraena*, pp. 17–18.

88. "Trial of Hutchinson," in Hall, ed., *Antinomian Controversy*, pp. 371–372.

CHAPTER 4   THE QUICKSANDS OF ANABAPTISTRY: GENERAL AND
PARTICULAR BAPTISTS

1. Johnson, *Wonder-Working Providence*, pp. 31, 132; Daniel Featley, *The Dippers Dipt, or The Anabaptists Ducked and Plung'd Over Head and Eares* (3d. ed., London, 1645), sig. B2ʳ.

2. See below pp. 98–100, and William McLoughlin, *New England Dissent, 1630–1833: The Baptists and the Separation of Church and State,* 2 vols. (Cambridge: Harvard University Press, 1971), 1:6.

3. See, for example, Tolmie, *Triumph of the Saints,* pp. 50–52, and McLoughlin, *New England Dissent,* 1:3–9.

4. Tolmie, *Triumph of the Saints,* p. 51.

5. McLoughlin, *New England Dissent,* 1:29.

6. Winthrop, *Journal,* 1:297; Gorton, *Simplicities Defence,* p. 113; Koehler, *Search for Power,* p. 324; Gildrie, *Salem,* p. 79; Tolmie, *Triumph of the Saints,* pp. 51–52.

7. See above, p. 74; Baillie, *Anabaptism,* pp. 96–97.

8. Thomas Shepard, "To the Reader," in George Phillips, *A Reply to a Confutation of some grounds for baptisme . . . put forth against mee by one Thomas Lamb* (London, 1645), sig. B1ᵛ; McLoughlin, *New England Dissent,* 1:28,30.

9. Edward Barber, *The Anabaptists Catechisme* (London, 1645), pp. 4–6; Hill, *World Turned Upside Down,* pp. 84–85.

10. Nuttall, *Holy Spirit,* p. 13; also see p. 122 and Peter Oliver, *The Puritan Commonwealth* (Boston: Little and Brown, 1856), p. 219; Hill, *World Turned Upside Down,* pp. 153, 193.

11. Tolmie, *Triumph of the Saints,* pp. 69–70; Whitley, *A History of the British Baptists,* pp. 20–28.

12. Tolmie, *Triumph of the Saints,* pp. 69–70; McLoughlin, *New England Dissent,* 1:5; Whitley, *British Baptists,* pp. 28–35, 40–45.

13. Tolmie, *Triumph of the Saints,* pp. 70–71.

14. Denison, *The White Wolfe,* pp. 37–38.

15. Gilpin, *Roger Williams,* pp. 52–53; Tolmie, *Triumph of the Saints,* pp. 72–73; Burns, *Christian Mortalism,* p. 91; Barclay, *Inner Life,* p. 222.

16. Tolmie, *Triumph of the Saints,* pp. 27, 34–40, 43–45; McLoughlin, *New England Dissent,* 1:58; Crosby, *English Baptists,* 1:307–321; Philip J. Anderson, "Letters of Henry Jessey and John Tombes to the Churches of New England, 1645," *Baptist Quarterly,* 28 (1979), 30–31; B. R. White, "Henry Jessey: A Pastor in Politics," ibid., 25 (1973), 98–110.

17. Marshall, quoted in Haller, *Liberty and Reformation,* p. 130; Louise Farago Brown, *The Political Activities of the Baptists and Fifth Monarchy Men During the Interregnum* (Washington, D.C.: American Historical Association, 1912), p. 6; Tolmie, *Triumph of the Saints,* pp. 55–65.

18. McLoughlin, *New England Dissent,* 1:6, and chap. 2 passim.

19. *Plymouth Church Records,* 1:92; on Gorton in Plymouth see below pp. 278–280.

20. *Plymouth Church Records,* 1:92–93; Bradford, *Of Plymouth Plantation,* pp. 313–314.

21. *Plymouth Church Records,* 1:92–107, especially 93–94, 97, 101. Felt (*Ecclesiastical History,* 1:531) notes that in 1644 William "Hewes" and his son John were presented at Essex County court "for deriding such as sing in the congregation, tearming them fooles," as well as for "saying Mr. [Samuel] Whiting preacheth confusedly." Firmin (quoted ibid., 2:63–64) noted that a member of the Rowley church who "denied singing psalms to be an ordinance of God" also was chastised.

22. *Plymouth Church Records,* 1:107; Hill, *World Turned Upside Down,* chap. 10 passim, notes the spiritual pilgrimages of many who eventually became Quakers. Also see Nuttall, *Holy Spirit,* p. 13; and *Visible Saints: The Congregational Way, 1640–1660* (Oxford: Basil Blackwell, 1957), p. 122.

23. McLoughlin, *New England Dissent,* 1:14, note 14; see also Felt, *Ecclesiastical History,* 1:403–404; Gorton, *Simplicities Defence,* p. 109, note 1; and *Winthrop Papers,* 4:159–160.

24. Deane, *History of Scituate,* pp. 59–90 passim.

25. McLoughlin, *New England Dissent,* 1:9; Hooker to Shepard, 2 November 1640, in Lucius R. Paige, *History of Cambridge, 1630–1877* (Boston: H. O. Houghton Company, 1877), pp. 49–50. Also see Winthrop, *Journal,* 2:67; Langdon, *Pilgrim Colony,* p. 62; *Plymouth Church Records,* 1:74; John Davenport to Cotton, c. 1640, in Isabel M. Calder, ed., *Letters to John Davenport, Puritan Divine* (New Haven, Conn.: Yale University Press, 1937), pp. 78–80, for a contemporary view of Chauncy's notion of baptism.

26. Felt, *Ecclesiastical History,* 1:443; Deane, *History of Scituate,* p. 89.

27. McLoughlin, *New England Dissent,* 1:11; Gaustad, *Baptist Piety,* p. 105; Tolmie, *Triumph of the Saints,* pp. 52, 56–57. Also see Thomas Patience, *The Doctrine of Baptism* (London, 1654), preface; and Edwards, *Gangraena,* pp. 56, 95, and 104, for his activities with William Kiffin.

28. Winthrop, *Journal,* 2:126, 177; Koehler, *Search for Power,* p. 240; Felt, *Ecclesiastical History,* 1:530–531, 568; McLoughlin, *New England Dissent,* 1:16–17. For other cases see Koehler, p. 242, and Felt, 1:543,568.

29. Winthrop, *Journal,* 1:310; Phillips, *Reply to a Confutation,* sig. c1ʳ, p. 2; Felt, *Ecclesiastical History,* 1:491–492; Foote, "George Phillips," p. 219.

30. Hubbard, *General History,* p. 412. On Lamb see chap. 3 above, note 71.

31. Whitefield, "A Farther Discovery," p. 136; on Gorton see chap. 10 below.

32. Gorton, "Letter to Morton," in Force, *Tracts,* 4, No. 7, p. 9.

33. Gorton, *Simplicities Defence,* p. 137, note 1; Chapin, *Documentary History of Rhode Island,* 1:262.

34. Gaustad, *Baptist Piety,* pp. 44–45.

35. Callender, *Historical Discourse,* p. 118.

36. Hooker, *The Covenant of Grace Opened . . .* (London, 1649); John Spilsbury, *A Treatise Concerning the Lawfull Subject of Baptism* (London, 1643). See Sargent Bush, Jr., *The Writings of Thomas Hooker: Spiritual Adventure in Two Worlds* (Madison, Wis.: University of Wisconsin Press, 1980), pp. 123–126, and B. R. Burg, *Richard Mather of Dorchester* (Lexington, Ky.: University of Kentucky Press, 1976), pp. 126–128.

37. Cotton, *The Grounds and Ends of Baptisme of the Children of the Faithful* (London, 1647), sigs. A3ʳ⁺ᵛ.

38. Thomas Cobbet, *A Just Vindication of the Covenant and Church Estate of Children of Members As Also of their Right to Baptisme* (London, 1648), passim, but especially p. 61.

39. Thomas Shepard, *The Church Membership of Children and Their Right to Baptism* (Cambridge, Massachusetts Bay Colony, 1663), p. 13.

40. Winthrop, *Journal,* 2:177. On the issue of baptism and the Half-Way Covenant see Morgan, *Visible Saints,* pp. 113–138; and Petit, *The Heart Prepared,* pp. 197–205. Also E. Brooks Holifield, *The Covenant Sealed: The Development of*

Puritan Sacramental Theology in Old England and New, 1570–1720 (New Haven, Conn.: Yale University Press, 1974), pp. 169–196.

41. Quoted in McLoughlin, *New England Dissent*, 1:23.

42. Tolmie, *Triumph of the Saints*, pp. 18–19, 26–27, 36–40; Anderson, "Letters of Jessey and Tombes," pp. 30–31; and *Winthrop Papers*, 3:57–63, 77ff., 126ff., 142–143, 188–189, 484–488; 5:204–205.

43. Anderson, "Letters of Jessey and Tombes," pp. 31–32.

44. Felt, *Ecclesiastical History*, 1:540; Anderson, "Letters of Jessey and Tombes," p. 36.

45. Ibid., p. 38.

46. *Winthrop Papers*, 5:23ff.

47. See below, pp. 198–200 and 219–220.

48. Winthrop, *Journal*, 2:259–260; Hubbard, *General History*, p. 413; Felt, *Ecclesiastical History*, 1:569–570; see also ibid., 2:12, 18 for other cases of protest against such laws.

49. Williams, *Complete Writings*, 6:188; also see p. 192. On Clarke see Thomas W. Bicknell, *Story of Dr. John Clarke* (Providence: The Author, 1915). On Lucar see A. H. Newman, *A History of the Baptist Churches in the United States* (New York: The Christian Literature Company, 1894), p. 50, and McLoughlin, *New England Dissent*, 1:11, note 7.

50. *Massachusetts Records*, 3:173–174.

51. The narrative is best followed in Gaustad, *Baptist Piety*, pp. 3–69.

52. John Clarke, *Ill Newes from New-England*, pp. 45–52, 55 for quotations here. Also see Williams, *Complete Writings*, 4:51 for Williams's chastisement of Cotton regarding the Clarke/Holmes episode.

53. Thomas Edwards, *The Third Part of Gangraena* (London, 1646), pp. 188–189.

54. Jeremiah Chaplin, *Life of Henry Dunster* (Boston: James R. Osgood and Company, 1872), pp. 101–144.

55. Ibid., pp. 121–123.

56. Ibid., pp. 128–131; also see p. 164.

57. On Goold see McLoughlin, *New England Dissent*, 1:49–72 passim; on Russell see Francis H. Russell, "A Cobbler at His Bench: John Russell of Woburn, Massachusetts," *New England Historical and Genealogical Register* 133 (1979), 125–133.

58. Russell, "John Russell," pp. 125–126, and passim; the "Woburn Memorial" is printed in Massachusetts Historical Society, *Collections*, 3d Ser., 1 (Boston, 1825), 38–44.

59. McLoughlin, *New England Dissent*, 1:51–52; Nathan E. Wood, *History of the First Baptist Church of Boston* (Philadelphia: American Baptist Publication Society, 1899), p. 42; pp. 25–124 for Goold's personal narrative. Also see Isaac Backus, *History of New England*, ed. David Weston, 2 vols. (Newton, Mass.: Backus Historical Society, 1871), 1:287–342.

60. Chaplin, *Dunster*, pp. 214–217, 276.

61. McLoughlin, *New England Dissent*, 1:53–56; and chap. 3 passim.

62. Ibid., chap. 2 passim.

63. See, for example, Morgan, *Visible Saints*, pp. 113–138; and Miller, *Colony to Province*, pp. 82–103.

64. See above, pp. 104–105, and below, pp. 145–151.

65. McLoughlin, *New England Dissent*, 1:7, 32, 36.

66. Shepard, "To the Reader," in Phillips, *Reply to a Confutation*, sig. A4^r; Richard Mather, *A Heart-Melting Exhortation* (Cambridge, Massachusetts Bay Colony, 1650), p. 77; and Featley, *Dippers Dipt*, sig. B3^r.

CHAPTER 5   CHRIST'S SECOND COMING:
MILLENARIANS AND QUAKERS

1. The best studies of radical millenarianism in seventeenth-century England are B. S. Capp, *The Fifth Monarchy Men: A Study in Seventeenth-Century English Millenarianism* (London: Faber and Faber, 1972); William M. Lamont, *Godly Rule: Politics and Religion, 1603–60* (London: MacMillan, 1969); John F. Wilson, *Pulpit in Parliament: Puritanism during the English Civil Wars* (Princeton, N.J.: Princeton University Press, 1969); also see P. G. Rogers, *The Fifth Monarchy Men* (London: Oxford University Press, 1966); and Peter Toon, ed., *Puritans, The Millennium and the Future of Israel: Puritan Eschatology 1600 to 1660* (Cambridge and London: Clarke and Company, 1970). On the Quakers see Hugh Barbour, *The Quakers in Puritan England* (New Haven, Conn.: Yale University Press, 1964); William Charles Braithwaite, *The Beginnings of Quakerism* (2d ed. revised, Cambridge, Eng.: Cambridge University Press, 1955), and *The Second Period of Quakerism* (2d ed., rev. by Henry J. Cadbury, Cambridge, Eng.: Cambridge University Press, 1961); Richard T. Vann, *The Social Development of English Quakerism, 1655–1755* (Cambridge: Harvard University Press, rev. by Henry J. Cadbury, 1969); and Melvin B. Endy, Jr., *William Penn and Early Quakerism* (Princeton, N.J.: Princeton University Press, 1973).

2. J. F. Maclear, "New England and the Fifth Monarchy: The Quest for the Millennium in Early American Puritanism," *William and Mary Quarterly*, 3d Ser., 32 (1975), 223–260; see p. 237. Throughout this chapter I am indebted to Maclear's insights in this important essay.

3. See R. G. Clouse, "The Rebirth of Millenarianism," in Toon, ed., *Puritan Eschatology*, pp. 42–65; Capp, *Fifth Monarchy Men*, pp. 23–49; and Tolmie, *Triumph of the Saints*, pp. 86–87; Thomas Hooker, *The Danger of Desertion* (London, 1641), rpt. in *Thomas Hooker: Writings in England and Holland, 1626–1633*, eds. George H. Williams, Norman Petit, Winifred Herget, and Sargent Bush, Jr., Harvard Theological Studies, 28 (Cambridge: Harvard University Press, 1975), 245–246 for quotation here.

4. Maclear, "New England and the Fifth Monarchy," pp. 229–230; also see Wilson, *Pulpit in Parliament*, pp. 223–230; Nuttall, *Visible Saints*, p. 148.

5. On the tragedy at Münster see George Hunston Williams, *The Radical Reformation* (London: Weidenfeld and Nicolson, 1962), pp. 362–386.

6. "Examination of Hutchinson at Newtown," in Hall, ed., *Antinomian Controversy*, p. 339.

7. See Ziff, *Career of John Cotton*, chaps. 2–3 and pp. 106–108; Everett Emerson, *John Cotton* (New Haven, Conn.: College and University Press, 1965), pp. 39–41; and Cotton, *A Brief Exposition of the Whole Book of Canticles* (London, 1642). C.f. Sacvan Bercovitch, "Typology in Puritan New England:

The Williams–Cotton Controversy Reassessed," *American Quarterly*, 19 (1967), 166–190.

8. Johnson, *Wonder-Working Providence*, p. 268. Also see Thomas Allen, "To the Reader," in Cotton, *An Exposition upon the Thirteenth Chapter of the Revelation* (London, 1655); Winthrop, *Journal*, 2:30; Lechford, *Plain Dealing*, pp. 51–52; also Maclear, "New England and the Fifth Monarchy," pp. 231–235.

9. Cotton, *The Churches Resurrection* (London, 1642), pp. 15–21.

10. *Winthrop Papers*, 4:85–87; J. Hammond Trumbull, "Introduction" to Lechford, *Plain Dealing*, pp. xx–xxix.

11. *Winthrop Papers*, 4:85–87; letter from Lechford to Hugh Peter, c. 1640, in *Plain Dealing*, p. xxi.

12. Cotton, *The Way of the Congregational Churches Cleared* (1648), in Larzer Ziff, ed., *John Cotton on the Churches of New England* (Cambridge: Harvard University Press, 1968), pp. 264–265.

13. Lechford, *Plain Dealing*, pp. xxi–xxii, xxiv–xxv.

14. Ibid., pp. xxv–xxvi.

15. "Note-Book Kept by Thomas Lechford . . . from June 27, 1638 to July 29, 1641," *American Antiquarian Society*, *Transactions and Collections*, 8 (Cambridge, 1885), 50.

16. Thomas Parker, *The Visions and Prophecies of Daniel Expounded* (London, 1645). On Parker's presbyterianism see the works of his co-minister in Newbury, James Noyes, especially *The Temple Measured* (London, 1647), pp. 63–67.

17. Ephraim Huit, *The Whole Prophecie of Daniel explained* (London, 1644); Thomas Hooker, *Survey of the Summe of Church Discipline* (London, 1648), especially the "Preface."

18. Winthrop, *Journal*, 1:284; Wheelwright, "Fast-Day Sermon," in Hall, ed., *Antinomian Controversy*, pp. 153–172 passim.

19. Chapin, *Documentary History of Rhode Island*, 2:19; also see Maclear, "New England and the Fifth Monarchy," pp. 240–242; and Andrews, *Colonial Period*, 2: chap. 1.

20. Ziff, *Career of John Cotton*, pp. 104–105; Worthington C. Ford, "Cotton's 'Moses His Judicials,'" *Massachusetts Historical Society*, *Proceedings*, 2d Ser., 16 (1903), 274–284.

21. Cotton, *Way of the Congregational Churches Cleared*, in Ziff, ed., *Cotton on the New England Churches*, p. 242. The efforts to evangelize the New England Indians are best studies in the so-called "Eliot Tracts," all of which are reprinted in Massachusetts Historical Society, *Collections*, 3d Ser., 4 (Cambridge, 1834).

22. Thomas Thorowgood, *Jewes in America, or, Probabilities, that the Americans are of that Race* (London, 1650), see especially pp. 129–138.

23. See, for example, Peter Toon, "The Question of Jewish Immigration," in Toon, ed., *Puritan Eschatology*, pp. 115–125; Cecil Roth, *A History of the Jews in England* (Oxford: Oxford University Press, 1941), especially pp. 149–172; and Mel Scult, *Millennial Expectations and Jewish Liberties: A Study of the Efforts to Convert the Jews in Britain . . .* (Leiden: E. J. Brill, 1978), pp. 17–34.

24. Whitefield, "A Farther Discovery," p. 128.

25. Ibid., p. 131.

26. Ibid.

27. John Eliot, *The Christian Commonwealth* (London, [1659]), "Preface," passim, but especially sigs. A4ʳ, B1ᵛ, C2ʳ; Maclear, "New England and the Fifth Monarchy," pp. 253–255.

28. *Winthrop Papers*, 5:126.

29. Hubbard, *General History*, p. 575.

30. Capp, *Fifth Monarchy Men*, pp. 92–93, 205, 200, 203, 213; Stearns, *The Strenuous Puritan*, pp. 368–369.

31. Ernest A. Payne, "Thomas Tillam," *Baptist Quarterly*, 17 (1957), 61–66; Thomas Tillam, *The Two Witnesses* (London, 1651), pp. 109–110; Thomas Weld, *Mr. Tillam's Account* . . . (London, 1657), suffix; Capp, *Fifth Monarchy Men*, pp. 137, 186. Tillam's later relation to the church at Hexham is recorded in the *Records of the Churches Gathered at Fenstanton, Warboys, and Hexham*, ed. Edward Bean Underhill (London: Haddon, Brothers, and Company, 1854), pp. 289–370 passim.

32. Nathaniel Briscoe to Thomas Broughton, 7 September 1652, in Massachusetts Historical Society, *Collections*, 3d Ser., 1 (1825; rpt. Boston, 1846), 32–34; Capp, *Fifth Monarchy Men*, p. 246; W. T. Whitley, "The English Career of John Clarke of Rhode Island," *Baptist Quarterly*, 1 (1922), 368–372.

33. Capp, *Fifth Monarchy Men*, pp. 92–93, 97, 101, 105, 117, 182, 200, 203; Brown, *Political Activities*, passim.

34. Maclear, "New England and the Fifth Monarchy," pp. 250–253; Battis, *Saints and Sectaries*, pp. 180–181, 187–189.

35. William Aspinwall, *A Brief Description of the Fifth Monarchy* (London, 1653), passim; W[illiam] A[spinwall], *Thunder from Heaven* (London, 1655), pp. 37–39.

36. Aspinwall, *Thunder from Heaven*, p. 38; also see Aspinwall, *The Legislative Power is Christs Peculiar Prerogative* (London, 1656), p. 27.

37. Aspinwall, *Thunder from Heaven*, p. 23. Aspinwall, *An Expectation and Application of the Seventh Chapter of Daniel* (London, 1653); *The Work of the Age; or, The Sealed Prophecies of Daniel opened and applied* (London, 1655).

38. Charles Edward Banks, "Thomas Venner: The Boston Wine-Cooper and Fifth Monarchy Man," *New England Historical and Genealogical Register*, 48 (1893), 437–44; William Hooke to John Winthrop the Younger, 13 April 1657, in Massachusetts Historical Society, *Collections*, 3d Ser. 1 (1825; rpt. Boston, 1846), 183–184.

39. Banks, "Venner," passim; Champlin Burrage, "The Fifth Monarchy Insurrections," *English Historical Review*, 25 (1910), 722–747; William L. Sasche, "The Migration of New Englanders to England, 1640–1660," *American Historical Review*, 53 (1947–1948), 257.

40. Banks, "Venner," pp. 442–443. Venner's trial is described in *A Relation of the Arraignment and Trial of those who made the late Rebellious Insurrections at London* (London, 1661).

41. Capp, *Fifth Monarchy Men*, pp. 195–227; Rogers, *Fifth Monarchy Men*, pp. 121–133. In 1660 John Davenport told John Winthrop the Younger about another of the colonists who had returned to England to become involved with the Fifth Monarchy Men, none other than Sir Henry Vane. "A company being mett some where in England . . . and Sir Henry Vane with them," Davenport reported, "it was propounded that, seeing Christ was not yet come, they should

thinck of some one that should be cheife among them, til he shall come." They chose Vane, and thereupon "one rose up with a viol of oile, which he poured on Sir Hen: Vaines head, and called him King of Jerusalem" (Massachusetts Historical Society, *Collections*, 4th Ser., 7 [Boston, 1865], 515–516).

42. See Capp, *Fifth Monarchy Men*, pp. 99–130; and Christopher Hill, *Antichrist in Seventeenth-Century England* (London: Oxford University Press, 1971), pp. 78–145.

43. The best account of the Quakers' arrival in New England still is Rufus Jones, *The Quakers in the American Colonies* (1911; rpt. New York: W. W. Norton and Company, 1966), pp. 3–110, but also see George Bishop, *New England Judged by the Spirit of the Lord* (1661; 2d ed., 1702; rpt. Philadelphia: Thomas William Stuckey, 1885), passim, for an extensive contemporary account. Also, Carla Gardina Pestana, "The City upon a Hill under Siege: The Puritan Perception of the Quaker Threat to Massachusetts Bay, 1656–1661," *New England Quarterly*, 56 (1983), 323–353.

44. One of the best accounts of Quaker spirituality is Endy, *William Penn*, especially pp. 54–92, 150–215.

45. Endy, *William Penn*, pp. 8–53; Johnson, "From Seeker to Finder," passim; Maclear, "'Heart of New England Rent,'" passim; Hill, *World Turned Upside Down*, pp. 186–207.

46. Felt, *Ecclesiastical History*, 2:142; Jones, *Quakers*, p. 40. As early as 1650, Thomas Parker of Newbury encountered Quakerism head-on. For several years previously, his sister, Elizabeth Avery, had been publishing prophetic books (see especially her *Scripture Prophecies Opened* [London, 1647]). New England ministers like Cotton, Wilson, and Noyes had written letters to her in England to try to recall her from the error of her ways, and finally Parker himself published *The Copy of a Letter Written by Mr.* THOMAS PARKER . . . *to His Sister*, MRS. ELIZABETH AVERY (London, 1650). She remained recalcitrant, however, and soon joined the Quakers. See especially pp. 5, 7–8, 13, 17.

47. Mather, *Magnalia*, Book VII, p. 22.

48. Gildrie, *Salem*, pp. 79–80, 131.

49. Ibid., p. 133; Fell quoted in Jones, *Quakers*, p. 64.

50. Jones, *Quakers*, pp. 64, 72; Langdon, *Pilgrim Colony*, chap. 6 passim; Felt, *Ecclesiastical History*, 2:182–183.

51. See above, pp. 104–105; *Plymouth Colony Records*, 2:17.

52. Leverich in Whitefield, "Strength out of Weakness," pp. 180–183.

53. Jones, *Quakers*, p. 40; *Plymouth Colony Records*, 3:111–112.

54. Felt, *Ecclesiastical History*, 2:73, 170.

55. See Langdon, *Pilgrim Colony*, pp. 71–78; Cudworth quoted in Bishop, *New England Judged*, p. 130.

56. Winthrop, *Journal*, 1:284; 2:41; Jones, *Quakers*, pp. 173–174.

57. Jones, *Quakers*, pp. 53, 79, 84, 172–173; and Bishop, *New England Judged*, pp. 101, 110, 119.

58. Gorton's letters to the Quakers first appeared in *An Antidote* but are more readily available in Staples's edition of *Simplicities Defence*, pp. 16–19.

59. Winslow, *Hypocrisie Unmasked*, p. 63; Felt, *Ecclesiastical History*, 1:458–459; *Good News from New-England* (London, 1648), rpt., Massachusetts Historical Society, *Collections*, 4th Ser., 1 (Boston, 1852); p. 207 for quote.

Thomas Underhill, *Hell Broke Loose: Or An History of the Quakers Both Old and New* (London, 1660), p. 13; and below, pp. 287–288. Also see Winslow, *Hypocrisie Unmasked*, pp. 48–49; and Morton, *New Englands Memoriall*, pp. 109–110.

60. Underhill, *Hell Broke Loose*, p. 12.

61. See below, pp. 284–287 for a description of the doctrine preached at Lamb's church; and Tolmie, *Triumph of the Saints*, pp. 69–84.

62. Quoted in John M. Mackie, "Life of Samuel Gorton, One of the First Settlers of Warwick, in Rhode Island," in Jared Sparks, ed., *Library of American Biography*, 2d Ser., 5 (Boston, 1864), 380–382; Gorton, *Simplicities Defence*, pp. 19–20; Humphrey Norton, *New Englands Ensigne* (London, 1659), p. 3.

63. Jones, *Quakers*, pp. 63–70; Bishop, *New England Judged*, pp. 7–175 passim, esp. pp. 95–125.

64. Jones, *Quakers*, pp. 70–94.

65. Morton, *New Englands Memoriall*, p. 157.

66. Massachusetts Historical Society, *Collections*, 4th Ser., 7 (Boston, 1865), 288. *Plymouth Colony Records*, 11:24. In 1672 Coddington reported to John Winthrop the Younger that George Fox recently had visited with him in Rhode Island and "spake to me to write to thee, viz: that Samuell Winthrope, thy brother, was with him at Barbadus. . . . And G. F. could wish that thou was like him, and that thou would stave off persecution in thy day, in thy jurisdiction, that thou mayst not be numbered amongst persecutors. . . ."

67. *Plymouth Colony Records*, 11:24.

CHAPTER 6   PURITAN IDEOLOGY: INHERENT RADICALISM

1. Baillie, *Dissuasive*, pp. 64–65.

2. Edwards, *Gangraena*, p. 62.

3. Foster, *Their Solitary Way*, pp. 46–47, describes the radical nature of the New England experiment, but at p. 166 notes as well its conservative elements. Michael Walzer, *The Revolution of the Saints: A Study in the Origins of Radical Politics* (Cambridge: Harvard University Press, 1965), especially chapter 5, also analyzes the Calvinist faith's radical potentiality; much of what he says can be applied to New England Puritanism. Ziff, *Puritanism in America*, also is interested in the radical/conservative poles of New England Puritanism; see especially chapter 4.

4. Miller, *Orthodoxy in Massachusetts*, pp. 73–101; Morgan, *Visible Saints*, pp. 64–112.

5. Cotton, *Answer to Williams*, in Williams, *Complete Writings*, 2:187.

6. Miller, *Orthodoxy in Massachusetts*, pp. 92–101; p. 98 for Canne.

7. Gildrie, *Salem*, pp. 75–87.

8. Miller, *Orthodoxy in Massachusetts*, pp. 88–90.

9. Massachusetts Historical Society, *Collections*, 1st Ser., 3 (Boston, 1810), 74; Foote, "George Phillips," pp. 202–204; Winthrop, *Journal*, 1:51–52.

10. See above, p. 37.

11. See above, p. 36.

12. Ziff, *Career of John Cotton*, pp. 95–98; Hall, "John Cotton's Letter," passim; Ziff, ed., *Cotton on the New England Churches*, pp. 41–68.

13. Ziff, *Career of John Cotton*, p. 97.

14. Winthrop, *Journal*, 1:112–113, 137; Gilpin, *Roger Williams*, pp. 39, 43–44.

15. Gildrie, *Salem*, pp. 51–54; Lechford, *Plain Dealing*, pp. 23, 38, 42.

16. Morgan, *Visible Saints*, chap. 3, especially pp. 98–100; Winthrop, *Journal*, 1:173–174.

17. Winthrop, *Journal*, 1:169, 177; 2:22–23; Morgan, *Visible Saints*, pp. 100–101; *Massachusetts Records*, 1:168.

18. Gildrie, *Salem*, pp. 51–54.

19. Foster, *Their Solitary Way*, p. 46.

20. Weld, preface to Winthrop, *Short Story*, in Hall, ed., *Antinomian Controversy*, p. 201; Winthrop, *Journal*, 1:219; *Massachusetts Records*, 1:197.

21. *Winthrop Papers*, 4:10–11; Cotton, *Of the Holinesse of Church Members* (London, 1650), p. 44.

22. Ziff, *Career of John Cotton*, pp. 207–208; Miller, *Orthodoxy in Massachusetts*, pp. 276–277; Winthrop, *Journal*, 2:139. Also see Thomas Parker and James Noyes, *A Reply of the Two Brethren to A.S.* (London, 1644).

23. Wall, *Massachusetts Bay*, chaps. 5 and 6; *Winthrop Papers*, 5:134–137; Hall, *Faithful Shepherd*, p. 97; Winthrop, *Journal*, 1:282; also see Winslow, *Hypocrisie Unmasked*, p. 100.

24. *Winthrop Papers*, 4:151. Callender, *Historical Discourse*, p. 75; Paul R. Lucas, *Valley of Discord: Church and Society along the Connecticut River, 1636–1725* (Hanover, N.H.: University Press of New England, 1976), pp. 38–40, 43. On Pynchon, see below, chap. 11. Also, Massachusetts Historical Society, *Collections*, 4th Ser., 7 (Boston, 1865), pp. 10–11.

25. Deane, *History of Scituate*, pp. 69–70; Ziff, *Career of John Cotton*, p. 210.

26. See Miller, *Orthodoxy in Massachusetts*, chap. 6, and Williston Walker, *The Creeds and Platforms of Congregationalism* (1893; rpt., Boston: The Pilgrim Press, 1960), pp. 194–237.

27. Winthrop, *Journal*, 2:139; Walker, *Creeds and Platforms*, pp. 137–139.

28. Gorton, *Simplicities Defence*, p. 46.

29. Bulkeley, *Gospel-Covenant*, pp. 256–257; Shepard, *Works*, 2:169; John Josselyn, *An Account of Two Voyages to New England* (1675), rpt. in Massachusetts Historical Society, *Collections*, 3rd Ser., 3 (Cambridge, 1833), p. 331.

30. Shepard, "Election Sermon of 1638," *New England Historical and Genealogical Register*, 24 (1870), 362–364.

31. Rutman, *American Puritanism*, pp. 111–113; also see Hall, *Faithful Shepherd*, pp. 99–100.

32. See Pettit, *The Heart Prepared,* passim; and Miller, "'Preparation for Salvation' in Seventeenth-Century Massachusetts," in *Nature's Nation*, pp. 50–77.

33. Stoever, "*Faire and Easie Way*," p. x.

34. Ibid., pp. 58–81.

35. Geree, *Antinomians*, sigs. A2$^{r + v}$; Giles Firmin, *The Real Christian* (1670; rpt., Boston, 1742), p. 53; Petit, *Heart Prepared*, pp. 184–190.

36. Bulkeley, *Gospel-Covenant*, p. 292 (misnumbered 922); Shepard, *Works*, 2:78, 332; 3:88.

37. See Hall, "Introduction" to *Antonimian Controversy*, pp. 3–20, where he discusses the centrality of Cotton's role in the controversy.

38. Foster, "New England the Challenge of Heresy," pp. 624–631 and passim.

39. Winthrop, *Journal*, 1:209; Cotton, *Answer to Williams*, in Williams, *Complete Writings*, 2:80–81.

40. Cotton to Shepard, c. 1636, in Hall, ed., *Antinomian Controversy*, p. 32; Cotton, *Way of the Congregational Churches*, in Ziff, ed., *Cotton on the New England Churches*, p. 241.

41. Stoever, "*Faire and Easie Way*," chap. 3; Cotton, *The Way of Life* (London, 1641), pp. 277, 335; *The Covenant of Gods Free Grace* (London, 1645), p. 30; *Way of the Congregational Churches*, in Ziff, ed., *Cotton on the New England Churches*, pp. 219–220.

42. Cotton, *A Briefe Exposition with Practicall Observations upon the Whole Book of Ecclesiastes* (London, 1654), p. 274; Cotton quoted in Stoever, "*Faire and Easie Way*," p. 169; and *The Way of the Churches of Christ in New-England* (London, 1645), p. 100.

43. Cotton, *Way of the Congregational Churches*, in Ziff, ed., *Cotton on the New England Churches*, pp. 240–241.

44. Hutchinson, *Collection of Papers*, 1:61.

45. Shepard, "Autobiography," in McGiffert, *God's Plot*, p. 74; Hubbard, *General History*, p. 302.

46. Gorton, *Simplicities Defence*, p. 122, Gorton's note; Oliver, *Puritan Commonwealth*, pp. 182–183; Cotton, *Way of the Congregational Churches*, in Ziff, ed., *Cotton on the New England Churches*, pp. 233–234.

47. See the bibliography in Emerson, *John Cotton*, pp. 163–165.

48. See Stoever, "*Faire and Easie Way*," chap. 4; Pettit, *Heart Prepared*, pp. 101–124.

49. *Winthrop Papers*, 3:326–332; Shepard, *Works*, 3:87.

50. Cotton, *Grounds and Ends of the Baptisme of the Children of the Faithful*, p. 43; *The Covenant of Gods free Grace*, p. 30.

51. Cotton to a "Beloved Brother" at Aquidneck, 4 June 1638, quoted in Rutman, *American Puritanism*, p. 107.

52. Ibid., pp. 114–123; 119 for quotation here.

53. Winthrop, *Journal*, 1:259–260; Foster, "New England and the Challenge of Heresy," pp. 654–657.

54. Foster, "New England and the Challenge of Heresy," p. 659.

55. Haller, "The Word of God in the New Model Army," *Church History*, 29 (1950), 28; also see below, pp. 225–228.

56. Hill, *Antichrist in Seventeenth-Century England*, pp. 78–145; *World Turned Upside Down*, chaps. 13 and 14; Lamont, *Godly Rule*, pp. 136–162.

57. Bercovitch, *American Jeremiad*, pp. 3–30; 23 for quotation here; also pp. 176–212.

58. Ibid., especially chap. 2.

59. See, for example, Emory Elliott, *Power and the Pulpit in Puritan New England* (Princeton, N.J.: Princeton University Press, 1975), passim, but especially chaps. 2 and 3; and Bercovitch, *American Jeremiad*, pp. 62–92.

60. Middlekauff, *The Mathers*, pp. 96–112; Hall, *Faithful Shepherd*, p. 86.

61. Timothy H. Breen and Stephen Foster, "The Puritans' Greatest Achievement: A Study of Social Cohesion in Seventeenth-Century Massachusetts," *Journal of American History*, 60 (1973), pp. 10–12.

CHAPTER 7   TOLERATION: THE GREAT CONTROVERSIAL BUSINESS
OF THESE POLEMICK TIMES

1. Ward, *Simple Cobler*, title and pp. 7–8.

2. Thomas Shepard, *Wine for Gospel Wantons* (Cambridge, Massachusetts Bay Colony, 1668), p. 10.

3. Miller, *Orthodoxy in Massachusetts*, pp. 263–313; Ziff, *Puritanism in America*, pp. 100–107; Haller, *Liberty and Reformation*, pp. 143–161.

4. Gilpin, *Roger Williams*, pp. 98–99; Williams, *Complete Writings*, 4:54.

5. Haller, *Rise of Puritanism*, pp. 238–248; H. John McLachlan, *Socinianism in Seventeenth-Century England* (London: Oxford University Press, 1951); W. K. Jordan, *The Development of Religious Toleration in England*, 4 vols. (Cambridge: Harvard University Press, 1932–1940), 3:376–412; Gerald R. Cragg, *Freedom and Authority: A Study of English Thought in the Early Seventeenth Century* (Philadelphia: Westminster Press, 1975), pp. 245–278.

6. Nuttall, *Visible Saints*, p. 95, quoting from *Calendar of State Papers, 1635*; Winthrop, *Journal*, 1:201; Richard Baxter, *Reliquiae Baxterianae* (London, 1696), Part 1, pp. 74–75. Also see James Kendall Hosmer, *The Life of Young Sir Henry Vane* (Boston and New York: Houghton, Mifflin, 1889).

7. Hutchinson, *Collection of Papers*, 1:79–113 for the relevant documents; quotations from pp. 84–85.

8. Winthrop, *Journal*, 1:286–287.

9. Gilpin, *Roger Williams*, pp. 96–116; Haller, *Liberty and Reformation*, pp. 151–158.

10. Haller, *Liberty and Reformation*, pp. 143–188; Wall, *Massachusetts Bay*, pp. 121–156.

11. Felt, *Ecclesiastical History*, 1:595; Pagitt, *Heresiography*, pp. 79–80.

12. Johnson, *Wonder-Working Providence*, p. 269.

13. Felt, *Ecclesiastical History*, 2:63; Thomas Shepard, *New Englands Lamentations*, p. 3.

14. Williams, *Complete Writings*, 4:325, 7:222.

15. McLachlan, *Socinianism*, pp. 5–54; Haller, *Liberty and Reformation*, pp. 249–253; on Pynchon, chap. 12 below.

16. Williams, *Complete Writings*, 3:13.

17. Ibid., pp. 41–54, and note 4 above.

18. Ibid., pp. 41–42.

19. Ibid., pp. 42–43.

20. Ibid., pp. 47, 53.

21. Cotton, *Answer to Williams*, in Williams, *Complete Writings*, 2:22. Gorton's account of his imprisonment is in *Simplicities Defence*, pp. 118–135.

22. Gorton, *Simplicities Defence*, pp. 125–132.

23. Ibid., p. 147.

24. See Tolmie, *Triumph of the Saints*, pp. 95–96; Haller, *Liberty and Reformation*, pp. 116–120; *Winthrop Papers*, 5:86–88; 95.

25. *Winthrop Papers*, 5:87.

26. Wall, *Massachusetts Bay*, pp. 157–210; the petition is printed in Hutchinson, *Collection of Papers*, 1:214–223. Also see George L. Kittredge, "Dr. Robert

Child the Remonstrant," Colonial Society of Massachusetts, *Publications*, 21 (1920), 1–146.

27. Hutchinson, *Collection of Papers*, 1:216, 220.

28. Ibid., p. 221; Williams, *Complete Writings*, 4:226–227; also see Winthrop, *Journal*, 2:307.

29. *Winthrop Papers*, 5:134–137; 125.

30. Wall, *Massachusetts Bay*, p. 211–224.

31. Winslow, *Hypocrisie Unmasked*, pp. 38–46.

32. Ibid., pp. 88, 92–96, 99–101.

33. Kittredge, "Robert Child," pp. 63–69, 72–81; Wall, *Massachusetts Bay*, pp. 219–221.

34. John Childe, *New Englands Jonas Cast Up at London* (1647), rpt. in Massachusetts Historical Society, *Collections*, 2nd Ser., 4 (1816; rpt. Boston, 1846), 107–120; pp. 111, 116–117 for quotations here.

35. Ibid., pp. 118–120.

36. Stearns, *The Strenuous Puritan*, p. 183; *Winthrop Papers*, 5:102;137–138; Connecticut Historical Society, *Collections* 21 (Hartford, 1924), 90–91.

37. Edward Winslow, *New Englands Salamander Discovered* (1647), rpt. in Massachusetts Historical Society, *Collections*, 3d Ser., 2 (Cambridge, 1830), 110–145; pp. 120–121 for quotations here.

38. Ibid., pp. 111, 112, 118; on John Goodwin see Haller, *Liberty and Reformation*, pp. 249–254.

39. Cotton, *Way of the Congregational Churches*, in Ziff, ed., *Cotton on the New England Churches*, pp. 169–264; pp. 290–292 for quotations here.

40. Firmin, *Separation Examined*, sig. B3^r.

41. Walker, *Creeds and Platforms*, pp. 236–237; and above, pp. 119–120.

42. Clarke, *Ill News*, pp. 13, 101.

43. Ibid., pp. 104–109.

44. The law is quoted in Russell, "John Russell," p. 129.

45. Massachusetts Historical Society, *Collections*, 3d Ser., 1 (1825; rpt., Boston, 1846), 38–44.

46. Ibid.

47. Thomas Cobbet, *The Civil Magistrates Power in matters of Religion* . . . (London, 1653), sig. A2^v.

48. Ibid., a2^r, C1^{r+v}, p. 2.

49. Ibid., pp. 15–16, 51.

50. Ibid., pp. 66–67, 86, 100.

51. Cobbet, *A brief Answer to a Scandalous Pamphlet*, appendix to *The Civil Magistrates Power*, sigs. B1^r, C1^v, C2^r.

52. Ibid., sigs. D2^r, E4^r, F1^r.

53. John Norton, *The Orthodox Evangelist* (London, 1654), "Epistle Dedicatory."

54. Isaac Penington, *An Examination of the Grounds or Causes, Which are said to induce the Court of Boston in New England to make that Order or Law* . . . *against the Quakers* (London, 1660), pp. 2, 5, 9.

55. Williams, *Complete Writings*, 6:234, 259; Norton, *The Heart of New-England Rent* . . . (1659; London, 1660), pp. 64, 65, 68, 78–79.

56. Ibid., p. 84.

57. Miller, *Colony to Province*, pp. 216–225.

58. See, for example, Lucas, *Valley of Discord*, chap. 6, and Hall, *Faithful Shepherd*, pp. 117–119, 198.

CHAPTER 8   NEW ENGLAND'S IMAGE: AT HOME AND ABROAD

1. Johnson, *Wonder-Working Providence*, pp. 23, 25.

2. Middlekauff, *The Mathers*, pp. 96–112.

3. See Bercovitch, *Puritan Origins*, passim; and Mason I. Lowance, Jr., *The Language of Canaan: Metaphor and Symbol in New England from the Puritans to the Transcendentalists* (Cambridge: Harvard University Press, 1980), especially pp. 113–246.

4. Gilpin, *Roger Williams*, pp. 56–62; McLoughlin, *New England Dissent*, chap. 1 passim.

5. Edwards, *Second Part of Gangraena*, p. 166.

6. Cotton, *The Powring Out of the Seven Vialls* (London, 1642), sig. Bbb4ᵛ; *Winthrop Papers*, 5:125. The classic study of this argument is Miller's in *Errand into the Wilderness*, pp. 2–15; also see Bercovitch, *American Jeremiad*, pp. 3–31, for a clarification of the theme of the errand in early New England history.

7. *Winthrop Papers*, 3:397–402.

8. "Trial of Hutchinson," in Hall, ed., *Antinomian Controversy*, p. 367.

9. Bulkeley, *Gospel-Covenant*, p. 14; Hooker to Shepard, 17 September 1646, quoted in Bush, *Thomas Hooker*, p. 80.

10. Baillie, *Dissuasive*, p. 94.

11. William L. Sasche, "The Migration of New Englanders to England, 1640–1660," *American Historical Review*, 53 (1947–1948), 226–271; Felt, *Ecclesiastical History*, 1:585–586; also see *Massachusetts Records*, 3:279–280, where one finds the complaint that "the first founders weare away apace, & . . . it grows more & more difficult to fill places of most eminence" because recent Harvard graduates "as soone as they are growne upp, ready for publike use . . . leave the country, & seeke for & accept imployment elsewhere."

12. Felt, *Ecclesiastical History*, 1:493.

13. William Hooke, *New Englands Tears, for Old Englands Feares* (London, 1641), p. 21; Massachusetts Historical Society, *Collections*, 4th Ser., 6 (Boston, 1863), 114; Winthrop, *Journal*, 2:295. Also see Nathaniel Mather to John Rogers, 23 December 1651, in Massachusetts Historical Society, *Collections*, 4th Ser., 7 (Boston, 1865), p. 4.

14. Edwards, *Second Part of Gangraena*, p. 61; *Gangraena*, p. 53.

15. John W. Thornton, *The Historical Relation of New England to the English Commonwealth* ([Boston: U.S.A. Press of A. Mudge and Son], 1874), p. 82.

16. Edwards, *Gangraena*, 2nd pagination, p. 77; *Second Part of Gangraena*, pp. 93–94; *Third Part of Gangraena*, pp. 109–110.

17. Dexter, quoted from Rhode Island Colony Records, in Bridenbaugh, *Fat Mutton*, p. 5; on the Hingham militia case see Winthrop, *Journal*, 2:229–245; and Wall, *Massachusetts Bay*, pp. 87–120.

18. *Winthrop Papers*, 5:126; Bulkeley, *Gospel-Covenant*, p. 143; Cotton, *The Churches Resurrection*, p. 21.

19. *Winthrop Papers*, 4:191; Penington, *An Examination*, p. 51. Also see James M.

O'Toole, "New England Reactions to the English Civil Wars, *New England Historical and Genealogical Register*, 129 (1975), 3–17, 238–249.

20. Gorton, *Simplicities Defence*, pp. 91–94, 119–135; Francis Jennings, *The Invasion of America: Indians, Colonialism, and the Cant of Conquest* (Chapel Hill, N.C.: University of North Carolina Press, 1975), pp. 262–272.

21. Winthrop, *Journal*, 2:177; Massachusetts Historical Society, *Collections*, 4th Ser., 6 (Boston, 1863), 537.

22. Wall, *Massachusetts Bay*, passim, describes in detail the various crises of the 1640s that made such readjustments necessary. Also see Bercovitch, *American Jeremiad*, pp. 62–92.

23. Erikson, *Wayward Puritans*, pp. 1–30, 183–206, and passim for a good discussion of Puritan control of dissent for a larger communal purpose; and Emil Oberholzer, Jr., *Delinquent Saints: Disciplinary Actions in the Early Congregational Churches of Massachusetts* (New York: Columbia University Press, 1956).

24. See, for example, Erikson, *Wayward Puritans*, pp. 137–160; Richard Slotkin, *Regeneration through Violence: The Mythology of the American Frontier, 1600–1860* (Middletown, Conn.: Wesleyan University Press, 1973), pp. 94–145; and Slotkin and James K. Folsom, eds., *So Dreadfull a Judgment: Puritan Responses to King Philip's War, 1676–1677* (Middletown, Conn.: Wesleyan University Press, 1978), pp. 3–54.

25. On Johnson's *Wonder-Working Providence* see Bercovitch, "The Historiography of Johnson's *Wonder-Working Providence*," *Essex Institute Historical Collections*, 104 (1968), 138–161; and Edward J. Gallagher, "An Overview of Edward Johnson's *Wonder-Working Providence*," *Early American Literature*, 5, No. 3 (1970–1971), 30–49.

26. Johnson, *Wonder-Working Providence*, p. 31.

27. Ibid., pp. 24, 25, 34.

28. Ibid., pp. 53, 60–61, 268.

29. Ibid., pp. 132, 152, 225.

30. See Bercovitch, "Cotton Mather," in Everett Emerson, ed., *Major Writers of Early American Literature* (Madison, Wis.: University of Wisconsin Press, 1972), pp. 92–149, see especially pp. 135–148.

31. Williams, *Complete Writings*, 4:31.

32. Connecticut Historical Society, *Collections*, 21 (Hartford, 1924), p. 61.

CHAPTER 9 ANNE HUTCHINSON AND THE "ANTINOMIANS"

1. Hutchinson herself never returned to England but assuredly had an effect on popular perceptions of radical spiritism. Her story, as reported in Winthrop's *Short Story* (1644), was frequently discussed by such prominent heresiographers as Baillie, Rutherford, and Pagitt; see, for example, Pagitt, *Heresiography*, pp. 93–102.

2. Gilpin, *Roger Williams*, firmly places Williams in several of the traditions of Puritan radicalism that I have discussed above. Earlier studies like Miller's *Roger Williams: His Contribution to the American Tradition* (Indianapolis: Bobbs-Merrill, 1953) and Edmund S. Morgan's *Roger Williams: The Church and State* (New York: Harcourt, Brace and World, 1967) still are valuable but focus more exclusively on his ecclesiology or politics.

3. The radical ideology of the decades of the 1630s, 1640s and 1650s can be profitably studied in, respectively, Haller, *The Rise of Puritanism* and *Liberty and Reformation*; and Hill, *World Turned Upside Down*; works like Tolmie's *Triumph of the Saints* and Capp's *The Fifth Monarchy Men*, among others, help to round out the picture.

4. Hubbard, *General History*, pp. 181–182.

5. Foster, "New England and the Challenge of Heresy," pp. 643, 647–648.

6. Clap, *Memoirs*, p. 33.

7. Winthrop, *Journal*, 1:209.

8. Shepard, *New Englands Lamentations*, p. 4.

9. Johnson, *Wonder-Working Providence*, pp. 128–129.

10. Hutchinson's early years are well described in Battis, *Saints and Sectaries*, pp. 7–62.

11. "Examination of Hutchinson," in Hall, ed., *Antinomian Controversy*, pp. 336–339.

12. Ibid., pp. 336–339, 322; and "Trial of Hutchinson," p. 380. This reference to the "Woman of Elis" long has puzzled historians. Edwards (*Second Part of Gangraena*, p. 29) noted that "*In the Isle of Ely (that land of errors and sectaries) is a woman preacher also.*" The anonymous author of *A Discoverie of Six Women Preachers . . .* (London, 1641) reported that "there likewise was one *Elizabeth Bancroft* in *Ely* in *Cambridgeshire*, where Bishop *Wren* first going to place Altars there, preached behind the minister upon a Saturday that it was fit upon Sunday to Sacrifice the Popes Bird upon his own Altar" (p. 4). Wren had been appointed Bishop of Ely in 1638, and Hutchinson left for New England in 1634; I have not been able to ascertain if Bancroft was active before her departure for New England. It well may be, however, that Elizabeth Bancroft was the "Woman of Elis" about whom Peter spoke.

13. Collinson, *Elizabethan Puritan Movement*, pp. 372–381; "Examination of Hutchinson," in Hall, ed., *Antinomian Controversy*, p. 314; Cotton, *Way of the Congregational Churches*, in Ziff, ed., *Cotton on the New England Churches*, p. 239.

14. Johnson, *Wonder-Working Providence*, pp. 127–128; Clap, *Memoirs*, p. 29.

15. Battis, *Saints and Sectaries*, pp. 106–107.

16. Winthrop, *Journal*, 1:201; Stephen Bernard Nutter, *The Story of the Cambridge Baptists in the Struggle for Religious Liberty* (Cambridge, Eng.: W. Heffer & Sons, 1912), p. 25; also see John Heard, Jr., *John Wheelwright, 1592–1679* (Boston and New York: Houghton Mifflin Company, 1930), pp. 110–111.

17. Shepard to Cotton, c. 1636, in Hall, ed., *Antinomian Controversy*, pp. 27–29.

18. Ibid., p. 32; Cotton to Bulkeley, c. 1636, ibid., pp. 37–38.

19. Johnson, *Wonder-Working Providence*, p. 124.

20. Winthrop, *Journal*, 1:195–197.

21. Ibid., 1:201, 204–207; Shepard, "Autobiography," in McGiffert, *God's Plot*, p. 65.

22. Winthrop, *Journal*, 1:207; Cotton, *Sixteene Questions of Serious and Necessary Consequence*, in Hall, ed., *Antinomian Controversy*, pp. 44–59; "The Elders Reply," ibid., pp. 61–77, p. 61 for quotation here; "Mr. Cottons Rejoynder," ibid., pp. 79–151, pp. 79, 82 for quotations here.

23. Winthrop, *Journal*, 1:208–210.

24. *Winthrop Papers*, 3:326–332; Winthrop, *Journal*, 1:209, 216.

25. Wheelwright's sermon is most easily available in Hall, ed., *Antinomian Controversy*, pp. 151–172.

26. Winthrop, *Short Story*, in ibid., pp. 249–250, 283.

27. Winthrop, *Journal*, 1:215–216; Hutchinson, *Collection of Papers*, 1:58; Battis, *Saints and Sectaries*, pp. 161–162.

28. Winthrop, *Journal*, 1:216–217; Cotton, *A Conference . . . Held at Boston*, in Hall, ed., *Antinomian Controversy*, pp. 175–198.

29. Bulkeley to Cotton, 25 March 1637, quoted in Rutman, *Winthrop's Boston*, p. 121; Winthrop, *Short Story*, in Hall, ed., *Antinomian Controversy*, pp. 253–254; Winthrop, *Journal*, 1:219, 226; Winslow, *Hypocrisie Unmasked*, p. 65.

30. See above, pp. 54–55; Jones, *Mysticism and Democracy*, pp. 79–84; Nuttall, *Holy Spirit*, pp. 178–180.

31. See above, pp. 56–58; and Stoever, *"Faire and Easie Way,"* pp. 138–160.

32. Cotton, *Way of the Congregational Churches*, in Ziff, ed., *Cotton on the New England Churches*, p. 226; Weld, preface to Winthrop, *Short Story*, in Hall, ed., *Antinomian Controversy*, p. 208.

33. Weld, preface to Winthrop, *Short Story*, in Hall, ed., *Antinomian Controversy*, pp. 212–213; Felt, *Ecclesiastical History*, 1:301.

34. Winthrop, *Short Story*, in Hall, ed., *Antinomian Controversy*, pp. 220, 223.

35. Ibid., pp. 226, 230, 239.

36. Ibid., pp. 233, 236, 239, 241.

37. Felt, *Ecclesiastical History*, 1:319; Wheelwright, "Fast-Day Sermon," in Hall, ed., *Antinomian Controversy*, p. 165; Weld, preface to Winthrop, *Short Story*, in ibid., pp. 210, 213.

38. Winthrop, *Short Story*, in ibid., p. 275; *Massachusetts Records*, 1:211; Felt, *Ecclesiastical History*, 1:332; Winthrop, *Journal*, 1:219.

39. Bulkeley, *Gospel-Covenant*, p. 293.

40. "Examination of Hutchinson," in Hall, ed., *Antinomian Controversy*, pp. 312, 314.

41. Ibid., pp. 315–318.

42. Ibid., pp. 320–321, 330–331, 334.

43. Ibid., pp. 337–338, 341, 347.

44. Johnson, *Wonder-Working Providence*, pp. 124–125; Winthrop, *Journal*, 1:259; "Examination of Hutchinson," in Hall, ed., *Antinomian Controversy*, p. 342.

45. "Report of Hutchinson's Trial," in ibid., p. 372; Maclear, "Hutchinson and the Mortalist Heresy," p. 87 and passim. Also see Jepser Rosenmeier, "New England's Perfection: The Image of Adam and the Image of Christ in the Antinomian Crisis, 1634–1638," *William and Mary Quarterly*, 3rd Ser., 27 (1970), pp. 435–459; and R[ichard] O[verton], *Mans Mortallitie* (Amsterdam [London], 1643); Morton, *World of the Ranters*, pp. 45–69.

46. Winthrop, *Short Story*, in Hall, ed., *Antinomian Controversy*, pp. 300, 301–302; Battis, *Saints and Sectaries*, p. 225.

47. Winthrop, *Short Story*, in Hall, ed., *Antinomian Controversy*, p. 301; Maclear, "Hutchinson and the Mortalist Heresy," p. 77.

48. Winthrop, *Short Story*, in Hall, ed., *Antinomian Controversy*, p. 302; "Report of Hutchinson's Trial," ibid., pp. 357, 358, 371–372.

49. "Report of Hutchinson's Trial," ibid., pp. 373–374, 383, 384.

50. Andrews, *Colonial Period*, 2:8; Battis, *Saints and Sectaries*, pp. 247–248; Winthrop, *Journal*, 1:277. For a clinical description of Hutchinson's miscarriage see Margaret V. Richardson and Arthur T. Hertig, "New England's First Recorded Hydatidiform Mole," *The New England Journal of Medicine*, 260 (1959), 544–545. Earlier that year Hutchinson's close friend Mary Dyer also had delivered a malformed baby, a fact that only fueled the Puritans' beliefs that God was punishing these heretical women; see Winthrop, *Journal*, 1:266–267.

51. Andrews, *Colonial Period*, 2:8–11; Battis, *Saints and Sectaries*, p. 248; Winthrop, *Journal*, 2:39, 276–277.

52. Battis, *Saints and Sectaries*, pp. 247–248; "Report of Hutchinson's Trial," in Hall, ed., *Antinomian Controversy*, p. 373.

53. Winthrop, *Short Story*, in Hall, ed., *Antinomian Controversy*, pp. 261–262, 281; Battis, *Saints and Sectaries*, pp. 91, 103, 106, 233.

54. Battis, *Saints and Sectaries*, pp. 106, 212, 301, 310; Stearns, *The Strenuous Puritan*, p. 215.

55. Battis, *Saints and Sectaries*, pp. 90–91, 177–179; 270, 278; 323; 225, 230; 261–262; 258; 324; 328; 323; 326; 327.

56. Winthrop, *Journal*, 1:284; 2:41.

57. Winthrop, *Short Story*, in Hall, ed., *Antinomian Controversy*, p. 261; Battis, *Saints and Sectaries*, pp. 180–181, 187–189, 270; Maclear, "New England and the Fifth Monarchy," pp. 250–253; Wheelwright, "Fast-Day Sermon," in Hall, ed., *Antinomian Controversy*, pp. 158–159.

58. Holden's story can best be followed in Gorton's *Simplicities Defence*.

59. Winthrop, *Journal*, 2:39; Samuel Greene Arnold, *History of the State of Rhode Island and Providence Plantations*, 2 vols. (New York: D. Appleton and Company, 1859), 1:152.

60. Williams, *Complete Writings*, 6:92.

61. Chapin, *Documentary History*, 2:78–79; also see Williams, *Complete Writings*, 6:257, for a letter dated 8 February 1653 from Vane to the "Inhabitants of the Colony of Rhode Island" in which he criticizes the "headiness, tumults, disorders, [and] injustice" among them.

62. Baxter, *Reliquiae Baxterianae*, Part I, pp. 74–75; Winthrop, *Journal* 1:233; Winthrop, *Short Story*, in Hall, ed., *Antinomian Controversy*, pp. 252–253.

63. Cotton, *Way of the Congregational Churches*, in Ziff, ed., *Cotton on the New England Churches*, p. 251; but also see Gorton, *Simplicities Defence*, p. 42.

64. *Winthrop Papers*, 4:414–415.

65. Winthrop, *Journal*, 2:166–167; and *Short Story*, in Hall, ed., *Antinomian Controversy*, pp. 278–279.

66. Wheelwright, *Mercurius Americanus*, pp. 188, 189–190, 199.

67. Ibid., pp. 191, 200–214, 215–217, 227.

68. Winthrop, *Journal*, 1:295, 309, 328; 2:27–28.

69. Ibid., 1:240, 275–276.

70. Ibid., 1:276–277; "Report of Hutchinson's Trial," in Hall, ed., *Antinomian Controversy*, pp. 371–372.

71. Wheelwright, *Mercurius Americanus*, pp. 191–192.

72. Winthrop, *Journal*, 2:27–28; Edwards, *Second Part of Gangraena*, p. 97.

73. Cyclone Covey, *The Gentle Radical: A Biography of Roger Williams* (New York: Macmillan, 1966), p. 168.

74. Levy, *Treason Against God*, pp. 225–226.
75. *Good News from New-England*, pp. 206–207.
76. Mather, *Magnalia*, Book VII, p. 14.

CHAPTER 10   SAMUEL GORTON

1. For the major historical accounts prior to the nineteenth century see Morton, *New Englands Memoriall*, quotation on p. 108; Mather, *Magnalia*, Book VII, pp. 11–12; Johnson, *Wonder-Working Providence*, pp. 222–225; Hubbard, *General History*, pp. 402–407; and Winthrop, *Journal*, 2:123–125, 147–150. Nineteenth-century assessments are found in John M. Mackie, "Life of Samuel Gorton," in Jared Sparks, ed., *Library of American Biography*, 2d Ser., 5 (Boston, 1864), pp. 317–341; Lewis G. Janes, *Samuell Gorton; A Forgotten Founder of Our Liberties . . .* (Providence: Preston and Rounds, 1896); Adelos Gorton, *The Life and Times of Samuel Gorton . . .* (Philadelphia: Gorton, 1907); and Charles Deane, "Notice of Samuel Gorton," *New England Historical and Genealogical Register*, 4 (1850), 201–220.

2. Deane, "Notice of Gorton," p. 211. Wall, in *Massachusetts Bay*, chap. 4, and Ziff, *Puritanism in America*, pp. 95–99, freshly examine Gorton's career, but neither explicates his theological affinities.

3. Erikson, *Wayward Puritans*, p. 11; Battis, *Saints and Sectaries*, pp. 254–255; Ward, *Simple Cobler*, p. 6.

4. Mackie offers the best biography of Gorton, but the outlines of his career are summarized in Kenneth W. Porter, "Samuell Gorton: New England Firebrand," *New England Quarterly*, 7 (1934), 405–444. Invaluable, too, is Staples's edition of *Simplicities Defence*, which provides extensive annotation to Gorton's life as well as to his treatise. Early Puritanism in the Manchester area is discussed in R. C. Richardson, *Puritanism in North-West England: A Regional Study of the Diocese of Chester to 1642* (Manchester, Eng.: Manchester University Press, 1972), chap. 1.

5. Winslow, *Hypocrisie Unmasked*, p. 65; Cotton, *Answer to Williams*, in Williams, *Complete Writings*, 2:15.

6. Morton, *New Englands Memoriall*, pp. 108–110. Gorton's side of the story is told in a letter sent to Morton, 30 June 1669, printed in Force, ed., *Tracts*, 4, no. 7.

7. *Plymouth Colony Records*, 1:105; Gorton, "Letter to Morton, in Force, ed., *Tracts*, 4, no. 7, p. 7; Morton, *New Englands Memoriall*, p. 108. Complicating events, Gorton rented half of Smith's house; once Smith was aware of Gorton's highly regarded meetings he sought to evict him, against the terms of the agreement on which Gorton had leased the home.

8. A minority party—headed by the Hutchinsonians and strengthened by Gorton and a band of his supporters who had moved with him from Plymouth—ousted Coddington from his "judgeship" during his absence from the settlement. Coddington moved to the southern tip of the island and established Newport; and, after his new base of power was consolidated, he acted to unite the island settlements under one government, a task aided by friction between Gorton and the Hutchinsonians. Gorton, *Simplicities Defence*, p. 3; Andrews, *Colonial Period*, 2:8–10; Mather, *Magnalia*, Book VII, pp. 11–12.

9. Lechford, *Plain Dealing*, p. 95; Mather, *Magnalia*, Book VII, p. 11. Also see Chapin, *Documentary History*, 2:179.

10. In Providence the battles were over land boundaries. For a description of the near-battle that resulted from Gorton's presence see Mackie, "Life of Gorton," p. 336. Also, Williams to Winthrop, 8 March 1641, in Winslow, *Hypocrisie Unmasked*, p. 56.

11. This petition is found in its entirety in an appendix to Gorton, *Simplicities Defence*, pp. 191–194. See also Winthrop, *Journal*, 2:53–54. It is important to note that Winthrop was *not* among the signers of the document, for Janes, *Samuell Gorton*, p. 35 n., questions the authenticity of Williams's letter to Winthrop because its tone seems inconsistent with Williams's usual graciousness.

12. Gorton, *Simplicities Defence*, pp. 52–54.

13. Ibid., pp. 61–62, 68. For an analysis of the European-Indian relationship in Rhode Island during this period see Jennings, *The Invasion of America*, pp. 262–272.

14. Gorton, *Simplicities Defence*, p. 83.

15. Ibid., p. 91. The Arnolds were trading with the Indians in the immediate area and evidently wanted to establish their legitimacy among the natives. The Gortonists' land had been purchased from Miantonomo, supposedly the head sachem of the area, and the minor sachem, Socconocco, had signed the deed with him. There still is dispute over whether Miantonomo was the chief in that area; further, Socconocco claimed that he had been forced into signing the deed. See Jennings, *Invasion of America*, pp. 262–272. Andrews, *Colonial Period*, 2:14, 24, suggests that the Arnolds may have been interested in maintaining the power of the minor sachems in the area because they themselves had purchased land from them.

16. Gorton, *Simplicities Defence*, pp. 112–116.

17. See above, pp. 194–196.

18. Gorton, *Simplicities Defence*, pp. 119–135 for an account of the trial.

19. Ibid., pp. 134–135, 147.

20. Baillie, *Dissuasive*, p. 145. Although Baillie and Williams had widely divergent theological and ecclesiastical views, their relationship was cordial, with Baillie referring to his "good acquaintence, Mr. Roger Williams"; see Laing, ed., *Letters and Journals of Baillie*, 2:211–212. Williams had returned to England in 1643 to secure a royal charter for the colonies in Rhode Island, a task he successfully completed in 1644; during this period he found himself at the center of theological and political controversy because of the publication of his *Bloudy Tenent of Persecution* (1644).

21. Baillie, *Dissuasive*, pp. 116, 145. On Milton's divorce tract see Hill, *Milton and the English Revolution*, pp. 117–139.

22. F. N. McCoy, *Robert Baillie and the Second Scots Reformation* (Berkeley and Los Angeles: University of California Press, 1974), pp. 94–111, presents a solid account of Baillie's activities in London between 1636 and 1646. Edwards, *Second Part of Gangraena*, pp. 174–175. In *The Third Part of Gangraena*, Edwards noted that he still had other sectaries to describe, "as *Gorton*, who hath lately set forth a book cal'd *Simplicities Defence* against *Seven-Headed Policy*, wherein are many dangerous and erroneous passages"; but he already had run out of room to in-

clude them. Thus he promised that the "fourth part of *Gangraena* will supply what's now wanting," but he did not complete this addendum before his death in 1647; see p. 249.

23. Lamb's conventicle was a frequent target of Edwards's wrath in the various parts of *Gangraena*; see below. Other information on him can be gleaned from Whitley, *British Baptists*, pp. 36, 38; Barclay, *Inner Life*, pp. 157, 162, 289; Brailsford, *The Levellers*, pp. 31, 137, 380; and *Dictionary of National Biography*, s.v. "Lambe, Thomas." On the General Baptists see above, pp. 97–100, and Whitley, *British Baptists*, pp. 17–62; Jordan, *Religious Toleration*, 3:452–453; Jones, *Studies in Mystical Religion*, pp. 396–427.

24. Edwards, *Gangraena*, 2nd pagination, pp. 23, 35, 36. On Denne see Whitley, *British Baptists*, pp. 68–70; Barclay, *Inner Life*, pp. 160–164; Jones, *Mystical Religion*, pp. 421–423; Crosby, *British Baptists*, 1:305; and *Dictionary of National Biography*, s.v. "Denne, Henry." On Oates see Whitley, *British Baptists*, p. 73, and Barclay, *Inner Life*, p. 256 n., 291. Baillie, *Anabaptism*, p. 94.

25. Edwards, *Gangraena*, 2nd pagination, pp. 23, 36; on lay exhorting in the conventicles see Barclay, *Inner Life*, pp. 274–307; and Jones, *Mystical Religion*, pp. 418–427.

26. Edwards, *Second Part of Gangraena*, p. 98; Winslow, *Hypocrisie Unmasked*, p. 53; Baillie, *Anabaptism*, p. 94. On Coppe's radicalism see Hill, *World Turned Upside Down*, pp. 168–171; Morton, *World of the Ranters*, pp. 70–114 passim.

27. Edwards, *Gangraena*, 2nd pagination, p. 31. On Attaway see Jones, *Mystical Religion*, pp. 419–421; Barclay, *Inner Life*, p. 157. On women preachers in England during this period see Keith Thomas, "Women and the Civil War Sects," *Past and Present*, 13 (1958), 42–62.

28. Edwards, *Gangraena*, 2nd pagination, p. 31; Baillie, *Anabaptism*, pp. 101, 118. For Williams's Seeker views see above, p. 74, and Morton, *New Englands Memoriall*, pp. 80–81; Winthrop, *Journal*, 1:309; Laing, ed., *Letters and Journals of Baillie*, 2:211–212.

29. Edwards, *Second Part of Gangraena*, pp. 10–11; 2nd pagination, pp. 113–115; Baillie, *Anabaptism*, p. 100. In his *Dissuasive* Baillie quoted directly from "Williams Paper" regarding Gorton's unorthodox ideas about divorce. "I thought good to let you [Baillie] see some particulars," Williams wrote, "wherein I could not close, nor goe along with them [the Gortonists]." After explaining the point of doctrine noted above (p. 283), Williams added that "the odiousnesse of this point was further manifested to me by the speech of *Ezekiel Hollimers* wife saying that she counted her selfe but a widow." Ezekiel Hollimer (or Holiman), who had gone to Providence from Salem, was the one who in 1639 rebaptized Williams and then joined him in forming the first baptist church in America; see Winthrop, *Journal*, 1:297.

30. On Calvert see Hill, *World Turned Upside Down*, pp. 301–302; Cohn, *Pursuit of the Millennium*, pp. 309–310, 317; and Morton, *World of the Ranters*, pp. 98, 106, 132–133. Calvert's shop was known to other New Englanders; for example, in 1651 William Coddington wrote John Winthrop the Younger to inform him that he had met his brother Stephen Winthrop at Calvert's "booke binder shope" (Massachusetts Historical Society, *Collections*, 4th Ser., 7 (Boston, 1865), 281. Edwards, *Third Part of Gangraena*, p. 241; *Second Part of Gangraena*, p. 98; for Gorton's whipping see note 8 above.

31. Underhill, *Hell Broke Loose*, pp. 12–13, also cited in C. E. Whiting, *Studies in English Puritanism from the Restoration to the Revolution, 1660–1688* (London: Macmillan, 1931), p. 294.

32. *Winthrop Papers*, 5:145; Gorton, "Letter to Morton," in Force, ed., *Tracts*, 4, no. 7, pp. 14–15; Winslow, *Hypocrisie Unmasked*, p. 69; and Tolmie, *Triumph of the Saints*, p. 137.

33. Gorton, "Letter to Morton," in Force, ed., *Tracts*, 4, no. 7, pp. 15–16. On the presbyterians' struggle to counter the increasing influence of the Independents see especially Haller, *Liberty and Reformation*, pp. 100–142.

34. Rutherford, *Survey of the Spirituall Antichrist*, pp. 183, 189–190, 192–193. Edwards, *Gangraena*, 2nd pagination, pp. 38, 95; *Second Part of Gangraena*, p. 113; also see Nuttall, *Visible Saints*, 46–47. No catechism by an "R. Beacon" is listed in Wing's *Short-Title Catalogue*, nor in Pollard and Redgrave. There was *A Breife Catechisme* published by an "R.B." in 1601, but it is a much shorter book than that from which Rutherford cites. John Corbet, in his *Vindication of the Magistrates and Ministers of Gloucester from the Calumnies of Mr. Robert Bacon . . .* (London, 1646), details Bacon's difficulties in Gloucester. On Barber see Whitley, *British Baptists*, pp. 57, 68; and Barclay, *Inner Life*, pp. 290–291.

35. Baxter, *Reliquiae Baxterianae*, Part I, p. 41. Calvert published Bacon's *Christ Mighty in Himself* (London, 1646), *The Spirit of Prelacie* (London, 1646), and *A Taste of the Spirit of God* (London, 1652). Rutherford, *Survey of the Spirituall Antichrist*, pp. 184, 186, 191.

36. Wall, *Massachusetts Bay*, pp. 150–152.

37. Edwards, *Gangraena*, p. 65; 2nd pagination, p. 19; *Third Part of Gangraena*, p. 30; Whitley, *British Baptists*, pp. 68–70; Gorton, *Saltmarsh*, sig. a4ʳ.

38. Wall, *Massachusetts Bay*, pp. 150–151; and Morton, *World of the Ranters*, pp. 62–68.

39. See Maclear, "'Heart of New England Rent,'" passim; Johnson, "From Seeker to Finder," passim; and Nuttall, *Holy Spirit*, for good introductions to the radical spiritists.

40. Rosenmeier, "New England's Perfection," discusses Cotton's position on Christ's role in the process of regeneration, one of the points at issue in the Antinomian Controversy; Winthrop, *Journal*, 2:145.

41. Hubbard, *General History*, p. 403; Janes, *Samuell Gorton*, pp. 88–89, 96, quoting from Gorton's unpublished "A Running Commentary on the Lord's Prayer," manuscript in the possession of the Rhode Island Historical Society, Providence, Rhode Island. Gorton to John Winthrop the Younger, 11 September 1675, in *Winthrop Papers*, Massachusetts Historical Society, *Collections*, 4th Ser., 7 (Boston, 1865), 603–607. See also Gorton's *Incorruptible Key*, passim, for extended treatment of his conception of Christ.

42. Rutherford, *Survey of the Spirituall Antichrist*, p. 183. "Swenckefield" was Caspar Schwenckfeld (1489–1561), a Silesian nobleman who became an exponent of evangelical spiritualism and mystical christology; "Muncer" was the famous Thomas Muntzer (1490?–1525), a German Protestant who led the peasants' uprising in Germany in 1525 and was viewed as the founder of the Anabaptists. "Becold" was John Beukels or John of Leyden (1509–1536), the Anabaptist "king" of the revolutionary theocracy in Münster. "David Georgius" was David Jorus (1501–1556), one of the leaders of the Münster uprising of 1533–1535;

"H. Nicholas" was Henry Niclaes (1502–1580), chief leader of the Family of Love, a radical spiritist group that by the late sixteenth century had conventicles in England. See Williams, *Radical Reformation*, pp. 106–117; 44–57, 75–81; 368–375; 380–386; 477–484; and Jones, *Mystical Religion*, pp. 428–444 and passim. By 1628 the *Theologia Germanica* of Hermes Trismegistus had been translated into English by John Everard, and it appeared in print in 1648. *The Bright Starre* was another compendium of mystical writings that circulated in England in the mid-1640s; see Benjamin Bourne, *The Description and Confutation of Mystical Antichrist, the Familists; or, An Information drawn up and published for the Confirmation and comfort of the Faithfull, against many Antichristian Familisticall Doctrines . . . particularly in those dangerous Bookes called Theologia Germanica, the Bright Starre, Divinity and Philosophy dissected* (London, 1646), pp. 5, 37, 39, 43, and passim.

43. See above, pp. 56–58; Rutherford, *Survey of the Spirituall Antichrist*, pp. 189, 191. Rutherford is referring to the sermon Dell preached before the House of Commons on 25 November 1646 and published as *Right Reformation: or, The Reformation of the Church of the New Testament, Represented in Gospel-Light* (London, 1646); see Haller, *Liberty and Reformation*, pp. 200–204.

44. Rutherford, *Survey of the Spirituall Antichrist*, pp. 186, 217, 246; on Saltmarsh's *Sparkles of Glory* see Haller, *Liberty and Reformation*, pp. 198–200; and Morton, *World of the Ranters*, pp. 45–69.

45. Rutherford, *Survey of the Spirituall Antichrist*, p. 193.

46. Gorton, *An Antidote*, sig. F2ʳ; *Incorruptible Key*, Part II, p. 25. See John Saltmarsh, *An End of One Controversie . . .* (London, 1646), and *Free Grace; or the flowings of Christs Blood freely to Sinners* (London, 1645), passim; and William Dell, *The Crucified and Quickened Christian . . .* (London [1652]), in *Several Sermons and Discourses of William Dell* (London, 1709), especially pp. 342–343. Also Gorton, *Incorruptible Key*, Part II, p. 119.

47. Gorton, *Simplicities Defence*, pp. 263, 268, 270; *Incorruptible Key*, p. 73.

48. Baillie, *Dissuasive*, p. 150; Gorton, *Incorruptible Key*, sig. c1ʳ; *An Antidote*, p. 17.

49. Gorton, *Incorruptible Key*, p. 2; Janes, *Samuell Gorton*, p. 93.

50. Winslow, *Hypocrisie Unmasked*, p. 44, paraphrasing Gorton, *Simplicities Defence*, pp. 71–72. Also see Dell, *The Way of True Peace*, in *Several Sermons*, p. 266.

51. Winslow, *Hypocrisie Unmasked*, p. 44; Gorton, *Saltmarsh*, "Introduction." Also see Whitefield, "A Farther Discovery," p. 137.

52. Ziff, *Puritanism in America*, p. 95. Gorton, *An Antidote*, sigs. G3ʳ, G4ᵛ; also pp. 27, 167; and *Incorruptible Key*, Part I, pp. 3–4.

53. Gorton, "Letter to Morton," in Force, ed., *Tracts*, 4, no. 7, p. 14; and Whitefield, "A Farther Discovery," pp. 135–137. For the radicals' distrust of university education see Solt, *Saints in Arms*, pp. 92–95; and "Anti-Intellectualism in the Puritan Revolution, *Church History*, 25 (1956), 306–316.

54. Gorton, *Incorruptible Key*, Part I, pp. 3–4, 83.

55. Gorton, "Letter to Morton," in Force, ed., *Tracts*, 4, no. 7, p. 9. By "generallists" Gorton probably was trying to distinguish himself and his General Baptist beliefs from those of people like Winstanley and Richard Coppin, who believed that all mankind would eventually be saved because a benevolent God

would not torture his creatures to eternity. See Hill, *World Turned Upside Down*, pp. 138–147, 177–179.

56. Gorton, *Saltmarsh*, sigs. a1ʳ, a3ᵛ.

57. See Mackie, "Life of Gorton," pp. 393–394 for a succinct analysis of Gorton's understanding of eternity; and Janes, *Samuell Gorton*, pp. 98–101, and Whitefield, "A Farther Discovery," p. 136. Gorton, "Letter to Morton," in Force, ed., *Tracts*, 4, no. 7, p. 12.

58. These letters first were printed as appendices to *An Antidote* but are more readily available in Staples's edition of *Simplicities Defence*, pp. 16–19. Quotation about Fox excerpted from a statement by an elderly Gortonist whom Yale president Ezra Stiles encountered on one of his trips to Providence in 1771. See Gorton, *Simplicities Defence*, pp. 19–20, and Mackie, "Life of Gorton," pp. 380–382. Humphrey Norton, *New Englands Ensigne* (London, 1659), p. 3.

59. Massachusetts Historical Society, *Collections*, 5th Ser., 8 (Boston, 1882), 200; 4th Ser., 7 (Boston, 1865), 276–277.

60. Ibid., 4th Ser., 6 (Boston, 1863), 549–550.

CHAPTER 11   WILLIAM PYNCHON

1. See McLachlan, *Socinianism*, passim; Haller, *The Rise of Puritanism*, pp. 245–253; T. Lyon, *The Theory of Religious Liberty in England*, passim; Jordan, *Development of Religious Toleration*, 3:376–412; Cragg, *Freedom and Authority*, pp. 245–278; and Hill, *World Turned Upside Down*, pp. 121–147.

2. No one has studied Pynchon's theological writings in any depth, and most accounts focus only on *The Meritorious Price of Our Redemption, Justification, &c. Cleering It from Some Common Errors* (London, 1650). Only McLachlan notes his association with latitudinarian thought (*Socinianism*, pp. 234–239). For good biographical accounts see Samuel Eliot Morison, "William Pynchon, the Founder of Springfield," Massachusetts Historical Society, *Proceedings*, 64 (1932), 67–107; and Ezra Hoyt Byington, *The Puritan in England and New England* (Boston: Roberts Brothers, 1896), pp. 185–218.

3. Battis, for example, comments on the "inherent Jacobinism of Protestant theology" that produced "a revolutionary dynamic . . . irrepressibly particularistic and anti-authoritarian" (*Saints and Sectaries*, pp. 254–255).

4. In addition to Morison, "Pynchon," passim, the best accounts of Pynchon's New England career are found in Joseph H. Smith, ed., *Colonial Justice in Western Massachusetts (1630–1702): The Pynchon Court Record* (Cambridge: Harvard University Press, 1961); E. H. Byington, "William Pynchon," Connecticut Valley Historical Society, *Proceedings*, 2 (1904), 20–40; and Ruth A. McIntyre, *William Pynchon: Merchant and Colonizer, 1590–1662* (Springfield, Mass., 1961).

5. See, for example, Perry Miller, "Thomas Hooker and the Democracy of Connecticut," in *Errand into the Wilderness*, pp. 25–30, where Miller makes much of the animosity between Cotton and Hooker; and Frank Shuffleton, *Thomas Hooker, 1586–1647* (Princeton, N.J.: Princeton University Press, 1977), pp. 197–210.

6. It is important to note that Pynchon's removal from Roxbury at the beginning of the colony's difficulties with the antinomians may have been linked to his recognition that the moderate Puritanism to which he had been exposed by his

association with John White of Dorchester was not to be nurtured in the Bay Colony. Morison links Pynchon to White's moderate Puritanism ("Pynchon," p. 70); also see Ralph J. Coffman, *Solomon Stoddard* (Boston, Twayne Publishers, 1978), pp. 27–31; and Francis Rose-Troup, *John White, the Patriarch of Dorchester* (New York: G. P. Putnam's Sons, 1930), passim. For Pynchon's role in early Valley government, see Smith, ed., *Colonial Justice*, pp. 12–14; and Henry M. Burt, *The First Century of Springfield . . .* 2 vols. (Springfield, Mass.: Henry M. Burt, 1898–1899), 1:156–158.

7. Morison, "Pynchon," pp. 83–87. Mason had been instrumental in the defeat of the Pequots in 1637; he also had been one of the first New Englanders interested in settling the Connecticut Valley. For Hooker's harsh condemnation of Pynchon see Mason A. Green, *Springfield, 1636–1886* (Springfield, Mass.: C. A. Nichols and Company, 1888), p. 33. Pynchon had to spend the next few years clearing his name from these charges of profiteering and oath breaking; see, for example, "Letters of William Pynchon," Massachusetts Historical Society, *Proceedings*, 48 (1915), 47.

8. Simeon E. Baldwin, "The Secession of Springfield from Connecticut," Colonial Society of Massachusetts, *Transactions*, 12 (1911), 70. Hooker was thoroughly incensed by the politicking of Pynchon, and the relationship of their personal disagreements to the various difficulties between Connecticut and the Bay is spelled out in a series of letters Hooker exchanged with Governor Winthrop in the late 1630s; see *Winthrop Papers*, 4:53–54, 75–79, 99–100.

9. For the most detailed accounts of the petitioners see Wall, *Massachusetts Bay*, pp. 157–224; and Kittredge, "Robert Child," pp. 1–146.

10. *Winthrop Papers*, 5:134–137. For Pynchon's interest in English political affairs see ibid., pp. 90, 115, 271.

11. Ibid., pp. 135–136.

12. See, for example, Rosenmeier, "New England's Perfection," passim.

13. Burt, *First Century*, 1:73–89.

14. Ibid., 1:82, quoting from *Massachusetts Records*, 16 October 1650.

15. Letter from John Cotton, Richard Mather, et al., to "some Brethren in Old England," in Burt, *First Century*, 1:122. On the degree to which *The Meritorious Price of Our Redemption* represented Socinian views see McLachlan, *Socinianism*, pp. 238–239. Also see Burt, *First Century*, 1:82–83. Norton completed his assignment in time for it to be given to Pynchon when he appeared before the court in May 1651; *A Discussion of That Great Point in Divinity, the Sufferings of Christ* was published in London in 1653.

16. Burt, *First Century*, 1:83–84.

17. The Bay's answer to Vane's letter (not extant) is found in Burt, *First Century*, 1:124–125, and also in Massachusetts Historical Society, *Collections*, 3rd Ser., 1 (Boston, 1825), 35–37. Vane had a significant degree of exposure to Socinian thought. In 1646, for example, he was one of five members of the House of Commons appointed to confer with the Socinian Paul Best, who then was being tried for his heretical opinions; and in that same year John Biddle, also arraigned for promulgating Socinian ideas, addressed a letter to him asking for assistance in his difficulties with Parliament. Vane, of course, was widely known for his liberal views on toleration. See McLachlan, *Socinianism*, pp. 155, 172.

18. Massachusetts Historical Society, *Collections*, 3rd Ser., 1 (Boston, 1825), 35–37.

19. Pynchon, *The Jewes Synagogue: Or, a Treatise Concerning the Ancient Orders and Manner of Worship Used by the Jewes in their Synagogue-Assemblies* (London, 1652); and *The Meritorious Price of Mans Redemption, or Christs Satisfaction Discussed and Explained* (London, 1655).

20. The two main attacks on Pynchon's position on the atonement were Anthony Burgess, *The True Doctrine of Justification Asserted and Vindicated from the Errours of Many, and More Especially Papists and Socinians . . .* (London, 1654); and Nicholas Chewney, *Anti-Socinianism, or . . . the Confutation of Certain Gross Errours . . . in a Dialogue . . . Called, The Meritorious Price of Our Redemption* (London, 1656). See McLachlan, *Socinianism*, pp. 136–137, 238.

21. Haller, *Rise of Puritanism*, pp. 195–201, where he notes that "one of the modes by which the humanist theologians expressed their scepticism concerning the Calvinistic dogma of predestination was by advancing heterodox notions concerning the atonement through which sinners become justified and by advocating some form of freedom of the will" (pp. 199–200 for this quotation). Also see Jordan, *Religious Toleration*, 3:88–89; and McLachlan, *Socinianism*, especially pp. 45–118.

22. The orthodox Puritan view of the atonement is succinctly expressed in Norton's *Discussion of That Great Point*, especially pp. 29, 106, 155, 174. Socinus's criticism of Trinitarian thought was based on his belief that scriptural revelation had to concur with human reason, a test that he believed the doctrine of Christ's divinity openly failed. He viewed Christ as superior in endowments, but not divine in nature, for to make him a member of the godhead was to mitigate his influence as a moral example to mankind. Although Socinus viewed Christ as an extraordinary person given unlimited powers by God, he maintained that if immortality was to be mediated by the example of his resurrection, he had to be human and so, able to die. God was omniscient and unitary, and Christ was his means of explaining our reward for obedience to God's moral law. See McLachlan, *Socinianism*, pp. 9–17. It should be noted that while in some particulars Pynchon's notion of Christ's role in redemption was akin to Socinus's, at no point in his writings did he approvingly quote him. In *The Covenant of Nature Made with Adam* (London, 1662), for example, he claimed that Socinus did not give enough weight to the merit of "the sufferings of Christ" (pp. 287, 329). But also see *Meritorious Price of Our Redemption*, sig. A2ᵛ.

23. Pynchon, *Meritorious Price of Our Redemption*, pp. 1–2, 83–84; Pynchon mentioned Christ's divine nature at pp. 93, 105, 111. The term "Novelismes" is Burgess's, quoted by Pynchon in *The Meritorious Price of Mans Redemption*, sig. C1ʳ; this volume also appeared under the variant title *A Further Discussion of That Great Point in Divinity[,] The Sufferings of Christ*. In his preface to Norton's *The Orthodox Evangelist* (London, 1654), Cotton noted that "such Protestants who . . . extenuate the bitterness of the Soul-sufferings of Christ" would greatly profit by Norton's treatment of the atonement. Concurring in his condemnation of Pynchon's opinions, Cotton urged critics of the orthodox view of the atonement to realize that "unless the whole guilt of our sin be imputed to him [Christ], and his perfect obedience to the Word be imputed to us, we shall fall short, both

of the matter and form of our justification" (sig. A4ᵛ). Pynchon clearly denied the first part of this proposition.

24. McLachlan, *Socinianism*, pp. 15–24.

25. Norton, *Discussion of That Great Point*, sigs. A3ʳ, A6ᵛ, A7ʳ, A4ʳ.

26. Ibid., sig. A5ᵛ.

27. Ibid., A6ʳ, prefatory leaf, A5ᵛ.

28. In *The Meritorious Price of Our Redemption* Pynchon made use of such divines as Calvin, Luther, Henry Jacob, St. Augustine, Hugh Broughton, and others and noted that he had corresponded with Henry Ainsworth concerning the wrath that Christ suffered (sig. A2ʳ, p. 57). It is worth noting, too, that in his opening remarks Pynchon said that the argument he was setting forth was "framed by Mr. Henry Smith a godly Preacher, neer thirty years since, in my presence." This was possibly the Henry Smith who in 1637 left Watertown to found Wethersfield in the Connecticut Valley. Samuel Peters notes that Smith left Watertown "in order to get out of the power of Mr. Cotton, whose severity in New-England exceeded that of the bishops in Old-England" (*General History of Connecticut* . . . [1781; New York: D. Appleton and Company, 1877], p. 138). Also see Sherman W. Adams, *The History of Ancient Wethersfield Connecticut* . . . , ed. Henry R. Stiles, 2 vols. (New York: The Grafton Press, 1904), 2:150–156.

29. Chewney, *Anti-Socinianism*, sigs. A2ʳ, a1ᵛ, p. 33. Chewney noted, for example, that "the weighty doctrine of a sinners justification before God, hath been notably canvased and discussed among Divines of all sorts," and he complained that Pynchon's work contributed to this doctrinal confusion because "by the fame and opinion of his learning and piety, [he] hath drawn in many professors of Religion, not only to a liking, but defending of his errors" (*Anti-Socinianism*, sig. A1ʳ).

30. Chewney, *A Cage of Unclean Birds*, in *Anti-Socinianism*, pp. 230–233. Biddle was one of the first overtly Socinian writers in England; see McLachlan, *Socinianism*, pp. 163–217.

31. Burgess, *True Doctrine of Justification*, sig. A3ʳ. Pynchon appreciatively noted Burgess's restraint. In *The Meritorious Price of Mans Redemption*, his answer to Norton's attack on his work, he noted that "after I had finished my Reply to Mr. *Norton*, and after a good part of it was printed, I received a Book lately published by Mr. *Anthony Burges*, called *The true Doctrine of Justification, The second Part*, wherein I found that he hath opposed some things in my Book of the *Meritorious Price*; but yet with a differing spirit from Mr. *Norton*, for he professeth that he likes not to be so deep in censuring, as he sees some others are" (sig. b4ᵛ).

32. McLachlan, *Socinianism*, pp. 149–217; and Jordan, *Religious Toleration*, 3:140, 203–208.

33. McLachlan, *Socinianism*, pp. 45–50; Haller, *Rise of Puritanism*, pp. 199–200; and Thomas Jackson, *The Life of John Goodwin*, 2d edition (London: Longmans, Green, Reader, and Dyer, 1872), pp. 34–41. The key works in this controversy were Samuel Wotton, *Mr. Anthony Wotton's Defence against Mr. George Walker's Charge* (Cambridge, Eng., 1641); Goodwin's *Imputatio Fidei, or a Treatise of Justification* (London, 1641); and Walker's answer to Goodwin, *Socinianisme in the Fundamentall Point of Justification Discovered* (London, 1641). See also McLachlan, *Socinianism*, pp. 50–54; Haller, *Rise of Puritanism*, pp. 199–203 (quotation on

p. 200), and *Liberty and Reformation*, pp. 249–253; and Jackson, *Life of Goodwin*, pp. 57–145.

34. Haller notes that "the name of Faustus Socinus soon became associated in England as elsewhere with that type of rationalistic simplification of Christian dogma which so generally led from the exaltation of conscience and reason to rejection of the doctrine of the trinity and denial of the infallibility of the church" (*Rise of Puritanism*, p. 195). It was, of course, Pynchon's seemingly impertinent questioning of "most, if not all, both ancient & modern divines" in the point of Christ's sufferings, to which the Bay magistrates so strenuously objected; see letter to Vane in Burt, *First Century*, 1 : 124. See also Laing, ed., *Letters and Journals of Baillie*, 2 : 111; and Edwards, *Second Part of Gangraena*, p. 136.

35. Haller offers a good summary of Acontius's thought (*Rise of Puritanism*, pp. 196–198); Jordan gives a more detailed account (*Religious Toleration*, 1 : 315–365). Haller speculates that Goodwin may have been the translator of *Satans Stratagems* (p. 199) and notes the possibility of Acontius's influence on Erastians like Chillingworth (p. 196). See also *Liberty and Reformation*, pp. 251–253; and McLachlan, *Socinianism*, pp. 55–57.

36. Chewney, *Anti-Socinianism*, pp. 131, 238, 117.

37. John Biddle, *Twelve Arguments Drawn Out of the Scriptures . . . against the Deity of the Holy Ghost . . .* (London, 1647). On Biddle see McLachlan, *Socinianism*, pp. 163–217; Jordan, *Religious Toleration*, 3 : 203–208; and Henry W. Clark, *History of English Nonconformity*, 2 vols. (London: Hall, 1911–1913), 1 : 353–354, 381–382. In February 1652 the orthodox Puritans, led by John Owen, had established a parliamentary committee for the propagation of the Gospel, and one of their first actions was to arraign Biddle for his errors. These same divines also wished to restrict toleration by making fifteen proposals for an established church to which dissenters had to pledge allegiance.

38. On the Racovian Catechism see McLachlan, *Socinianism*, pp. 18–19, 187–193. The relationship between the latitudinarians and the more radical groups is described ibid., pp. 208–210; see also Haller, *Rise of Puritanism*, pp. 202–203; and Christopher Hill, *Milton and the English Revolution*, pp. 290–293.

39. In speaking of justification Chewney states that with regard to this subject Pynchon and he were of similar opinions, "yet if he [Pynchon] be acquainted with *Socinian John* (as I believe he is) on that doctrine, a mighty stickler in this case, he may soon be drawn away, and easily perverted, to comply with him and his party even in this matter also" (*Anti-Socinianism*, p. 95). Since Chewney wrote at the time of the controversy over Biddle and spoke of his "party," he may well have intended the reference to that Socinian. In all his writings, however, Pynchon nowhere quoted Biddle but did mention Goodwin; see, for example, *The Covenant of Nature*, pp. 170, 274, 283.

40. *Jewes Synagogue*, sig. A2ʳ. On Goodwin's similar ecclesiastical views see Haller, *Rise of Puritanism*, pp. 199–203, and *Liberty and Reformation*, pp. 249–253; and Jackson, *Life of Goodwin*, especially pp. 30–145. Goodwin's writings are numerous; especially pertinent here is *Hagiomastix . . .* (London, 1647), in which he criticized civil rulers for claiming the right to impose their understanding of the word of God on all citizens.

41. Pynchon, *Jewes Synagogue*, p. 80. While E. Brooks Holifield and Paul R.

Lucas believe that Stoddard imbibed his doctrines at the fount of English Puritan sacramental theorists, to whose works he was introduced in the mid-seventeenth century, it is fascinating that his notorious predecessor in the Connecticut Valley could have espoused so similar a theory, derived partially from English Puritan rationalists and partially (no doubt) from Connecticut presbyterialists. See Holifield, "The Intellectual Sources of Stoddardeanism," *New England Quarterly*, 45 (1972), 372–392; and Lucas, *Valley of Discord*, pp. 143–188.

42. Lucas, *Valley of Discord*, especially pp. 87–188.

43. Pynchon, *Jewes Synagogue*, p. 80.

44. Lucas, *Valley of Discord*, pp. 23–86.

45. Pynchon, *The Time When the First Sabbath Was Ordained* (London, 1654), p. 2. The least significant of Pynchon's theological writings, this treatise, which also appeared under the title *A Treatise of the Sabbath* (1655), was part of the large body of literature in the controversy over the observation of the Sabbath; see Winton U. Solberg, *Redeem the Time: The Puritan Sabbath in Early America* (Cambridge: Harvard University Press, 1977), pp. 167–196. "Being . . . intreated by some godly persons in New England" who were disturbed by the New England Puritans' observation of the Sabbath from sundown to sundown, Pynchon advocated an observance by the "natural" day, from midnight to midnight. See pp. 66, 120, sig. u3⁴.

46. Pynchon, *Meritorious Price of Mans Redemption*, p. 439.

47. Ibid., sig. b3ʳ, pp. 19, 70, 103–104, 220–221; Anthony Wotton, *De Reconciliatione Peccatoris* (Basel, 1624).

48. Pynchon, *Meritorious Price of Mans Redemption*, pp. 220–221; compare Wotton's claim in *De Reconciliatione Peccatoris* that "Christ's obedience is the meritorious cause of justification" (p. 70, quoted in McLachlan, *Socinianism*, p. 48) to Pynchon, *Meritorious Price of Our Redemption*, pp. 95–96, 102.

49. Pynchon, *Meritorious Price of Mans Redemption*, pp. 103–104.

50. Edward Holyoke, *The Doctrine of Life, or of Mans Redemption* (London, 1658). Felt, *Ecclesiastical History*, 2:205, suggests that they frequently exchanged ideas. One of the few histories to mention Holyoke is Ziff, *Puritanism in America*, pp. 160–164.

51. Holyoke, *Doctrine of Life*, pp. 325, 353, 355.

EPILOGUE   TOWARD THE GREAT AWAKENING AND BEYOND

1. Simon Bradstreet to Increase Mather, Massachusetts Historical Society, *Collections*, 4th Ser., 8 (Boston, 1868), 478.

2. See Pope, *Half-Way Covenant*, passim, but especially pp. 43–74; Morgan, *Visible Saints*, pp. 113–138; Hall, *Faithful Shepherd*, pp. 201–205; and Holifield, *The Covenant Sealed*, pp. 171–182.

3. Pope, *Half-Way Covenant*, pp. 54–72; Holifield, *The Covenant Sealed*, pp. 179–182.

4. Hall, *Faithful Shepherd*, chap. 10; Miller, "Declension in a Bible Commonwealth," in *Nature's Nation*, pp. 50–77.

5. Pope, *Half-Way Covenant*, pp. 239–260; Hall, *Faithful Shepherd*, pp. 150–157; Holifield, *The Covenant Sealed*, pp. 169–224; Charles E. Hambrick-Stowe, *The*

Practice of Piety: Puritan Devotional Disciplines in Seventeenth-Century New England (Chapel Hill, N.C.: University of North Carolina Press, 1982), p. 33.

6. Johnson, *Wonder-Working Providence*, p. 173; Thomas Shepard, *Eye-Salve; Or, A Watch-Word From our Lord Jesus Christ unto his Churches* (Cambridge, Massachusetts Bay Colony, 1673), pp. 24–25, 38.

7. Mather, *Magnalia*, Book VII, pp. 21–29; p. 26 for quotation; Hill, *World Turned Upside Down*, pp. 296–297.

8. Charles Chauncy, *Seasonable Thoughts on the State of Religion in New England* (Boston, 1743), pp. iii–xxx; 221, 225, 277, 342; c.f. pp. 201–208. Alan Heimert and Perry Miller, eds., *The Great Awakening: Documents Illustrating the Crisis and Its Consequences* (Indianapolis and New York: Bobbs-Merrill, 1967), pp. 140, 148, 319, 351, 380, 419; Jonathan Edwards, *Religious Affections*, ed. John E. Smith (New Haven: Yale University Press, 1959), pp. 287, 322–323. Also compare Robert Ross, *A Plain Address to the Quakers, Moravians, Separatists, Separate-Baptists, Rogerenes, and Other Enthusiasts; on Immediate Impulses and Revelations* (New Haven, 1762); Alexander Garden, *Regeneration, and the Testimony of the Spirit* (1740; rpt. Boston, 1741), p. 24; and Edward Wigglesworth, *A Letter to the Reverend Mr. George Whitefield* (Boston, 1745), pp. 3–4.

9. Alan Heimert, *Religion and the American Mind from the Great Awakening to the Revolution* (Cambridge: Harvard University Press, 1966), passim; and Nathan O. Hatch, *The Sacred Cause of Liberty: Republican Thought and the Millennium in Revolutionary New England* (New Haven: Yale University Press, 1977).

10. Joseph Haroutunian, *Piety versus Moralism: The Passing of the New England Theology* (1932; rpt. New York: Harper and Row, 1970), p. 282.

INDEX

ABOUT THE AUTHOR

Philip F. Gura's research is rooted in his own Massachusetts background: he was born in Ware, was graduated from Harvard College (B.A., 1972), received his Ph.D from Harvard (1977), and was a fellow at the Charles Warren Center for Studies in American History at Harvard University in 1980–1981.

Gura received the MLA's Norman Foerster Prize in 1977 and is professor of English at the University of Colorado at Boulder. In 1985–86 he was an NEH Senior Fellow at the Institute of Early American HISTORY AND Culture in Williamsburg, Virginia. He is the author also of *The Wisdom of Words: Language Theology and Literature in the New England Renaissance* (Wesleyan, 1981) and, with Joel Myerson, *Critical Essays on American Transcendentalism*. His home is in Boulder.